NELSON *to* VANGUARD

NELSON *to* VANGUARD

WARSHIP DESIGN AND DEVELOPMENT
1923–1945

David K Brown

Naval Institute Press
ANNAPOLIS, MARYLAND

Frontispiece
Vanguard, The last Big Gun battleship.
(Admiralty photo, courtesy R A Burt)

This edition first published in Great Britain in 2012 by
Seaforth Publishing,
Pen & Sword Books Ltd,
47 Church Street,
Barnsley S70 2AS

Published and distributed in the
United States of America and Canada by the
Naval Institute Press,
291 Wood Road, Annapolis,
Maryland 21402-5034

www.nip.org

Library of Congress Control Number: 00-104386

ISBN 978 1 59114 602-5

Printed and bound in China

Contents

Foreword and Acknowledgements

THIS BOOK continues the theme of *The Grand Fleet*,[1] and deals with the history of British warship design and construction from the Washington Treaty of 1921 to the end of the Second World War. The technologies of the naval architect will be covered in detail, those of the marine engineer less fully, while other specialisations such as weapon design will be considered only in so far as they affect the ship. The big ships of the era have been well covered by other authors and hence I have tried to emphasise the problems of lesser vessels.

The inter-war years were dominated by three main constraints; treaties limiting the number and size of ships, budgetary restrictions and a very strong mood of pacifism in the country. The main treaties were the Washington Treaty of 1921, the London Treaty of 1930 and the London Treaty of 1936. The last of these was never ratified but the majority of RN ships designed during the rearmament of the late 1930s conformed to the limits which that treaty would have imposed, although several other navies paid little attention to the limits which they had accepted.

Funds for warship building were never great and diminished even further during the depression of the

1 D K Brown, *The Grand Fleet, Warship Design and Development 1906-1922* (London 1999).

For much of the war, British warships were designed in the Grand Pump Room Hotel, Bath, since demolished. (Author's collection)

early 1930s, though the effects are often exaggerated. It must be remembered that the Washington and later limitation treaties were governments' way of limiting naval expenditure. There were no such treaty limits on the Army or the RAF and they were even worse off than the Navy. It will be argued that the RN benefited from the limitations imposed as these appeared to set an internationally agreed size of the fleet. The Army and Air Force had no such basis for argument.

The size and hence the capability of major warships was limited by the treaties but there were no such limits on the power of most weapons. This was brought out clearly by Stanley Goodall, Director of Naval Construction (DNC) from 1936 to 1944, in a paper of 1937[2] which forms a skeleton for this book. From 1932 onwards Sir Stanley Goodall's outspoken diaries are also a major source, which will be used extensively, mainly as footnotes.[3] It is unusual to get such a clear view of the action as seen from the top. A brief biographical note follows.

To some extent, British naval thinking concentrated on a rerun of Jutland in which Fleet Air Arm torpedo bombers would slow the enemy battlefleet which would then be engaged and sunk by the guns of the RN. As Controller and as First Sea Lord Admiral Chatfield dominated the Board. He stated his priorities as being 'to rebuild the battlefleet, to increase our cruiser strength to a minimum of 70 and to free the Fleet Air Arm from Air Ministry control.' As Beatty's Flag Captain at Jutland, Chatfield had become a firm advocate of heavy armour which had a major effect on the design of battleships and carriers. One may also see the influence of Admiral Henderson in advancing many aspects of technology.[4] It was, indeed, an era of great men – Churchill, Chatfield, Henderson, Oswyn Murray (Permanent Secretary to the Board) and Goodall himself.

Smaller ships were not entirely forgotten but successive reviews of anti-submarine warfare (ASW) suggested that trade protection against German submarines could be provided by older destroyers and the few sloops with trawlers in coastal waters. The ASW picture up to the fall of France goes far to justify this approach. After many failures, successful prototype landing craft for men and light tanks had been developed by 1939.

At the end of the previous volume, it was suggested that many promising technical developments died about 1923. Machinery lagged further and further behind the USN while welding made only very slow progress, and longitudinal framing was only introduced for destroyers in 1937. The first post-war ships had a very heavy anti-aircraft armament for the day but this lead was lost, particularly in control aspects. Much thought was given to protecting battleships from high-

level bombing and torpedoes but it was thought that for smaller ships their manoeuvrability was sufficient protection. For what seemed good reasons the threat of the dive bomber was discounted.

Directors of Naval Construction[5]	**Engineers-in-Chief**
Eustace Tennyson d'Eyncourt 1912-23	George Goodwin 1917-22
Edward Berry 1924-30	Robert Dixon 1922-8
Arthur Johns 1930-6	Reginald Skelton 1928-2
Stanley Goodall 1936-44	Harold Brown 1932-6
Charles Lillicrap, 1944-51	George Preece 1936-9
(All knighted)	(All Engineer Vice-Admiral, Sir)

This book concludes my series on British warship design: *Before the Ironclad*, *Warrior to Dreadnought* and *The Grand Fleet*. I was too much involved in later ships to attempt a dispassionate account though there may be a more personal memoir. The first generation of post-war ships are, however, included as showing the perceived lessons of the war.

Acknowledgements

One must make special mention of John Campbell who up to his death in 1998 was such a help on armament matters to so many writers. George Moore allowed me to use the fruits of his research in the PRO and other record collections. He and Iain McCallum read all my drafts and made most valuable suggestions. Many of those who worked on these designs are still alive and have made important contributions – J C Lawrence, E McNair, A J Vosper, and F H Yearling. The author served in several of the ships described during training for the RCNC. John Roberts has been most helpful with illustrations. Thanks are due to L Leventhal for permission to use material in Chapter 7 and to Ian Buxton for permission to use his work in Chapter 11. Robert Gardiner and his team at Chatham have done their usual splendid work.

As before the selection of photos has been assisted by the secretaries of the Naval Photograph Club and the World Ship Society, presently F Lindegaard and Dr R O Osborne. Both societies hold sales of photos which I have attended over the last half-century and it has not been possible to trace the origin of all those used and I apologise for any unwitting use of someone's material.

My thanks are also due to J D Brown, D W Chalmers, J F Coates, G M Hudson, H R Jarman, I Johnston, A Lambert, K McBride, C Marsh, R O Morris, R H Osborn, G Penn, P Pugh, J Shears, T Shaw, R Todd, G Till, and J Wraight.

2 S V Goodall, 'Uncontrolled Weapons and Warships of Limited Displacement', *Trans INA* (1937).

3 Sir Stanley V Goodall's diaries are held in the British Library. They are listed in Appendix 1. They will be referenced simply as Goodall, date. Off-the-cuff criticism of individuals has either been disguised or omitted.

4 See Appendix 11.

5 Controllers were – Rear-Admiral Cyril T M Fuller (1923-5), Vice-Admiral Sir Ernle Chatfield (1925-8), Rear-Admiral Roger R C Backhouse (1928-32), Rear-Admiral Charles M Forbes (1932-4), Vice-Admiral Sir R G H Henderson (1934-9), Bruce A Fraser (1939-42), Wake Walker (42-).

Sir Stanley V Goodall, RCNC

'I will impart the enthusiasm'

FOR A LARGE PART of the era covered in this book Stanley Vernon Goodall (1883-1965), was responsible for warship design. This brief note outlines his career.[1] He was born on 18 April 1883, educated at Owens School, Islington, and intended to become a naval engineer officer but, very soon, in July 1901, transferred to the Royal Corps of Naval Constructors. He graduated from the RN College in 1907 with one of the highest marks of all time and excellent records in tennis and rugby.[2]

After a short appointment to Devonport Dockyard he went to work under Edmund Froude at the Haslar ship model tank (AEW). In 1908 he married Helen, the daughter of C W Phillips of Plymouth. By 1911 he was at the Admiralty in charge of the design of the novel light cruiser *Arethusa*. He was later to describe this design in a lecture to US constructor students which forms the best description of the way in which designs were carried out in that era.

At the outbreak of the First World War Goodall was the lecturer at the RN College, a prestigious post, but was recalled for other wartime duties. He was part of a team which studied damage to RN ships after the Battle of Jutland, though his report was later suppressed. When the USA entered the war, he was sent to Washington as Assistant Naval Attaché, working within their design office and serving as the focus for exchange of information between British and American designers. It was a valuable experience meeting senior US officers and corresponding directly with the

1 A fuller account may be found in Conway's *Warship Annual* 1997-98, p52.

2 He even found time for occasional tennis during the war when he was nearing 60.

Sir Stanley Goodall (right) with Queen Mary on the steps of the Pump Room Hotel on 30 September 1941. He was furious during the rehearsal when he, 'the Principal Technical Adviser to the Board' was placed third in the receiving line but all was well on the day. (Diary 27 & 30 Sep 1941). (C Marsh)

Director of Naval Construction (DNC), Sir Eustace Tennyson d'Eyncourt. His views on US ships were reported at length and summarised in *Engineering* in 1922. His work was acknowledged with the MBE and the US Navy Cross.

Returning to the UK, he worked under E L Attwood (an outstanding designer) on the design of post-war battleships and battlecruisers, culminating in the mighty 'G3', ordered in 1921 but cancelled under the Washington Treaty. Goodall's sense of fun can be seen in a bet with the DNC that none of the class would meet their design speed, still in the ship's cover. After a short time in Malta Dockyard he returned to head the destroyer design section – and the departmental concert party. It was in this appointment that, responding to a rather dull draft from his assistant, he wrote that he just wanted the facts and 'I will impart the enthusiasm', a phrase which might be seen as his motto. A number of his proposals for novel designs failed to materialise in the quest for economy.

He became Chief Constructor in 1930 and Assistant Director in 1932, mainly concerned with the modernisation of older ships and trials of protection though including the early studies for the *King George V* class battleships. He wrote an interesting paper to the INA pointing out that ships were limited by treaty but weapons were uncontrolled. In 1934 he was awarded the OBE which he tried to refuse seeing it as an insult to an officer of his rank.

In 1936 Goodall became DNC and the award of the CB in 1937 and the KCB in 1938 went far to offset the earlier, insulting, OBE. He took a very direct view of his responsibility for the design of a ship; in signing the building drawings he took personal responsibility for success or failure. This responsibility and poor health seem to have caused the loss of his sense of humour – several of his staff use the word 'austere' to describe his wartime manner, though he was always seen as fair.[3] He preferred to sort out problems over the drawing board and diary notes of such visits usually end '. . . gave decision'. There is some evidence of a reluctance to delegate, *eg* he handled the supply of blankets for firewatchers

himself! He would probably claim that many of his staff needed his eye on them, After one visit he wrote '. . . it is bad that no one locally tackles such a matter energetically and it is left to me to find it out and get busy.'

The DNC department was moved to Bath in September 1939 which Goodall opposed as he lost the personal contact with Ministers and other Board members which he saw as essential; this was partially remedied in October 1942 when Goodall and a small staff returned to Whitehall. In the early part of the war, Churchill was First Lord of the Admiralty and Goodall saw him frequently and admired him greatly – though some of the minister's bright ideas could irritate. As well as the overall direction of the Department, Goodall continued to carry out a number of personal duties such as the viva voce examination of constructor students.

During the war 971 major warships from battleships to fleet minesweepers were built, together with innumerable landing craft, coastal forces etc. In addition, some 1700 requisitioned merchant ships and trawlers were converted for war purposes and about 300 US-built ships joined the RN. Repair work did not come under DNC but he was responsible for ensuring that professional standards were maintained.

Goodall's attitude to retirement is interesting. On 18 April 1943 he wrote, '60 today. To my joy I now feel that I am free. I have always felt that I undertook to serve until I was 60.' However, to help the war effort, he agreed to stay on. After discussion with Controller and Lady Goodall he decided that he should give up the key DNC post to Lillicrap whilst the latter was still on the peak of his form. Lillicrap took over in January 1944, Goodall retaining the post of Assistant Controller (Warship Production) which he treated as an 'elder statesman' role, leaving the key decisions to Lillicrap.

After retirement he continued an active professional life as Prime Warden of the Worshipful Company of Shipwrights, Vice President of the Institution of Naval Architects and with the British Welding and Ship Research Associations. He died on 24 February 1965 at his home on Wandsworth Common.

3 Many diary entries end with the words 'A thick day' or even 'A very thick day'.

Introduction

The Ten Year Rule

In 1919, well before the Washington Treaty, the Chancellor of the Exchequer, Winston Churchill, introduced a guideline for defence spending; namely that there would be no war for ten years.[1] This 'Ten Year Rule' was very sensible in 1919 with all the major powers (except Japan) suffering from the casualties and cost of the late war. In 1924-5 the Admiralty suggested that the rule implied readiness for war in 1929 and tried to justify a much enhanced building programme. The only result was that the rule was changed to a rolling ten-year target, a change formalised in 1928. However, it was abandoned in March 1932 following the Japanese invasion of Manchuria. Though much criticised both at the time and later, it is likely that the rule merely reflected the reality of the times and had little direct effect on budgets.[2]

The Washington Treaty of 1921

The terms of this treaty left the RN equal to the USN in battleship tonnage and considerably superior to that of Japan, but British ships were older, worn by wartime hard steaming and, generally, had smaller guns. In recognition of these points the RN was allowed to build two new battleships, *Nelson* and *Rodney*.[3] These two ships were designed within the new displacement limit of 35,000 tons but the weight-saving measures adopted were too successful and they completed well under the limit. The Washington Treaty left the RN as numerically the largest navy in the world.

The maximum displacement permitted for cruisers was 10,000 tons and the calibre of their guns was not to exceed 8in. These limits immediately became the norm and the treaty makers were blamed for an escalation in the size and cost of cruisers. This was most unfair, for they were still smaller than the big protected and armoured cruisers of the turn of the century and a logical development of the wartime *Hawkins* class. Surface raiders were still seen as the main threat to trade routes and the requirements for the 'County' class were well set to counter such a threat (see Chapter 4).

Each of the naval limitation treaties called for full and accurate disclosure to the other signatories of the main characteristics of new ships. It is probably true that all the countries bent the rules and most broke them. The RN's only serious breach was the design of the *Unicorn*, declared as a depot ship but completed as a fully-fledged carrier with a heavy armament and an armoured hangar. This was almost accidental as the significance of a series of changes was not appreciated.[4]

1 This introduction is largely based on D K Brown, 'Naval Rearmament, 1930-41: the Royal Navy' in J Rohwer (ed), *The Naval Arms Race* (Stuttgart 1991).

2 G C Peden, *British Rearmament and the Treasury 1932-39* (Edinburgh 1979), pp6-8. The whole of this book forms an invaluable background to this chapter.

3 D K Brown, *The Grand Fleet*, Ch 12.

4 When consulted, Naval Law department said that if she was not a carrier, she could be declared as a battleship! D K Brown, 'HMS *Unicorn*: The Development of a Design' *Warship 29* (London 1984).

The Washington Treaty permitted the RN to build two new battleships to match the new ships of the USA and Japan. *Nelson* is seen late in the Second World War. (Author's collection)

The cruiser limits were easy to agree as the USA wanted 10,000 tons and 8in guns, and the RN wanted to keep the *Hawkins* class (HMS *Hawkins* seen in 1942) and Japan was planning similar ships. (Author's collection)

The battleships of the *King George V* class were approved at a design displacement of 35,500 tons but this was on the assumption that, as with the *Nelson*, they would complete at a lower figure. There were other lesser tricks such as quoting a displacement corresponding to a smaller number of shells than the full stowage.

The USN had a controversial interpretation of the rules which meant that *Lexington* and *Saratoga* had a displacement of 36,000 tons when other navies thought that the maximum was 33,000 tons. The USN also argued amongst themselves that Washington Treaty definitions applied to material in existence in 1922, so new equipments, light AA guns, radar etc, were not included in reported 'standard' displacement! Other countries cheated much more blatantly.[5] The table gives a small sample only.

Cheating

Ship	Nationality	Displacement (tons) Declared	Actual
*Gorizia**	Italian	10,000	11,712
Scharnhorst	German	26,000**	32,100
Hipper	German	10,000	14,050
Mogami	Japanese	8500	11,200

* The true size of *Gorizia* was revealed when she was in collision off Tangiers in June 1938 and had to be docked in Gibraltar for repairs.
** Itself a breach of the Versailles Treaty which limited Germany to 10,000 tons.

It is often not realised that 10 per cent more displacement will usually give much more than a 10 per cent increase in capability. There are many equipments for which only one or two units are needed, regardless of ship size. For example, more guns will not require more directors and fire control equipment – and their crews –

5 Goodall, 30 Nov 1936. '*Gorizia* at least 11,000 standard. What could we do with *Fiji*, *Belfast* with 10% more'. 2 Nov 1937. 'Went into German *Scharnhorst*. I believe the Hun is cheating.'

6 Based on ADM 1 8702/151 originally PD 0813/23 and 01849/23 which differ slightly.

7 ADM 167 67.

while longer ships require less power per ton for the same speed.

The post-Washington 1923 plan

A 'Special Programme of Naval Construction' was compiled in 1923. The object was to bring forward some of the more important items of future programmes in order to alleviate unemployment. The programme died with a change of government but is of interest as showing the Board's priorities in the immediate post-Washington era. The programme included:[6]

Capital ships. Fit bulges to *Queen Elizabeth*s by 1929
Aircraft Carriers. Convert *Glorious* on completion of *Furious* and follow with *Courageous* (or build new by 1929). Lay down new carrier about 1928.
Light Cruisers. Complete eight 'light' cruisers with 8in guns by 1929. Complete ten smaller cruisers by 1929.
Destroyers. Lay down two flotillas of a leader and eight destroyers per year from 1927-8
Depot Ships. Fit *Sandhurst* and *Greenwich* for foreign service and lay down two new destroyer depot ships (later reduced to one). Lay down one large submarine depot ship in 1924/5 and two MNB (Mobile Naval Base) depot ships before 1929 (may be conversions).
Submarines. Lay down seven overseas patrol and one fleet or cruiser submarine each year from 1925-6.
Minelayers. Lay down three controlled minelayers before 1929.
Anti-Submarine Craft. Allocate £200,000 per year from 1925-6.
CMB. One per year from 1924-5
Store Carriers. Convert two by 1929.
Triad. Replacement by 1929

This programme would have cost £67.8 million over eight years and seems to have been reduced to £23,249,940 over five years.[7] The Treasury agreed that

design work could start and that preliminary discussions with shipbuilders could take place, but no expenditure was to be made or committed.

Industry

Though the size of the post-Washington fleet was adequate and was all that could be afforded, nevertheless the reductions had a devastating effect on industries involved in warship building. It was recognised at the time that ordnance companies and armour makers would be hardest hit, a prophecy that was found to be all too correct when rearmament began. Armstrongs collapsed in 1927 and was bought by Vickers. The Coventry Ordnance Works closed in 1925, Beardmores in 1929 and Palmers in 1932, to name but the biggest.

Bulging the *Queen Elizabeth* class was seen as a priority task but took some time to accomplish. (Author's collection)

The Fleet Air Arm developed slowly. *Furious* is seen here with a flight of six aircraft, the standard unit. (Author's collection)

The main consequence of the 1930 London Treaty was the scrapping or demilitarisation of the *Iron Duke* class, a sentimental loss but they would have been a liability in war. *Iron Duke* herself became a training ship with reduced armament and side armour removed. There were thoughts of 'modernising' her during the war but there were no resources to waste. (Wright & Logan)

Many smaller companies also closed. To help industry survive, building in the Royal Dockyards was greatly reduced and Pembroke was closed, Rosyth reduced to 'care and maintenance' while Haulbowline was handed over to Eire.[8] There were further cuts in the intended building of cruisers and destroyers.

The London Treaty of 1930

The Wall Street Crash of October 1929 made further cuts in governmental spending inevitable. Another general disarmament conference was held in Geneva in 1927 but broke up without agreement.[9] Then a naval limitation conference was held in London in January 1930 following informal and good-tempered contacts between the British and US government including a visit by the Prime Minister, Ramsay MacDonald, to the USA in 1929. Initially, the same five countries as at Washington participated but Italy and France soon withdrew. The RN wanted numbers and were willing to accept smaller size to get them within a realistic budget.[10] In particular, they pressed for battleships to be limited to 25,000 tons with 12in guns.

Agreement to further reductions was reached between the three remaining governments. The main effects on the RN of the treaty are given in Appendix 5. The limit of fifteen battleships meant the scrapping of the *Iron Duke* class and the *Tiger*.[11] These ships had little military value, much less even than the *Royal Sovereigns*, but there was strong sentimental attachment to them. The ten-year ban on building new battleships was extended to 31 December 1936.

The London Treaty of 1936

Before the five main naval powers assembled in December 1935 there had been prolonged discussions both within the Admiralty, with the Foreign Office and with the USN. At a meeting between the First Sea Lord and the USN Chief of Naval Operations friendly relations were restored and the US assured the British that they would not press for a numerical limit on RN cruiser strength. The RN were still arguing for 25,000-ton battleships and 12in guns but with little prospect of success since France and Italy were well advanced with 15in gun ships. Japan withdrew and Italy did not sign but implied that they might sign in 1938.[12] Agreement was reached on the size of individual ships in the major categories and limits on numbers or total tonnage were removed. Battleships were limited to 35,000 tons and 14in guns (see Chapter 1).[13] The RN were pleased that the minimum size of the battleship was 17,000 tons and the maximum size of cruisers was 8000 tons, thus abolishing 'pocket battleships'. In a complicated series of bilateral discussions, Germany and the Soviet Union accepted the limitations on displacement and armament.[14] There was also a protocol prohibiting unrestricted submarine war on merchant ships which was signed by over forty nations (see Appendix 6).

Rising tension and rearmament

During the early 1930s there were plenty of signs of impending trouble. Following the Mukden incident of September 1931, Japan occupied Manchuria and fighting in Shanghai led to war with China a year later in 1932. The collapse of the Geneva conference on general disarmament in 1932 showed that not all the great powers were committed to peace. The rise to power of the Nazi Party in Germany and the Italian attack on Abyssinia were further pointers. The Spanish Civil War (1936-9) with active involvement of German, Italian and Soviet forces was the last warning.[15]

The Defence Requirements Committee considered the 'deficiencies' in the three services during 1933 and planned to make good such deficiencies by 1942 (later advanced to 1937) coming up with a report in February 1934 recommending a five-year programme costing £93 million, an enormous sum for the day.[16] With a commitment to sound finance, promises to restore emergency cuts and an election impending, it is no surprise that the Government cut this figure to £77 million – indeed, one may be surprised that they accepted such a high figure.

It must be remembered that the other two services were in much worse state than the Navy. The RN was still the world's biggest, but the RAF had sunk to fifth place and the Army numbered 206,000 men compared with the pre-war figure of 259,000, with hardly any post-war equipment.[17] It should also be noted that Sir Warren Fisher, Permanent Secretary to the Treasury, was a leading advocate of defence spending. It is a convenient myth to blame the Treasury for shortage of funds; their role is to administer government policy and ministers of all parties welcome the Treasury taking the blame for unpopular measures. Baldwin's victory in the election of November 1935 made it possible to start rearming, though on a small scale and without publicity. In February 1937 a Defence Loans bill was passed permitting borrowing of £400 million for defence over five years. It took a little longer for the general public to realise the growing threat: in 1937 a large majority voted for appeasement in a Gallop poll.[18]

The combination of the Great Depression and naval limitation treaties had badly hit the shipbuilding and marine engineering industry and particularly the armament firms. Of twelve major armament concerns operating in 1914 only one was fully capable in 1933, with four others retaining some very limited capability.[19] The twin 5.25in gun was most affected and several of the *Dido* class cruisers completed with a turret missing or, in two cases, with a main armament of 4.5in guns (see Chapter 4). Armour was seen as a problem but a big purchase of non-cemented armour from Czechoslovakia for the carriers and *Fiji* class cruisers relieved the situation. In 1930 there were 459 building slips over 250ft in length, a number reduced to 266 in 1939 with 134 slips available for warship building.[20]

Though new battleships could not be started until 1937, some work had been done to update the existing ships. Their torpedo protection had been improved by fitting bulges and their AA armament and control had been improved. However, in 1933 it was pointed out that the RN had spent only £3 million on updating battleships whilst the USN had already spent £16 million and were about to commit a further £16 million, and it was also thought that Japan had spent about £9 million.[21] In March 1934 *Warspite* was taken in hand for a complete reconstruction which was to take three years and cost £2,362,000 (see Chapter 9). Three other ships were taken in hand for similar work before the war started.

8 The small operating bases at Dover, Scapa and Invergordon also closed.

9 Relations between the RN and the USN were very acrimonious at that time.

10 McDonald was impressed by the views of Richmond and Ackworth favouring coal-burning battleships of 7000 tons (see Chapter 1).

11 *Iron Duke* herself was partially demilitarised (armour removed and armament reduced) and used as a training ship. *Emperor of India* and *Marlborough* were used as weapon trials ships before scrapping. The older battleship *Centurion* remained in service as a radio-controlled target ship.

12 The treaty was only ratified by France and the USA.

13 It was agreed that if Japan did not accept these limits, guns could be increased to 16in. If any power built outside the limits, the 35,000-ton displacement limit would be raised or removed.

14 S Roskill, *Naval Policy between the Wars* (London 1976), Vol I, Chapter X.

15 I was only allowed by my parents to have warship models after the Spanish Civil War broke out!

16 Multiply by 20-30 for today's figure.

17 Peden, *British Rearmament*, p7. The RAF's problems are well covered by J James, *The Paladins* (London 1990).

18 G A H Gordon, *British Seapower and Procurement between the Wars* (Basingstoke 1988), p171.

19 Ibid, p79, quoting CAB 21/371.

20 I L Buxton, *Warship Building and Repair During the Second World War*, Research Monograph No 2, The British Shipbuilding History Project (Glasgow 1997).

21 It is suggested in Chapter 5 that US shipbuilding costs were about double those in the UK.

Dragon was fitted with the prototype multiple pom-pom, a 6-barrel mount, in B position (under the tarpaulin in this photograph). Delay in getting this into production is about the only delay for which the Treasury can be blamed. (Ben Sharp)

In 1936 the Admiralty put forward a programme for greatly enhancing the AA defence of the fleet by 1945, a date subsequently advanced to 1938. It included 32 twin 4.5in, 138 twin 4in and over 200 other mountings together with 13 High Angle Control Systems. This list was soon increased and the cost was to be additional to other new programmes. The proposed purchase was divided into two parts, fleet and trade protection with the first part approved in April 1936. Part II was approved in complicated negotiations some 18 months later.[22] The delay in Part II was probably due more to lack of capacity than to economies.

The Admiralty obtained authority to order the guns for the first two ships of the *King George V* class six months ahead of the orders for the ships. With the assistance of the Treasury, the orders for the guns of the three ships of the 1937 programme were also placed early in a technical breach of the rules. Flushed by their success, the Admiralty then ordered twenty turrets for the *Fiji* class at a cost of £1.5 million without even Treasury consent. The Treasury's reaction was to obtain retrospective authority rather than to criticise the Admiralty.

New standard

In April 1937 the Board began to consider the implications of the Defence Requirements Committee review of strategy.[23] They had recommended, and ministers had accepted in principle, that the Navy should be strong enough to send a fleet to the Far East which would 'cover' the Japanese fleet while retaining enough strength in home waters to prevent the strongest European power from commanding the vital sea areas.

In May a paper on the 'New Standard of Naval Strength' was discussed informally with the Treasury, who were very worried by the cost. This was about

£104 million above the normal spending on the Navy for seven years. It might be possible to make a small reduction by extending the life of some ships and, if new treaties could be agreed with Japan and Germany, further reductions would be possible though not in battleships. The Defence Plans (Policy) Committee of the Cabinet were sympathetic but it does not seem that the New Standard was formally agreed. Nevertheless it formed the background to the last pre-war estimates and even into the early war years.

It seems most unlikely that such a programme could have been sustained, particularly in the light of requirements from the other two services.

Armour from Czechoslovakia

By 1936 it had become clear that the requirement for armour plates needed in the re-armament programme would greatly exceed the supply.[25] The three manufacturers, Beardmore, Colville and English Steel could produce about 18,000 tons per year against a forecast requirement of 44,000 tons in 1938-9. In mid-1936 approval was given to expand UK plants at Admiralty expense for a capacity of 40,000 tons. This left a near term shortfall of about 15,000 tons.

During 1937 matters deteriorated with too many plates failing test. In a series of meetings in January 1938 (fifteen in all) it was agreed that attempts be made to purchase armour abroad.[26] It was thought that British cemented armour was so much better than that of other countries that only NC should be purchased abroad. Approaches were made to Germany(!), the USA, France, Sweden and Czechoslovakia but only the latter was willing to assist.

Early in March 1938 the Controller (Henderson) and Offord (Head of DNC armour section) visited the Skoda factory at Vitkovice and, after some debate, the Treasury agreed to place an order for 12,000 tons. A further 2200 tons was planned and, by the time war broke out, some 10,000 tons had reached the UK.[27] The armour was used for the flight decks of *Illustrious* and *Victorious* and both the flight deck and hangar deck of *Formidable* as well as most deck and bulkhead armour for *Trinidad* and *Kenya*. Other delays, particularly in the supply of gun mountings, made the delay in armour production less critical.

Estimate and approval procedures

The financial year began on 1 April and money voted by Parliament had to be spent within that year.[28] The money also had to be spent for the purpose approved by Parliament and an underspend under one heading could not be used to offset an overspend in another without the agreement of Parliament. To ensure that money was spent in the approved manner, the total Admiralty grant was split into seventeen 'Votes'.

New Standard Tentative Building Programme[24]

	1936	1937	1938	1939	1940	1941	1942	1943	1944	1945
Battleships	2	3	2	3	2	2	2	1	1	-
Fleet Carriers	1	1	1	1	1	1	1	-	1	-
Trade Protecn Carriers	1	1	1?	1	1	-	-	-	-	-
Large 6in Cruisers	2	5	5	5	5	5	4	4	2	-
8in Cruisers	-	-	-	-	-	-	-	-	3	5
Small 6in Cruisers	5	2	2	2	2	1	2	2	-	-
Fast Minelayers	-	1	-	-	-	-	-	1	-	-
Destroyer ('Tribal')*	1	1	1	-	-	-	-	-	-	-
Destroyer**	1	1	1	1	1	1	1	1	1	1
AA Sloops	-	1	-	1	1	-	-	-	-	-
M/S Sloops	5	4	5	4	5	4	5	3	2	2
Coastal Sloops	1	2	2	2	2	2	2	-	-	-

* Flotillas of 8
** Flotillas of 9

Planning was a continuous process, with preliminary discussion on the requirement for the following year commencing as soon as the current year estimates had been approved. The departments responsible for each vote would bid for the amount they wanted in the following year. In many categories, such as pensions, there was little scope for variation and, should the Government decide on a reduction, this would fall very largely on ship construction and stores. Since there was little scope for reduction on contracts already placed, cuts would fall heavily on new work.

The individual departmental bids would first be scrutinised by the Financial Committee of the Board where unrealistic over-bidding could be removed. The full Board of Admiralty would then discuss and agree the 'Sketch Estimates' before they went to the Treasury. There would then be a lengthy period of correspondence between the Ministries, formal and informal, partly for clarification and partly to adjust – cut – the total estimates to match Government policy. Finally, the Cabinet would approve a figure in line with its policy and the bids from other Ministries. The Treasury could take a more active role: Peden suggests that they overrode the Air Ministry in insisting on more fighters in the late 1930s.

Great men

The 1930s was unusual in that the principal personalities changed little and were men of outstanding ability. The Secretary of the Admiralty from 1917 to 1936 was Sir Oswyn Murray. He was very able, well liked and a strong supporter of the Navy. Chatfield, as Rear-Admiral, was Controller from 1925 to 1928 and First Sea Lord from 1933 to 1938. The second volume of his autobiography gives an unusual view of life at the top.[29] The Minister – First Lord – was Sir Bolton Eyres-Mansell from 1931 to 1936, who was a little known politician but fought hard for the Navy.

The Treasury is seen by both politicians and civil servants as the centre of power and, as such, attracts able men. The Chancellor from 1931 to 1937 was Neville Chamberlain who has been described as a human dynamo with a tremendous grasp of detail. He was supported by Sir Warren Fisher as Permanent Secretary and by Sir Richard Hopkins, first as Controller and later as Second Secretary. The Treasury team were dedicated to balanced budgets and to preserving the value of the pound but, increasingly, saw the need to increase defence expenditure. The Treasury was responsible for controlling the financial policy set by the Government and so was expected, as a matter of course, to challenge the spending proposals of other Ministries. This proper challenge was usually seen as opposition, particularly by service officers. This view of Treasury policy is linked to a view put forward by Chatfield, Goodall and many others that defence should be 'above politics'. No government could accept that one of the biggest items of expenditure should be outside their control.

The Prime Minister in the early 1930s was Ramsay MacDonald, who was seen by Chatfield as generally sympathetic to the Navy and willing to listen.[30] The government was advised on defence policy by the Committee of Imperial Defence whose secretary from 1912 to 1935 was Sir Maurice Hankey, a man of immense influence. Chatfield paints a rosy picture of friendly agreement with his colleagues from the Army and Air Force. Nevertheless, at lower levels the battle for funds was fought with some bitterness.

Some economic figures

Date	Price Index (1866=100)	Wages (1930=100)	National income (£m)
1923	129	100.0	1920=3664
1924	139	101.5	
1925	136	102.2	3980
1926	126	99.3	
1927	122	101.5	
1928	120	100.1	
1929	115	100.4	
1930	97	100.0	3957
1931	83	98.2	
1932	80	96.3	
1933	79	95.3	
1934	82	96.4	
1935	84	98.0	4109
1936	89	100.2	
1937	102	102.8	
1938	91	106.3	4671
1939	94	—	

These figures may be compared with those for the three years 1912-14 when the price index was 85. In other words, the value of money in the 1930s was fairly similar to that before the War.

Navy Estimates 1923-39 (£m)

Date Estimate	Estimate	Date	Estimate
1923	58	1932	51
1924	56	1933	54
1925	61	1934	57
1926	58	1935	60
1927	58	1936	70
1928	57	1937	78
1929	56	1938	94
1930	52	1939	69
1931	52		

22 Gordon, *British Seapower and Procurement between the Wars*, p211

23 Roskill, *Naval Policy between the Wars*, Vol II, p327.

24 ADM 205 80 per G Moore.

25 D K Brown, Note on p9 of *Warship International* 1/98.

26 Goodall, 4 Jan 1939. 'Situation bad. Controller, as usual, faced it like a sportsman but I feel we should have been alive to it earlier.'

27 Len Batchelor, then a young draughtsman, brought the last trainload across Germany at the end of August 1939. He told me how hard German Rail worked to fulfil their contract. On return he was interviewed by Goodall himself, then almost unheard-of for such a junior officer.

28 These procedures were still in use for much of the author's career.

29 Admiral of the Fleet Lord Chatfield, *It Might Happen Again* (London 1947).

30 Chatfield thought he was inclined to believe that the day of the battleship was over or, at least, could be replaced by the 7000-ton mini ship advocated by Richmond and Ackworth (see Chapter 1).

From 1911 to 1913 the total Navy Estimate varied from £45-£52 million. Allowing for inflation the total sums voted in the 1930s were about the same as for the peak years before the start of the First World War even though the Gross National Product had doubled. However, the pattern of spending was very different.

Shipbuilding expenditure 1930-9

Date	Estimate (£m)	Shipbuilding (£m)
1930	51.7	5.3
1931	51.6	5.3
1932	50.5	6.8
1933	53.6	8.4
1934	56.6	10.2
1935	60.0	10.5
1936	70.0	13.9
1937	78.1	28.0
1938	93.7	34.8
1939	69.4	46.1

In the last three years before the First World War the expenditure on shipbuilding was £25-£30 million. Prior to the Second World War, far more of the Admiralty's money was spent on other services – pay, pensions etc. This shows how a very small change in a large total Estimate may have a disproportionate effect on a component vote.

The pie chart shows the amounts spent on major types between 1930 and 1939. Any discussion of a different type of fleet must bear in mind that no government could have increased the total; indeed, there was great difficulty in spending the money allocated. The

Breakdown of spending by ship type

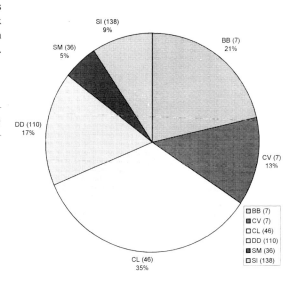

total was also limited by shipyard capacity, particularly number and length of building slips and by the availability of skilled labour. There is some evidence that men were leaving shipbuilding for the expanding – and better paid – aircraft industry.

Trials of attack and defence between the wars

There were a considerable number of full scale trials carried out between the wars to test and develop weapons and defence against them. These trials were carried out in secrecy[31] and, even today, their extent and

Terror's 15in guns were used for several trials of protection after the war. (World Ship Society)

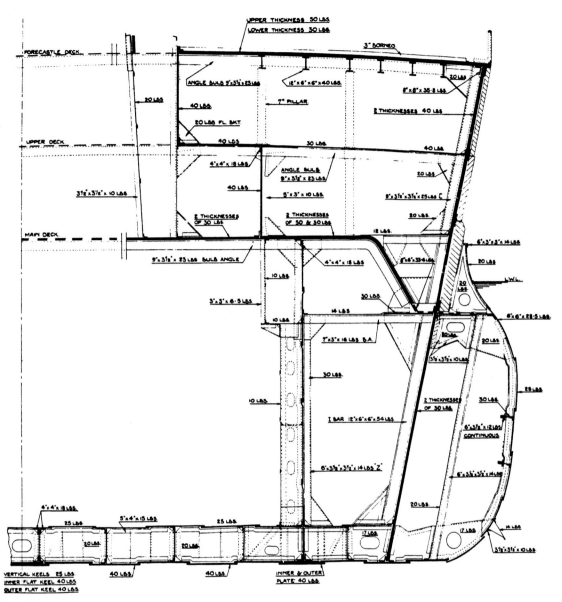

Hood's deck protection was very weak. Several thin decks are far less effective against shells than one thick one. (Author's collection)

value are usually not fully recognised. Trials involved shells, bombs, torpedoes and other devices.

Early trials of shells

These trials are described in more detail in the previous volume, *The Grand Fleet*, and are only summarised here.[32] In 1919 new-type 15in shells were fired against a target representing the protection of *Hood*. The weakness of the 7in upper belt was apparent but nothing much could be done as the ship was already grossly overweight. In 1921 the monitors *Erebus* and *Terror* fired thirty-one new-type 15in shells against the ex-German battleship *Baden* at velocities representing ranges of 15,500 and 21,800yds. The best performance was penetration at the higher velocity of a 14in plate at

18½° to the normal by an APC shell filled shellite. Both APC and CPC could penetrate thick plates and burst, reliably, about 40ft later.[33]

Pre-war trials with old type APC shells had shown them as comparatively ineffective, bursting without penetrating thick plates. The high-capacity HE shell seemed a more serious threat and much of the weight available for protection was devoted to medium-thickness armour, to burst such shells outside the ship. The performance of the new APC shells was such that it was clear that all attention should be given to the thickest possible armour over the vitals with the rest of the ship unprotected – the so-called 'all or nothing' system, pioneered by the USN in the *Pennsylvania*.

A mock-up of the protection[34] proposed for the new

31 In February 1936 Lord Strabogli asked a question in the House of Lords suggesting that no trials had been carried out on bombing against battleships. In drafting a reply for the First Lord, Viscount Monsell, Goodall wrote that ignorance of these trials was 'a tribute to those officers who have kept silence'. This section follows Goodall's notes closely with some additional material since he was personally involved in most of them. His papers (British Library ADM 52792) are in three parts, a suggested reply, a brief for the First Lord only on the background and Goodall's own conclusions, not passed to First Lord. Regrettably, the diary entry for 12 Feb reads 'First Lord v Strabogli yesterday: didn't put in much of my guff.'

32 D K Brown, *The Grand Fleet*, pp170-1.

33 See W H Garzke and R O Dulin, *Battleships–Allied Battleships in World War II* (Annapolis 1980).

34 14in sloped belt, 7¼in deck.

Several torpedo protection systems were attached to *Gorgon*'s bulges for trial. (World Ship Society)

battlecruisers ('G 3') was built into the *Superb* using some of *Baden*'s plates. This was successful in resisting 15in shells at 'battle range' in May 1922. Some concern had been felt over the strength of the supports but they were satisfactory apart from some minor weld failures. *Monarch* was fired on by both cruisers and battleships in January 1925. [35] Her thin protective deck was penetrated by splinters from 6in and 13.5in APC[36] penetrated the 11in barbette, exploding behind. A few experimental CPC shells were fired with a TNT filling and a gaine which caused very severe blast damage. At last the RN had effective shells.

Bombing trials

The first problem was that it was extremely difficult for an aircraft to hit a ship, even when stationary, using contemporary bomb sights. However, trials at Shoeburyness in 1920 showed that bombs could be fired from a gun at targets representing the deck of a ship.[37] In 1921 tests were carried out firing 435lb bombs from a 9.2in gun and 1500lb and 2000lb AP from a 13.5in gun. These tests showed the penetration to be expected from such weapons and bombs were positioned at appropriate locations within *Baden*, a fairly new ship but with old-fashioned protection.[38]

35 For a detailed account and impressive photo see R A Burt, *British Battleships of World War I* (London 1986).

36 Filled Shellite – a mixture of lyddite and dinitrophenol, much more stable than lyddite alone.

37 There is some evidence that firing from a gun disturbed the fuse which did not function normally.

38 Repeated in the later *Bismarck*!

Bombing trials against *Baden* 1921

Number	Wt of Bomb (lbs)	Charge wt (lbs)
4	520	360
1	1800	960
1	550	180

Reports from the USA suggested that severe underwater damage could be caused by near-miss explosions from large bombs. In 1922 bombs from 250lb to 2000lb were exploded close to the bulges of the *Gorgon* causing only slight damage. The following year a 60ft long structure representing the side protection of *Nelson* was built onto the *Monarch*. A charge of 2082lb TNT (representing a 4000lb bomb) was exploded 7ft 6in from the side and 40ft below the waterline. The structure stood up to this severe test quite well; though the main bulkhead was considerably distorted, it remained watertight and the gun turrets were unaffected. Eight boilers were alight and the machinery was running. The only weakness lay in the circulating water inlets, and in 1924-5 a number of model tests were conducted in a successful attempt to develop a better design.

In 1924 there were further bombing trials against *Monarch*. The DH 9a bombers flew in flights of two or three of which only the leader had a bomb sight. The ship was at anchor, the weather was clear and conditions ideal. Each flight had at least one practise run and the leader usually had two or three sighting shots with 9lb practise bombs before the real drop. The results were as shown in the table (left).

None of these dummy bombs succeeded in penetrating the 60lb upper deck in a fit condition to burst. Later, bombs were developed with greater penetration and in 1936 Goodall wrote that such bombs were 'a most serious form of attack. Protection against such bombs is essential.'

Bombing trials against *Monarch*, 1924

Bomb wt (lbs) & type	Case thickness (in)	Dropped	Hits	Within 10ft	10-20ft	25-50ft	Over 50ft
550 heavy case	3/4	16	5	0	1	0	10
520 light case	1/10	16	3	2	1	3	7
1650 SN	5/16	14	0	0	1	0	13
250 heavy	1/2	11	3	0	1	0	7

A number of bombs were then positioned internally and exploded. A particular objective was to study the effect of bombs exploding within the funnel and the effectiveness of armour gratings. It was found that bombs exploding in the funnel opened up the boiler casing and the uptakes which would have caused a loss of pressure in the stokehold and a momentary flash-back, possibly starting a fire. The support to the armour gratings needed to be stronger and it was recommended that gratings be fitted both at upper and middle deck levels since a heavy-case bomb could penetrate a single grating.

The general damage caused was severe but localised. Damage from splinters was confined to a narrow band radiating from the largest diameter of the bomb. Most of the splinters were small but those from AP bombs were bigger and could penetrate two ¼in bulkheads. The blast zone was complicated; basically there were two 45° cones from either end of the bomb and a band round the middle but this pattern was modified by reflection from the structure nearby. Within the damaged area, all ventilating fans and trunking, heaters, pipes and electric cables were destroyed by splinters or by tearing as the bulkheads to which they were attached were destroyed or severely distorted. Damage to voice pipes and to the fire main were seen as the greatest problems.

Between 1924 and 1930 the Shoeburyness guns lobbed bombs from 50lb GP to 450lb AP against targets representing the decks of *Queen Elizabeth*, *Royal*

Agamemnon (top) was the first radio-controlled target ship, replaced by *Centurion* (left). Many influential trials were carried out on her, particularly those of early dive bombing. (Author's collection)

39 The original intention was *Ajax* but *Centurion* was substituted at the last moment. Ships Cover 449.

40 Designed by E L Attwood and K Watkins.

41 Goodall, 3 July 1935. 'Read Air Ministry minutes of bomb experiments which show *Centurion* results to be window dressing.'

42 This gave rise to a Goodall entry, 20 Sept 1933. 'As a result of *Centurion* bombing DNC wants all M pompom to fire right forward in old capital ships.'

43 Burt, *British Battleships of World War I*.

44 Goodall, 4 April 1932, 'Air Vice Marshal Dowding surprised how little effect from light case (HE) bombs on *Marlborough*.' (Goodall did not get on with Dowding.)

45 Based on notes from John Campbell supplemented by R A Burt.

46 Hence *Nelson*'s inboard belt.

47 The thick bulkhead was set in 3in and it was thought that it could have resisted a much heavier charge.

48 I was told by a senior constructor that he carried out gunfire trials on the effect of shells on surfaced U-boats. Nothing less than 4.7in was any use and even they bounced off quite often. I have not been able to find a report on such trials.

49 I find this hard to believe.

50 D K Brown. 'Attack and Defence', *Warship 24* (London 1982).

51 The Air Ministry contributed to the cost. Ships Cover 540.

52 Designed by D E J Offord and D W Smithers.

53 All mention of Job 74 in the press was forbidden under a D notice.

54 Rather small for this size of charge. I would have expected about 36ft long. About ¼ chance of a 24ft hole.

55 Two thicknesses of 35lb plate riveted together.

56 Though this full size section resisted a 1000lb charge the similar protection in *Prince of Wales* failed against a 330lb charge. See *Warship 1994*, p193 and also Chapter 10 where a not very successful attempt is made to explain the difference.

57 Goodall was very worried when *Ark Royal* was torpedoed and sank but relieved when the inquiry showed that the bulkhead did not fail (see Chapter 10), also 1 Nov 1935, 'Job 74 looks all right as extent of damage but welding looked bad'.

Sovereign and *Hood*. These trials showed that the most effective way in which to use a given weight of armour was in a single thickness, and that the thickness needed in the upper deck for strength would defeat the small (20lb) GP bombs then carried by fighters. In 1930 another target was tried with 450lb AP and 250lb SAP to provide information for the modernisation of *Barham* which led to a 4in deck.

The last pre-Dreadnought, *Agamemnon*, was used as a radio-controlled target from April 1923 till December 1926. She proved most valuable and was replaced by a more modern ship, *Centurion*.[39] Her side armour was thought adequate for practice shells but 3in of mild steel plate was fitted, mainly on the upper deck. The uptakes were protected with 6in armour (C) removed from *Renown*. The turrets were removed and the openings covered with 3in mild steel. Despite the extra protection, she was still light and 5000 tons of shingle ballast was installed to keep the bottom of the side armour well under water.[40] She was converted to oil firing and it was hoped she could steam at 19½kts. (This seems to have been optimistic and 16kts was about her best.) She could steam under radio control for three hours. Accommodation for her steaming crew of 230 had to be provided under armour though living spaces above were also available – but liable to damage! There were many exercises in which bombs were dropped against *Centurion*, confirming the difficulty of hitting a ship from medium or high level.[41] On the other hand, a trial of dive bombing against *Centurion* in September 1933 scored nineteen hits with forty-eight bombs. This success seems to have had an important effect on Admiralty thinking.[42] A full record of exercises and trials has not been found.

In 1931 the *Marlborough* became due for scrapping under the treaties and Goodall arranged a further series of trials. It was clear that magazines were still a problem as a charge was exploded in B magazine badly distorting the bulkhead to A magazine.[43] Cordite should not be exposed to the direct effect of bombs or shells and adequate venting was essential particularly when protection was weak. This trial had an important effect on the modernisation of *Warspite* and later ships. Further trials in 1932 involved dropping dummy 250lb and 500lb bombs followed by exploding similar bombs together with 450lb AP and 1080lb HE placed within the ship. The lessons were that heavy decks were necessary against SAP, that HE bombs were ineffective and that the effect of near-misses was very small.[44]

Emperor of India gunfire trials, June 1931

The *Emperor of India* was allocated for firing trials[45] and left Portsmouth under her own power on 8 June 1931 only to run aground on the Owers Shoal. Salvage proving very difficult, and early attempts to refloat her having failed, it was decided to fire on her where she lay. On 10-11 June she was hit by twelve rounds of 13.5in

from the 'worn out' guns of *Iron Duke*. The first four were fired at 12,000yds and the rest at 18,000yds. The most damaging hit was on the bottom edge of the belt making a hole 2ft by 1ft 8in before passing through the inner bottom and the bunkers and exploding over a boiler in B boiler room. It was concluded that the belt on all RN ships was too shallow which affected the design of the *King George V*. Plans were drawn up to deepen the belt on *Nelson* but were not implemented.

Underwater protection

In 1920 a replica of the *Hood* bulge (with tubes) was built onto the Chatham Float and successfully resisted a 500lb charge of TNT with only slight leakage round rivets. By the following year interest had shifted to a scheme with several longitudinal bulkheads somewhat similar to that used in the USA. The difference was that the American ships had all bulkheads the same thickness whilst the British scheme had a thick inboard bulkhead. Scale models of both were made and tested on the Float using a 20lb charge to represent a full scale 1000lb charge (see Appendix 7). These tests seem to show that the British design was superior though there was some concern as it was known that similar tests in the USA had reached the opposite conclusion. The British tests concluded that venting the explosion outside the armour was effective.[46] A full scale replica of the *Nelson* protection was built onto the Chatham Float and resisted a 1000lb charge.[47]

As a result of these tests the fleet was overconfident on torpedo protection. During an exercise in January 1932 Blackburn Darts from *Courageous* and *Glorious* dropped 57 torpedoes against the fleet at anchor obtaining 17 hits – of which 11 were allowed under exercise rules. The effect of these hits was estimated as follows.

Torpedo exercise January 1932

Ship	Hits	% loss of speed	Remaining speed (kts)
Queen Elizabeth	2	15	20
Resolution	7	30	14
Ramillies	2	10	18
Royal Oak	1	10	18
Devonshire	1	10	30
Sussex	1	10	30
Curlew	3	100	SUNK

Can anyone seriously think that any battleship, let alone *Resolution*, would only lose 30 per cent speed with seven torpedo hits? In January 1933, thirty-one torpedo bombers attacked a cruiser squadron steaming at 24kts and manoeuvring violently. Even so, six hits were scored. Shortly afterwards, thirty-two aircraft scored twenty-one hits against a slower force.

Further early trials included the effect of depth charges on surrendered U-boats[48] and the trials with *Gorgon* and *Monarch* referred to above. Money was scarce and only model tests could be carried out. A strong box (10ft x 12ft) was built at Portsmouth in which different arrangements of bulkheads could be tried. Known as the 'bulge model' it lasted well into the Second World War by which time 130 tests had been carried out together with another 240 on an even simpler model.

In 1929 the monitor *Roberts* was saved from the scrapyard and used as a pontoon for fairly large models of protection (⅓ or ¾ scale). Charges of up to 16½lbs were used to represent 1000lbs full scale. By 1935 eleven trials had taken place and it was known that protection 12ft deep (side to holding bulkhead) would resist a 1000lb charge[49] whilst 9ft was insufficient to resist a 500lb charge. Arrangements with air-water-air spaces were best and the spaces should be roughly of equal depth.

Several vent plates failed to function leading to the conclusion that, after all, venting was not necessary. Welding eliminated the old problem of leaking and tearing along riveted seams though great care was needed in designing and welding the details.

In 1934 the design of *Ark Royal* was in hand as were studies for the new battleships.[50] The DNC, Sir Arthur Johns, persuaded the Board to build a large new test vehicle for trials of protection against various forms of attack despite an estimated cost of £165,000.[51] It was 72ft long, 50ft deep, the beam varying with the depth of protection fitted, and known as 'Job 74'.[52] Internal compartments were fitted out to battleship and cruiser standards. For the first series of trials Job 74 was given a

sandwich system on one side and a modified d'Eyncourt bulge on the other leading to an overall beam of 100ft.[53] The sandwich was 20ft deep to the holding bulkhead, of two thicknesses of 35lb plate, riveted together. The outboard compartment was air to allow the gases from the explosion to expand freely. Then there was a liquid-filled space, initially water, later filled with fuel oil. This spread the pressure load and also stopped fragments of the torpedo and the shattered hull. There was another air-filled space in front of the thick bulkhead. It was expected that the thick bulkhead would distort and hence leak so there was a watertight compartment inboard used for non-essential services.

A 1000lb charge was exploded against each side in turn, both making a hole about 25ft x 16ft in the outer plating.[54] In the sandwich the two intermediate bulkheads were destroyed over a length of about 36ft and the main protective bulkhead deflected 18in but were not ruptured.[55] The rapid deflection of this bulkhead caused a pressure pulse in the oil tank behind which caused some damage to the innermost bulkhead.[56] On the other side, the bulge failed, the main bulkhead being ruptured over an area 14ft long by 28ft deep. In a later trial (April 1937) a welded holding bulkhead, 60lbs, as used in *Ark Royal* failed through the welds.[57]

During the 1930s there was much concern over the threat from the B bomb, which was designed to be dropped ahead of a ship and had a large air chamber making it buoyant so that it would come up under the bottom of its victim. It was conceived in 1927 as a 2000lb bomb, reduced to 1100lbs and then to 250lb in 1933. It entered service in 1939 but was never used operationally. In tests the B bomb was devastating and no effective protection was found. Job 74 had a double

Bruce was expended in a trial of the Duplex (magnetic) pistol in an 18in torpedo. It seems to have worked this time but was unreliable and soon dropped. (Author's collection)

bottom 7ft deep which was 'no good'.[58] Even the 250lb version (127.5lb charge) would flood the compartment above–two compartments if it exploded within 15ft of a bulkhead. A triple bottom had been tried earlier without success, but double bottoms gave some protection if half full of liquid.

Offord (and Goodall) were very worried about the safety of the above-water torpedo tubes in *Hood* and to quantify this concern, three 750lb warheads were exploded on the main deck of Job 74. This led Offord to tell the inquiry into the loss of *Hood* that her torpedoes were to blame, a view which he continued to hold.[59]

Bombing trials were carried out, confirming the difficulty in hitting a small target,[60] but thirty hits were scored with bombs totalling 10,000lbs weight. Her thick (5in) armour deck seems to have done well.[61] There were turret flash trials and charges in 6in and 8in magazines were ignited. An aircraft hangar was fitted on deck to study hangar fires. There were a number of trials of magazine and shell room safety.

Other trials included the use of the old submarine *L 19* for shock trials until scrapped in 1937 when a special test section, Job 81, was built. After trials in 1938 she was tested to destruction and another section, Job 9, was built and remained in use until after the war, mainly to study the resistance of batteries to shock. The Duplex (magnetic) torpedo pistol was also tested, sinking the destroyer *Bruce* off the Isle of Wight on 22 November 1939.[62]

Chemical warfare

The threat of gas attack was taken very seriously between the wars. The first trial was against the *Ramillies* in 1920, when it was found that her open bridges were very vulnerable and little could be done. There was a further trial with *Courageous* in 1922 and with *Monarch* in 1924 with similar results. A copy of USN studies was received in 1923 which reached much the same conclusion as the RN; that it was impossible to protect a ship, particularly after damage and that individual gas masks were the best that could be done, with protective clothing against mustard gas when available. The *Nelson* and the *King George V* classes had gas filter arrangements to the bridge tower but there was little faith in their value. The importance attached to gas warfare is well described by Bywater in his fictional account *The Great Pacific War* which was largely based on gossip in the Whitehall pubs; written in 1925, it forecast a war in 1931 and contains many thoughts of the day.[63]

Armour

The full story of armour development remains obscure but from 1935 a number of experimental plates were made by The English Steel Corporation, Firth-Brown and Beardmores. The early plates had a hard face some 20-25 per cent of the thickness but later ones had as much as 33 per cent hard face,[64] and considerable attention was paid to alloying elements and heat treatments to give a gradual transition from the hard face to the tough back. The thick face would break up shells with enough velocity to penetrate so that they would be unfit to burst. Most tests were on 440lb plates attacked by 13.5in APC but some thicker plates up to 600lb were used against 15in APC. From 1937 onwards a bonus was paid for plates which performed better than specification.

The results were very satisfactory; the armour of the *King George V* and later ships being about 25 per cent more effective than First World War armour. German developments were similar as shown by post-war tests on plates removed from *Tirpitz*. The USN failed to achieve similar advances, and the armour of their Second World War ships was no better than those of the earlier war.[65] When it was realised that UK armour production was inadequate, it was decided that only non-cemented armour could be ordered abroad as British cemented armour was so much superior.

Parliament

There was an interesting sequel to the trials just described when, in November 1936, a sub-committee appointed by Parliament reported 'On the Vulnerability of Capital Ships to Air Attack'.[66] There had been a great deal of ill-informed comment in the press and even in Parliament that battleships were too vulnerable to air attack and that their role could be carried out by bombers at less cost. The report was unclassified but refers to the study of a large number of secret reports, presumably on the trials described in this chapter. In almost every aspect the Admiralty and the Air Ministry were in agreement.

The report mentions numerous trials on the chance of bombs hitting, on their penetration and their effect in exploding. It also described and considered USN trials, the report concluding that British experience was much greater. They also concluded that, while no protection could be perfect, that provided in recent ships and modernisation was soundly based. Account was taken of level bombing, dive bombing and torpedo bombing.[67]

The efficacy of AA fire was the only aspect where the two service departments were at odds. Both did agree that few planes would actually be shot down, but the Admiralty maintained that the psychological effect on aircrews would be a considerable deterrent, a view not accepted by the Air Ministry.[68] The ministries agreed that the cost of building, running and maintaining a single battleship was equal to that of forty-three twin engined bombers.

Their final conclusion was that the views of the air enthusiasts were that the UK should stop building battleships–'If their theories turn out well founded, we have wasted money; if ill founded, we would, in putting them to the test, have lost the Empire.'

58 Goodall, 25 Feb 1936. He continued–'. . . closeness of watertight subdivision could be overdone . . . went into the dock under the Job, the real problem is that of sound bulkheads unpierced by the inner bottom. 'Also 21 April.' Conference on Job 74. Watson a valuable critic though I think him wrong.' (Goodall is often referred to as an autocrat but this passage and a few others shows that he valued informed opposition.)

59 Letter to the author in 1980.

60 Goodall's diary for 20 Feb 1935. 'At Chatham. Job 74 looks small. I wonder if AM will ever hit it.' Goodall often used AM to refer to the Air Force, presumably for Air Ministry. 24 June, '500lb SAP a good weapon.'

61 During the war Job 74 was used as an air raid shelter–Offord wrote 'the shelterers had a certain amount of confidence in her.'

62 Goodall, 1 July 1932. 'DTM got away with proposal for magnetic pistol with 350lb warhead.'

63 H C Bywater, *The Great Pacific War* (London 1925). Amongst his other forecasts is a class of diesel engined cruisers. It has been claimed that Yamamoto planned his war on Bywater's model.

64 This figure comes from Scott, other accounts suggest 3½in face on a 15in plate. Since the transition was gradual, the difference probably lies in the definition of 'face'.

65 This result was confirmed by trials in both countries. See Garzke and Dulin, *Battleships–Allied Battleships in World War II*, p231 quoting J D Scott, *Vickers–a History*.

66 A subcommittee of the committee of Imperial Defence, chaired by Sir Thomas Inskip. Report Cmd 5301, 1936.

67 There is no mention of the B bomb, still secret.

68 A Queen Bee, a radio-controlled target aircraft, had flown round the fleet, under fire, for an hour at 85mph without being hit!

Battleships | *One*

THE NUMEROUS STUDIES for both battleships and battlecruisers carried out prior to the Washington treaty showed what the Royal Navy wanted in the early 1920s. These studies are described in the previous volume and elsewhere but the main particulars of the ultimate battlecruiser 'G 3' and the battleship 'N 3' are included in the table below for comparison.

The Washington Treaty limits are outlined in Appendix 4 but, briefly, for battleships displacement was limited to 35,000 tons with guns up to 16in. No new battleships (other than *Nelson* and *Rodney*) were to be started before 1931.

The first design in January 1927 was for a 28,000-ton ship of *Nelson* style but with 14in guns.[1] In July a second design was prepared with four twin turrets, fore and aft, which was preferred even though it was 1200 tons heavier due to the longer citadel. The displacement of both was later increased by 500 tons to give better protection against 'diving shells', which hit the water short of the ship and could hit below the belt. It is notable that, despite the pressure on size, the heavy deck protection was retained.[2]

Staff requirements 1931

Under the Washington Treaty the replacement of older battleships could begin in 1931, and discussion began in 1928 on their requirements.[3] The discussions at Geneva in 1927 showed that a reduction from 35,000 tons would not be acceptable to other navies and it was decided to look at ships of this size with both 16in and 14in guns. Both calibres would be of new design with heavier shells fired at lower velocity.[4] A new design of 16in turret would be required to overcome the problems found in *Nelson* but the twin 14in design could be modelled on the 15in turret with only slight changes.

There was to be a secondary armament of twin 6in turrets, better protected than in *Nelson* and spaced further apart. The anti-aircraft guns were to be 4.7in of a new design, probable in four twin BD mounts. Consideration was given to a dual-purpose secondary armament but it was thought the AA and anti-destroyer requirements were incompatible.[5] There were to be six bow torpedo tubes as in the submarine *Oberon*, probably 21in with a 1000lb warhead. Protection was to be against 16in shells and 2000lb bombs. Speed was to be 23kts.

Sketch designs, 1928-9

Design 16A in the table below had four twin 16in turrets, two at each end, and was the only 35,000-ton ship. Both the two 14in ships had four twin turrets and had an 11in belt.[6] 14B had a speed of 23kts, while 14A was more powerful and longer; probably reaching 25kts. It was originally hoped that the 14in ship could be kept to 28,000 tons but, as the table shows, this figure was considerably exceeded.

There were eleven 12in designs of which only the preferred four are shown in the table. The reasons for rejection are of interest. The two 27kt ships were too big (at 28,150 and 27,750 tons), well in excess of the proposed 25,000-ton limit. All those with triple turrets went: two with three triple, one with two triples and a twin. The four remaining all had four twin turrets, all eleven had a 10in sloping belt and were said to be better protected against 12in shells than was *Nelson* against 16in. They were all over the 25,000-ton target and though this could be achieved by reducing the thickness of the armour, this was thought unwise. DNC warned that the displacement would probably rise and it would be wise to assume that a 12in ship should be associated

1 Some papers refer to 13.5in guns. The design was for 14in but it was decided to press for a 13.5in limit at Geneva.

2 It is a reasonable guess that this was due to Chatfield who was then Controller.

3 See A Raven and J Roberts, *British Battleships of World War II* (London 1976), p149 for a fuller discussion of designs of this era.

4 16in = 2250lbs, 2575ft/sec MV. 14in = 1500lbs, 2550ft/sec.

5 See Appendix 8.

6 Presumably resisting 14in shells.

Battleship designs of the 1920s

Design	LxBxT (ft)	Dspt (tons)	Armt	shp = kts	Belt (ins) @°	Deck (ins)
1921 'G 3'	850x106x32.5	48,400	9-16in	160,000=32	14@18	8-4
1921 'N 3'	815x106x33	48,000	9-18in	50,000=23	15@18	8
1927a	600x100x33	28,000	9-14in	45,000=23.25	12	6¾-4½
1927b	630x100x33	29,200	8-14in	45,000=23.25	12	6¾-4½
1928 16A	692x106x30	35,000	8-16in	45,000=23	13	6¼-4¼
1928 14A	660x104x27	30,700	8-14in	60,500=?	11	6¼-4¼
1928 14B	620x104x27½	29,070	8-14in	43,500=23	11	6¼-4¼
1928 12B	610x100x26	25,430	8-12in	40,000=23	10	6-4
1928 12D	620x102x26	26,800	8-12in	55,000=25	10	6-4
1928 12G	612x102x26	26,070	8-12in	48,000=24	10	6-4
1928 12J	629x102x26	26,700	9-12in	55,000=25	10	6-4
1928 10A	620x96x25	21,670	8-10in	54,000=24	8	5½-3½
1928 10C	600x98x25	22,000	8-10in	48,000=24	8	5½-3½
1928 11A	600x98x26	23,300	8-11in	48,000=24	9	4¾-3¾

Notes: Length is between perpendiculars. Displacement, standard. Where deck protection has two figures, the first is over magazines, the second over machinery.

This pair of photos, *Rodney* (1937, top) (Wright & Logan) and *Nelson* (1945, right) shows the enormous growth in the number of light anti-aircraft guns during the war. Neither ship had had a proper refit and both were worn out by the end of the war.

Battleships

27

with a 27,000-ton limit. The smaller, 10in and 11in, ships seem to have been purely exploratory and dismissed quickly. There seems to have been little discussion of the fate of a 12in ship with a 10in belt if engaging an older ship with 16in guns. The RN would have been quite content with the 12in limit but neither the USN nor Japan were interested.

Considerable thought was given to protection from 'diving shells'.[7] It was thought that the fuse would explode the shell some 30ft after impact and that the shell would turn broadside on after about 25ft. Three different armour schemes were drawn out. 'A' was similar to *Nelson* but with thinner armour extending the main belt further down. 'B' and 'C' had the belt on the outside of the ship with torpedo protection venting through hinged flaps. This venting system was not liked and all the 1928-9 designs had scheme 'A'.[8] The London Treaty of 1930 (see Appendix 5) retained the Washington limits but extended the moratorium on battleship building to 1937.

It will be noted that these new 12in designs were much heavier than the 1928-9 ships.[9] This was mainly due to a very considerable increase in the weight of armour with a corresponding growth in hull weight.[10] They all had twelve 6in singles in sided batteries and twelve 4.7in AA in twin mounts (see Appendix 8 for discussion of medium-calibre guns). N and P were preferred and DNC produced alternative designs without the 6in guns and with increased numbers of 4.7in (twenty-eight in N, twenty-four in P). They had a quintuple 21in torpedo mount on either beam. Speed was 23kts for all designs.[11] France had already built two ships of about this size, included in the table for comparison, with very light weight machinery and quadruple turrets. It was thought that France, Germany and Italy would agree to ships of about 28,000 tons even though all three were planning much larger ships with 15in guns. There was no chance of the USA or Japan agreeing to smaller ships, so all later designs were of 35,000 tons.

The 1935 studies

The first eleven studies for 35,000-ton ships included three with 16in guns,[12] two with 15in[13] and six with 14in.[14] They all had ten twin 4.5in BD mounts, and protection included a 12-14in belt with deck over magazines of 5-6in and 3-5in over the machinery. Nine had speeds of 27-30kts with just two at 23kts. The faster ones were described as battlecruisers in early papers.

These designs were compared in a lengthy paper by the naval staff which can only be summarised here.[15] A key factor was the penetration of deck and side armour by different sizes of shells and bombs. The USN presentation of 'immunity zones' was clearer than that used in Britain but it is obvious that the two navies were working on very similar principles.

1934 Designs with 12in guns

Design	LxBxT (ft)	Dspt (tons)	Armt	shp = kts	Belt (ins)	Deck (ins)
12 N	570x102x29	28,500	8-12in	45,000=23.0	12½	5½-3½
12 O	570x102x29	28,130	9-12in	45,000=23.0	12½	5½-3½
12 P	590x103½x28½	28,500	10-12in	45,000=23¼	12	5-3
12 Q	590x103½x28½	28,500	9-12in	45,000=23¼	12	5-3½
Dunkerque	685x102x28½	26,500	8-13in	112,500=29.5	9¾	5

Ranges below which side armour is penetrated by AP shell at normal impact (yds)

	Shell		
Armour thickness	14in, 1590lb	15in, 1938lb	16in, 2375lb
14in	13,700	17,200	20,000
13in	15,800	19,400	22,000
12in	18,000	21,700	24,500
11in	20,500	24,500	28,000
10in	23,700	28,000	32,000

Ranges above which deck armour is penetrated by AP shells (yds)

	Shell		
Armour thickness	14in	15in	16in
6	Immune	32,500	31,000
5	32,000	29,500	
4	28,000	26,000	
3	24,000	22,000	
2	20,000	18,000	

Heights above which deck armour is penetrated by bombs (ft)

	Bomb			
Armour thickness (ins)	2000lb AP	1500lb AP	1000lb AP	500lb SAP
7	9000	13,000	immune	immune
6	7000	10,600	15,000	immune
5	5000	7800	10,500	immune
4	3000	5000	7000	12,000
3	1000	2500	4000	7000
2	-	-	2000	3200

Offord pointed out that for deck armour 'our information re bomb resistance is fairly comprehensive and re shell resistance is at least good enough for comparisons

7 At Jutland, *Lion* was hit by five such shells and *Malaya* by two. After the war, there were numerous such hits on the target ships *Agamemnon* and *Centurion*.

8 It was proposed to fit the lower extension in *Nelson* and *Rodney* but this was never done.

9 Goodall, 2 Feb 1934. 'Four twin 12 inch + good protection = 28,000 tons, 10 - 12 inch means moderate protection on 29,000 tons.'

10 Goodall, 15 Sep 1933. 'Started work on new battleship; a balanced design according to old ideas of balance will have 24,000 tons but with heavy protection will be 33,000.'

11 Goodall, 27 Jul 1933. 'Looked at his new battleship design – if it matures we should be laughing stock of the world.' And 28 Nov 1933. 'Looked at H-- struggle with a form for the new capital ship. Really his design ignorance is "Kolossal"'.

12 Two with nine guns, one with eight guns.

13 Both with nine guns.

14 Four with twelve, one with eight and one with ten guns.

15 Given in full in Raven and Roberts, *British Battleships of World War II*.

16 D Offord. Head of Vulnerability section, DNC, 'Protection of New Battleships' (1 Jan 37, unreferenced). Paper passed to National Maritime Museum. Note that Offord's view is exactly the opposite of the staff view quoted by Roberts (p279). Offord was the expert.

Ranges

RN Ship	Opponent	Date	Opening Range (yds)
Renown	*Gneisenau*	9 Apr 1940	19,000. Hit after 10 minutes
Warspite	*Cesare*	9 Jul 1940	26,000. Hit 1st salvo
P of Wales	*Bismarck*	24 May 1941	26,500. Hit around 14,500yds
Rodney	*Bismarck*	27 May 1941	23,400. Hit 2nd salvo
D of York	*Scharnhorst*	26 Dec 1943	12,000. Hit 1st salvo (radar)

Development of the *King George V* class

Design	LxBxT (ft)	Dspt (tons)	Armt	shp = kts	Belt (ins)	Deck (ins)
14L	700x104x28	35,000	12-14in, 20-4.5in	100,000=28.0	14	6-5
14O		35,000	12-14in, 16-5.25in	100,000=28.5	14-13	5½-4½
14P	700x103x28	35,000	10-14in, 16-5.25in	100,000=28.5	15-14	6-5

Anson on trials in 1942. Note that she is very wet even in this very moderate sea. The requirement of the guns of A turret to fire forward at depression severely limited the sheer of the forecastle deck and hence the freeboard at the bow (compare with *Vanguard*'s raised forecastle). (Imperial War Museum: A10153)

to be made . . . our data re side armour of this thickness is far less definite.'[16] He went on to say that there was evidence that armour mounted on the flexible structure of a ship was more effective than during butt tests. He also pointed out that there were problems in the manufacture of very thick plates (over 13in) and it was not certain that increase in thickness would give a proportionate increase in resistance. It was assumed that 'decisive range' would be 12,000-16,000yds. The table above shows some of the longest ranges at which British battleships opened fire in the Second World War which suggests the staff were right in selecting decisive range.[17]

It was concluded that it would be impossible to give adequate protection to a 30kt ship with 16in guns and the 14in had insufficient penetration. The ship with nine 15in guns incurred some risks at decisive range but it was thought these were acceptable.

At 27kts a well-balanced ship could be designed with nine 16in, nine 15in or twelve 14in guns. Overall, the 15in version was preferred as protection of the 16in ship was on the light side. At 23kts, a well protected ship with nine 16in was possible. No more guns could be mounted if the calibre was reduced to 15in so the smaller gun had no advantage. On the other hand, twelve 14in could be mounted, which was likely to score more hits. However, the greater penetration of the 16in was preferred.

The staff paper quoted DNC as saying that the weight saving in a *Nelson*-style design would not be as great in a ship with numerous AA guns and with aircraft arrangements. He also said that it was unlikely that the machinery could be accommodated aft in a 27 or 30kt ship.[18] The staff had a strong preference for one turret bearing aft, but they did not express a clear preference for any particular speed.

On 20 September 1935 the paper was discussed by the Sea Lords who decided on nine 15in guns and 29kts. In October it was learnt that the USA would agree to a 14in limit on guns provided that Japan agreed. Since it was hoped to order the guns for the first two battleships before the end of 1935 a decision had to be made very quickly. On 10 October, the Sea Lords decided on twelve 14in and 28kts (note modernisations are covered in Chapter 9).[19]

Design L (see table left) was the first response to the Sea Lords' decision. It was thought that the shafts were too long and design N, which otherwise was the same as L, had the machinery moved 32ft aft. It also had one

funnel to make it more difficult to estimate its inclination. These designs were considered in January 1936 when the following points were discussed. The speed was 28kts in standard condition but only 27kts with full fuel (4000 tons) and water in the torpedo protection (2000 tons). DNC agreed to consider putting 2000 tons of fuel in the protection instead of water. E-in-C came up with an extra 10,000 shp as 'design overload' giving 28.8kts standard, 27.5kts deep at the cost of 100 tons of machinery weight.

There is a lengthy passage in Goodall's diary (13 March 1936) concerning Chatfield's views on these studies.

Controller, I gather, is thinking he won't get Chatfield to walk back and agree to 14 O study. He put Chatfield case very politely and said it was the psychological shock of what he saw at Jutland. I pointed out that *Queen Mary* and co went up through cordite fires and Controller said 'Yes; Chatfield knows and I know. Nevertheless the effect on Chatfield is such that he feels under no circumstances will he be responsible for a ship that has the faintest chance of blowing up.' This is the constructors' tragedy . . .

Goodall had another concern with the 14 O design.

DNC sent me down to Controller (R Backhouse, First Sea Lord, also present) with rough drawing of 14 O. Both very pleased but Controller said 'What about weight?'; when I explained, he said 'In other words it's cheating'. I said yes it is. Told DNC who was very sad and said he would look into weights and tackle that part of the job himself. . . . It's all very well for DNC to cut our weights but he will be gone when the crunch comes.

A much bigger change, proposed by ACNS, was to raise the armour deck from middle deck to main deck with a corresponding increase in the depth of the belt. Pengelly[20] pointed out the advantages of raising the deck:

A 500lb SAP exploding near the ship's side on the armoured main deck should not compel the ship to [return] to a base immediately for repair but a hit on the middle deck would. The reserve of buoyancy and stability with the ends riddled is greatly increased and the main deck gives strength for heavy weather with the upper deck wrecked. Escape from below is facilitated, the middle deck is the crown of the boiler room and difficult to armour. Communications are better protected if the armour is at main deck level.

Furthermore, with two structural decks below the main deck there was no need for a splinter deck as in USN ships. The thick upper deck was sufficient for de-capping. To keep within the 35,000-ton limit the thickness

of the deck was reduced by ½in and the upper belt by 1in. The secondary armament was changed to sixteen 5.25in – hindsight suggests that the original twenty 4.5in would have been more effective. The reduction in thickness was not liked and, after discussion of various alternatives, it was agreed to reduce the main armament to ten 14in guns.

There was an interesting discussion, recorded in Pengelly's work book, as to the position for the twin mounting.[21] This note shows one example of the numerous interacting factors in a design.

Y Weight aft reduced, lowering docking stress.
    Less blast on aircraft and hangar.
    Shell rooms easier.
A Move citadel forward and improve arrangement at Y.
    Reduce sagging stress.
    Can fine lines forward.
B Move citadel forward.
    Greatest weight saving.
    Less blast on bridge.

In the end weight-saving was paramount and B position was selected.

The design of the quadruple 14in mount was begun in October 1935, when trial guns were ordered, and in May 1936 orders were placed for four quadruple and two twin mounts. It soon became obvious that the amount of drawing office work had been grossly underestimated and there was a shortage of skilled labour to build them.[22] The first quadruples were 11 months late and the twins were 6 months late.

King George V

Now that the main particulars were decided, the detail design could proceed. Compared with post-war procedures, the design process of the late 1930s was simple. In November 1936 the ship design team consisted of one constructor, two assistant constructors, two senior draughtsmen and sixteen draughtsmen and the work was completed in a few months.[23] Following Goodall's promotion to DNC in 1936, battleship design was headed by H S Pengelly, a tough and capable constructor, well trusted by Goodall.[24]

Protection

As shown earlier, the design was dominated by protection. The cemented armour was much improved due to slight changes in composition and heat treatment and had a resistance to penetration about 25 per cent greater than older armour.[25] There were initial problems in achieving the design performance but these were solved.

The very deep main belt extended from 8½ft below the designed (standard) waterline to the main deck, a total depth of 23½ft.[26] It was arranged in three strakes

17 However, note that the monitor *General Wolfe* fired at 36,000yds in 1918.

18 I do not understand this, the 'G 3s' with that layout were much more powerful, though bigger.

19 There is an excellent history of this and related decisions in ADM 205/23.

20 Head of battleship section. It was DNC Section No 1 and usually had the pick of the staff.

21 Now in the National Maritime Museum.

22 Goodall, 23 Mar 1936. 'Afraid I'm beginning to worry guts. Oh that we could be left alone quietly to get on with the job.'

23 In addition, there would be contributions from DNC specialist groups dealing with protection, galley design and many other topics. There would also be Engineer and Electrical groups.

24 By the time I met Pengelly c1953, he had mellowed and was a charming gentleman. There is an amusing pair of entries in his work book for the *King George V*. First thing in the morning he notes a visit by Goodall – 'Told DNC he was wrong'. The day concludes on a note of triumph – 'Convinced DNC he was wrong'!

25 Details of the changes have not been found. Similar changes were made in Germany about 1930 but the USA were not aware of the improved performance until 1939, too late for improved armour to be fitted in any USN battleship. Postwar tests, both in the UK and USA, including some on plates removed from *Tirpitz*, confirmed these figures.

26 Depth of belt is rarely quoted in comparisons of rival ships but it is a very important parameter.

Duke of York, Berwick and *Liverpool* in dock at Rosyth 11 November 1943. Note that the gap for the catapult has been filled in and the anti-aircraft armament has been enhanced. (Imperial War Museum: A20162)

of about equal depth with plates in each strake keyed to those above and below and to neighbouring plates at the butts.[27] The upper two strakes were 15ins thick abreast the magazines and the lowest one tapered from those thicknesses to 5½ and 4½ins at the bottom.

Within the citadel, the main deck was 6ins thick over the magazines and 5ins over machinery, all non-

cemented plate.[28] The lower deck forward was 5ins at the citadel tapering to 2½ins at the forward bulkhead. The lower deck aft was 4½ins with 5ins over the steering gear.

Torpedo protection

The torpedo protection was a triple sandwich of air-, liquid-, and air-filled spaces between the shell and the main holding bulkhead which was of two thicknesses of 30lb plate riveted together. The initial force of the explosion would be dissipated in the outer air space while the liquid-filled space would slow down fragments from the ruptured shell plating and would also spread the load.[29] The inner air-filled space would prevent the shockwave in the liquid from impinging directly on the holding bulkhead. The intermediate bulkheads were 15lbs. Even so, the rivets in the bulkhead might

27 It is interesting that when armour was introduced in *Warrior* (1860), plates were keyed to each other. This feature was soon abandoned as it was thought that the joint could spread damage to adjacent plates; it was also realised that the replacement of a damaged plate would be very difficult.

28 Several passages in Goodall's diary during March 1936 refer to

5½in new deck armour equivalent to 6¼in of the old material.

29 It was originally intended that the liquid should be water but to carry sufficient oil without undue size of ship it was decided to fill with oil. If it was necessary to burn this oil it would be displaced by water.

30 Goodall, 29 Apr 1938. 'Sir Thomas Inskip saw KGV damage model, seemed very impressed and

wants MP's Committee to see. Controller said All right'. Then 10 June 1938. 'A BF committee of CID came to see KGV flooding model. They seemed more keen on improving air attack than anti aircraft defence, a wrong attitude for an insular naval power.'

31 *Prince of Wales* fired fifty-five rounds out of a possible seventy-four.

tear and leak so there were inner spaces to limit the extent of any such flooding. This protection was designed to resist a 1000lb warhead and was proved at full scale on Job 74 (see Introduction). It did not perform as well as expected during the Japanese attack on *Prince of Wales*, discussed in Chapter 10.[30]

Armament

The reason for the selection of 14in guns and the reduction to ten guns has been explained and seems inevitable in the circumstances. The 14in gun could penetrate at least 12in armour (British or German) at 18,000yds – the face plate of *Bismarck*'s B turret was penetrated at long range by either a 14in or 16in shell and the conning tower (14in thick) is said to resemble Swiss cheese. The problem lay in the mounting which was unreliable.

Problems in the *Prince of Wales* against *Bismarck* could be excused since she was barely complete but *King George V* only got off 339 rounds against *Bismarck* compared with 380 from *Rodney* with a slower-firing gun.[31] Even at the end of 1943 *Duke of York* only got off 68 per cent of possible rounds at North Cape.

Part of the problem lay in the requirement to pass ammunition into the turret at any angle of training. This involved a transfer ring, moving independently between ship (magazine) and turret. The designers of the ring did not allow enough for the flexibility of a ship and its bending due to heating of the upper deck in sunshine and the action of waves. Either could bend the ship several inches.

Goodall compares some of the secondary features in battleships of 1935 with those of 1912.

The forward 14in guns of *Duke of York* seen in Rosyth in 1945. The choice of the 14in gun was dictated by political considerations but the damage inflicted on the *Bismarck* shows that it was a fully adequate weapon. (Imperial War Museum: A20166)

Prince of Wales in 1941 showing her hoisting her Walrus amphibian. Aircraft arrangements absorbed a great deal of weight and space and the need to keep them from severe gun blast constrained upper deck layout. (The Naval Photograph Club)

32 Goodall, 3 Apr 1939. 'Discussed aircraft aft in 1939 battleships. (This would have led to poor damaged stability.)'

33 In which case why were RN destroyers armed with the smaller 4.5in?

34 It seems that the inadequate ventilation system of these ships was due to the assumption that they would operate in European waters.

35 Vice-Admiral Sir Louis Le Bailly, *The Man around the Engine* (Emsworth 1990), Ch 11.

36 This seems unlikely since the *KGV* estimates were based on the actual weights of *Nelson*.

37 Quoted in Raven and Roberts, p283.

Percentage of standard displacement

Feature	1912	1935
Secondary armament	2	5
Torpedo protection	2.5	5
Horizontal protection	5	16
TOTAL of these	10	25

Aircraft arrangements not only took up a great deal of space but were difficult to accommodate as they had to be kept away from gun blast.[32]

The earlier studies had a 6in armament against destroyers and 4.7in AA. The 5.25in gun finally decided upon was seen as dual-purpose but it was often said that its 80lb shell was too small to attack destroyers.[33] Furthermore, rates of training and elevation and rate of fire were too slow for effective AA work and it was unreliable as well.

Comparison of stability

Ship/date	Dispt (tons)	GM (ft)	Max GZ (ft)	Max Angle°	Range°
Design	40,990	8.51	5.35	37	72.5
KGV/1940	42,245	8.14	4.87	35.5	70.4
Howe/1944	44,512	7.25	3.98	34	65.5
Nelson	39,245	9.4	6.0	38	

Stability

The citadel was relatively much longer and deeper than that in *Nelson* which meant that the metacentric height in the intact condition could be reduced while still preserving adequate stability after damage. The table (below left) shows the stability in the deep condition, as completed and in 1944.

Machinery

The problems encountered with British machinery are detailed in Chapter 5 but must be mentioned here. There was progress during and soon after the First World War which made possible the modernisation of some older ships, but from the early 1920s only slight progress was made.

Machinery weights

Ship	lbs/shp
Queen Elizabeth, as built	86.1
Hood	65.9 Small tube boilers
Queen Elizabeth, modernised	43.9
King George V	37.3

Note: USN machinery was lighter and more compact but comparisons are not possible since electrical equipment was under machinery in US records and under hull in the British system.

Battleships

33

The price for obsolescent machinery was paid in endurance. The Staff Requirement read 'Sufficient for 200 hours at 16 knots with steam for 18 knots, plus 18 hours at full speed, plus 16 hours at 18 knots with steam for full speed.' This was to be achieved with fouling equivalent to six months out of dock and with a 35 per cent allowance for bad weather and maloperation. The total was not to be less than that needed for 14,000 miles at 10kts. The USN's anti-fouling paint was considerably superior, helping their endurance still further. In temperate water frictional resistance, which accounted for most of the power required at lower speeds, would increase by some ½ per cent per day with the British material – 90 per cent in six months out of dock – whereas the US material fouled at about half that rate. Eventually, their composition was made in Portsmouth under license.

Chatfield (as First Sea Lord) thought this endurance could be reduced if the class were to operate only in European waters.[34] It was assumed that the fuel consumption at 10kts in trial condition would be 2.4 tons per hour but in service it was 6.4 tons per hour, due in part to the innumerable steam leaks from joints in the piping.[35] The realistic endurance of the class was 6000 miles at 10kts or 5000 miles at 20kts with 3770 tons of oil. (The small difference between these figures reflects the very heavy consumption of the auxiliaries.) In 1942 the USS Washington operated with the Home Fleet and Admiral Tovey reported that her fuel consumption was 39 per cent less than King George V at lower speeds and still superior at higher speeds which with a fuel stowage gave the US ship double the endurance of the British battleship

Weight growth

The original design calculations showed a displacement (standard) of 35,900 tons but it was hoped that savings during building as in Nelson would bring this down to 35,000 tons before completion.[36] Weight began to creep up and when the legend was prepared for Board approval in September 1936, the calculated displacement was 36,401 tons. Goodall altered the figure to 35,500 tons.[37] Though this change was arbitrary, a real effort was made to achieve the lower figure: Pengelly's workbook shows that an attempt was made to save 213 tons by reducing the thickness of armour by 5-10lbs. However, weights still increased despite a memo to all departments in August 1936 calling for savings. In fact,

Anson being broken up in 1959, looking aft. The bulkhead in the foreground is that between the forward boiler and engine room. To the right of the picture (port side) the bulkheads of the torpedo protection system may be seen. (Dr I L Buxton)

Howe at sea in 1944 showing the extra deckhouse in place of the catapult and the increased anti-aircraft armament. (Courtesy John Roberts)

the calculated weights of September 1936 were very accurate.

Breakdown of weights

Group	Weight (tons)		
	Legend	Calculated	As completed
Hull	12,500	13,750	13,830
Machinery	2685	2687	2768
Armament	6050	6144	6567
Armour	12,700	13,215	12,413
Equipment	1050	1120	1149
TOTAL	34,985	36,916	36,727

Cost breakdown (Vote 8 ex Dockyard)

Item	Cost (£x1000)
Hull and Electrics	2050
Main and Auxiliary Machinery	825
Armour	1425
Guns	550
Gun mountings and air compressors	1514
Ammunition	805
Aircraft (4 TBR)	34
" Torpedoes and Bombs	21
Boats	20
Incidentals	27
Dockyard labour and materials	25
TOTAL	£7493 thousand

Comparison of battleships

Ship	KGV	N Carolina	S Dakota	Littorio	Bismarck	Richelieu	Yamato	S Soyus
Dspt, st (tons)	35,500	36,600	38,664	41,167	41,700	38,199	62,315	58,220
Dspt, deep (tons)	42,000	46,700	44,519	45,272	46,000	43,992	69,990	64,120
Armt	10-14in	9-16in	9-16in	9-15in	8-15in	8-15in	9-18.1in	9-16in
Belt (ins)	15	12	12¼	13.8	12½	13½	16.1	16¾
Deck (ins)	5-6	3.6-4.1	5	4-6	3.2-4.7	6-6.8	7.9-9	5.9
Torpedo (ft)	13	18½	18½	25	18	20	17	
vs charge (lbs)	1000	700	700	1100	550		880	
Speed (kts)	28.5	27	28	30	30	31.5	27.5	28

Note: Where two figures are given for deck thickness, the thicker one is above magazines and the other over machinery. Torpedo protection is given as depth to main bulkhead on the upper line, the charge weight to be resisted below.

Duke of York in the Pacific in 1945. Note the two-tone paintwork, extra AA guns and radar. (Courtesy John Roberts)

The estimated costs above were used as the basis for a single tender order for *King George V* and *Prince of Wales* (both c£3,500,000 for hull and machinery only) whist the actual cost was some 20 per cent less.[38] (See Chapter 11 for excess profits, Gordon for tendering.)

The first two ships (1936 Programme) were laid down on 1 January 1937, the first day after the Treaty moratorium expired. Somewhat reluctantly, it was decided that the three ships of the 1937 programme should be of the same design and they were laid down later in 1937.

The figures in the table opposite (below) are chosen, with difficulty, to represent the design intention.[39] Most grew in weight whilst building, after the war started. The hull form of the US ships was selected so that the maximum depth could be maintained over a great length. They attempted to provide protection to the inner tail shafts by fitting skegs to the outer ones.[40]

One can see that the RN put priority on protection with the thickest belt and deck of any ship near the 35,000-ton limit[41] and with torpedo protection designed – and tested – to resist a 1000lb charge. The depth of the protected citadel, bought at great price, was also much greater than in most other ships. Speed was less important and, seemingly gun power even less so. However, a recent inspection of the wreck of the *Bismarck* suggests that the 14in gun was at least adequate.

Hindsight – a personal view

An internal paper by Offord suggested that the side armour would have to be reduced by about 2ins and the deck by ½in for a ship with twelve 14in guns. The range at which the deck could be penetrated by 14in fire would have been reduced by 1500yds and the belt would have lost about 2500yds effectiveness at normal impact, less at oblique impact. I think this would have been worthwhile. If politics permitted I would have gone for nine 16in guns with twelve 14in as the fallback. I would not have fitted any secondary armament nor any aircraft (which might have enabled some of the armour to be thickened).

Ackworth's mini battleship

During 1937-8 Captain B Ackworth advocated small battleships with coal or dual firing. One such ship claimed to mount six 13.5in guns on 11,980 tons with a speed of 17kts.[42] He also advocated coal or dual firing for other categories. Politicians including the Prime Minister were attracted by the claims for a cheaper fleet and DNC had to waste a great deal of time rebutting these claims. Ackworth read a paper on dual firing to the INA in April 1938.[43] Both Goodall and the E-in-C spoke in the discussion giving the true facts.[44] It is, perhaps, of interest that during the oil crisis of the early 1970s, various studies were made into the use of coal.[45] The cheapest and most satisfactory answer was to convert the coal into oil on shore and use conventional machinery.

Lion

Technically, the *Lion* design was a slightly enlarged *King George V* with nine 16in guns and needs little discussion. All options had been considered during the development of the *King George V* and within the constraints of time, money and industrial capacity it was

38 The original proposed name for the second ship was *Edward VIII*, changed by the King (Moore).

39 I am grateful to Phil Sims for comments on USN displacement and to Andrew Smith for French and Italian figures. The USN had an interesting interpretation; that the Washington Treaty was not binding on equipment not invented in 1922. Therefore, light anti-aircraft guns, radar etc were not included in the standard displacement of their ships!

40 These led to very severe vibration problems which took a long while to solve. In the author's opinion, it is doubtful if they provided much protection.

41 Note that British and German armour was 25 per cent superior to US material. The quality of other countries' armour is unknown.

42 B Ackworth, *Britain in Danger* (London 1937).

43 B Ackworth, 'Alternative Firing of British Men-of-War', *Trans INA* (1938).

44 Goodall, 6 April 1938. 'Spoke at INA v Ackworth, not very pleased with myself.' There are several other entries of this period complaining about the way ministers fell for Ackworth's ideas.

45 One study led to a cartoon of a coal burning Type 42 with four tall, thin funnels and a ram bow!

King George V in 1946. The AA
armament has been reduced to
save on maintenance work.
(Wright & Logan)

46 Raven & Roberts, *British
Battleships of World War II*.

47 Russia, Germany and Italy also
signed later.

48 Goodall, 4 May 1938. 'RB (1st
Sea Lord) wants 12-16in and thinks
US will do it on 45,000 tons. I said
we couldn't do it whatever the
speed unless we gave up docking at
Portsmouth and Rosyth. CNS said
out limit was 40,000. Later D of P
said US attitude was stick to 35,000
or go to 45,000 – no compromise
between.'

49 ADM 205/23 for this and later
decisions.

50 Goodall, 24 Jan 1940.' I was
horrified that First Sea Lord
(Pound) wants still more capital
ships; he is willing to give up
anything to get them.'

51 Goodall, 16 Feb 1942. (At
Haslar) 'Looked at *Lion* with
propellers forward – Horrid is the
first impression.'

52 ADM 229 26 of 18 June 1942.

53 ADM 205/23.

54 This was used, briefly, to justify
the conversion of *Vanguard* to a
carrier.

55 Goodall, 25 Jan 1944; also 2 Feb
'Winston all out for battleships.
There is now a pro battleship set
back in the Admiralty.'

56 Early proposals frequently
referred to such ships as
'battlecruisers' in the light of their
comparatively light armament.

thought that this design was the best which could be achieved.

The earliest studies, in April 1937, were for a 35,000-ton ship with protection as in *King George V* and two triple and one twin 16in turret. The displacement came out at 36,150 tons and various schemes to cut this down were considered.[46] By early 1938 reports had been received that the new Japanese ships were very large, possibly with 18in guns, and on 31 March Britain, USA and France invoked the escalator clause raising the displacement limit. The new limit was set at 45,000 tons at US insistence, though Britain said it would not exceed 40,000 tons.[47] Before this limit had been agreed, DNC produced a number of design studies including a monster of 48,500 tons (55,000 tons deep) with twelve 16in.[48] These studies seem to have confirmed that a 40,000-ton ship made best use of resources, did not have

serious docking problems and had the capability in both attack and defence to deal with any likely opponent.

A new study was approved at the end of June and detailed design commenced. The standard displacement was 40,750 tons with the usual expectation of savings during build. There were nine 16in guns of a new design firing a heavy shell (2375lbs), sixteen 5.25in DP and protection as *King George V* except that the belt over the machinery was increased to 15ins.

The two ships of the 1938 programme were laid down in mid-1939 and it was intended to order the two 1939 ships in mid-summer. On 28 September 1939 it was decided to suspend work on the ships though work on the gun mountings for the first two would continue.[49] The First Sea Lord, Pound, made frequent attempts to get these ships re-started and some re-

Comparison of *Lion* with larger and smaller designs, 1942[52]

	Lion 1938	*Lion 1942*	*Small A*	*Small B*	*Large*
Length wl (ft)	780	810	630	740	1000
Dspt stanrd (tons)	40,000	48,000	33,000	37,000	85,000
Dspt deep (tons)	46,500	56,500	39,000	43,500	97,000
shp x1000/speed (kts)	120/30	140/29½	75/25	110/28	250/31½
Armament	9-16in	9-16in	6-16in triple	6-16in twin	9-16in
	16-5.25in	16-5.25in	12-4.5in	16-4.5in	16-5.25in
	6x8pp	8x8pp	16-40mm	16-40mm	8x8-40mm
		24-20mm	24-20mm	24-20mm	24-20mm
Armour side (ins)	15	15	15	14	18
deck (ins)	5-6	5-6	5-6	5-6	9

design was undertaken.[50] Early in the war, they had grown to 56,500 tons, 810ft x 115ft.[51]

Goodall, in a covering note, pointed out that even the big ship was not invulnerable to underwater attack. He saw the future as lying with the aircraft carrier.

On 14 September 1942 Goodall came back from Deputy First Sea Lord's meeting (Admiral C E Kennedy-Purvis) and wrote in his diary 'It was decided that the carrier should be the core of the fleet of the future. Hurrah!'. The official notes alter the conclusion somewhat.[53] 'After discussion, it was decided that it would be better not to refer to the aircraft carrier as "the core of the fleet" '. It was agreed that 'the carrier is indispensable.'[54] Pound's successor, Cunningham, was also a battleship enthusiast. Goodall was given a retirement lunch on 25 January 1944 when Cunningham said that '. . . there won't be an aircraft carrier afloat in twenty years time. I said I thought the battleship was dead. We are poles asunder.'[55]

Vanguard

When the 'large light cruisers' *Courageous* and *Glorious* were converted into aircraft carriers their 15in gun tur-rets were put into store. In the late 1930s there were a number of proposals to use these turrets in a modern battleship.[56] A DNC study of February 1937 showed that it would be possible to design such a ship within the 35,000-ton limit. This seems to have died but in March 1939 Director of Plans came back to the idea, asking for a 30kt ship of 40,000 tons. E-in-C wanted to use *Lion* machinery, the design of which was nearly complete, and this brought the speed at normal power to 29¼kts. The basic design of *Vanguard* was similar to *Lion/King George V* but changes were made using the lessons of the war. There were several proposals to build sister-ships taking guns from the *Royal Sovereign*s, but it was clear that there was insufficient effort to spare and none of these schemes was pursued.

In February 1940 it was decided to fit splinter protection to the waterline forward and aft of the citadel and to increase the protection of the eight 5.25in turrets. By April 1940 other changes had been made and it was decided to reduce the belt by 1in. Underwater protection was the same as *King George V* but after the loss of *Prince of Wales* it was deepened one deck height. It was soon realised that the original light AA of six 8-barrel pompoms was inadequate and there were several

Vanguard in 1953. The increased sheer forward is clear. This made her much dryer than previous British battleships – and USS *Iowa*. (Courtesy John Roberts)

A close-up of *Vanguard* in
1946. Note the numerous 6-
barrel Bofors. (Wright & Logan)

changes. For example, on 28 August 1941 Goodall wrote 'VCNS wants aircraft aft in *Vanguard*. Damn!' (a very rare expletive in the diaries). She finally had seventy-three 40mm barrels in a variety of mounts.

Changes to the old turrets were not easy; they had been designed when magazines were above shell rooms and to reduce the work needed *Vanguard* had cordite handing rooms on the lower deck, above her shell rooms which, in turn, were above her magazines. The two old forward turrets became A and Y for *Vanguard*; the other two needed more work to give them the longer trunks to B and X.[57] The face plates were increased to 13in and the roof to 6in NC. Flash protection was brought up to modern standards and the elevation increased to 30°. She was intended to use supercharge propellant charges but these were never issued.[58] Remote power control of training was fitted.

In July 1942 it was proposed to convert *Vanguard* into an aircraft carrier, this being a reflection of the enthusiasm referred to above which led to the carrier being described as 'the core of the fleet'. Though DNC confirmed that this was possible, it was recognised that the result would be to lose an excellent battleship and gain a mediocre carrier, and the scheme was therefore abandoned. The original design had aircraft arrangements as *King George V* but these were omitted to improve the AA arrangements. There was a proposal to fit a hangar aft but DNC was scathing and this, too, was dropped.

Vanguard had a transom stern giving a bonus of ⅓kt and improved stability. In September 1942 it was decided to increase the sheer forward very considerably

which made her a far better seaboat than *King George V* (and *Iowa*). Inevitably, wartime changes meant that she completed much overweight – 51,420 tons deep instead of the final design of 48,140 tons. Stability had deteriorated but was still adequate though her stresses were a cause of concern. Additions could only be accepted if compensating weight were given up. She was the first British design with cafeteria messing which was initially unpopular but soon became a model for the future.

A personal view

Because of her 'second-hand' guns *Vanguard* is often seen as a second-rate ship. However, she was much superior to *King George V*; compared with *Iowa*, her 15in shells should have had little difficulty in penetrating the thin belt of inferior armour. On the other hand, the heavy US shells would have caused much damage. Much would depend on who got the first hits; *Vanguard* could range to 36,500yds and it is unlikely that *Iowa* could hit at greater ranges. I would even have given her a good chance against the much larger *Yamato*.

But it won't lie down!

Late in the war and even after there were attempts to revive the *Lion*. Two were planned for the 1945 programme with two more 'projected.'[59] On 22 November 1944 the second pair were cancelled but the others were to proceed slowly. At this time it was envisaged that they would displace 43-50,000 tons with nine 16in, twelve 4.5in and ten 6-barrel Bofors. Long endurance at

57 Though the turrets came from *Courageous* and *Glorious*, the barrels were changed. The complicated story is told in a letter to *Navy News*, September 1999 (p8), by Arnold Hague.

58 This change involved stiffening the supports to take the increased recoil force.

59 This passage is based on research by G Moore and used with permission.

60 CAB 66 60.

61 Appendix 9, size of docks.

62 I have been told that there were studies with a 12in deck.

63 ADM 1 18659.

high speed was thought necessary and 6000 miles at 25kts was desirable. The roles were carrier escort and shore bombardment. It is suggested that shore bombardment was far less effective than usually claimed (see Appendix 10).

There seems to have been considerable opposition in the War Cabinet to this attempt to continue the battleship programme. The sinking of the *Tirpitz* by 12,000lb bombs was seen to mark the end.[60] The First Lord's reply made the usual points that aircraft, particularly from carriers, could not be sure of sinking a battleship in bad weather and that battleships were an essential part of the carriers' protective screen. Perhaps for the first time, it was suggested that guided weapons would swing the balance away from aircraft. The sinking of the *Tirpitz* was countered by the failure to sink *Scharnhorst* and *Gneisenau*, only 150 miles from British air bases.

The new DNC, Charles Lillicrap, reported on 25 January 1945. Studies had shown that a battleship with this armament would be between 950 and 1000ft long with a beam of 120ft and displace 67-70,000 tons.[61] There would be a 15in belt and 6in deck over the magazines.[62] Some drawing work had been undertaken to examine magazine protection. A total of 18,300 tons was absorbed in protection and Lillicrap thought that this should be reduced. Sea speed would be 26kts, 30.25kts standard. Lillicrap minuted 'he cannot but view with considerable concern the size of this ship . . . a ship even of this size is far from invulnerable.'

A small committee was set up to study the requirements of a smaller battleship of about 44,000 tons.[63] They took a Sea Lords' minute of May 1944 as their starting point: 'The basis of the strength of the Fleet is the battleship. . . . A heavier broadside than the enemy is still a very telling weapon in a naval action.' Armament was reduced to six 16in in two triples forward, the belt came down to 12.5ins but a 6in deck was retained (with 4ins over machinery) and speed, standard, to 29kts. It was hoped that this would equate to 45,000 tons. There were still hopes for a final class of four ships. The 1945 programme included two such ships at £13,250,000 each but it never reached the Cabinet.

It is often said that the battleship died because it was vulnerable. This is incorrect; it was replaced by the fleet carrier which was much more vulnerable. The battleship died because it was far less capable than the carrier of inflicting damage on the enemy.

Vanguard, 8 September 1948. Note the transom stern, the only battleship so fitted. It gave an increase in top speed of ⅓kt and would have improved stability particularly following damage aft of amidships. The hull form is a good, conventional one compared with the *Iowa*, which sacrificed a little hydrodynamic performance for the sake of more effective torpedo protection. (Imperial War Museum: FL20866)

Two | Fleet Carriers

The aircraft carrier presents the naval constructor with some of the most difficult problems encountered in warship design. On a hull possessing most normal warship features, provision must be made for the operation and maintenance of several squadrons of aircraft. If operated ashore, a carrier's aircraft would require an airfield extending over several square miles with air control, hangar, maintenance shops, petrol stowage, bomb dumps, barrack blocks and messes, transport and runways thousands of feet in length. In the carrier this has to be compacted into a ship about 800 feet long with a flight deck area of less than two acres. (J H B Chapman RCNC)[1]

Indomitable entering No 2 Dock at Rosyth. Note the forward gun battery which had good arcs of fire at the expense of obstructing the flight deck. In the background may be seen (left to right) the cruiser *Emerald*, a *Royal Sovereign* class battleship, a 'Town' class, and *Newark* (G47). (Imperial War Museum: A23371)

EARLY IN 1919, of the existing RN aviation ships, it was intended to retain *Furious*, *Argus*, *Vindictive*, *Nairana*, *Pegasus*, *Vindex* and *Ark Royal* and also to complete *Eagle* and *Hermes*. But *Nairana* was on the disposal list by the end of the year and the other seaplane carriers, except *Pegasus*, were disposed of. It was soon decided to lay up *Vindictive* pending her re-conversion to a cruiser and *Furious* was also to be laid up until her future was decided. The projected battle fleet comprised forty-one capital ships and it was thought that these should be supported by no fewer than eleven aircraft carriers with a total of 175 aircraft plus another thirty-eight planes carried on the turrets of the fleet.

Top: Eagle as first commissioned for trials with only one funnel and lacking the mast. There was still doubt over the feasibility of 'island' designs but trials in this configuration proved successful. (World Ship Society)

Lower: Eagle during the war, little changed from her pre-war appearance. (Imperial War Museum: A7586)

By July 1920 a more realistic approach was adopted[2] and at a meeting a number of decisions were made which would have a major effect on the shape of the Fleet Air Arm (FAA) up to the Second World War. Based on the early trials in *Eagle*, it was thought that a carrier could launch six aircraft fairly rapidly after which there would be half an hour to prepare the next flight of six.[3] It was also accepted that funds would allow for no more than five carriers and hence each should carry as many planes as possible. Studies then in hand for *Furious* (discussed later) showed a double hangar which it was hoped might accommodate some forty-five planes. The figure of five carriers was to be the basis of the RN bid at the Washington conference.[4]

There was some doubt concerning the double hanger as the flight deck would be so far above water that high lateral accelerations would be generated there when the ship was rolling. For this reason, it was decided not to modify *Eagle* with a double hangar. *Furious* was less high than *Eagle* and it was thought that she would be acceptable. The conversion of *Furious* was much cheaper–though less effective–than building a new ship and for this reason it was clear that it would be necessary to convert her half-sisters, *Courageous* and *Glorious* along similar lines.

Furious

Design work began under Narbeth on a verbal request from the Controller on 5 July 1920. Despite the apparent success of the mock-up trial of an island on *Argus*, it was decided that she should be flush-decked, the

1 J H B Chapman, 'The Development of the Aircraft Carrier', *Trans RINA* (1960).

2 The changing policies of the post war era are covered in detail in N Friedman, *British Carrier Aviation* (London 1988).

3 It was this reasoning which led to the flight of six as the basic FAA unit. The decision that only six aircraft would take off at a time was to influence the design of carriers. Cf the big strike from USS *Lexington*.

4 It was argued that at least seven carriers were needed to keep five operational at any one time.

Furious during the war. The small island was for weapon control only and the ship was still navigated from the fore end of the flight deck. The lower flight deck has been abolished and the freeboard increased. (Author's collection)

thought of operating much larger aircraft influencing the decision. Ducting the exhaust gases was a far greater problem than in *Argus* since her power meant there was six times as much gas to get rid of. Narbeth decided to give her a double hangar accepting the risk of high lateral forces when rolling. This led to prolonged debate on hangar height but, eventually, it was decided that both hangars should be 15ft high, which led to a height above water only 3ft more than *Argus*, and that both lifts should serve either hangar. Some thought was given to fitting a gyro stabiliser but, presumably as a result of the trials of such a device in the destroyer *Vivien*, it was not fitted. The lifts could bring a plane to the deck in about 40 seconds from the lower hangar and 30 seconds from the upper hangar. They could take planes of 47ft span and 46ft long.[5]

Furious grew by 756 tons due to alterations during conversion and the original calculations for this novel ship seem to have been in error as her GM was only 3.0ft (even with bulges) instead of the 5ft intended, a very low figure for such a ship. The flight deck (roof of the upper hangar) was the strength deck and the increased depth of the ship kept the stresses below those accepted in the original cruiser design. For structural reasons the flight deck was 25lbs thick, sufficient to keep out the 20lb bombs used by contemporary fighters. The fore end of the flight deck was elliptical in both plan and profile as a result of wind tunnel tests.

The upper hangar ended about 200ft from the stem and big doors could be opened so that the small fighters[6] of the day could take off directly from the hangar over a lower flight deck sloping to the bow. The lower hangar opened onto the quarter deck where seaplanes could be lifted on board by cranes.[7] Initially, there was

an elaborate arrester gear with longitudinal wires to prevent planes from falling over the edge. This was soon found useless – even dangerous – and was removed in 1927.

There were control positions at the fore end of the flight deck with flying controlled at the port side while the ship was driven from the starboard side. There was a retractable chart house in the centre with a navigating position on top. The two side positions were connected by a passage under the deck off which opened the chart house, signal office, radio direction finder and intelligence office. In 1939 the AA armament was greatly increased and a small island was fitted to carry the director; it was not used for navigation.

She completed in September 1929 and trials were generally satisfactory, showing that all types of aircraft could land and take off safely. There were various problems with heat and smoke, discussed later in comparison with *Courageous* and *Glorious*.

Courageous and *Glorious*

There had been suggestions even during the war of fitting these two ships with a flying-off deck forward as in the first conversion of *Furious*. More serious design work began in 1921-2 but first came a lengthy debate on the gun armament required. The biggest USN and Japanese carriers mounted 8in guns in turrets and various plans for up to ten such guns were considered for *Courageous* and *Glorious*. The supports and hoists obstructed the hangars and Narbeth suggested a funnel on the starboard to regain some space. When it was finally decided to give an all-AA armament the funnel and a small navigating space survived.[8]

5 Same design lifts as *Hermes*. Lifts in carriers present problems as the whole ship flexes in a seaway disturbing the alignment of the guide rails with the platform.

6 In 1927 the AA guns at the side of the lower flight deck were removed for a successful trial with larger aircraft prior to the completion of her half-sisters.

7 Seaplanes were used for flying in harbour when there was insufficient wind over the deck for conventional take-off and landing.

8 Narbeth preferred to call these two ships 'funnel carriers' rather than island. See *The Grand Fleet*, pp118-19 for photos of wind tunnel models.

9 Previously Captain of *Furious* and a pioneer in many aspects of technology. See Appendix 11.

Courageous, showing the double flight deck arrangement which was well liked when fighters were small and took off quickly. (Author's collection)

Aircraft arrangements

	Furious	*Glorious*
Number of aircraft	33	42
Upper hangar (ft)	520 x 50	550 x 50
Lower hangar (ft)	550 x 30/50*	550 x 50
Main flight deck (ft)	576 x 91.5	576 x 91.5
Aviation fuel (Imp Gallons)	20,800	35,700

*Furious's lower hangar was partially obstructed by offices and workshops.

Ducting the exhaust cost *Furious* stowage for nine aircraft with smaller and awkward hangar, poor ship control and about 200 tons in weight high in the ship. The temperature adjacent to the ducts was 146° F and the after end was always hot and dirty, sometimes intolerable.

On the whole, these three ships were successful and they enabled the RN to experiment in the use of air power at sea, particularly in 1933 when the three operated together under Rear-Admiral Henderson.[9]

Glorious showing weather damage to her lower flight deck. (Author's collection)

Treaty limits

The RN went to Washington hoping for five carriers of about 25,000 tons. The Americans wanted fewer but larger ships and the final agreement was fairly satisfactory to everybody. Britain and the USA were allowed 135,000 tons of carriers with an individual limit of 27,000 tons but two conversions of ships under construction could be of 33,000 tons. The USN declared *Lexington* and *Saratoga* as 33,000 tons but used a controversial interpretation of a clause permitting existing capital ships to grow by 3000 tons for improvements in protection to allow these ships to complete as 36,000 tons. Carriers under 10,000 tons were not included in the total. The Washington Treaty permitted battleship building to re-commence in 1931 and the Admiralty were keen to get some new carriers before new battleships took all the money. The older carriers were deemed 'experimental' and could be scrapped at any time.

New designs

The first thought, in May 1923, was to explore the carrier of under 10,000 tons, unlimited in numbers by the Treaty. Studies were carried out by Payne, working under Narbeth. The flight deck aft was for landing on only, terminating forward in a 'bridge' below the flight deck. Forward, there was a catapult which could be rotated into the relative wind. It was hoped to carry up to twenty-seven fighters (*Hermes* twenty-one) at a speed of 27kts. She would have mounted five 5.5in guns against destroyers and three 4in AA. It would seem that it was a very 'tight' design and would probably have grown in the detail stage. The smoke was ducted to the stern but the machinery was as far aft as possible, limiting the length of the ducts. The idea was briefly resurrected in 1930 but once again rejected.

A year or so later Payne designed the seaplane carrier *Albatross* for the Australian navy. On a displacement of 4800 tons she carried nine amphibians with a speed of 21kts. She was transferred to the RN in 1938 when there was a proposal to convert her to a real aircraft carrier with an island. Payne also produced two larger designs in 1923, one of 16,500 tons and the other of 25,000 tons. Both had sided funnels[10] though controls were at the fore end of the flight deck as in *Furious*. It was estimated that ducting the smoke would add 1-2000 tons to the displacement. The bigger ship would have mounted six 8in guns in twin turrets restricting hangar space.

New design carriers

Displacement (tons)	9800	16,500	25,000
No of Aircraft	27	35	50 (Fighters, wings spread)
Tons/plane	363	471	500

In November 1923 the Board instructed DNC to develop the 16,500-ton ship with an AA armament of six 4.7in and the legend and sketch design was approved on 28 November. It was hoped to include one ship in an emergency building programme intended to relieve unemployment but this fell with a change of government. Work on the design continued and by early 1924 it had grown to 17,200 tons due to the addition of a 5.5in anti-destroyer battery and an increase in power shown necessary by model tests.[11] It was intended for inclusion in the 1925-6 programme but was deferred, first to 1929 and then as the financial situation was even worse, to 1932. However, by 1924 the design was already beginning to seem obsolescent with a 15ft hangar height and a narrow flight deck. It was also desirable to carry more aircraft. One may see the 1934 *Ark Royal* as the ultimate development.

There were also problems in obtaining and manning sufficient aircraft. In 1929 it was calculated that five carriers in commission would need 176 planes and a further 75 would be needed for battleships and cruisers but at that date there were only 141 available. The Admiralty proposed to remedy this shortage by 1938, ordering two new flights per year. However, as a result of the financial crisis no new flights were ordered in 1929 and there was a desperate battle to get the 1930 order. Before the war, the cost of the aircraft complement was about 5 per cent that of the ship, rising to 10 per cent by the end of the war.[12] There were too many types on each ship involving different spares and maintenance work. The Admiralty pointed out that in 1929 the USN had 229 aircraft and that this number would rise to 400 by 1938, whilst the Japanese already had 118. There was also a shortage of pilots as neither the RN nor the RAF saw service as a Fleet Air Arm pilot as a stepping-stone to high rank.[13]

More Treaties

In preparation for the abortive Geneva conference of 1927 the DNC looked at 23,000-ton studies which would be roughly similar to *Glorious*. He thought that 24-25,000 tons would be better allowing for aircraft development. By the London Treaty of 1929-30 the Admiralty was looking for a 25,000-ton limit with, possibly, only four ships. The 1935 London conference (1936 Treaty not ratified) reduced the limit on individual ships to 23,000 tons but removed the limit on total tonnage. By that time *Ark Royal* was committed to 22,000 tons.

Flight deck machinery[14]

During the First World War and for some years later there seemed little need for arrester gear as the landing speed was so low that in a light wind aircraft would soon come to rest even without brakes. Indeed, this low

10 Friedman, *British Carrier Aviation*, p93.

11 Reported 25 March 1925.

12 P Pugh, *The Cost of Seapower* (London 1986), p202.

13 S Roskill, *Naval Policy between the Wars* (London 1976), Vol 2, p195.

14 D K Brown. 'Ship Assisted Landing and Take Off', *Flight Deck* 1/86 (Yeovilton 1986). A much more detailed account than can be given here.

15 Mitchell later designed the steam catapult.

16 The gear fitted in *Unicorn* could accept 20,000lb planes but it was so strong that, initially, it would pull a Seafire in two! Modified settings cured the problem.

17 D K Brown, 'The British Shipboard Catapult', *Warship 49* (London 1989).

18 A catapult had a cradle for the aircraft; an accelerator launched the plane on its wheels.

Hermes early in the war. Note the enormous gunnery control top. She was too small to be an effective fleet carrier. (Author's collection)

landing speed led to another problem, that the light aircraft might be blown sideways and over the deck edge. For this reason, early British carriers had longitudinal wires engaged by hooks on the undercarriage to keep them central along the deck. In *Furious* and *Hermes* these wires were supported above the amidships portion of the flight deck which was lower than the fore and aft sections. The upwards ramp at the fore end was useful in bringing planes to rest and was incorporated in *Courageous* and *Glorious* even though they did not have longitudinal wires.

About 1920 a Joint Technical Committee on Aircraft Arrangements was set up with a membership of airmen, engineers and constructors, W A D Forbes RCNC acting as secretary. Forbes designed a prototype arrester gear which was rejected by the RAF after some perfunctory trials at the Isle of Grain, much to his annoyance. The patent for this gear was sold to the USN for $20,000 and used in *Langley*. Then, in the late 1920s, Forbes saw a newsreel showing a developed version of his gear in a US carrier. He produced a new design, the Mk I, which was made in Portsmouth Dockyard and tried at Farnborough. Forbes had great experience in aircraft carrier work. He had been wounded as a Territorial Army private in 1914 and, after service in DNC department, went to sea in *Furious* on the staff of Admiral Commanding Aircraft (Sir R Phillimore).

The Mk I arrester gear was not successful nor was the Mk II by Forbes and Drysdale but the Mk III designed by C C Mitchell at McTaggart Scotts was a success and used in all wartime carriers.[15] It featured a gradual build-up of retardation to a maximum of 1½g followed by a gradual diminution. It was tried in 1931 in *Courageous*, the flagship of Rear-Admiral (Carriers), Henderson, who was impressed by its value. and installed in *Ark Royal* with the capability to arrest an 8000lb aircraft at 60kts. Later units in *Indomitable*

could accept 11,000lbs at 60kts.[16] The difficulties in the design of such a device are not often realised. First there is the impact as the hook engages the wire and has to start it moving from rest. As the wire begins to pull out a mass of pulleys and tackles have to be set in motion – fast – and only then does the hydraulic ram begin to function.

Crash barriers were an American invention which revolutionised flight deck operations. They consisted of a strong net supported off stanchions which would catch and stop any aircraft which missed the arrester wires and stop them crashing into the planes in a forward deck park. They were introduced in *Ark Royal* which had a pull-out of 40ft. The Fleet Air Arm still usually operated in small numbers and little use was made of barriers until about 1941 when deck parks became universal. The barrier would damage the plane which hit it but it was usually repairable and the pilot uninjured. Aircraft lifts and weapon lifts added to the complexity of flight deck operation.

Accelerators[17]

The light aircraft of the 1920s had a short free take-off run and there was no requirement for assisted take-off, particularly in the light of RN policy of small strikes which did not require a big range on deck. The first catapults were installed in *Courageous* and *Glorious* in 1934 and could launch a 7000lb plane at 56kts.[18] They were operated by a compressed-air ram working through wire and pulleys. It was found that contemporary aircraft were not strong enough to launch in this way on their wheels and a cradle was used. *Ark Royal* had similar catapults but could launch 12,000lb planes.

This design was further developed into the BH III, used in all carriers up to the *Majestic*, launching a 14,000lb plane at 60kts in its final form. The BH V used

Ark Royal just before the war. Note the accelerators port and starboard which could launch a 12,000lb plane at 56kts. (Author's collection)

in *Majestic*, *Ark Royal* and *Albion* was generally similar but capacity was increased to 14,000lbs at 85kts. The track length was 140ft 9in and peak acceleration 3.25g (mean 2.6g) during which ram, wires and pulley as well as cradle and plane had first to be accelerated after which the assorted ironmongery had to be brought to rest (maximum deceleration 11.25g). The 1942 *Ark Royal* could launch every 40 seconds from each catapult with three pumps running, every 60 seconds with two. The wires lasted some 900-1000 launches after which they needed replacement which took 38 hours during which time the ram would be re-packed. During the Korean War, *Theseus* carried out 400 launches in each

eight-day operating period and had to renew the wires after two such periods. With practice, this could be done in 24 hours.

Preliminary designs, 1931

The DNC (Johns) and Forbes argued strongly for a permanent deck park, probably with a single hangar. However, at a meeting in Controller's office on 15 April 1931 it was agreed that the new carrier should have an island, two flight decks (as *Glorious*) and a double hangar, without a deck park. The following targets were also set

High speed 30 knots, 32 preferred. Endurance at least equal to *Nelson* (10,000 miles at 10 kts).
To carry 60 aircraft (later increased to 72 bigger planes) AA guns only, protection against 6in shell and 500lb bombs below the hangar, 20lbs for hangar, torpedo with 750lb warhead.
Displacement should not exceed 22,000 tons as it was then believed that this would be the new treaty limit.

The 32kt, two flight deck design came out at 23,000 tons – too big. DNC suggested carrying half the aircraft in a deck park which would save 1500 tons and also suggested that a reduction of 2kts would save 1200 tons, pointing out that the introduction of arrester gear much reduced the time required for landing and hence made very high speed less important. The single, full-length flight deck ship was developed; a third lift was added to speed the return of aircraft but this meant lengthening the hangar though the ship could be shorter. Beam had to be increased – greatly reducing the number of docks available – and, overall, the 30kt ship grew 445 tons giving a deep displacement of 27,600 tons (22,000 tons standard) at which the speed would be 29.75kts. This study encouraged the Admiralty to press, unsuccessfully, for a 22,000-ton limit.

Ark Royal

It had been hoped to include a new carrier in the 1933 programme but the financial crisis made this impossible. Work on the design was resumed in mid-1933 under Forbes with a target of 22,000 tons in the hope that such a limit could be agreed at a future conference. The initial requirement asked for a flight deck 900ft long but this was soon seen as impractical[19] and it was reduced to 800ft.[20] It was hoped to stow seventy-two aircraft in the double hangar. The design section was

tiny; five men until the detail drawings of *Ark Royal* were started when it rose to twenty.

There was considerable debate over the nature and position of the gun armament. It was originally intended to fit sixteen of the new 5.1in then under development but, after trials, it was abandoned as its 108lb fixed round was too heavy. The next choice was the 4.7in but there was no modern AA gun available and, eventually, the new 4.5in was selected. Early studies showed single mounts at lower hangar deck level but space was very limited and, eventually, twin mounts were fitted at upper gallery deck level. This permitted limited cross deck firing if there were no planes on deck but cost an extra 150 tons. There were also to be six 8-barrel pom-poms.[21] Prior to radar and homing beacons it was hardly possible for single-seater fighters to go out of sight of the ship because the pilot was too busy to be able to navigate back. Attempts to use a two-seater as a navigational leader for single-seaters were not very successful so fleet fighters had a crew of two with consequent inferior performance.

Ark Royal had protection against 6in shells and 500lb bombs over magazines, aviation fuel and machinery. This consisted of a 4.5in belt and a 3.5in lower hangar deck. The flight deck was 30lb D quality amidships and 25lb at the ends which was thought adequate to keep out 20lb bombs.[22] The torpedo protection was intended to resist a 750lb warhead and was tested on one side of Job 74 (see Introduction). The sandwich protection consisted of a 2ft 6in inner air space, 7ft 6in liquid and 3ft air outboard. The main bulkhead was a single 60lb D quality plate with welded joints.[23] Initial trials seem to have been satisfactory but in a later trial the welded holding bulkhead failed through lines of weakness along the weld.[24] Her loss and the lessons from it are described in Chapter 10.

It was clear that there would soon be a new genera-

19 There were very few docks which could take a 900ft ship and its manoeuvrability was questionable. I would be very doubtful of keeping a 900ft ship within 22,000 tons.

20 A lengthy report of March 1934 described model tests at Haslar which showed that the new ship would handle better than *Glorious* as her profile was more balanced. A model of the above water form was towed upside down in the tank at various yaw angles to estimate wind forces. A large cut up, a larger (single) rudder and the flow over that rudder from the centre propeller contributed. Various different model rudders were tried during the whole of 1934.

21 Two were not fitted initially as the crash barrier was not ready and it was thought that planes might end up in the pompom sponson!

22 In October 1935 a smaller design with an armoured hangar was considered and rejected (Friedman, *British Carrier Aviation*, p124).

23 D quality was difficult to weld (Appendix 15) and it is amazing that a welded joint was used in such a thick plate.

24 Goodall, 19 April 1937. By that date it was too late to alter the ship and Goodall was very worried when she was lost and relieved when it was clear that this problem did not contribute to her loss (Chapter 10).

Ark Royal as completed with a short funnel. The multiple pom-poms amidships were not installed until the crash barrier was fitted as it was thought that they might be hit by an errant plane. (Author's collection)

Ark Royal at war in the
Mediterranean. This view
shows the raised funnel. *Ark
Royal* was never fitted with
radar and her planes were
directed using *Sheffield*'s radar
with flag signals between the
ships. (Imperial War Museum:
A2298)

25 Two 25,000 gallon tanks and
sixteen of 3125 gallons.

26 It is said that the size of the lift
was constrained by stresses in the
flight deck. This seems unlikely as
the depth of the hull ensured that
these stresses were low anyway.
Design stress in the flight deck was
7.6 tons/in² hogging and 5.6 tons/in²
sagging. Quite low for a big ship.

27 I suspect the intention was to use
the lower hangar for maintenance
and the upper one for operations.

28 S V Goodall, 'HMS *Ark Royal*',
Trans INA (1939). It would seem
that much of this paper was drafted
by Forbes. Goodall notes, 4 Mar
1939. 'Lillicrap looked through *Ark
Royal* paper and said "No"! I
revised final copy'. On 29 March he
notes 'My paper and discussion
went off well. Power, CO *Ark
Royal* was very good.'

29 I had occasion to examine these
estimates in connection with the
design of the three shaft CVA 01.
There was no obvious error – the
interaction between the hull and a
centre line shaft was – is – difficult
and the smoother welded hull
forward all helped.

30 Let it not be forgotten that the
Skua was the first dive bomber to
sink a major warship, *Königsberg*, in
1940.

tion of high-performance monoplanes which would be
bigger and it was not clear if the wings of such aircraft
could be folded. This led to a long debate on hangar
height but eventually it was accepted that the penalties
on increasing the original 16ft (clear) were too great.
Both hangars had a width of 60ft, the upper was 568ft
and the lower 452ft long giving a total deck area of
60,960 sq ft (*Glorious* 53,170 sq ft). Re-appraisal of the
stowage showed that the maximum in the hangars
would be sixty aircraft and this was undesirably
cramped and the normal stowage would be forty-eight
to fifty-two. During the war the maximum actually carried was fifty-four. There were three fire barriers in the
lower hangar and four in the upper.

Faster aircraft burnt more fuel and the stowage was
increased to 100,000 Imperial gallons – which would not
have been adequate for the intended seventy-two aircraft.[25] An air pressure delivery system was used in
place of water displacement as in earlier ships to reduce
contamination of the petrol. These were stowed in
cylindrical tanks isolated from the ship's structure and
jacketed. It was noted that though there was considerable whipping when *Ark Royal* was torpedoed, there
was no petrol leakage or fire. There were three lifts,
each 45ft x 22ft.[26] Each lift had two platforms and travelled through one deck height. This was intended to
speed the movement of aircraft but to get a plane from
the lower hangar to deck involved three movements.[27]

Far more extensive use was made of welding than in
previous large ships[28] (see Chapter 4 for the state of
welding in general). The builders, Cammell Laird, were
the only major shipbuilder to have shown interest in
welding having built the small, all-welded merchant
ship *Fullagar* in 1920 (398 grt). Some 65 per cent of *Ark*

Royal's structure was welded including bulkheads,
decks, shell above the lower hangar deck and the whole
of the forward 100ft. The upper hangar deck was plated
transversely with an edge butt at every deep girder, 8-
12ft apart. Stiffeners and beams were generally T bars.

A welding shop (including a school) was set up at the
head of the slip with 150 welders employed on board
and 50 more outside. The shop had a 10-ton crane to
lift weldments and the skids supporting weldments
were 5ft high so that welders could work underneath.
Seven million feet – 260 tons – of electrodes were used.
Distortion was seen as the major problem and a contraction allowance of 1 in 96 was used. There was no
serious overall movement but bowing of plates between
frames was a problem. At that date, it was thought that
welding was slightly more expensive than riveted construction but it saved 500 tons of weight. The legend
and sketch design were approved on 21 June 1934 subject to the displacement being reduced from 22,800 tons
to 22,000 tons, easily accomplished, on paper, by reducing the weight of bombs and ammunition declared in
the figures.

There was a good deal of reasoned debate over the
ship's endurance with general agreement that flying
operations necessitated more fuel than capital ships.
Various formulae were tried and these were eventually
equated to 11,200 miles at 16kts, much less than comparable USN ships. She was a three-shaft ship as the
power (103,000shp) was thought too much for two and
four would have been heavier. On trials in May 1938
she made 31.7kts with 103,055shp at 22,381 tons compared with the estimate of 30.75kts with 102,000shp at
22,000 tons. In other words, she could have made the
design speed with under three-quarters of the installed

power. This is important; the lower power could have been put through two shafts with a much less difficult run of uptakes and deeper torpedo protection.[29]

Ark Royal may be seen as a qualified success from which a much better Batch II could have been derived. However, British carrier design was to undergo a major change. Some comparison of USS *Yorktown* and HMS *Ark Royal* (10 per cent larger) may be of interest. In the table below only the most important figures are given

Comparison of *Ark Royal* and *Yorktown*

	Yorktown	*Ark Royal*
Standard displacement (tons)	19,900	22,000
Aircraft	63	54 (normal, in service)
Length of flight deck (ft)	781	720
Hull and fittings (tons)	14,451	13,651
Aircraft fuel (US Gallons)	186,860	120,090

These figures illustrate the advantages and disadvantages of the open hangar (US) and closed hangar (British) style. The deeper hull (to the strength deck) of the closed hangar leads to a lighter hull. The difference between the two ships above is consistent with studies for HMS *Malta* (discussed later) where it was estimated that the closed hangar ship would be 1000 tons lighter. The price to pay was in aircraft stowage and, in particular, ability to launch large numbers of planes in a single strike.

The Royal Navy took very elaborate precautions against fire involving aircraft fuel after the loss of the *Ben-my-Chree* in 1917. These were successful in that there were no major fires in British carriers but, again, the price was high in reduced stowage, an embarrassment in Pacific operations.

Armoured hangars – *Illustrious*

All RN carriers had paid considerable attention to the safety of the hangar and the aircraft within. In the earlier ships this involved a closed hangar, separated from the rest of the ship and entered only through air locks together with sub-division by fire curtains. In 1935-6 a number of aspects came together making improved protection both desirable and feasible. The warning time (before radar) was diminishing with the introduction of faster aircraft, particularly land-based, whilst single-seat fighters were virtually confined to visual distance of the carrier. The Controller, Henderson, had, as Rear-Admiral Aircraft Carriers, directed trials of dive bombing leading to the requirement for the Blackburn Skua.[30]

Firing against the slow, radio-controlled target aircraft had shown how ineffective was the fleet's AA gunnery. On the other hand, the abolition of the Treaty limit on total tonnage combined with the government's willingness to spend a little more on defence reduced the need to cram the maximum number of aircraft into each ship. By 1935 plans were being based on eight fleet carriers, five smaller trade protection carriers and a training carrier, and Henderson could be sure of backing for increased protection from the First Sea Lord, Chatfield, who was a dedicated proponent of armour (see Chapter 1).

Initially, the trade protection carrier was given prior-

W A D Forbes was responsible for most British carrier developments between the wars such as arrester gear and barriers as well as the design of *Ark Royal* and *Illustrious*. He was seen as a possible successor to Goodall. (Author's collection)

Formidable in near original condition. (Imperial War Museum: A11660)

ity and a number of studies were prepared with and without armoured hangars. They were all seen as too expensive and the concept changed into large and small fleet carriers. In January 1936 Henderson instructed Forbes, head of carrier design, to protect the hangar against 500lb bombs and 6in shellfire.[31] The DNC, Johns, was ill and Henderson worked directly with Forbes. They were good friends and frequently travelled in together with a formal meeting every Friday afternoon (one week Forbes was away and the assistant, Stevens went instead; it was most unusual for Controller to deal with such a junior officer).[32] After considering several options it was decided to make the deck 3ins thick which would stop 500lb bombs from dive bombers or similar bombs from level-flying aircraft at over 7000ft. The sides were 4.5ins thick and would resist shellfire beyond 7000yds. (The deck became vulnerable to plunging fire at over 23,000 yards.)

The hangar bulkheads were 4½ins thick and had

doors through which aircraft were moved to the lifts, one at either end (these bulkheads were extended to the ship's side at 2½ins). Since the lifts were outside the armoured box, they were designed so that they would still function even if surrounding structure was distorted.[33] The structural design of the flight deck with 1500 tons of armour was a very difficult task with the limited structural theory of the day – and no computer. Weight economy was vital, both to comply with the Treaty and to help stability and the armour was worked structurally.[34] The main deck beams were 6ft deep but, even so, Forbes was to quote a leading structural expert as saying that he would have used twice as much material. The structural design was a magnificent feat of engineering, reflecting great credit on the assistants, Sherwin and Stevens. Procuring the armour presented something of a problem and most of that for the first three ships came from Czechoslovakia.[35]

The price to pay for the armour was a heavy one; *Illustrious* could carry only thirty-three aircraft[36] as

Indomitable was originally intended to be a fourth ship of the *Illustrious* class. The hangar side armour was reduced to 1½in making it possible to increase the depth by 14ft, the height of the upper hangar. A half length lower hangar was 16ft high and served only by the after lift. Aircraft complement was 48. (Author's collection)

compared with *Ark Royal*'s nominal sixty.[37] Freeboard was reduced from 60ft to 38ft with the elimination of the second hangar.[38] The sketch design was completed in June 1936 and circulated by Henderson for early comment, a brave decision since there was no staff requirement and plans called for a small carrier. The partnership of Henderson and Forbes had achieved a remarkable result at great speed.[39] However, all went well and the design was approved with very minor changes on 21 July. Two ships were included in the 1936 programme and the detailed design was approved in December. When bombed *Illustrious* suffered seven hits, probably all 500kg, and lived to fight again.[40]

Two more similar ships were planned under the 1937 programme but the second one, *Indomitable*, was redesigned with 14ft more depth which permitted one and one half hangars. The upper, full-length hangar had only a 14ft headroom but the lower, short hangar had 16ft. Weight was saved by reducing the thickness of the hangar sides to 1½ins. Weapon stowage and petrol had to be increased by 50 per cent which caused some problems. An extra 25,000 gallons[41] of petrol (89 tons) was stowed at the expense of 350 tons of ship's fuel, showing how the British safety stowage of petrol reduced the amount carried.[42] (British and USN views on petrol stowage are compared in the next chapter under escort carriers.)

During this period, 1935-8, there were a number of studies for much smaller carriers.[43] At the bottom end an 11,000-ton ship would have twelve aircraft, a lightly armoured flight deck, eight 4.5in guns, a speed of 28kts and would cost £2.5 million. The comparison with *Illustrious* at £4 million shows that the small ship was extremely poor value for money. It probably was a response to those who still saw the role of the carrier and its aircraft as search only, guiding in the battle fleet for the kill. By 1945 the complement had risen –

Goodall, 10 July 1945 – 'CO *Illustrious* said 2200 men in ship designed for 1300 were quite happy'!

The 1938 carrier – *Implacable*

The original intention was a slightly faster *Illustrious*, still working to the 23,000-ton treaty limit. It was felt that the power required, 140-152,000shp, was too great for three propellers and a four-shaft plant was adopted with longer machinery and hence citadel. This involved weight reduction, mainly in armour, the hangar deck coming down to 100lbs and the hangar end bulkheads to 80lbs.

It was then decided to increase the aircraft complement to forty-eight Albacores which had a height of only 13ft,[44] This led to sketch designs with a 14ft upper hangar and a 16ft lower hangar. Hangar sides were reduced to 60lbs but in April 1939 it was approved to increase the thickness to 80lb with the lower hangar reduced to 14ft in compensation.[45] Further changes were made during construction; the flight deck aft was raised, the forward lift increased to 45 x 33ft to take

Indefatigable, a bigger double-hangar ship. Hangar height was only 14ft making it impossible to operate Corsairs. (Author's collection)

31 Forbes' own account (written from memory) is given in D K Brown, *A Century of Naval Construction* (London 1983).

32 Conversation with L G Stevens, Forbes' assistant, who summed it up 'Forbes was brilliant' a complement paralleled by Forbes (*Naval Review* (July 1965), p298) 'I received splendid support from L G Stevens and later from C E Sherwin'.

33 This appears to have worked when *Illustrious* was bombed.

34 This kept design stresses very low, generally around 4 tons/in².

35 D K Brown, Note in *Warship International* 1/98, p9, summarised in the Introduction to this book.

36 Increased to fifty-four with a deck park by 1945. However, aviation fuel stowage was not increased and frequent replenishment was needed.

37 There is a suggestion that one reason for reducing the nominal capacity of *Ark Royal* from seventy-two to sixty was to minimise the difference to *Illustrious*. Goodall 13 Dec 1938, '60 aircraft in *Ark Royal* in lieu of 72 as this will look the reason for 22,000 tons'.

38 There is a splendid film clip showing seas breaking over the flight deck of *Illustrious*.

39 Goodall, 27 April 1937. 'Told DDNC I had my eye on Forbes to

succeed me' – and several similar notes later.

40 Letter from Pierre Hervieux 30 Oct 1983.

41 In August 1944, *Victorious* used 12,000 gallons in one strike on Padang (*Naval Staff History*, Vol IV p217).

42 J D Brown, *Aircraft Carriers* (WW II Fact File) (London 1977).

43 Friedman, *British Carrier Aviation*, p142.

44 The Albacore was intended to act as a dive bomber as well as a torpedo bomber.

45 It seems likely that they completed with 60lb sides.

46 J D Brown, *Aircraft Carriers*.
Used extensively in this chapter.

47 *Eg* Goodall, 10 Aug 1942. 'Twin
rudders for *Ark Royal*, can't make
my mind up yet . . .' and 17 August
'Nothing in Haslar experiments to
give clear lead but single rudder not
sufficiently good to back in face of
opposition, decided on twins but
asked Gawn (Superintendent, AEW,
Haslar) for more experiments'. 9
Sept ' Haslar report on twin rudder,
no lead.' Note that twin rudders are
no better than one in resisting
damage. They were linked and, if
one was jammed, so was the other.

48 Goodall, 26 Mar 1943. 'Horsea
[lake] steering of *Ark Royal* with
bow rudder only not good, rudder
too small. Everyone agreed we need
better facilities for manoeuvring
tests.' (The manoeuvring tank at
Haslar, 400ft x 200ft, was opened by
Prince Phillip in 1960.)

49 This made it impossible to build
at Swan Hunter.

50 Disposing of one of the
advantages of the open hangar–see
later section.

51 I A Sturton, '*Malta*', *Warship
International* 3/71.

Seafires, the bow was modified and diesel generators were fitted, all of which delayed completion. In the Pacific *Implacable* operated forty-eight Seafires, twelve Fireflies and twenty-one Avengers. She carried 94,650 gallons of aviation fuel, enough for only five sorties per aircraft.[46]

A repeat *Implacable* was included in the 1940 Supplementary Programme, to be ordered in the spring of 1941. It was hoped to improve the flight deck protection, carry more aircraft (fifty-four) and aviation fuel with a wider flight deck. All this had to be achieved without basic changes from *Implacable* while retaining satisfactory stability. Improvement to the flight deck protection was impossible but DNC found it possible to accommodate fifty-two aircraft even though the lower hangar had to be reduced in length to find room for the extra air crew and handling parties. A packet of essential changes was agreed and the design began in March 1941. It was clearly departing more and more from *Implacable* and approval to order was refused. In August 1941 a new series of studies began:

(a) *Implacable* with a 4in flight deck, 23,500 tons
(b) A bigger carrier with a 4in deck and long double hangars, 27,000 tons
(c) A 3in deck and big double hangar, 25,000 tons.

It was then realised that current 500lb bombs could penetrate any of the decks under consideration and a fourth study (d) was produced with a 1½in flight deck as a burster and a 6in lower hangar deck, at 26,500 tons. Option (b) was chosen for development and a new design began in October 1941, ending the line of *Illustrious* derivatives.

Ark Royal (1940 Programme)

Even with the reduced height of 13ft 6in it did not seem possible to carry sixty-four aircraft because the lower hangar had to be reduced in length from 208ft to 150ft in order to accommodate the additional men. Other improvements included a 45ft x 33ft forward lift for non-folding aircraft and a 10ft wider flight deck. There was a 4in flight deck in most of the studies. By September 1941, Staff opinion was hardening in favour of the biggest – 27,000 ton – option with a 4in deck. On 28 November approval was given to proceed with the improved *Implacable* but it was cancelled two days later.

New Staff Requirements were issued for a much bigger ship. The machinery was in two units, widely separated, particular care being given to the run of uptakes. Each unit had two boiler rooms, an engine room and a gearing room. The beam was increased to provide protection against a 1000lb contact charge with a 100lb holding bulkhead and subdivision was tight.

There was great discussion over the number and arrangement of rudders to provide quick turning and some ability to steer after damage. It has never been clear whether the requirement for a warship is a small turning circle, a minimum loss of speed in the turn or a rapid movement away from the original course. They are not the same and have different solutions. Many favoured twin rudders but Goodall was worried as numerous entries in his diary show.[47] Twin rudders were thought to cause vibration, add to resistance and cause a considerable loss of speed on the turn. On the other hand, twin rudders did give a rapid initial movement. Damage to *Bismarck*'s rudder had been a major factor leading to her sinking and a bow rudder was investigated for *Ark Royal*.[48] As fitted, it gave some steering if the main rudders were fore and aft but the small bow rudder could not over-ride a stern rudder jammed at an angle. The bow rudder was soon removed. The transom area was increased beyond the optimum in order to give greater longitudinal separation of the propellers as a further damage limitation exercise.

Late in 1942 the Joint Technical Committee reviewed the size and performance of future naval aircraft. The expected weight would increase from 11,000lbs to 30,000lbs with a corresponding increase in dimensions. In particular, clear hangar height should rise to 17ft 6in, already the USN standard. The free take-off distance would be 500ft. A stalling speed of 75kts had to be achieved by the accelerator and accepted by the arrester gear, both at the increased weight. Folded width was reduced to 13ft 6in enabling aircraft to be stowed four abreast.

The new hangar height required the depth of the ship to be increased by 6ft which, in turn, meant another 4ft on the beam.[49] The standard displacement rose to 32,500 tons. Eventually four ships were ordered; *Ark Royal* was the 1940 Supplementary ship, *Audacious* (later renamed *Eagle*) and *Eagle* under the 1942 programme and *Africa* under the 1943 programme – the lat-ter two being cancelled after the war. Changes to the design continued in the light of wartime experience. Bigger and stronger lifts were required and the forward one had to be moved, hangar ventilation was increased sufficiently to allow eighteen aircraft to be warmed up simultaneously,[50] bomb lifts enlarged, better fire control for the 4.5in guns and Bofors in place of pompoms. The nominal aircraft complement was eighteen fighters and forty two TBR (including deck park, forty of each). Aviation fuel stowage was increased from 103,000 gallons to 115,000 but even this was only about enough for two days operation. Many more changes were incorporated post-war. Weapon stowage was another problem. In 1944 *Ark Royal* was intended to carry forty TBR aircraft with 80-1600lb AP, 80-1000lb MC/GP, 320-500lb SAP, 160-500lb MC, 160-250lb B bombs, and 160 depth charges; a total of 250 tons.

Malta

The much bigger aircraft envisaged by the Joint Technical Committee inevitably led to the thought of bigger carriers.[51] The Future Building Committee discussed possible requirements in November 1942 and considered improvements to speed, protection, hangar height, accommodation, improved protection to hangar sides and flight deck arrangement with regard to armament. Improvement in any of these areas would increase the size of the ship.

Initially, thought concentrated on speed and it was recognised that while speeds above 30kts were not essential, a genuine 30kts deep, in tropical waters, was needed, as was the ability to accelerate quickly from cruising speed to 30kts. DNC hoped to meet these requirements by a much lengthened *Ark Royal*. From the start, there was debate over the choice of an open or

Eagle as completed. (World Ship Society)

closed hangar. DNC saw the closed hangar as the more efficient ship style and his views were strengthened following a visit to the USA by Forbes – 'Forbes back from USA, thinks our closed hangar is right and armour should be on the flight deck but we should have accommodation just below flight deck and bigger lifts (3); also believes double hangar necessary, in size we must think big, both for ship and aircraft.'[52]

Initial studies began in February 1943 covering a very wide range of options.[53] Initial studies were for 850-900ft long (wl) and up to 54,000 tons deep with either single or double closed hangars. The 850ft variants were soon dropped even though there was concern that there were only three building slips which could take the longer design and few docks (see Appendix 9). Both four- and five-shaft machinery were investigated.[54] It was hoped to have 4in flight deck armour over a 5in lower deck. Two designs were submitted on 17 July 1943, B with a single closed hangar and C with a double hangar. Design C, 55,000 tons deep, was approved on 8 October. An open hangar design was prepared for comparison with an unarmoured flight, a 4in hangar deck and a 6in deck below. It was 61,060 tons deep.

Three ships were ordered in July 1943 even though the design was still uncertain. Departments which had argued for the open hangar appeared to have been convinced by the arguments for the closed hangar. The air group was 108, 50/50 fighters and TBR. This implied a complement of 3300 – and rising. There was still concern over the size of the ship and another design which would fit in No 10 Dock at Devonport was produced but it was not attractive. The design stress in all these ships was very high, about 9.5 tons/in² compared with 6.5 tons/in² in *Ark Royal*.[55]

Design C was developed and was ready for submission in April 1944 when the Fifth Sea Lord, Boyd, resurrected the question of an open hangar. On 19 May 1944 the Sea Lords decided that an open hangar design should be adopted, to DNC's (Lillicrap) annoyance since the closed hangar design was well under way: 'I am bound to say that apart from any over-riding operational requirements it is my opinion that the closed hangar has great advantages.'[56] The change of policy would delay the ship about 8 months. In a detailed study of the use of the deck park, Lillicrap pointed out that fifteen aircraft could be put into the air every 5 minutes and, using the after lift, aircraft could be brought up from the hangar in time to complete warming up before take off. DNC investigated a closed-hangar ship with a side lift and also an arrangement with the after end of the upper hangar open so that ten aircraft could warm up in that area. The open-hangar design X was submitted in August with no flight deck armour but a 6in deck above the citadel. Torpedo protection was intended to resist a 2000lb charge but a full-scale test section failed against a 1000lb charge. There were two side lifts and two centreline lifts. The deep

displacement had risen to 60,000 tons and there was concern as to whether such a large ship could even enter Portsmouth or Plymouth. DNC was asked to look at smaller options with waterline lengths of 850 and 750ft. The studies came to the obvious conclusion that the bigger ship gave more aircraft per ton (or per £). However, the Board decided that the 900ft ship was too big and settled for a compromise at 850ft, design X1.

There was a great deal of discussion over the protection to be provided. Design X had a 6in NC main deck and a 3in belt. There was pressure to thicken the deck and raise it to hangar level but DNC could only offer 6.9in main deck at the expense of all side armour. The staff then asked for the magazines and bomb rooms to be protected against a 3000lb, rocket-assisted weapon. DNC said this would need 13in C or 15in NC on both deck and side. The eventual choice was for a 4in deck, mainly at hangar level, lower at sides, 4in C side armour and a strip of armour below water on the holding bulkhead against diving rockets. The torpedo protection system was thought adequate to resist 1200lbs TNT (liquid, liquid, air, holding, coffer dam). Machinery of 200,000shp on four shafts would give 33½kts standard, 32kts deep.

Comparison of carriers X1 and X with USN CV41

Design	X1	X	CV41
Length, flight deck (ft)	888	938	932
Dspt, deep (tons)	56,800	60,000	59,950
Oil (tons)	7600	8800	10,210
Endurance/speed (kts)	6000/20	6000/24	
Complement	3300	3300	3500
Aircraft TBR/F	40/40 or	45/45 or	
	27/54	30/60	
Petrol (gallons)	180,000	190,000	277,000

The large number of boats carried by the British ships in comparison with the USN was notable.

An open and shut case

Both the open and closed hangar styles have important advantages and disadvantages which may explain why the lengthy debate in the UK was conducted without undue rancour. It is probable that the closed hangar was best suited to an operational concept of small strikes; the open hangar to big strikes. The British desire to protect aircraft from weather as well as enemy attack led both to the closed hangar and, later, to the armoured hangar (see Appendix 12).

Strength and weight

Any ship may be regarded as a hollow beam loaded by the distribution of buoyancy in waves (see Appendix 12). In the closed-hangar ship the flight deck is the

52 Goodall, 12 Dec 1942.

53 These can only be summarised here – for more detail see Friedman.

54 The five-shaft derived from the Bucknill report on the loss of *Prince of Wales* which suggested that a centreline shaft was, to some extent, protected. Goodall, 14 July 1943.' New carrier; said unless Haslar experiments opposed I was for raising stern (Steering gear above waterline), 2 rudders, 5 screws, long cut up.'

55 See Appendix 12. Under the criteria then in use there were sound reasons for permitting higher nominal stresses in long ships.

56 ADM 229 34 DNC's minute of 26 April 1944.

57 C.f. the deep hull of the 'County' classes, Chapter 4.

58 These figures for hull weight are probably not directly comparable as definition of 'Hull' may well be different. They are sufficient to show that the closed hangar design is considerably lighter.

59 Three such joints in an *Essex*.

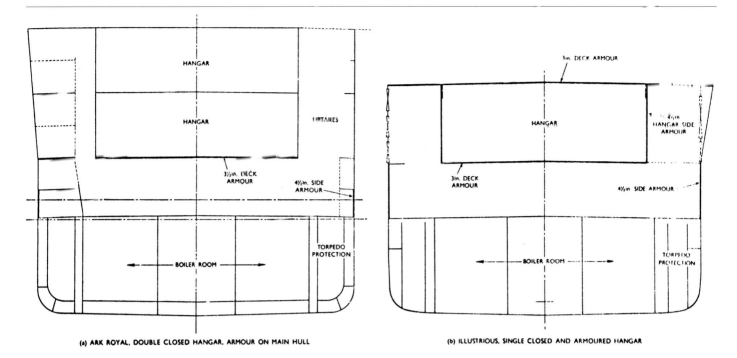

(a) ARK ROYAL, DOUBLE CLOSED HANGAR, ARMOUR ON MAIN HULL   (b) ILLUSTRIOUS, SINGLE CLOSED AND ARMOURED HANGAR

Aircraft carriers – comparison of sections through the hangar. (Author's collection)

upper flange of the girder whilst the hangar deck is the upper flange in the open-hangar ship. In general the deeper girder will be the lighter and stronger means of resisting any given loading and the difference can be considerable;[57] for example, the hull weight of the *Ark Royal* (1934) was 13,655 tons, that of the smaller *Enterprise* was 14,951 tons.[58] Goodall claimed that *Hermes* would have come out 1000 tons heavier as an open-hangar ship.

The stresses in the closed-hangar ship will be low.

Stresses in open- and closed-hangar ships (tons/in²)

	Ark Royal				Illustrious			
	Hogging		Sagging		Hogging		Sagging	
	Deck	Keel	Deck	Keel	Deck	Keel	Deck	Keel
	7.6	4.0	5.6	3.8	5.1	4.1	3.0	4.0

Even with these low stresses it is undesirable to cut large holes in the primary structure – deck and sides, a point which will be considered under lifts. Note, that a centre-line lift in an open hangar ship cuts into the hangar – strength – deck. The USN were able to accept much higher stresses due to their advanced welding procedures and materials. In the open hangar, the flight deck and its supports form a superstructure above the hull. In order to ensure that it is not strained when the hull flexes it will be divided into fairly short sections by expansion joints.[59] There will inevitably be a stress concentration at the root of these joints and local cracking is all too likely.

The asymmetrical weight of the island structure is a problem in both styles. The solution usually tried in the closed-hangar ship was to move the whole hangar structure to port but this was often unsuccessful as the extra space alongside the hangar to starboard tended to be filled giving a starboard weight bias again. Both styles probably ended with permanent ballast, fuel restrictions or even asymmetrical bulges.

The *Essex* class suffered damage to their open bow structure in heavy weather but this is not a necessary failure of the open hangar style as shown in their postwar modernisations and also in the final version of *Malta*. It is sometimes said that openings in the side of the hangar would admit heavy seas but few if any such incidents have been recorded.

Fire

Because of the fire on *Ben-my-Chree* when she was sunk, the RN was always very conscious of the fire hazard in the hangar (see also petrol stowage). The closed hangar was separated from the rest of the ship by air locks and with the lifts up was reasonably airtight so there was insufficient oxygen to support a major fire. The closed hangar automatically provided a perfect blackout, very difficult to achieve in an open hangar relying on curtains along the side. The hangar was then divided by fire curtains (usually three) so that an accidental fire could be contained to a small section. If an enemy weapon exploded in the hangar these precautions would be less effective as the curtains would almost certainly be destroyed by blast and the entry hole would admit air. However, the fire would be unlikely to spread to the rest of the ship.

There could be no such limits placed on the spread of fire in an open hangar. Access below was from the hangar deck and there were cases of burning petrol leaking into spaces below[60] and of men trapped below an inferno.[61] On the other hand, ventilation in tropical waters was excellent – conversely, the closed hangar was warmer in cold climates! Refuelling aircraft in the open hangar was probably safer as it was less likely that petrol vapour would build up.

Space

The open hangar extended to the side of the ship and hence provided greater deck area whilst the greater width made it easier to fit in aircraft of different sizes and shapes. The British response to this problem was the double hangar which provided the deck area but was still narrow and introduced problems in getting planes to the deck from the lower hangar. The great depth of the hull was an embarrassment, particular as increased hangar height was demanded.[62] There was concern over roll acceleration in a high hull whilst windage made ship handling difficult. The deck park was equally applicable to both styles though the RN was reluctant to adopt it before the war as it would lead to weather damage.[63]

Operational factors

Aircraft engines could be run up in the open hangar and a large strike brought quickly to the flight deck. This became slightly less important when immersion heaters were fitted in the oil system of aircraft so that they could be 'warmed up' within a closed hangar. This was to be seen as the overriding argument for the open hangar in the *Malta* class. The strength of the closed hangar enabled the principal guns to be mounted high in the ship giving better arcs of fire. However, the intrusion of cut-outs in the flight deck for the gun mountings was seen as a serious problem in RN carriers.

Lifts

As was said earlier, it is undesirable to cut large holes in load-bearing structure and hence lifts in British carriers tended to be small, accentuating the problems of rapid movement to the flight deck. With the axial flight decks of wartime carriers the side lift was a great advantage and it was virtually impossible to fit a side lift to a closed hangar.[64] The hangar side and the ship's side formed the web of the hull girder carrying the shear forces. The cyclic time of a lift serving a double hangar was inevitably long.

Protection

The debate between the open and closed hangar is quite separate from that of armoured hangar. Closed hangars can be either armoured (*Illustrious*) or unarmoured (*Ark Royal*, 1934). Open hangars can have an armoured

deck, though the supporting structure was very heavy – *Midway*, *Malta* – but not armoured sides. The open sides were vulnerable to attack by the smallest weapons. Appendix 13 lists action damage to armoured hangar carriers and does not provide very convincing evidence in support. There were eight hits by suicide bombers on RN carriers. The only one causing serious damage was on *Illustrious* where the bomb exploded in the water close alongside, the hangar protection being irrelevant. There was one hit on the armour deck where the fleet thought the protection had been invaluable; in the others it was thought that the structure of an unarmoured deck would have resisted the glancing blow. More fighters would have been better protection than armour. For the same area of hangar, the double hangar will need only about half the armour of a single hangar. In particular, the lift wells were the Achilles heel of the armoured deck. The open sides of the open hangar were vulnerable to the most trivial attack – machine guns, splinters as well as light bombs.

Post-war

Post-war designs of all navies were required to resist nuclear blast and fallout, the closed hangar becoming universal but this does not necessarily imply it was the right choice earlier. It was almost impossible to protect either deck or side against the latest weapons such as big rockets. It was found that modernisation of armoured, closed hangar ships was so expensive (*Victorious*) as to be impractical but modernisation was not considered at the design stage. *Hermes* had a considerable number of changes suggesting that modernisation of unarmoured, closed hangar ships was feasible though still more expensive than an open hangar.

Summary of advantages

Open Hangar. Good ventilation, easy to warm up planes, mount large strike, side lifts, more planes.
Closed Hangar. Stronger, lighter hull. Much safer against fire, easy to armour, planes protected from weather and some enemy action.

The choice was not easy, depending on the weight attached to the different aspects. Goodall made these points in July 1943 under four headings – Aircraft operation, Size and strength of the ship, Protection and Fire risk. He saw the open hangar as having a small lead in operation, closed with a big lead in strength and protection and little difference in fire risk.[65] Overall, he favoured the closed hangar. I would suggest that both the RN and USN were right for the wars they planned to fight, the RN in narrow seas, facing shore-based aircraft while the USN expected to engage the Japanese fleet in the open Pacific.[66] The author's choice for the RN in the late 1930s would have been an improved *Ark Royal* with better lifts and cleaner run of uptakes.

60 *Ticonderoga*, 21 Jan 1945.

61 It should have been possible to trunk access to the gallery or even to the flight deck.

62 A tortuous and congested run of uptakes became almost inevitable.

63 Friedman suggests that the RN may have seen a later increase in aircraft by a deck park as a concealed bonus. I am inclined to doubt this as a deck park would be inconsistent with the limited petrol stowage.

64 *Hermes* and *Ark Royal* (upper hangar only) were given side lifts after the war – a magnificent feat of engineering – but the structure was very heavy and the opening quite small. They were removed when the angled deck was introduced.

65 ADM 229 30 of 14 July 1943.

66 There are well-known stories of a serious plan to swap the six RN armoured carriers for six *Essex* class.

Smaller and Cheaper Carriers *Three*

BY ABOUT MID-1940 it had become apparent that the guns of the fleet provided little protection against a determined attack from land-based bombers. The fleet needed fighter protection but two of the best carriers had already been sunk. The first thoughts were for battleships to carry their own fighters in hybrid style, perhaps remembering the 1918 Grand Fleet when most battleships and some cruisers carried fighters.[1]

In October 1940 the Director of Air Material proposed adding ten fighters to the *King George V* class ships.[2] This was found to be quite impractical but DNC was asked to carry out a number of studies into hybrid battleships and cruisers.[3] None of these showed much promise, the absurdity being shown by Goodall's comparison of a hybrid squadron with a mixed force of conventional battleships and carriers.

Hybrids vs mixed force

Squadron	Tonnage	Guns	Aircraft
5 Hybrids	225,000	30-15in	70
3 *Lion*s, 3 *Indomitable*s	200,000	27-16in	144

Goodall concluded 'Which of the two above forces would you rather command?'.[4]

To name but a few of the problems of the hybrid, there was blast on aircraft, the long and tall, lightly protected hangar on a ship intended to fight a gun duel etc.[5] The hybrid was dead.

A more promising option was the so-called 'aircraft destroyer'[6] There were four main variants but a typical option would carry twelve fighters at 31-32kts on 10,550 tons, deep. It had guns to fight off a single destroyer and torpedoes to attack a heavier ship at night or in bad weather. No-one, DNC nor staff, was happy with any of them. This led to further consideration of a fighter carrier with, initially, three possibilities: conversion of a liner such as *Winchester Castle*, conversion of *Hawkins* class cruisers or a new ship. It was soon clear that the conversions would not be very effective and work started on a new design. This is one of many examples in which the pursuit of a crazy idea (the hybrid) leads to something different and useful.

The *Colossus* class light fleet carriers

Draft requirements were agreed on 26 December 1941 and passed by Controller to DNC four days later. DNC's carrier section under A Mitchell came up with a sketch design on 14 January 1942, the main features being: a 600ft flight deck with a hangar 14ft 6in high holding fifteen fighters. The two lifts were 45ft x 34ft[7] and could take 15,000lb aircraft. The speed would be 25kts and there was an armament of two twin 4in, four 4-barrel pompoms and eight Oerlikons. Building time was 21 months. Informally, they were described as 'Woolworth carriers'.

The proposals were generally accepted but a number of changes were asked for. In particular, the flight deck was to be lengthened 20ft to allow for rolling take-off of Typhoons.[8] Because DNC was overloaded, design work was handed over to Vickers who had experience in

1 D K Brown, *The Grand Fleet*, Ch 8.

2 N Friedman, *British Carrier Aviation*, pp218 et seq. See also R D Layman and S McLaughlin, *The Hybrid Warship* (London 1991); p113 has a sketch of this proposal and others.

3 N Friedman, *British Carrier Aviation*. Also Goodall, 2 Feb 1941. 'Cogitated on cruiser on *Audacity* lines. Lillicrap damping my enthusiasm.'

4 ADM 1 11051 DNC submission of 16 July 1941.

5 It is wasteful to provide all the workshop and store facilities for only a few aircraft. This factor was to damn later projects for small Harrier carriers.

6 It was not a destroyer with aircraft as sometimes suggested but a destroyer *of* aircraft – a fighter carrier.

7 Big enough for the most up-to-date RAF fighters with unfolded wings.

8 The idea of operating Typhoons with the unreliable Sabre engine over the ocean is frightening.

Venerable was the quickest to build of her class (25 months). She was built by Cammell Laird. (Imperial War Museum: A27089)

both merchant ship and warship work.[9] Their chief naval architect, J S Redshaw, was to come up with one of the outstanding warship designs of all time, both simple and efficient.

The first Vickers sketch design was inspected on 23 January 1942, incorporating the first wave of changes which had increased the building time to 24 months. Further changes were then required of which the most important were an increase in hangar height to 16ft 6in and aviation fuel stowage to 100,000 gallons. The final sketch design was submitted to the Board in February with a building time of 27 months and an estimated cost of £1.8 million. The First Lord insisted that the building time be cut to 21 months by omitting all non-essentials, but the 'approved' building time was later agreed at 24 months. Changes continued; not surprising in the light of the speed with which the ships had been conceived.[10] Towards the end of 1942 it was decided to extend the flight deck aft which meant the loss of the 4in guns and their control. The First Lord kept up the pressure for a 24-month building time and suggestions came from both shipbuilders and Deputy Controller for simplification.[11] It was clear that the hull and machinery were the major factor in building time and that no great improvement could be achieved.

Contracts were placed for the first three ships in March 1942 (one more later) and for nine more in August. A review in September showed that it was possible to build two more at Harland and Wolf and one at Devonport making a total of sixteen ships. Vickers were responsible for the design and for supplying building information to the other builders. Some drawing work was farmed out to these other builders subject to Vickers' approval. Individual builders could vary structural drawings to suit their own procedures subject to maintaining strength and no significant increase in weight. *Venerable* (Cammell Lairds) was the fastest in 25 months but 27 was more typical; cost averaged £2.5 million (*Ocean* required 20,772 man months of shipyard work).

Machinery and subdivision

The machinery was based on half the *Fiji* class installation. Machinery had already been ordered for the *Bellerophon* and this was used for the first two ships.[12] The actual arrangement was novel with two widely separated machinery spaces each containing two boilers and a turbine.[13] There were two compartments containing aircraft fuel between the machinery spaces, each 24ft long, making it unlikely that a single torpedo could put both units out of action.[14] There was no torpedo protection system but there were a large number of transverse bulkheads.[15] It was claimed that they would float with four main compartments flooded. Wing spaces were arranged abreast machinery, magazines and bomb rooms and the main petrol stowage and these were filled with empty drums to maintain buoyancy and stability after damage. This was a very effective form of protection (see performance of armed merchant cruisers against torpedoes in Chapter 10). There was no armour except for mantlets over the thirty-two torpedo warheads carried. The inner bulkhead of the wing drum spaces gave some splinter protection.

Colossus as completed

Displacement: 18,040 tons deep, 13,190 tons standard.
Dimensions: 650ft (wl) x 80ft (wl) (112ft 6in over sponsons) x 23ft 5in mean, deep.
shp: 40,000 = 25kts deep, clean, temperate waters.
Armament: late 1945, varied, typical six 4-barrel pom-poms, seventeen single Bofors.
Oil: 3190 tons giving endurance of 8500 miles at 20kts.

Aircraft arrangements

The flight deck was 690ft long with a width of 75ft abreast the island, narrowing to 45ft at the bow. There were two lifts 45ft x 34ft with a 15,000lb working load and a 36-second working cycle.[16] The hangar was 342ft x

Triumph in 1946, built by Harland and Wolff. (Author's collection)

52ft with a 17ft 6in height. The hangar had four fire curtains and was fitted with spraying arrangements. There was a BH III catapult with a capacity to launch 20,000lb aircraft. Originally, there were eight arrester wires with four Mk 8 operating mechanisms but two more wires were added after trials. These wires could accept a 15,000lb aircraft at 60kts. Two safety barriers were fitted which could accept the 15,000lb aircraft at 40kts.

The intended aircraft complement was changed several times involving increased complement and correspondingly poorer habitability. The design complement was 1054 which had risen to 1336 by the time they completed. The four which reached the Pacific carried twenty-one Corsair and eighteen Barracuda, not far from the capability of the much bigger *Illustrious* class with up to fifty-four aircraft. Aircraft fuel was 80,000 gallons (*cf Illustrious* 50,000) and was stowed in three groups of tanks. Weapon stowage was provided for 36 2000lb, 216 500lb SAP, 72 500MC, 216 100lb A/S bombs, 32 torpedoes and 1½ million rounds of aircraft gun ammunition.

Stability was good: *Colossus*'s inclining in November 1944 gave;

	Deep	Light
Metacentric Height (ft)	8.6	4.9
Max GZ	5.65	2.84 Hangar free flooding
Angle of max GZ	36½	36

Stresses were low with a maximum of 7.5 tons/in² in the flight deck which was the strength deck (hogging – tensile). The structure was basically merchant ship style though slightly lighter than Lloyd's rules. This gave rise to incorrect stories that they were intended to convert to liners after the war. Their machinery arrangement and subdivision would have made that almost impossible. They were constructed from mild steel which, at that date, was sensitive to temperature, becoming brittle at low temperatures. This became apparent during cold-weather trials, 'Operation Rusty', in 1948-9, when there was a very serious crack extending much of the way across the flight deck of *Vengeance*.

Trials showed there were few problems other than overcrowding. There was considerable vibration in the island, ameliorated by local stiffening.[17] They were excellent ships and formed the backbone of the RN for many years. In particular, most of them served with the RN force off the west coast during the Korean War. During that war, *Ocean* achieved a class record with 123 sorties in a day. Her Sea Furies got down to a landing interval of 18.6 seconds with Fireflies at 20.2 seconds. The other light fleet carriers achieved comparable performances.[18] *Theseus*'s ability to re-wire the accelerator has been described in the previous chapter. Designed for a short life, at least one may see the millennium out! Eight ships completed as the *Colossus*

class, two became maintenance ships and the last six became the *Majestic* class.

Majestic class

The last six ships were re-arranged early in construction to suit the new central messing scheme. In September 1945 further changes were agreed and they were redesignated the *Majestic* class. The changes were intended to permit the operation of bigger aircraft, up to 20,000lbs, and were to take place in two phases. In the first the flight and hangar decks were to be stiffened and the catapult improved while retaining the existing machinery. Pompoms were to be replaced by Bofors, the radar and radio fit was to be updated and improved replenishment-at-sea gear would be installed. Phase two would have involved fitting new lifts, 50ft x 34ft, new arrester gear (20,000lb aircraft at 75/80kts) and a third barrier installed.

None of these six ships served in the RN though five were completed, to varying standards, for Commonwealth navies. *Terrible*[19] was completed for Australia as *Sydney* and *Magnificent* for Canada, both roughly as described above. *Majestic*, *Powerful* and *Hercules* were modified much more drastically, receiving steam catapults. The remaining *Colossus* class ships in the RN were improved along similar lines in 1949-51. This enabled them to operate 20,000lb aircraft with some limits on wind speed over the deck.[20]

Hermes class – 1943 Programme

It had originally been hoped to order eight slightly improved *Majestics* under the 1943 programme. However, at the end of 1942, the Joint Technical Committee made a series of recommendations on future aircraft.[21] The most important of these as regards carrier design were that weight could be 30,000lbs with a stall speed of 75kts (governing both accelerator and arrester gear performance).[22] There was no way in which a *Majestic* could be adapted to meet these requirements and a new design was needed. It was clearly going to be a bigger ship and more speed was needed to get wind over the deck. This more expensive ship was thought to need better protection than the earlier ships, both in the form of guns and passive protection, adding further to the cost.

A sketch design was prepared to loose requirements, the legend giving the following figures in June 1943.

Displacement: 18,000 tons standard, 23,800 tons deep.
Dimensions: 685ft wl x 90ft wl x 24ft 8in.
shp: 76,000 = 29kts deep, temperate, clean. At least 25kts operational, worst case
Armament: Four twin 4.5in, two 6-barrel Bofors, ten twin, seven quad Oerlikon, four twin Oerlikon
Oil: 4000 tons, endurance 6000 miles at 20kts

9 The detailed statement of requirements, based on the DNC study was taken to Vickers on 7 January 1942. It is contained in ADM 229/25 described as 'Fighter Support Ship'.

10 Goodall, 23 Jan 1942. Woolworth carrier design 'everybody added something in spite of my repeated warning that this meant more work and getting the ship late.'

11 Friedman, *British Carrier Aviation*, pp223-5.

12 *Colossus, Edgar*.

13 The boilers used forced draught and hence the engines were under pressure as well.

14 Goodall pointed out that the two propellers were vulnerable but he still thought they were less vulnerable to torpedo attack than any cruiser.

15 The author had to plan the new damage control marking system for *Glory* in 1950.

16 The lifts had only one set of operating machinery instead of the usual two as an economy measure.

17 Much later, studies suggested it was a torsional vibration associated with lack of strength in the after lift area.

18 J Winton, *Air Power at Sea* (London 1987); J R P Lansdown, *With the Carriers in Korea* (Worcester 1992).

19 The only carrier to be built in a Royal Dockyard.

20 They could operate Gannets, Vampires and Venoms. See Friedman, *British Carrier Aviation*, p229 for details.

21 Ibid, p245.

22 Note the pre-war figure was 11,000lbs!

Bulwark late in her life as a
helicopter carrier (probably
c1979). She was broken up in
1984. (Author's collection)

The original aircraft complement was numerically the
same twenty-four as in the 1942 ships but they were bigger; 30,000lbs all-up weight instead of 24,000lbs. The
flight deck was 732ft 9in by 90ft (84ft min). There were
two lifts, 54ft x 44ft for 35,000lb load. The hangar was
381ft x 62ft x 17ft 6in, 23,522 sq ft. There were twelve
arrester wires (Mk 11) with a pull-out of 162ft. As completed, there were four barriers, two for jets, two for
propeller-driven planes. One, later two, BH 5 accelerators were installed. Stowage was provided for 80,000
gallons of petrol. The bomb room had stowage for nine
loads for twenty-six strike aircraft, a load being either 2
x 1000lb or 4 x 500lb bombs. There were also 32 18in
torpedoes, 2000 3in rockets and 316,000 20mm cannon
rounds. The bomb lift could take 4000lbs and it was expected that sixteen aircraft could be loaded in 40 minutes.

The structure was a mixture of merchant ship practice
– transverse frames were bulb angles – and warship, with
DW steel for the flight deck, longitudinal protective
bulkhead, middle deck over machinery and lower deck
over petrol stowage etc.[23] The rest was mild steel. The
protective bulkhead was 1in and there was 80lb NC
over magazines and bomb rooms. There was close subdivision and it was claimed that they could float with six
main compartments flooded amidships or five towards
the ends.[24] There were two machinery units, half the
Ark Royal plant, each consisting of a boiler room with
two boilers, an engine room and a gearing room.

The First Lord thought the ships were too elaborate,
and hence expensive, and that they would not complete
before the war with Japan was over. He therefore decided to refer the issue to the Cabinet.[25] In the meantime,
Controller ordered work on the design to continue and

eight ships were ordered on 12 July 1943.[26]

Four ships were cancelled at the end of the war and
the others proceeded very slowly. In 1947 there was a
major redesign which can only be outlined. The aircraft
complement was increased to twenty-four bombers and
sixteen fighters, the lifts were widened to 44ft, a second
accelerator was fitted and more 40mm and 20mm guns
added. Machinery weight increased by 80 tons making a
total increase of 560 tons, largely offset by the original
margin of 350 tons. The 4.5in guns and their controls
were deleted, mainly to help accommodation as the
complement had risen from 1400 to 1823. Three ships
were completed more or less to this design though their
very lengthy building times allowed further changes.
Bunks were provided for the crew in lieu of the traditional hammocks.[27] The fourth, *Hermes* (ex-*Elephant*),
was to be redesigned to a much more radical plan with
an angled deck and a side lift etc.[28] Despite the changes
stability and strength were very good.

Aircraft maintenance ships

During the period covering the Italian invasion of
Abyssinia (1935-6), the RN learnt a great deal about the
intensive operation of aircraft from carriers. It was estimated that a month's flying could lead to 20 per cent
crashed or damaged beyond repair and 10 per cent
needing major repair. Repair and even the major maintenance work could not be carried out in the hangars of
an operational carrier without interfering with flying
and hence it was decided to build a maintenance ship.
The development of this design was a long and difficult
process which can only be outlined here.[29]

She was to service three *Illustrious* class each carrying thirty-three aircraft. The new ship, to become *Unicorn*, was to be able to carry forty-eight aircraft with wings folded and a further eight being worked on with wings unfolded. She was to have a heavy armament, an armoured flight deck but a speed of only 13½kts. After considering various options, the speed was increased to 24kts. By now, *Unicorn* was looking more and more like an aircraft carrier and the UK had already used or allocated its quota of such ships. The Naval Law Department advised that it might be a battleship! It was finally declared as an auxiliary which happened to look like an aircraft carrier. When war broke out, it was reclassified as a carrier and served briefly as such during the Salerno operation. Lack of accommodation for officer pilots was the main problem.[30] For the rest of the war and also during the Korean War she served successfully in her intended role.[31]

With hindsight, one may feel that the original requirement was over-elaborate, leading to an expensive ship with a lengthy building time. On the other hand, the armament and protection was comparable to contemporary submarine and destroyer depot ships of the day. It is interesting that she was not seen as a starting point for the 1942 light fleet carriers (the *Colossus* class).

During the planning of the Fleet Train for the Pacific it was realised that two more maintenance ships were needed – quickly. A new design was prepared[32] – 17,000 tons, 685ft (oa) x 92ft x 16ft 6in. A study showed that a new design would not be ready in time and it was decided to convert two of the *Colossus* class. They were to carry out major maintenance work, fuselage repair and functional testing, but only minor engine and component work as other ships were being converted for these tasks. Since it was not intended to fly aircraft on or off, all aircraft equipment was deleted and the armament was much reduced making room for a large number of workshops and stores. *Pioneer* reached the Pacific in time for two months' operational duties and seemed satisfactory; *Perseus* was just too late.

The Best is the Enemy of the Good Enough?

The ships described in the first part of this chapter represent, in the main, attempts to provide much of the capability of a fleet carrier in a ship which was much cheaper and could be built more quickly. At first sight, the escalation from the simplicity of the first ideas for a 'Woolworth carrier' to the more elaborate *Colossus* and *Majestic* classes as built followed by the big jump to the *Hermes* class suggest a loss of control.

However, it is hard to fault any of the changes which were incorporated into the *Colossus* class and the actual building times were not much greater than the original, possibly over-optimistic, estimate. Changes to the *Majestic*s were small and mainly to improve living conditions, even in wartime recognised as poor in the earlier group. The big increases in size, speed and cost of the 1943 design may be seen as the inevitable consequence of the increasing size of aircraft, particularly the dependence on US aircraft.

The *Colossus* carried an air group only a little smaller than that of *Illustrious* and had appreciably more aviation fuel stowage. The main sacrifice was in protection with no heavy AA battery, no armour and no torpedo side protection. Since none of these ships was attacked, let alone hit, it is not possible to say how important was this reduction in protection. The close subdivision of the light fleets should have done very well against torpedoes and their closed hangars, even if unarmoured, gave fair protection against damage.

Escort carriers

The earliest proposal for ships to carry aircraft in defence of trade came in an Admiralty suggestion to the Air Ministry in 1926. The idea seems to have been to launch seaplanes by catapult and recover them from the sea using cranes. The idea was not developed and no design was prepared. In 1932 DNC (Johns) was asked to consider designs for a small carrier converted from a

23 Goodall, 26 June 1943. 'Light Fleet Structural sections bad. Trouble is draughtsmen's standard is very low especially so in this section.'

24 Designers thought she was better able to resist underwater attack even than *Ark Royal*. The Constructor Commander with the Falklands task force referred to *Hermes* as 'Like a bloody great steel fort.'

25 Building time was estimated as 31 months and the war with Japan was expected to last until the end of 1946. See A V Alexander's view in ADM 205/32.

26 Goodall signed the building drawings on 21 Jan 1944, his last as DNC, noting that his first was a China gunboat. It was his last day as DNC.

27 The author worked on the drawings as an apprentice – wasted effort as the design was changed.

28 As with *Ark Royal*, the side lift was a technical triumph which showed that such an arrangement was not really compatible with a closed hangar.

29 D K Brown, 'HMS *Unicorn*: The Development of a Design 1937-39', *Warship 29* (January 1984).

30 Goodall, 21 Aug 1942.

31 During the Korean War she carried out a shore bombardment with her 4in guns, perhaps the only carrier to do so.

32 Drawing in ADM 116 5151.

Two of the *Colossus* class were converted to aircraft maintenance ships. This is *Pioneer*. (Author's collection)

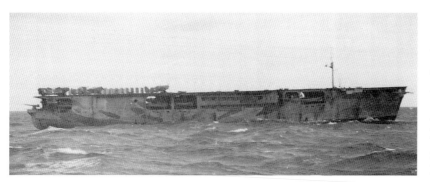

Audacity was a very simple conversion of the captured German merchant ship *Hannover*. Her life was short but showed great promise. (World Ship Society)

Activity was originally known as an improved *Audacity* but her conversion was much more elaborate. This photo gives some idea of the difficulty of landing on such a small flight deck. (Author's collection)

merchant ship, but due to shortage of staff the work was not carried out till 1934. A range of sizes was considered from 14-20,000 gross tons and speeds from 15 to 20kts. There was a catapult forward and a hangar with a single lift. The landing deck was 285-300ft long and 65-80ft wide. It was estimated that conversion would take 9-12 months. Belatedly, it was realised that a landing deck abaft a bridge and funnel was impractical and attention was centred on diesel-engined ships where the exhaust could be moved to one side or even trunked aft.[33]

An outline requirement for converted liners was drawn up by the staff in 1935 and by February 1935 DNC had produced two sample design studies, one based on the *Winchester Castle* of 20,000 tons and the other on *Waipawa* of 12,500 tons. The latter was thought to be too small but in 1937 five liners (including *Winchester Castle*) were identified as suitable. Nothing more was done before the war, largely because it was proving very difficult to get enough planes for the fleet

carriers then on order. By 1940 the need for trade protection carriers was urgent and a range of suitable requirements was drawn up.

Trade protection carriers

	A	B	C
Max speed (kts)	20	18	16½
Aircraft Hangar/deck park	16/9	12/3	4/6
Lifts	2	1	1
Flight deck length (ft)	550	500	450
Arrester wires	6	6	4-5
Barriers	2	2	1
Petrol stowage (1000 gallons)	75	50	33

Audacity

The first ship was smaller and less capable than any of these. The captured German merchant ship *Hannover* was allocated for conversion by Blyth Shipbuilding on 2 January 1941, advance information was supplied by Mathias on 17 January and finalised on 7 March. She completed as HMS *Audacity* on 26 June for ten days' trials and a month's work-up.[34]

Masts, funnels and superstructure were cut away and a flight deck 435ft x 60ft built above. The shelter deck remained the strength deck and hence three expansion joints were fitted in the flight deck (see Appendix 12). There was no hangar, no island and only two arrester wires, together with a safety wire and a single barrier. Six Martlet (Wildcat) fighters were carried on deck. *Audacity* took part in four convoy operations before being torpedoed on 21 December 1941. She was seen as highly successful and there were plans for more similar ships to be converted in the UK as well as six in the USA.

Activity and other British escort carriers

Various other schemes were considered including five to the pre-war *Winchester Castle* design but suitable ships could not be spared. Eventually the *Telemachus*, building at Dundee, was allocated, known originally as 'Improved *Audacity*'. She was converted in ten months to 1940 standard C as the *Activity* incorporating some experience from *Audacity*. The requirements grew and grew. The first idea was that all six aircraft should be kept on deck with room for one, with wings spread, in a workshop hangar below.[35] This grew first to four disassembled Swordfish and finally the hangar could hold six folded Swordfish though her normal complement was three Swordfish and seven Wildcats.

In late 1941 there was a proposal to build new-design escort carriers.[36] These would have had a speed of 18kts with twin diesel-driven shafts. The hangar would hold six folded planes and six non-folding fighters with a single lift, 45ft x 33ft, to a flight deck 550ft x 75ft. There was to be a considerable gun armament, protection to

Pretoria Castle was the largest British-built escort carrier. She was used for training, the photo shows an Albacore being catapulted off with the ship at anchor. (Author's collection).

33 D K Brown, 'The Development of the British Escort Carrier', *Warship 25* (January 1983).

34 Goodall took a keen interest in *Audacity* (briefly *Empire Audacity*), visiting her on 25 April and noting her rapid progress. He was keen to build many repeats and also considered a cruiser conversion on similar lines.

35 Ships cover 667.

36 Friedman, *British Carrier Aviation*, p185.

37 *Nairana*, *Vindex* and the larger and faster *Campania*.

38 D K Brown (ed), *Design and Construction of British Warships* (London 1995), Vol 1, pp87-8.

39 See Friedman, *British Carrier Aviation*, above, and his *US Aircraft Carriers* (Annapolis 1983). Also D K Brown, *Design and Construction*. Both are needed to get a full picture.

40 The fifth ship, *Charger*, was retained by the USN for training RN pilots and the sixth, *Tracker*, was completed to a different design.

magazines, petrol stowage and machinery, and they were required to float upright with three main compartments flooded. There was, of course, no capacity to build such ships.

Further attempts were made to obtain liners for conversion and one, *Pretoria Castle* serving as an AMC, was so converted generally to Type B standard, taking about 12 months. She was the largest British escort carrier, with a hangar for fifteen aircraft and was employed for flying training and trials. Three more cargo liners were requisitioned at an early stage of construction and converted, taking about two years.[37] The flight deck was the strength deck but, unusually, the hangar extended to the ship's side with access below the hangar deck. Fifteen aircraft could be stowed. These ships differed slightly but the particulars of *Campania* in the next section are generally typical except that the first two were 2kts slower.[38]

These three ships were largely of riveted construction and, for this reason, were preferred to welded ships for Arctic work. Brittle fracture at low temperatures was not fully understood at the time but it was believed that a riveted seam would stop a crack from extending further – this was usually, but not always, true. It is said that deck landing accidents were less frequent on these ships than on US-built RN carriers.

US-built escort carriers for the RN

The US designed and built escort carriers can only be covered very briefly for comparison.[39] In January 1941 the US was asked to build six escort carriers for the RN based on an improved *Audacity*. However, the USN had already started their own first escort carrier and it was decided that the RN ships should be similar to the *Long Island*. The first ship was the *Archer*, based on a C-3 hull, the next three incorporated both USN and RN experience.[40] *Archer* had no island, her merchant style bridge wings projected beyond the flight deck

Archer was the first US-built carrier for the RN. Her multiple diesel installation proved very unreliable and she was laid up in 1943. (Author's collection)

Avenger was much improved but her engines gave problems too. She was torpedoed on 15 November 1942 and exploded. This led to much improved safety measures for the bomb rooms. (Author's collection)

Stalker was one of the *Tracker* class which may be seen as the first definitive US escort carrier class. (Author's collection)

either side; the next three had a small island. *Archer*'s flight deck was 438ft long, the other three were originally 410ft, later extended to 442ft and carried nine TBR and six fighters.

Archer had two Sulzer diesels geared to a single shaft. These were very unreliable so that she was laid up in August 1943 and became the merchant ship *Empire Lagan* in March 1945. The others had Doxford diesels and were little better. They were intended to have a two compartment standard of flooding, but stability was inadequate and some 1000 tons of ballast was fitted (this was increased later).

On 15 November 1942 the *Avenger* blew up after a torpedo hit. The inquiry found that splinters from the torpedo had detonated bombs and depth charges stowed in the bomb room against the ship's side. A longitudinal bulkhead was installed in surviving ships to ensure that charges were 10-15ft from the ship's side; the USN made similar changes. *Dasher* sank on 27 March 1943 following a petrol explosion blamed by the USN on poor procedures in the RN and by the British on bad design of stowage and handling. It would seem that both were right; the extreme care taken in British petrol arrangements allowed rather sloppy obedience to rules on smoking etc. Petrol stowage was reduced dramatically in the British operated ships – *Archer* from 87,500 gallons to 36,000, the others from 75,000 gallons to 36,000.[41]

Tracker was a steam turbine C-3, 2kts faster than the diesel ships and more reliable once teething troubles were overcome. She formed the basis for a class of eleven ships in the RN and thirty-three in the USN. They were much better subdivided with nine bulkheads to the main deck and two more to the lower deck. The hangar was longer and there were two lifts with the same aircraft complement.[42]

These ships were followed by twenty-three similar, but improved ships of the *Smiter* class, compared in the table below with *Campania*, the best British design.

These US-built ships were excellent carriers but expensive. Few costs have been located – *Activity* £850,000, *Campania* £1,520,000 against the much superior US *Commencement Bay* at $11 million.

The RN required a number of modifications to suit British operating procedures, improve safety and to enable them to carry out other duties such as the support of landings. These changes included lengthening the flight deck and fitting a round-down at the after end, larger hangar and improved arrangements, flight deck lighting, fitting ballast, altering (reducing) petrol stowage, additional bomb room and protective bulkhead and ventilation to the hangar.

The USN were upset by the time taken to get the escort carriers into service which might include 6-12 weeks making good defects found on trial, 2 weeks passage, 7 weeks modification time in the UK and 5-6 weeks work-up. Eventually, a facility was set up in Vancouver which corrected defects and carried out modifications together in 6 weeks, working on three ships at a time.

Later, some ships were further modified for specific roles – the basic escort carrier, fighter carriers for the Gibraltar run, and assault carriers, while others were unaltered as aircraft transports.[43] During 1944, after the Battle of the Atlantic had been won, the number of

operations of different types was as follows.

Convoy escort	64
Ferry	42
Landing support	23
A/S hunt	17
Shipping strike	70
Minelaying	9
Blockade runner hunt	1

Escort carriers sank ten U-boats and shared another six, almost all on the Murmansk run as the main battle of the Atlantic was over before most of them entered service. All but two of the kills were by Swordfish which, contrary to popular belief, were flimsy and much more prone to accidents than the Avenger. Accidents occurred on 3.9 per cent of sorties. The Swordfish was slow, could not carry a full load in light winds and the crew tired quickly in the open cockpit and the radio was poor. Typically, they would fly about sixteen sorties a

Campania was the best British escort carrier (see table). She remained in service until 1955 having served as an exhibition ship and supporting atom bomb trials. (Author's collection)

41 The USN did not agree that these changes were necessary but later reduced their petrol stowage by a lesser amount.

42 All the first fifteen ships had American H2 catapults which could not launch British aircraft.

43 Friedman, *British Carrier Aviation*, p188.

Escort carriers

	Campania	Smiter
Displacement, deep (tons)	15,970	15,160
hp = speed (kts)	13,250 bhp=18	8500 shp=18
Flight deck length x width (ft)	515 x 70.5	450 x 80
Lifts/size (ft)ft	One 45 x 34	Two 42 x 34
No. of catapults	One C2	One H4
Hangar dimensions	198 x 73.5 x 17.5	260 x 62 x 18
No. of arrester wires	4	9
Aircraft	15	18
Petrol (gallons)	52,000	43,200
GM Deep (ft)	4.95	3.7
Max GZ @ angle (deg)	5.62@46½	? @48

day with up to twenty-seven recorded. About 23 per cent of operating days were limited by weather.

MAC ships (Merchant Aircraft Carriers)

Early in 1942 thought was given to fitting a flight deck etc to merchant ships 'for self protection'. The original requirement was for ships with a speed of 14-15kts and a 490ft flight deck. It was soon clear that ships of this performance would not be available and revised requirements were prepared for ships with a speed of 11kts, a flight deck 390ft long and 62ft wide and with a hangar for four Swordfish. These ships can only be described very briefly. The outline design was prepared by the Controller of Merchant Ship Repairs with advice from the Admiralty based on experience with *Audacity*.[44]

Six grain carriers were converted while building and all were given names beginning '*Empire Mac . . .*'.[45] The first was ordered in June 1942 and handed over in April 1943. The hangar was 142ft long with a single lift 42ft x 20ft. There were four arrester wires and no barrier.

Later, it was decided to convert nine existing tankers and convert four more still building. Conversion took about 6 months and added 3 months to building time. The tanker MAC ships did not have a hangar but carried six Swordfish on deck. By the time the MAC ships entered service the Battle of the Atlantic had been won. Only one convoy with a MAC ship was attacked and they sank no U-boats. However, MAC ships took part in 217 convoys and flew 4174 sorties.

The weight of the flight deck and its supports posed stability problems but the grain ships managed about 4ft GM, the new tankers 3ft and the conversions 2ft. There were also structural problems in the tankers with the flight deck in four sections with three expansion joints. The grain ships had a longitudinally stiffened, continuous flight deck. Projections beyond the side were strictly limited so that they could load and unload at normal berths. The merchant and naval parts of the crew had accommodation (and pay) to their own normal standards, but this seems to have caused little conflict.

44 J Lenaghan, 'Merchant Aircraft Carrier Ships', *Trans INA* (London 1947), p96. (Also *Design and Construction of British Warships*.)

45 One was named *Empire MacKendrick* after the CO of HMS *Audacity* which was, to some extent, a model for these ships.

Cruisers | *Four*

AT THE END OF the First World War the Royal Navy had some fifty modern cruisers (including nine building).[1] All but five of these were small ships with 6in guns, very suitable for North Sea or Mediterranean duties, but lacking endurance for the ocean trade routes. The Admiralty had fought a successful battle to complete most of the cruisers under construction when the war ended and there was no chance of funds for new-design ships. The five *Hawkins* class were the only bigger ships.[2] With a displacement of 9750 tons and an armament of 7.5in guns they were a major factor in the discussions concerning cruisers at Washington. It was known that Japan had ordered four big cruisers with at least four more to follow. The naval staff claimed that the RN needed eight similar ships for fleet duties and nine more to deal with any of the Japanese operating on the trade routes.

Since US studies had suggested ships of roughly *Hawkins* size with 8in guns and the Japanese had started the *Furutaka* class with 7.9in guns and only a little smaller, as completed, agreement was soon reached that the limit on cruiser size should be 10,000 tons with 8in guns.[3] There was to be no limit on numbers or on total tonnage. It is often said that the Treaty encouraged an escalation in cruiser size but it is clear that the major navies were already thinking of such ships which were still smaller than the First Class cruisers of the beginning of the century which had mounted 9.2in guns.

Effingham was the only one of the *Hawkins* class to be modernised. She was given nine single 6in in place of her 7.5in and would receive four twin 4in. (Not mounted in this 1938 photo.) The *Hawkins* class were the inspiration for the Treaty limits of 10,000 tons and 8in guns for cruisers. (Author's collection)

1 A Raven and J Roberts, *British Cruisers of World War Two* (London 1980), p103.

2 Includes *Vindictive* with reduced armament as an aircraft carrier and *Raleigh*, wrecked in 1922. It is remarkable that two of these five ships were lost in grounding accidents – The second being *Effingham*, Norway 1940.

3 The RN might have preferred a 7.5in gun but, since a new model was required, a change of calibre was easily accepted.

The requirement for seventy cruisers

A paper by Plans Division in 1923 set out the requirement for cruisers.[4] It began by noting that the wartime figure of 101 cruisers, all fully employed, had been reduced to 51 by 1923. The most probable enemy was Japan which left the Empire less well situated geographically than in the late war when the British isles lay across German access to the ocean. British cruisers were needed to protect trade routes and to form the scouting line for the main battlefleet. Japan had twenty-five cruisers which could be used with her main fleet if they decided to accept a battle or on the trade routes while, as the aggressor, she could choose a time when all her ships were available.

The RN requirement thus became an equal number with the battlefleet plus a 25 per cent margin for refits etc, a total of thirty-one. 'A most thorough investigation', which has not been found, concluded that thirty-nine more were needed on the trade routes, together with a number of armed merchant cruisers.[5] The thirty-nine cruisers should all be less than 15 years old but the risk of having up to ten over this age was acceptable. It was noted that twenty-six of the existing cruisers were war-built ships, designed for North Sea work and hence with endurance inadequate for the trade routes.

It was proposed to build eight 10,000-ton cruisers by 1929 and a further ten smaller cruisers. These would form part of the 'Special Programme of New Construction' proposed in 1923 to relieve unemployment by bringing forward new warship building, which died with the change of government (see Introduction). Since other navies would be building up to the 10,000-ton limit, it was essential that the RN had similar ships in the scouting line. This very simplistic justification of a force of seventy cruisers was treated as sacred writ until April 1937 when the 'New Standard' for a Royal Navy fighting a European war at the same time as a war in the Far East envisaged a force of 100 cruisers.

The 8in cruisers

In Britain, the first step was a new-design 8in gun and mounting. Single, twin and triple mounts were considered but it was not possible to mount a sufficient number in single mounts and, since the RN lacked experience with triples, this was ruled out as too complex. A very advanced twin mount was selected; initially it was hoped to fire at 12 rounds per minute per barrel with at least 65° elevation for long range anti-aircraft fire.[6] The rate of fire was soon reduced to 5 rounds a minute which proved hard to achieve reliably.[7] Since the new cruisers were intended to carry four 4in AA guns and two 8-barrel pompoms as well, their anti-aircraft capability was remarkable for the 1920s.[8]

Speed was the second desirable after heavy AA capability and all five of the first set of design studies submitted on 1 August 1923 were capable of 33kts at standard displacement. However, they were all thought to be lacking protection; even design D, the most heavily armoured, had protection only for magazines and shell rooms (4in sides, 3in deck and ends). Eventually, after three more design studies it was decided to reduce the power from 100,000 to 75,000shp at a cost of 2kts in top speed. The E-in-C subsequently found it possible to obtain 80,000shp without increasing weight or space and this, together with some fine-tuning of the hull form, recovered ½kt. These changes made weight available for splinter protection to the machinery, one inch side, one and a half deck (total weight of armour 1025 tons). They had a small torpedo bulge (5¼ft wide), too small be of much value against contemporary torpe-

Berwick (*Kent* class) as completed with short funnels. Designed with wartime experience these were probably the best of the early 'Treaty' cruisers. (World Ship Society)

York, an attempt at a smaller and cheaper cruiser, still with 8in armament. She had a very high bridge as it was originally intended to fit a catapult on B turret – shown in the Dinky toy model! (Author's collection)

does, let alone those under development.

The armament continued to give trouble; the 8in turrets were grossly overweight.

Weight of 8in turrets (tons)

	Original estimate	As completed	Excess
Mk I *Kent*	155	205	50
Mk I *London*	159.5	210	50.5
Mk II[9] *Dorsetshire*	168.8	220.3	51.5

Only as the first ships were completing was it discovered that their Mk V torpedoes were not strong enough for the 27ft drop from the upper deck to sea and they had to be modified. Multiple pompoms were not in production when the ships completed and they began life with four singles.

d'Eyncourt suggested a novel form of weight saving. By increasing the depth of the ship from keel to upper deck, the bending loads in a seaway can be accepted by a lighter structure.[10] This cannot be carried too far as other weights go up but Lillicrap did use a very deep hull which, in turn, led to the high freeboard making them very dry ships, so maintaining speed in rough seas, whilst the 'tween deck height gave them airy mess decks.[11] He noted that this depth gave plenty of room for the deep beams associated with longitudinal framing and also space for big vent trunks. d'Eyncourt suggested stresses of 10 or even 11 tons/in^2. Luckily, Lillicrap did not adopt such extreme values. Five *Kent*s were ordered under the 1924 programme and two more were ordered for Australia.

Great care was taken to save weight during building; overseers having the authority to reject fittings which they saw as overweight, while 40 tons were saved by using rivets with a smaller head! As a result they all completed well under the 10,000-ton limit, giving some

scope for updating. It had always been hoped that there would be weight to spare for a catapult and this was fitted during the 1930s. There were few teething problems other than with the armament. The first *Kent*s to complete showed that the funnels were far too short and they were raised 15ft (18ft in the Australian ships). There were vibration problems aft, soon cured by minor stiffening.[12] Four generally similar ships of the *London* class were ordered under the 1925 estimates. The shallow bulge was omitted and this, together with refinement of the lines, was expected to give them an extra ¾kt.[13] The two *Norfolk*s of the 1926 programme mounted the Mk II turret but were generally similar to the *London*s.

Shortage of funds made the idea of smaller but more numerous ships seem attractive and in August 1925 DNC submitted three studies of about 8200 tons for discussion. They all mounted six 8in in three, twin Mk II mounts.[14] They were required for trade protection but might have to serve with the fleet so that a minimum speed of 32kts was required. In the design selected a 3in belt was fitted over the machinery. Most of the weight saving was in the hull, the depth being reduced by one deck height from amidships aft.[15] It was intended to fit an aircraft catapult on the roof of B turret but it was realised that this would interfere with the balance and training of the turret. By that time the first ship, *York*, had been given a very high bridge structure to clear the catapult. She was to be the first cruiser to carry the new and heavy director control tower (DCT) (other than the trial fit in *Enterprise*) and the weight of this, high up, led to a considerable increase in beam. *York* was ordered under the 1926 Estimates.

It had been intended to order two more under the 1927 programme but only one was ordered (HMS *Exeter*). In appearance she was radically different. *York* was intended to have the same three-funnel style as the *Kent*s but the forward two were trunked to keep the smoke away from the bridge. Studies under the Director of the Senior Officers Technical Course in

4 ADM 8702/151, originally OP 01849/23 of 22 Dec 1923.

5 Other papers give a figure of fifty (later fifty-six) armed merchant cruisers.

6 This is a strange requirement. 65° is not needed for long-range AA fire – see Appendix 16.

7 *Norfolk* off Norway in 1945 seems to have fired at 5 rounds/min for some time with the Mark II mount.

8 Though still lacking an effective AA control system.

9 The Mk II had simplified loading arrangements and elevation was reduced to 50° to improve reliability and reduce weight. It seems to be a law of nature that a 'lightweight' Mk II weapon weighs more than the Mk I.

10 C S Lillicrap, Workbook, in National Maritime Museum. 2 Nov 1922. 'DNC does not wish to be bound by anything we have done before. Increase depth/length to reduce weight.'

11 He seems to have assumed hull weight varied as L²B (draught/depth) but his book is not entirely clear on this.

12 Most foreign ships also had vibration problems reflecting the light hull adopted to save weight. Light weight does not necessarily mean vibration but makes it more likely, particularly with the fairly crude structural design methods available in the 1920s.

13 I doubt if the small bulge would make much difference to speed and trials results seem to show little difference between the three groups.

14 The after mount was slightly modified to suit the reduced freeboard.

15 This break of forecastle caused a stress concentration amidships which would lead to severe cracking in some later classes.

Exeter, originally a sister of *York* but modified with a lower and simpler bridge and with upright funnels to make it more difficult to judge her course. Both these ships originally had three funnels, the forward one being trunked with the second in an attempt to reduce the amount of smoke on the bridge. (Imperial War Museum: A3882)

16 I A Sturton, 'HMS *Surrey* and *Northumberland*', *Warship International* 3/77, p245.

17 It is tempting to attribute this trend to Chatfield as Controller and, later, First Sea Lord.

18 D K Brown, 'Second World War Cruisers: Was Armour Really Necessary', *Warship 1992*, p121.

19 Cured by bigger bilge keels.

20 It had been agreed, informally, among the Treaty powers that 300 tons of growth was acceptable.

21 For details see Raven and Roberts, *British Cruisers*, p244.

22 The AA improvements included a pair of HACS and four twin 4in replacing the singles. (Some received an interim fit of two twins, two singles.)

23 Armour £72,000, aircraft £54,000, AA defence £43,000.

24 For details see Raven and Roberts, *British Cruisers*, p256.

25 Goodall 15 Sep 1941. 'Lillicrap to make *London* strength investigation and analysis of cruisers that have had troubles.'

26 The neutral axis is the axis about which a girder or a ship bends. See Appendix 12.

27 N G Holt and F E Clemitson, 'Notes on the Behaviour of H M Ships during the War', *Trans INA* (1949). Discussion by R J Daniel, p101. The number of structural problems in cruisers is notable.

28 This paragraph is based on a manuscript note passed to the National Maritime Museum.

1928 came out strongly in favour of vertical funnels to make it more difficult for an enemy to estimate the ship's inclination. At the same time, the number of complaints over the windy bridges of the *Kent*s led to a new design bridge for *Exeter*, lower and fairly free of wing extensions. The style of all future RN cruisers can be traced to the *Exeter*. The compass platform was given a bullet-proof roof. She also had the Mk II* turret at a cost of 90 tons. It is interesting that these two smaller ships needed the same power for the same speed as the earlier, bigger ships, mainly because of their reduced length.

In 1927 consideration was given to a ship with five twin turrets and virtually no protection other than to the magazines. It was rejected, partly because of the poor protection but also because the fifth turret was difficult to fit in and led to serious blast problems. The alternative, design 'X', had 5¾in protection to the after boiler room and engine room with 1-2in on the forward machinery.[16] In April 1928 design 'Y' was offered with all machinery heavily protected at the cost of a reduction in power to 60,000shp and speed to 30kts. There seems to have been a good deal of debate with the balance coming down in favour of 'Y' with a slight reduction in side protection to allow for 1in on the turret trunks. A change to an *Exeter*-style bridge and two vertical funnels was also made. The two proposed ships, *Surrey* and *Northumberland*, were cancelled in January 1930 as a result of the financial crisis and, following the London Treaty later that year, Britain gave up building cruisers with 8in guns.

Judgement

The merits of the *Kent* class can be judged, firstly by the changes made in later classes of British 8in cruisers and, secondly, by comparison with foreign ships of similar date and size though the *Norfolk* was ordered before *Kent* went to sea. Both *York* and *Surrey* show the increasing importance being attached to protection.[17] The general issue of protection in inter-war cruisers has

been considered at length elsewhere and will be returned to later in this chapter.[18] It would seem that there was a strong minority opinion favouring speed.

Comparison with foreign ships is not easy as several countries cheated, building ships well over the 10,000-ton limit. The balance between protection and speed is much less difficult to resolve given an extra 1000 tons! Then there are other factors to be considered: the British ships could fire 5 rounds a minute for a short time whereas the other navies fired at about 2 rounds a minute. It is likely that the British director system was superior at this date though used with spotting, 2 rounds a minute was all that was possible. Furthermore, France and Italy ran trials with the machinery heavily overloaded, recording very high speeds which were not attainable in service.

The first two USN ships, the *Pensacola*s, were not very successful. Their low freeboard made them wet and they rolled heavily.[19] Their turrets were cramped, the guns were mounted in a common cradle and their general fittings were inadequate. The next two groups were only a little better but the *New Orleans* class of 1931 were vastly superior ships. Their advanced machinery made it possible to give them a 5in belt and armoured turrets (6in face, 2¼in roof). With these ships the USN took a decisive lead in cruiser design which they were to retain.

Personally, I would certainly claim the *Kent* as the best of the early ships; after all, no other navy had the depth of wartime experience. It is a pity that this lead was not maintained due to obsolescent machinery design and the general backwardness of British industry.

Pre-war modifications

The changes made to the 8in cruisers prior to the outbreak of war show how staff views altered. Since they were underweight there was scope for some limited additions. During the early 1930s they were all given a catapult and aircraft. The two 8-barrel pompoms were

Cumberland in 1942 with a cut-down quarterdeck in partial compensation for additional armour. (Author's collection)

part of the original design and were fitted as they became available. During 1933-4 a number of schemes were considered for extensive improvements to the five *Kent* class ships. The amount by which they were under the Treaty limit varied from ship to ship as did the weight growth since completion.[20] In consequence, the schemes considered differed from ship to ship.[21] The principal addition would be an armour belt over machinery spaces. A 5½in belt would give some protection against 8in shell above 10,000yds and immunity over 15,000yds, with immunity against 6in above 5000yds. A 4½in belt gave no immunity against 8in shell but would protect against 6in above 8000yds.

After discussion, the Controller gave the following order of priority: (a) armour, (b) aircraft equipment, (c) anti-aircraft armament. However, a 5½in belt would preclude aircraft equipment and a 4½in belt was agreed. The changes actually made still varied from ship to ship but the base line involved 288 tons of armour, 120 tons of aircraft equipment and 34 tons AA defence (total 442 tons).[22] The cost was £161,000–£215,000 per ship.[23] Once again, one notes the emphasis on protection. Discussions on the *London* class began in 1936 and continued for two years. A much more fundamental change was looked for and schemes included all new machinery or the old machinery re-arranged in a unit system.[24] In the end a scheme was agreed with a 3½in NC belt and the superstructure remodelled as a *Fiji*.

London had received a number of minor additions during the years from completion to 1937. Even so, it was a surprise to find from an inclining in February of that year that her standard displacement was already 10,203 tons instead of 9750. This would imply a displacement after modernisation of 10,687 tons as planned in January 1939 and which turned out to be 11,015 tons (14,578 tons deep) on completion in February 1941. This great increase in the load on a light hull was to cause problems; by May 1941 reports were received of leaking rivets and cracks in the upper deck, particularly around the boiler room uptakes.[25] She was taken in hand from October 1941 to January 1942 when an extra 63 tons of strengthening was added to the upper deck. These repairs were ill-conceived as strengthening the upper deck raised the neutral axis increasing the stress on the bottom.[26] Sure enough, the bottom began to leak, contaminating the feed water, and she was taken in hand for further stiffening from December 1942 to May 1943 after which she was as satisfactory as any ageing, hard-worked ship.[27] The remaining *London*s and the *Dorsetshire*s did not have any major modernisation but their AA armament was increased and a high-angle control system (HACS) fitted.

Early small 6in designs

Even before the Washington Treaty, some thought was given to smaller cruisers but no design studies were undertaken. By February 1925 requirements had been completed for a ship of 7500-8000 tons with four twin 6in turrets. The endurance of 5500 miles at 12kts was inadequate and a new study prepared with 7000-mile endurance and a displacement of 8500 tons. With 100,000shp, as in *Enterprise*, the speed would be 34½kts.

In connection with this design, DNC asked for a re-examination of the philosophy of machinery design.[28] A review in 1925 had led to a Board decision that no risks should be taken with the machinery of the big cruisers; DNC noting, sourly, that he had had to take considerable risks with the structure of these ships to save weight. Saving of weight in machinery was of increased importance in smaller cruisers and if British machinery was heavier than that of other navies RN ships would either be slower or inferior in military capability. DNC deduced that the early Italian cruisers of the 'Condottieri' class had 95,000shp for about 1400 tons or 68shp/ton. The new British ships would have 60,000shp for 1325 tons, 45.3shp/ton. DNC pressed for larger boilers and lighter machinery (see Chapter 5).

In January 1929 five designs were presented to a Light Cruiser Conference, all of 6000 tons. This displacement was chosen as it was required to maintain 27kts in a 'Force 4-5 sea'.[29] Armament varied with five 6in or six 5.5in open shields, or three or four twin 6in turrets. Reports from trials of *Enterprise*'s twin 6in were good and the idea of open mounts was dropped.[30] Protection was required against 6in above 10,000yds and below 16,000yds and against 4.7in above 7000yds (sheet immune against 4.7in at all ranges). This equated to 3in NC side and 2in deck.

The 5.5in gun had many advantages in a hand-worked mount but in a powered turret, the heavier shell of the 6in was clearly superior and a design with four twins was selected. With an endurance of 6500 miles at 16kts the displacement was 6500 tons. A legend and sketch design was approved on 3 June 1929 with four twin 6in on a displacement of 6500 tons.

Leander[31]

A considerable number of changes were made during the development of the design of this class, the most important being improved subdivision of the machinery spaces. The sketch design had two boiler rooms ahead of two engine rooms with 20,000shp on each outer shaft and 10,000shp on the inners. This was changed to three boiler rooms each with two boilers and two engine rooms with a separate gearing room. The new arrangement of machinery occupied a length of 179ft instead of the 160ft of the original layout. Extra bulkheads are always expensive as access is required to equipment each side of the bulkhead. More machinery spaces also put up the engine room complement and the additional men had to be squeezed into less space since the ship was only lengthened by 12ft. Living conditions were poorer than in the 'County' class and no better than the cramped wartime ships. The boiler rooms were

together so that the uptakes could be trunked into a single funnel making it more difficult to estimate inclination. Both the funnel and bridge were streamlined in a successful attempt to reduce the amount of smoke on the bridge.

The horsepower was increased to 63,000 to maintain speed, bringing the displacement to 7000 tons. Experience with the 'County' class showed that boiler pressure could be raised from 250lbs/in² to 300lbs/in² increasing the power to 72,000shp and the speed to 32½kts. Model tests at Haslar with a range of bulbous bows showed that a bulb with a cross section 4 per cent of that of the midships section would reduce resistance by 1¾ per cent and increase speed by ⅛ knot between 25 and 32kts.[32] Later tests gave 1-2¼ per cent less resistance at top speed with a penalty of 3¼-3¾ per cent at 25kts.

Changes to aircraft equipment, machinery and armour brought the calculated displacement up to 7154 tons which was approved in June 1931. During building a further increase of 300 tons was calculated but DNC expected that much of this would be offset by the extensive use of welding and she, in fact, completed at 7289 tons, 135 tons over the approved figure.[33] At about £1.6 million, *Leander* was not particularly cheap compared with a 'County' at £2 million.

The London Treaty of 1930 has been discussed in the Introduction. As far as RN cruisers were concerned it meant an end to the building of 8in ships and limited the total tonnage of those with 6in guns to 192,200. This made ships like *Leander* seem very attractive and four similar ships were ordered, three in 1930 and one in 1931.[34] The beam was increased by 1ft at the waterline, holding the original beam at the deck to improve stability.[35] There were slight changes to the armour arrangement but, as DNC had predicted, the experience with welding in the *Leander* led to much bigger weight savings in the follow-on ships. The next three completed at 7030-7070 tons and the last, *Ajax*, at 6840 tons.

29 It is unclear what this means. 'Force' relates to wind speed with only an indirect relationship with wave height. The use of 'Sea State' was not common in 1929 but this may have been an early example. Sea State 5 implies waves up to about 12ft high in which a typical 6000-ton cruiser should just about make 27kts. Speed in a seaway depends on length, draught and freeboard, only indirectly linked with displacement. See Appendix 19.

30 As seen at the time the open mount had many advantages apart from cheapness. It could develop a higher rate of fire for a short time, it was more reliable and presented a smaller target. On the other hand, the turret needed a smaller crew who were better protected and the lower rate of fire was consistent with director control and spotting.

31 K McBride, ' "Eight Six-inch Guns in Pairs". The *Leander* and *Sydney* Class Cruisers', *Warship 1997-1998*, p167.

32 The DNC history says that fitting of the bulb was approved but, apparently later model tests were less favourable and the bulb was not fitted. (Raven and Roberts, *British Cruisers*, p206). However, the body plan as laid off in Devonport Dockyard in 1931 shows a bulb. I do not think it was fitted but the evidence is unclear either way.

33 Her weight calculations were probably based on *Exeter* and there is a belief that scaling-down from a bigger ship is more likely to lead to error than scaling up.

34 The DNC history distinguishes the *Leander* class as different from *Leander* herself.

35 While this would improve initial stability (GM) it would not help much at larger angles.

36 The author served in *Euryalus* of the *Dido* class in 1950 and remembers the wet upper deck.

Leander in 1942 serving with the Royal New Zealand Navy. She still retains pole masts and shows no sign of radar. (Author's collection)

There were few problems in peacetime service; the upper deck abaft the break of forecastle was wet and the boats stowed there in *Leander* were damaged the forecastle was extended and the boats raised.[30] There were the usual leaky rivets which led to some stiffening. The closed bridge was not liked as the windows got obscured if closed and it was very draughty if they were open. In war they were able to stand up to severe damage and still get home.

Amphion class

In the second ship of the 1931 Programme it was decided to adopt a unit system of machinery alternating boiler room, engine room, boiler room, engine room. Either boiler room could feed either engine room and there was a good chance that the ship would still be mobile with any two spaces flooded. This additional security was gained at a price; the length of the machinery spaces went up by 9ft to 188ft and the length over which the side armour extended to the upper deck was 141ft instead of 84ft in the earlier ships. The length of the ship was increased by 8ft but it was clear that they would be even more cramped than the *Leander* class, and the unit system of machinery demanded even more men making matters worse. Originally the required complement was 650 but there was thought to be room for only 600. It is unclear how this was resolved but their nominal complement on completion was 570. There were four boilers instead of six and there was equal power on each shaft.

This arrangement of the machinery spaces was used in all later British cruisers which were built. While it should have greatly increased the resistance to damage, there was a very serious flaw which detracted greatly from its value. The two boilers in the after room were in line amidships to allow the outer shafts to run outboard of them, This left two small wing compartments. Calculations showed that the heel produced by flooding one of these spaces was very small. However, if the ship was torpedoed in that region two or probably three main compartments would be flooded greatly reducing the stability so that the asymmetric buoyancy of the other wing compartment would cause a very large heel and, in all probability, capsize the ship.

Fleet cruisers

The small war-built cruisers were very satisfactory as fleet cruisers, leading destroyers and shadowing and no thought was given to replacing them until 1929 when, during discussions which led to the *Leander*, it was suggested that such ships were too big for fleet work where small size was actually desirable. The limit on total tonnage imposed by the London Treaty also made small size attractive while it was hoped that the smaller ships would be cheaper.

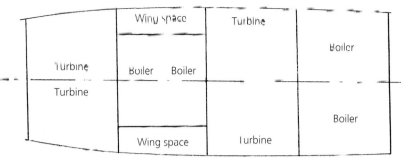

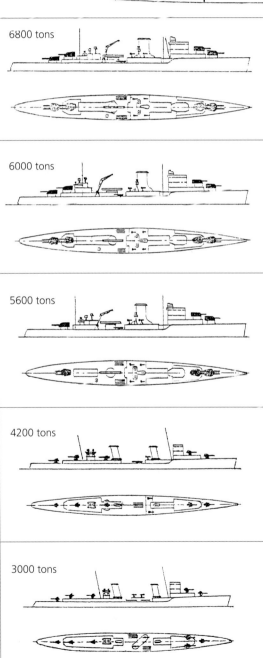

Studies for the fleet cruiser (1929) which led to the *Arethusa*.

Machinery Layout and Capsize

From *Amphion* onwards, British cruisers had machinery arranged with two boilers side by side in the forward room, then two turbines driving the outboard shafts. The after boiler room was arranged with boilers along the centre and wing spaces outboard. The after engine room drove the inboard shafts.

Flooding a wing space alone would only cause a small angle of heel. However, a torpedo hit in this area would probably flood both engine rooms, the after boiler room and one wing space. Stability would be greatly reduced and the asymetric buoyancy of the other wing space would capsize the ship – very quickly.

1929 Fleet cruisers

Design	A	B	C	D	E
Dispt (tons)	6800	6000	5600	4200	3000
Main armt	4-6in twin	4-6in twin	3-6in twin	5-6in	6-5.5in
Speed (kts)	31½	33	33	36	38

Only Design 'A' had protection to the machinery and 'E' did not even have protection to the magazines. Two more designs of about 4800 tons were prepared, both with three twin 6in and 3in side armour to magazines and machinery. They had a general style of the *Leander* with one funnel and three boiler rooms together. Minor additions during the development of the design brought the displacement up to 5000 tons and a legend was approved in March 1931.

It was not possible to place orders immediately because of the financial crisis and, during the wait, DNC started to look at unit machinery. This brought the displacement up to 5500 tons, unwelcome in the light of the Treaty limit, and the cost had risen to £1,428,000, also unwelcome. After discussion of various alternative schemes it was decided to go ahead with the bigger ship, reduced to 5450 tons by savings in the machinery. The remaining tonnage under London 1930 would permit five of these ships (the *Arethusa* class) and nine *Leander*s.[37]

Welding

Welding was used to an increasing extent from *Leander* onwards. Cammell Laird was the leading private yard

and they welded all the main bulkheads of *Achilles*. For *Arethusa*, Chatham Dockyard welded the shell and strength deck for the forward 80ft, all internal decks and the superstructure, framing in the double bottom, bulkheads and much minor work. In a paper dealing with this work, Sherwin said that distortion was a difficult, but soluble, problem.[38] During the discussion, Lillicrap, head of the cruiser section, made two important points. Though successful welds had been made in D quality steel (see Appendix 15), failures were too common for any confidence in such work. The cost of welded structure was about the same per ton as riveted (1931) but since the welded structure was lighter, the overall cost was less (see *Seagull*, Chapter 7).

Bigger cruisers

The Admiralty's plans for numbers of small cruisers were thwarted when other countries, particularly Japan, began to build large cruisers with numerous 6in guns. The *Mogami* class were declared at 8500 tons with fifteen 6.1in guns which caused a sensation. In fact, their true design displacement was 9500 tons corresponding to a trial displacement of 11,169 tons, they completed at 12,962 tons (trial) and, when their numerous problems had been cured, they weighed in at 14,112 tons (trial).[39]

Considerable thought was given in all major navies to the value of the big 6in ship as against those armed with 8in. The 6in could fire more quickly, 6-8 rounds per minute[40] as opposed to 2 for the 8in (5 possibly for the RN turrets), which also had longer range, better penetration of armour and caused more damage when it hit. The key question was whether the slow-firing 8in could inflict fatal damage on a 6in ship between 28,000 and

Arethusa in mid-war condition; tripod masts, air warning and gun direction radars with numerous 20mm Oerlikons. (Author's collection)

20,000yds, the maximum effective ranges of the 8in and 6in gun respectively. Most navies seem to have favoured the 6in ship, although Japan took the opposite view and re-armed her big 6in ships with 8in guns. The USN built large numbers of both types and introduced much heavier shells for both guns.[41] Wartime experience strongly suggests that hits on a manoeuvring target at over 20,000yds were rare, justifying the 6in armament.[42]

In 1933 DNC produced four studies based on *Amphion* but with four triple 6in turrets, three twin 4in and 5in side armour. Speeds ranged from 30 to 32kts and displacement from 7800 to 8835 tons. Perhaps surprisingly, the biggest was chosen for development – and it got bigger. The length of the armour belt was increased though its thickness was reduced to 4½ins. A fourth twin 4in was added together with two multiple pompoms. There was considerable debate over the aircraft arrangements ending with approval for an athwartships heavy catapult and a hangar either side of the fore funnel. The Controller, Henderson, decided on raking funnels ostensibly to get the smoke clear of the bridge but probably mainly for aesthetic reasons.[43] All cruisers since the 'E' class had a knuckle forward intended to keep water off the deck but someone must have had doubts since *Birmingham* was built with a conventional flare. No comparative trials of the bow shape were carried out but a young constructor, J C Lawrence, went to Capetown in *Birmingham* to observe her behaviour.[44] Despite his favourable report, Controller decided to rebuild her with a knuckle though the outbreak of war meant that the work was not undertaken.[45] The CO of *Birmingham* said that sea trials showed no advantage in her bow.[46] Later, in January 1939, she met very heavy weather between Hong Kong and Manila and, in the CO's view, the bow was very effective.[47]

After the first five were built, a little more money became available and the last three had an extra DCT aft

and three HACS. The last, *Gloucester*, had a 2in deck in place of the 1¼in of the earlier ships. Power was increased in the last three to maintain speed at 32kts.

Catapults[48]

At the end of the First World War the Grand Fleet (excluding aircraft carriers) carried 103 aircraft on simple flying-off platforms, usually over a gun turret.[49] Such arrangements obstructed the arcs of fire, sometimes forced the ship to steam into the wind and were less useful as planes got bigger and faster. A specification for a powered catapult was issued in 1916 and two different catapults were tested in 1917, one ashore, the other on a self-propelled lighter, HMS *Slinger*.

In 1922 a new specification was issued for a catapult to launch a 7000lb aircraft at 45kts with a maximum acceleration of 2g. The Carey catapult had a compressed-air ram which worked the trolley through wires and pulleys. It was installed on *Vindictive* in 1925 and proved very satisfactory leading to similar installa-

Birmingham of the 'Town' class. She was the only British cruiser of the period to be built without a knuckle in her bow sections. Opinions still differ on the value of a knuckle. (For the author's view look at the 'Castle' class OPV.) (Imperial War Museum: A12924)

37 Goodall 20 Feb 1935. 'Walked along upper deck of *Arethusa* – looks a big ship for only six 6in guns.' And 12 Aug 1936 visiting- '*Penelope* full of everything except guns and armour'.

38 C E Sherwin, 'Electric Welding in Cruiser Construction', *Trans INA* (1936), p247. Sherwin told the author that this paper was based on the notes left by his predecessor, A J Sims, used with permission.

39 E Lacroix and L Wells, *Japanese Cruisers of the Pacific War* (London 1997).

40 Probably more like 4 when spotting fall of shot at long range.

41 The 8in shell went from 260lbs to 335lbs, the 6in from 105lbs to 130lbs.

42 D K Brown, 'The Cruiser', in R Gardiner (ed), *The Eclipse of the Big Gun* (London 1992), p64. Particularly cruiser actions at Matapan and the Komandorskis.

43 There is a small piece of paper in the cover with a sketch of the funnels and Henderson's writing says make it like this. The result, in this writer's opinion was one of the most beautiful warships of all time and one which strongly influenced the Type 43 destroyer cancelled in 1980. See D K Brown, *A Century of Naval Construction*, p269.

44 Conversation with the author.

45 The value of a knuckle depends on the length, freeboard and speed of the ship compared with the length and height of the waves

encountered and it is hard to generalise. In the author's opinion knuckles are of value from ships of OPV size (I designed the 'Castle' class) to cruisers.

46 ADM 229 22 of 22 July 1939.

47 This is what I would expect. The knuckle is most effective in moderate seas and its value will diminish when seas rise well above the deckline.

48 A fuller account is given in D K Brown, 'The British Shipboard Catapult', *Warship 49* (London 1989).

49 D K Brown, *The Grand Fleet*, p122.

The old seaplane carrier *Ark Royal* (later renamed *Pegasus*) was used for numerous trials of catapults between the wars. (Wright & Logan)

50 Goodall, 22 Nov 1933 re *Barham* catapult trial. 'I believe the catapult is only a toy to get the Navy air minded. Practical value NIL as once the plane is gone, it's gone for ever until the ship returns to port.' It was intended that they should land on the sea and be hoisted back but this could only take place in calm weather. The Hein mat gear was tried from *Ark Royal* but seems to have had little success.

51 S V Goodall. 'Uncontrolled Weapons and Warships of Limited Displacement', *Trans INA* (1937).

52 See G A Rotherham, '*It's Really Quite Safe*' (Belleville, Ont. 1985).

53 S V Goodall. 'Uncontrolled Weapons and Warships of Limited Displacement', *Trans INA* (1937), p1.

54 Their size enabled them to mount six twin 4in.

55 MFO 658/36 passed to the National Maritime Museum.

56 There are numerous, critical entries in Goodall's diary. 13 Mar 40. 'Told First Lord of trouble with *Edinburgh*, he is very nice to me so far'. And finally 28 Jan 1941. Lillicrap re *Edinburgh* '. . . these *Southampton*s are a groggy lot'. (See also Appendix 12.)

57 Again, why were smaller guns fitted in destroyers?

58 ADM 138 555.

59 Goodall 2 Feb 37 'Inspected *Dido* drawing; Jackman has done well.'

60 Of those torpedoed near the aft boiler room, *Bonaventure*, *Naiad*, *Hermione* and *Charybdis* capsized rapidly as did *Spartan*, hit by a guided bomb in the same area. Only *Cleopatra* survived, thanks to excellent damage control.

61 Goodall 27 Mar 1940. 'Finished *Dido* strength; made small alteration at break of forecastle in ships not too far advanced'. 6 July 1940. 'Found problem with *Naiad* A turret'. 16 August 1940. '*Dido* with 4 twin 5.25 and doubling deck around A turret'. 10 Sept 1940. '*Dido* gun mountings all give trouble except *Bonaventure*'. (When the author was serving in *Euryalus* in 1950 A turret was permanently out of action due to problems with the roller path) – Also 9 Mar 1941 '*Dido* cracked plate . . . more damned square vent holes in strength members'. (Goodall hardly ever swore; he must have been very angry) 12 March 1941. 'Square corner vent hole in stringer which makes me mad'. (His underlining)

62 Joining *Euryalus* in 1950, I was given the cabin furthest aft 'so that I could learn about vibration!'. Vibration aft was only reduced from about 1960 with the introduction of five-bladed propellers.

tions in *Resolution* and the submarine *M 2*. The RAE catapult used telescopic tubes and was fitted to *Barham*, *Royal Sovereign* and, later, *Resolution*.[50] *Hood* was given a catapult on its low quarterdeck, Goodall remarking (4 April 1932), '*Hood*'s catapult is a washout literally. Must hasten midships arrangement.'

After some other experimental units, the Extending Structure catapult was designed by W A D Forbes on similar lines to the Carey catapult and it was fitted to a number of ships. This was followed by the Slider catapult designed in the E-in-C Department. Mention must be made of the role played by the seaplane carrier *Ark Royal* (later *Pegasus*) which tried fifteen catapults, usually with several types of aircraft.

By the mid-1930s, battleships and cruisers had similar aircraft arrangements with two hangars ahead of a fixed, athwartships catapult which was double acting, *ie* could be fired in either direction. By this time aircraft arrangements were taking up some 20 per cent of the weather deck area in cruisers.[51] Considerable importance was attached to these shipborne aircraft. They were used to search for the enemy and to spot for gunfire.[52] The most powerful catapults could launch a 12,000lb plane at 70kts but great care was needed to avoid damage to the relatively flimsy aircraft or the crew. The maximum acceleration had not to exceed 1.25 times the average, the build up should be smooth over the first 10ft (0.4 seconds) and the acceleration must diminish steadily from the maximum to the end of the run. For a launch speed of 66kts, reached in 96ft, the mean acceleration would be 2g with a maximum of 2.5g. Catapults were phased out in 1942-3 with the increasing number of carriers and the need to use the space for other purposes.

Warships of limited displacement

Goodall, in his paper quoted under battleships, comments on the growth of certain features of cruisers between 1920 and 1935.[53] Anti-aircraft armament had increased from less than 1 per cent of the standard displacement to nearly 3 per cent, deck protection from about 2 per cent to 10 per cent whilst the percentage of weather deck area occupied by aircraft and their equipment had risen from almost zero to 20 per cent. All these increases had to be accommodated within a hull limited in size by the Treaties.

Edinburgh and *Belfast*

The *Southampton* armament of twelve 6in guns appeared less than that of US and Japanese cruisers with fifteen guns, although the difference was less than it would seem as one turret of the foreign ships had very limited arcs of fire. It was, however, desired to match such ships in the improved 'Towns' and they were intended to carry four quadruple 6in turrets. But the quadruple mount proved difficult to design and it was decided that the two ships of the 1936 should have four triples, which enabled them to be a little shorter than originally planned and the deck armour was increased to 2ins.

The machinery block was moved aft, presumably to get smoke away from the bridge, which led to a very awkward ammunition supply to the 4in guns and ruined their appearance.[54] The official docket seeking and obtaining Board approval of the final design has survived, showing how simple the procedures were prior to the war.[55] The minute, signed by F Bryant for DNC who was sick, runs to half a page of foolscap. Some of the wording is of interest, for example, it says that other departments have been 'consulted' as opposed to agreed. It concludes by saying that invitation to tender will be sent out in 6 days time, prior to approval. There is then three pages of description and the Legend form. Board approval was given in one sentence, less than a month later.

They had a break of forecastle amidships and the side and deck armour stepped down a deck within a few feet. This double discontinuity in the structure led to a weakness and *Belfast* broke her back at this point when mined (see Chapter 10). *Edinburgh* was already cracking at the same place as were some of the earlier *Southampton*s under normal seaway loading.[56] The forecastle was slightly extended and stiffening fitted.

Fleet cruisers

In 1934 the Board was still uncertain of the design for a fleet cruiser. After considering proposals from DNC (table opposite) they listed the desired characteristics as:

Small enough to be built in reasonable numbers.
Large enough to keep up with the fleet in a seaway.
Maximum gun power.
Speed and handiness.
Small silhouette.

Design 'V' was to be developed into the 'Tribal' class destroyer (see Chapter 5) but suggestions that it could fulfil cruiser roles were rejected. None of the designs in the table were favoured as cruisers. It gradually became apparent that a mixed armament of 6in and 4in AA was extravagant in weight and space and that a dual purpose weapon was needed. The 5.25in gun, selected as the secondary armament of the *King George V* class battleships, was chosen for the cruisers as having the smallest shell effective against destroyers.[57] It was hoped to obtain 12 rounds per minute but this was optimistic. It entered service with a nominal 10 rounds per minute but 8 was more realistic and even at this rate there were frequent breakdowns, and rates of training and elevation were too slow for effective AA fire. Four early studies all mounted ten 5.25in guns and two 4-barrel

pompoms with a speed of 32kts. Armour varied slightly but most had a 3in belt and 1in deck (2 or 3ins over magazines). 'B' and 'Q' had unit machinery (as *Amphion*) and two funnels while 'A' and 'P' had boiler rooms (2 and 3 respectively) ahead of two engine rooms and a single funnel.[58] 'A' and 'B' had vertical funnels, the others were raked.

Design 'P' was developed as the *Dido* class which carried ten 5.25in guns on 5450 tons.[59] The concept was excellent but spoilt by various problems. The gun was never really satisfactory and the problem of heel and capsize with asymmetric flooding in the region of the after boiler room was more serious in these smaller ships.[60] There were more structural problems, particularly in the region of A turret which jammed if the roller path was distorted.[61] Priority for the 5.25in turrets was given to the battleships so *Dido* and *Phoebe* completed with a 4in star shell gun in Q position and *Bonaventure* in X. *Scylla* and *Charybdis* had four twin 4.5in mounts ordered for the re-arming of the old 'D' class cruisers, making them much better AA ships but with a surface capability not much better than a large destroyer. They seem to have been well liked in service. After the 'Counties' most reports on the new cruisers commented on the lack of vibration 'except for the usual problem aft'.[62]

Fleet cruiser designs 1934

	A	B	R	S	T	U	V
Dispt (tons)	4500	5000	4500	4500	5500	3500	1830
Speed (kts)	30¾	33	33	33	33	38	36¼
Main Armt	6-6in	6-6in	6-6in	7-6in	6-6in	8-6in	10 4.7in
AA Armt	1 4in	4 4in	2-4in	2 4in	2 x4 pp	Nil	Nil
Belt (ins)	4	1	4	1	4	Nil	Nil

Edinburgh, a 'Town' class derivative. These ships all had a weakness as the break of forecastle amidships was close to the point at which the armour stepped down a deck height. In this photo the forecastle has been extended to alleviate the problem. (Imperial War Museum: A6160)

Top: Dido with all five twin
5.25in turrets and with few
wartime modifications except
radar. (Imperial War Museum:
A23709)

Lower: Scylla. 5.25in turrets
were in short supply and she
and her sister, *Charybdis*,
completed with four twin 4.5in
originally ordered for the old
'D' class cruisers. (Author's
collection)

The 8000-ton cruisers

The new London Treaty of 1936 came into force on 26
July 1937. After Japan withdrew, Britain and the USA
agreed to remove all limits on the total tonnage of ships
but a new limit of 8000 tons on individual cruisers. At
this size, it was desirable to combine the roles of fleet
cruiser and trade protection cruiser. The first three
studies in mid-1936 had three triple 6in, speeds between
30 and 32.5kts and side armour from 3ins to 4.5ins. Two
of them mounted four twin 4in AA and two multiple
pompoms whilst one gained two more 4in mounts by
removing aircraft equipment.

The Board wanted a heavier armament and two more
studies were prepared, one with ten 6in guns and the

other with twelve in the proposed quadruple mount.
The new 5.25in was then investigated, seven studies
having seven twin mounts and the other eight. At first,
opinion favoured the designs with 5.25in guns but eventually a 6in ship was chosen since such cruisers might
have to fight enemy 8in ships and, while the 6in ship
would have a chance, the ship with 5.25in guns would
not.

Design proceeded on a study 'K31' with four 6in
triples, four twin 4in and a 3½in belt.[63] Variations on
this design led to the *Fiji* class in which the belt was
reduced to 3¼ins and power increased to 80,000shp
giving 32¼kts. The aircraft outfit was changed from
three Walrus to two larger Sea Otter which meant a bigger catapult, 32 tons heavier.[64] By June 1937 the design

legend displacement was 8170 tons with the usual hope that savings would bring this down below 8000 tons, particularly as the use of welding was to be further extended.[65] However, as war approached weights continued to rise and by 1939 the displacement was estimated at 8268 tons with a further 32 tons when torpedo tubes were fitted.[66]

The five ships of the 1937 programme were ordered in December of that year and the four similar ships of the 1938 programme in March 1939. There was considerable debate over the 1939 ships with much support for design 'K34' with only nine 6in and thicker armour (4½ins if possible). There was concern that French and German 6in guns had a higher muzzle velocity and hence more penetrating power. Goodall wrote a powerful minute disagreeing with the view that *Fiji*'s protection was poor; if the intelligence on foreign guns was correct it could be argued that her armament was inferior. He strongly supported the heavier armament of the *Fiji*, which was better protected than any RN cruiser except *Belfast*, rather than the heavier protection of the 'K34'. It was eventually agreed that more armour was not worth a reduction of 25 per cent in armament. However, the three ships of the 1938 and 1939 programmes did end up with nine 6in as the *Uganda* class, with enhanced AA armament. There were three similar ships of the *Swiftsure* class with a foot on the beam under the 1941 estimates and five more of the *Tiger* class with a further foot on the beam under the 1941 supplementary and 1942 Estimates (see Appendix 14).

In general these ships were reduced *Southamptons* but the long stalk 6in turrets reduced the manpower requirement, though they were still cramped and with wartime additions soon became much worse as the design complement of 710 (738 as flagship) rose to over

900. The machinery spaces were shorter and there were no diesel generator spaces which, together with a larger superstructure helped accommodation. Other improvements to the quality of life included a laundry, pantry with washing-up machine, smoking room for CPOs, padded mess stools, ship side lining, hot lockers for broadside messes. Washing arrangements were improved with hot and cold taps to each basin! Some additional space for CPO and POs washplaces was found by combining into one space the separate fitting shops for ERAs, OAs and EAs. Each officer's cabin would have a basin with hot and cold water. The cold and cool rooms were about 50 per cent bigger than in previous practice. Writing 63 years later, it is hard to imagine life before these 'improvements'.

They were the first ships, other than *Adventure*, with a transom stern giving a small increase in top speed and more space aft.[67] The formal submission docket said '. . . that difficulty may be experienced in maintaining steady revolutions at a certain speed when with this form of stern a rapid change in wake formation occurs.'[68] Goodall used to review his work critically twice a year and his comments on the *Fiji*s were; (1940) 'The *Fiji*s better than I foresaw' and a year later '*Fiji*s are doing well'.

Fast minelayers

Three fast minelayers of the *Abdiel* class were ordered under the 1938 programme, another the following year and two slightly modified ships in 1941. They were intended to carry 100 Mk XIV or XV mines in the standard condition and 50 more with loss of speed. The speed was to be 40.2kts in the standard condition (2640 tons) giving, it was hoped, 35.2kts in the deep condi-

Trinidad (*Fiji* class). Her armour was largely made in Czechoslovakia. She had the misfortune to torpedo herself and after repairs in Murmansk was sunk by air attack. (Imperial War Museum: A7683)

63 Goodall 1 Oct 1936. 'Kennett on 8,000 ton, 12-6 inch. He has done the trick but is rather a stick in the mud.'

64 Goodall 4 Mar 1937. 'Had a good go at 8,000 ton cruiser. Johns has done well.'

65 Goodall 8 May 1937. 'John came in to say that he had under estimated *Fiji* GM. Went into this and put up beam 8 inches and cut down upper deck by about 1'6 (left exact figures to him). John a bit downhearted (a good man I still think) tried to cheer him up.'

66 Goodall 10 July 1939. 'Lillicrap says *Fiji* coming out heavy with appreciably less GM than estimate. Ship safe but we must set our face against all additions.'

67 It is probable that the transom would have improved resistance to flooding aft by reducing trim. However, in days before the computer such calculations were almost impossible.

68 Goodall admitted elsewhere that he had been over-conservative on the subject of transom sterns.

tion.[69] They were roughly destroyer style with two boiler rooms, each containing two boilers, one engine room and a gearing room for 72,000shp.

During the development of the design the displacement increased and on trial *Manxman* reached 35.6kts off Arran with 73,000shp at 3450 tons, and similar results came from other ships of the class, figures entirely consistent with the original estimates. Trials are run with a clean bottom and the machinery in best condition; there is little chance of such speeds being exceeded in service.[70] Both trial and model data were re-examined with great care during the design of the abortive Type 19 frigate, intended for a trial speed of 43kts – luckily it was cancelled. Stability intact was good but the large open mining deck would be a hazard if flooded – as with a RO-RO ship – and the two later ships were fitted with portable coffer dams to divide this space. They were quite highly stressed and when used as a high-speed store carrier, a frequent task, cargo was limited to 200 tons on the mine deck.[71] The later *Apollo* cost £807,000, without guns and ammunition.

Cruisers up to the War

The policies for cruiser building seem sensible and the changes in policy were justified by changes in the world situation. The initial concentration on big cruisers for trade protection was justified anyway but emphasised by the abundance of small war-built ships. Similarly, the shift to small cruisers was not merely a reflection of the rules of the London Treaty but those rules were

pressed by the RN in an attempt to get a more numerous force.

The designs to satisfy these policies were generally good. It has been argued that the *Kents* were the best of the first wave of post-Washington ships. The *Leander* and follow-on ships were good examples of small cruisers. It is ironic that these ships, which were seen as the smallest with a decisive superiority over an armed merchant ship, included *Sydney* which was sunk by such a raider. The concept of the *Didos* was admirable, nullified by the lack of performance and reliability of the 5.25in mount.

There was a steady increase in power per unit weight of machinery in these ships, mainly associated with higher steam pressures from 250 lbs/in² to 400lbs/in² in *Fiji* and *Dido*, partially offset by the extra weight of unit layout.

Power of pre-war cruisers

	shp	M/C Wt (tons)	shp/ton
Kent	80,000	1830	43.7
Exeter	80,000	1750	45.7
Leander	72,000	1504	47.8
Amphion	72,000	1310	55.0
Arethusa	64,000	1221	52.4
Southampton	75,000	1492	50.3
Belfast	80,000	1498	53.4
Fiji	80,000	1440	55.6
Dido	62,000	1146	54.1

For comparison, the shp/ton of machinery in USN ships ranged from 60.6 in *Salt Lake City* to 54.1 in *Cleveland* and 59.6 in *Baltimore*. Too much should not be read into this comparison as the definition of weight groups can vary from one office to another but see passage on USN machinery (see Appendix 17). Most of the weight saved went into increased protection, a trend slightly reversed in *Fiji*.

Though the performance of these ships in war, including resistance to damage, was good, there were still too many detail errors in design. Structure was a particular problem with discontinuity and sharp corners too common.[72] Asymmetric flooding of the wing compartments was a bad feature which should have been recognised even though this was not easy in pre-computer days.

Wartime changes

(Note; this section applies to most other categories of ship) The first lesson of the war was the need for exposed personnel to be protected against splinters which involved weight, high up, but no demand on space. Increasing top weight–aerials, light AA guns, zarebas, and heavier directors meant that the main armament of many ships had to be reduced to compensate.

The introduction of radar had more complex effects. First came the aerials, often requiring tripod or lattice masts. Then there were the radar offices demanding more men and at the same time encroaching on accommodation space. The interpretation of the radar picture led to fairly elaborate action information organisation (AIO) spaces again increasing complement and reducing mess deck space. Radar was so secret that its significance could not be explained to all and sundry (still sometimes a problem with very secret gadgetry). In consequence, there was some doubt and even resentment over the fitting of this gear–even Goodall had doubts (29 June 1942): '*Argonaut* full of gadgets. I only hope that all this RDF [radar] is of real value.'[73]

The congested AIO spaces needed air conditioning, adding to the demands for electric power. Turbo generators were uprated and, where possible, supplemented by diesel generators which made a valuable contribution after damage leading to loss of steam. Close-range AA guns were added in considerable numbers once they became available and their crews added to congestion.

69 This was, of course, an artificial condition. The standard condition excludes fuel and hence there can be no speed.

70 It is amazing that nonsensical claims for much higher speeds are still made.

71 Goodall 8 Sep 1942. '. . . *Welshman* to carry petrol on mine deck. Told him to phone ERO re work not conforming to petrol regulations.'

72 See Appendix 12. The RN College notes had had a section on the dangers of discontinuities and sharp corners since 1913. The notes of the 1930s were brief but quite specific on the problems associated with break of forecastle and sharp corners to openings. There was little excuse.

73 Two weeks earlier, ACNS(W) had visited *Argonaut* and came back 'a physical wreck' from climbing over high coamings. Goodall noted 'Then I get blamed for ships sinking'. His own visit caused him no great physical problems even though he was a much older man!

Royalist, a modified *Dido* with four twin 5.25in, a lower bridge and vertical funnels. (Wright & Logan)

The first relief came in about 1943 when it was appreciated that aircraft in cruisers were of little value. Catapults were heavy and their removal helped the weight situation whilst hangars provided office and mess space. This was still not enough and, later in the war, most cruisers had a turret removed.

Habitability

Though some thought had been given to ventilation and associated topics like insulation before the war, habitability was unacceptable in extreme conditions such as the Arctic and the tropics.[74] It was found that harbours were much colder than the open sea; in the former temperatures could fall to -20°F (-30°C) whilst at sea the temperature was unlikely to fall below +10°F (-12°C). The aim was to keep the temperature in living spaces at 60°F (15.5°C) using steam heaters in the supply down to +10°F and fit electric radiators for harbour use. This was accompanied by more effective insulation.[75] It took a long while to implement this standard and smaller ships suffered.

Arcticisation[76]

Ice caused problems of all sorts. Gun mountings, directors, rotating aerials would all jam with ice and heaters had to be fitted. Even the upper deck crews had to kept warm. Damage to waterline plating from floating ice

was a problem, particularly in lightly-built destroyers. Accumulation of ice could endanger stability and could usually be removed only by hand chipping.[77] For arctic service more heating and lagging was required.

Tropics

In the tropics it was too hot, conditions anticipated outside were 88°F (31°C) dry bulb, 80°F (27°C) wet bulb. In harbour, conditions would be much worse but the effects could then be alleviated by the use of awnings, side screens etc. A special squadron of *Hood, Repulse* and five 'D' class cruisers had made a world cruise in 1923-4 with study of living conditions as a major objective.[78] In 1938 a ventilation committee was set up with some of the country's leading experts, chaired by Admiral Andrew Cunningham but the war broke out before its recommendations could be implemented.

Pengelly, Fleet Constructor, Eastern Fleet, 1942-4 said that the design standards were adequate but many systems had been badly installed and badly maintained and failed to deliver the intended output. Fans installed back to front were not uncommon. Additional equipment installed during the war increased the heat load and increased the number of men while reducing the living space available.[79] Ships' staff were not trained to make the best use of what was fitted. Vent trunks

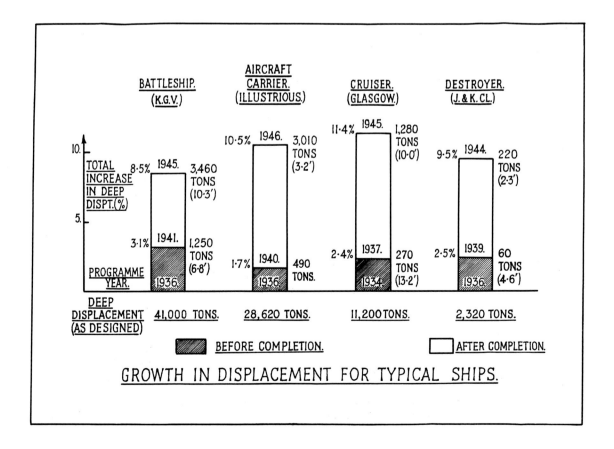

GROWTH IN DISPLACEMENT FOR TYPICAL SHIPS.

Y - HERE WAS Y TURRET
Removed for topweight compensation for fighter direction, R/T, HF/DF, pom-pom RPC and Target Indication.

X - HERE WAS X TURRET
Removed for topweight compensation for gun control Radar and additional WS sets.

D - HERE WAS THE DCT
Removed.
No longer required.

B - HERE WAS B TURRET
Removed to make room for AIC

A - HERE WAS A TURRET
Removed for topweight compensation for 4-inch RPC

stuffed with socks to keep warm in the Arctic did not function well in the tropics.

Time to change the air in a space (minutes)

Living spaces, bathrooms, heads	5
Wireless offices etc	2-3
Galleys	½
Bakeries	2
Main machinery, laundries	1

The peacetime Navy had, understandably, avoided the worst conditions. Visits to the Arctic were very rare and certainly not in winter. The Eastern fleet went north during the worst of the summer etc. Ships which did experience extreme heat opened everything up and certainly did not close down to action stations.

There are two questions to be asked over these changes – could the need have been foreseen before the war? And, if so, was implementation prevented by cost considerations or Treaty limits? Radar is easy, for it had not been invented and could not have been foreseen and much the same applies to AIO (and hence air conditioning). The need for close range AA guns had been foreseen in the multiple pompom but there were insufficient barrels and the muzzle velocity was too low. To a considerable extent, the need for more barrels was a consequence of the dramatic improvement in aircraft performance in the late 1930s.

The effect of splinters on exposed personnel should have been obvious from trials, and even within Treaty weight limits something could have been done. Peacetime exercises tended to avoid the extremes of temperature and also avoided bad weather where possi-ble. More realistic exercises could have shown the need for heaters, better ventilation and more lagging, though the 1938 committee clearly showed some awareness.

Bow propellers

The loss of cruisers due to flooding and the disabling of *Bismarck* by a torpedo hit aft drew attention to the vulnerability of machinery spaces, propellers, shafts and rudders. Goodall instructed the cruiser section to study:[80]

Smaller machinery spaces
Separated machinery spaces,[81] and
Bow propellers. (He suggested ¼ power on two bow propellers.)

Model tests were carried out both on bow propellers and bow rudders.[82] Bow propellers were tested for *Lion* and a cruiser and contemplated for the aircraft carrier *Malta*. The cruiser was 630ft long with a displacement of 12,300 tons. It had two bow propellers with 10,000shp each and two stern propellers with 30,000shp each. The full speed was estimated as 31¼kts compared with 32¾kts using four propellers at the stern with 20,000shp each. Goodall had written before the tests 'Do not be shocked over the loss of speed. I am quite prepared to say to the staff "You can have this arrangement if you are prepared to sacrifice 1½ or 2 knots of speed." '

The speed with bow propellers only was 10½kts if the stern propellers were locked or 17¼kts if the stern shafts were trailing. The propulsive coefficient was 0.54 compared with 0.66 on four conventional propellers.

A light-hearted view of weight growth and compensation is shown in this contemporary cartoon. (Re-drawn by John Roberts)

74 A J Sims, 'The Habitability of Naval Ships under Wartime Conditions', *Trans INA* (1945), p50 and discussion.

75 This was usually in the form of sprayed limpet asbestos which would kill so many (including several friends of mine) in the years to come. The asbestos was sealed by a layer of special cement to prevent condensation within the insulation.

76 The full treatment was called Arcticisation and was intended for ships which might operate in thin ice. A lesser treatment, Winterisation, was given to ships working in cold but less extreme weather.

77 It was believed that one RN whaler was lost due to ice formation.

78 W G Sanders, the Squadron Constructor, discussion on Sims, 'Habitability', p65.

79 Wartime electronics used the thermionic valve which gave off far more heat than modern equipment.

80 ADM 229 27 Minute of 29 March 1942.

81 See machinery layouts in Chapter 10.

82 Goodall, 12 Feb 1942. 'Looked at *Lion* with propellers forward. Horrid is the first impression.'

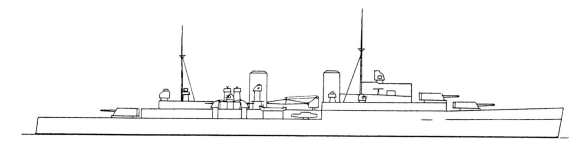

K34, a 1939 design based on *Fiji* with heavier armour and one less turret. After lengthy debate, guns won. (Drawn by Len Crockford for G Moore)

83 G Moore. 'From *Fiji* to *Devonshire* – a Difficult Journey', *Warship*, 123 & 124 WSS 1995-96

84 This was far from the only occasion on which Churchill, either as First Lord or as Prime Minister, asked for an outrageous design and then refused the resources to build it. Design work had started for a new triple 8in but no work had been done on a 9.2in gun or mount.

85 ADM 1/11344 says four ships in 1941 building up to a total of sixty such ships or, as a fall back, twenty 15,000 tons and forty intermediate with forty new design light cruisers as well!

86 One inch over sides with a 2in turtle deck.

87 Accommodation was to be to 'submarine standards'.

88 The choice of *Southampton* is surprising as the weakness of the hull was known at the time.

89 ADM 116/5150 Future Building Committee – Cruiser Policy.

90 ADM 116/5151 Comparison of 5.25in and Improved *Belfast* Cruiser of 26 Jan 1944. Also Goodall, 30 Nov 1942. 'Future Planning Committee. 6in or 5.25in cruiser. *Bermuda* too big but USS 15-6in fine. (ACNS(W))'.

91 The 1944 paper equates damage to weight of burster; more recently, one would take as square root of burster.

92 ADM 116/5150.

93 A new, longer 21in torpedo was to be carried.

94 Legend in ADM 167/118. It is of interest that the staff wanted a single funnel to reduce smoke interference with the directors but both DNC and E-in-C objected. Goodall, '5.25 inch cruiser, 8 gun won, will be rumpus over reduced speed'.

95 ADM 116/5150. Both papers showed that staff knowledge of history was shaky!

96 Legend in ADM 167/127 which also includes a four-turret ship.

Bow propellers have some advantages but efficiency is not one of them!

Cruiser designs 1939-45

The numerous cruiser designs can only be outlined here.[83] Only enough will be given to see the changing thoughts on the role of the cruiser and the conflict with available resources.

1939 heavy cruiser

Very soon after the outbreak of war the Controller asked for sketch designs of heavy cruisers with 8in guns. DNC produced six studies with an extra one later. Speed was to be greater than that reported for *Hipper* and was chosen as 33½kts standard. The most attractive had three triple 8in turrets and eight 8-barrel pompoms with 6ins belt and 3ins deck. It would have taken three years to build. Then the First Lord, Churchill, asked for a design with twelve 9.2in.[84] This 22,000-ton ship would have cost £5½ million and taken four years to build. It was then expected that *Vanguard* could complete in Spring 1944 and the 9.2in cruiser early in 1945 (8in cruiser by mid-1944). Staff opinion was virtually unanimous that two *Vanguards* were a better buy than three big cruisers, so that was the end of the 9.2in ship. The figures below for the effectiveness of the armour on one variant are of interest.

7in belt effective against 8in shell (normal impact) at 10,800yds
3½in deck effective against 8in to 29,000yds (2¾in deck to 25,000yds)

Against bombs:	3½in deck	2¾in deck
250lb	Any	8500ft
500lb	9500ft	6000ft
1000lb	5500ft	3500ft

1940 heavy cruiser

There was still interest in heavy cruisers and DNC was asked to produce studies for ships with nine 8in of 12,000 and 15,000 tons. The bigger ship had improved subdivision and would cost £4½ million against £3½ million for the smaller; either would take 4 years to complete. It was decided that five of the 15,000-ton 8in ships should be ordered in November 1940, completing between December 1943 and November 1944 at a total cost of £22½ million.[85] The *Lion* class battleships *Conqueror* and *Temeraire* would be cancelled in compensation.

There was a lengthy re-examination of cruiser policy in 1941 during which the views of Cs-in-C were obtained. Inevitably, these views differed but one may see a majority wanted more deck armour and more speed. Importance was attached to the greater range at which RDF (Radar) could spot the fall of 8in shells. Home Fleet wanted numbers but most saw a need for some bigger ships. There were the usual complaints that the ships were larger than necessary for their armament. Director of Plans attempted to sum up as a requirement for twenty heavy cruisers (with nine 8in guns), forty medium (six 8in or nine 6in) and forty light (6in or 5.25in).

The anti-aircraft cruiser

Eight sets of destroyer machinery were building at Metropolitan Vickers for the Soviet Union and in April 1940 it was thought that it might be possible to use these units in two cruisers. By June it was decided not to use Russian machinery but the project continued for another month with either 'L' class or fast minelayer engines.

The torpedo cruiser

At the end of February 1940 Churchill proposed a cruiser with a main armament of torpedoes. It had a low freeboard, a protected hull[86] with six bow tubes and eighteen torpedoes. There was a 4-barrel pompom and the speed was 35kts. The 120,000shp machinery took up 260ft of the 400ft length and more space was needed for the large engine room complement.[87] It came out at 4900 tons and died quickly and quietly.

1941 heavy cruiser

There was still considerable support for 8in ships, particularly as the 8in was the smallest gun whose splash would show on contemporary radar. It was hope to start four ships in the autumn at a cost of £3½ million each (compared to £2¾ million for a *Fiji*). The hull was to be based on *Southampton* and it was to carry nine 8in

and sixteen 4in (4.5in preferred).[88] By October the standard displacement was 16,930 tons and priority
dropped though one set of gun mountings was ordered
in November. In December the displacement reached
17,500 tons and the profile was to resemble *King
George V*. There was a study for a small version with
four 8in and eight 4in but even this came out at 11,140
tons and it was quickly dropped. The order for the guns
was cancelled in July 1942 which really marked the end
of the heavy cruiser though it was not until June 1943
that the Sea Lords finally decided that there should be
nothing between a small cruiser and a battleship.

The 1944 light cruiser

In September 1942 there was a prolonged discussion on
the characteristics of the future cruiser.[89] Existing
designs were outdated because of their unsatisfactory
main armament (low-angle), inadequate close-range
AA and far too short an endurance. (Note that departmental views changed from time to time and the following account has been simplified to keep a reasonable
length.) The roles were seen as anti-aircraft protection
of carriers and surface reconnaissance in bad weather

There was a careful study of the capability of 5.25in
and 6in guns in ships with (a) eight 5.25in HA/LA, (b)
nine 6in LA, and (c) twelve 6in LA.[90] The 6in ships
would have six twin 4.5in AA. The 6in gun was clearly
superior in armour penetration, perforating 3in side
armour at 12,500yds compared with 9500yds for the
5.25in. The bigger gun would go through a 2in deck at
ranges over 22,000yds whilst the 5.25in would not per-
forate at any range. While the superior ballistics of the
5.25in shell made the effective range the same, the bigger splash of the 6in shell made visual spotting easier,
with the use of radar, however, there was little difference. The new 5.25in gun could fire 12 rounds per
minute against 5 for the 6in. The burster weights were
3.25lb and 3.75lb respectively.[91] It was argued that with
comparable control the relative number of hits would
be as: (a) 1.9, (b) 1.0, (c) 1.3. It was concluded that the
5.25in was superior in low-angle fire, while the eight
5.25in would be as effective in AA fire as twelve 4.5in.
The 5.25in armament was superior to any available 6in
armament.

DTSD considered that 28kts would be sufficient and
would need only half the power of a 32kt ship which
would give improved subdivision as well as reducing
the size and cost of the ship. Endurance was agreed as
6000 miles at 18kns. Aircraft were not needed but,

rather reluctantly, torpedoes were included. It was
hoped that the ships would float after two torpedo hits.

In November 1942 there was further discussion and a
design with three of the new twin 5.25in was preferred.
However, it was decided that orders for cruisers in 1943
would delay destroyers and carriers which were needed
even more.[92] Further designs were prepared in March
1943, when it was decided to develop a ship with four
twin mounts, eight twin 'Buster' Bofors, twelve twin
Oerlikons and two quadruple torpedo tubes.[93] The
speed was dropped to 28kts, halving the power
required, and endurance was increased to 7700 miles at
18kts.[94] Protection was against 5.25-5.9in shells at
medium range and against 500lb bombs from 2500ft.
Underwater protection was to be provided by numerous thick transverse bulkheads carried intact as high as
possible. The after engine and boiler rooms would have
a centre line bulkhead. Five ships were included in the
1944 programme but the new First Sea Lord,
Cunningham, wanted 6in guns and the 5.25in-gun ship
died.

Most of the staff accepted the requirement for the
small cruiser but a substantial number of officers
believed that a larger cruiser was needed as well. In
March 1943 there was a paper supporting the large
cruiser by DTSD and D of P and another against such
ships by DAWT and CAOR.[95] In April, AC (WP) tried
to summarise the conflicting views. To incorporate adequate protection, it seemed that the small cruiser would
be limited to about 28kts, and there could be occasions
in which it could not keep up with a carrier. There was
also the possibility of attack by a large, enemy cruiser in
bad weather though it was argued that two smaller ships
could deal with a single big ship as in the River Plate. It
was not thought likely that the big ship would be much
more resistant to damage than the smaller cruiser.

Neptune

Work then started on a 6in cruiser known as 'improved
Belfast' but very different. The preferred option mounted four triple Mk XXIV 6in (10-12 rounds/minute, 60°
elevation, later changed to 80°) twelve 4.5in, twenty
40mm, twenty-eight 20mm and sixteen torpedo tubes.
Speed was 32½kts and endurance 6500 miles at 20kts.
Work stopped in March 1946. The *Neptune* design was
replaced by the *Minotaur* design in 1946.[96] This would
have had five twin 6in DP and eight twin 3in/70 on
15,070 tons. It was the last true cruiser designed for the
RN.

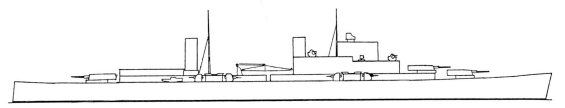

The 1941 8in cruiser. This
variant was 16,500 tons
(standard) with nine 8in and
sixteen 4in. Speed was 32¼kts.
(Drawn by Len Crockford for G
Moore)

Five | Destroyers

T HE 'V' CLASS destroyer leaders, designed by Hannaford in 1915-16, and the later 'V' and 'W' class destroyers set the style for destroyers of many navies in the 1920s and early 1930s.[1] They had geared turbine machinery, advanced for its day, four guns (4in, later ships having 4.7in[2]), four, later six, torpedo tubes and, with a high forecastle and bridge well aft, they were the best seaboats of their size anywhere.

Amazon and *Ambuscade*

With plenty of excellent 'V' and 'W' class destroyers in service there was no need to build new ones after the First World War. However, in 1924 two experimental destroyers were designed and built by Thornycroft and Yarrow, following a sketch by Hopkins, the head of DNC's destroyer section. They may be seen as Batch II 'V' and 'Ws' with similar armament but super-heated boilers with a slight increase in steam pressure which, with improved materials throughout the machinery, led to a considerable increase in power, raising trial speed to about 37kts. *Ambuscade* had two large boilers and one smaller one instead of the usual three of equal size.

They used the new D quality steel in highly-stressed members (see Appendix 15).

There were favourable comments when these ships joined the fleet but – a recurring complaint – they were thought to be too big (1173-1352 tons[3]) adding to their cost and making them too visible in night torpedo attacks. A new – and larger – director meant a much bigger bridge, increasing their silhouette. Though USN destroyers serving in British waters in the late war had demonstrated many features which improved the quality of life on the lower deck, no improvements were made in these experimental destroyers and in 1927 even the fitting of refrigerators was criticised as unnecessary.

Role of destroyers and the 'A' – 'I' classes[4]

In July 1926 the Controller called a meeting to consider the requirements for a class of destroyer to be built under the 1927 Estimates. It was agreed that emphasis should be placed on torpedo attack, a requirement which was to dominate destroyer design into the Second World War. In particular, it led to an emphasis on a small silhouette. This view seems strange in the

Ambuscade from Yarrows was much lighter at 1173 tons than Thornycroft's *Amazon* at 1352 tons to the same requirements but both could reach 37kts on trial. (Author's collection)

light of the lack of actual success of ship-launched torpedoes up to and including Jutland although it can be argued that *fear* of the torpedo had a major influence on tactics.[5] In this connection further questions about the value of torpedo attack could have been raised by an exercise in May 1937 when four destroyers launched a night attack on four ships simulating an enemy battle line. Each destroyer fired eight torpedoes at ranges between 600-1000yds scoring fifteen hits on the leading target, one on the second and none on the other two. This unequal distribution of hits showed that co-ordinated attacks were not possible until the introduction of reliable voice radio and, possibly, radar.

The 'A'–'G' class destroyers (built between 1929 and 1935) mounted two quadruple torpedo tubes,[6] the 'I' class introducing the quintuple mount in 1936. By the late 1930s most ships carried the 21in Mk IX torpedo which was reliable and as fast and powerful (warhead 727lbs TNT, later 810lbs torpex) as those of any other navy except Japan, whose advances were then unknown.[7] The 'A' class introduced the new 4.7in Mk

IX QF with 30° elevation (see below). Separate ammunition was used to improve magazine safety but the old 50lb shell was retained. The 1926 discussions led to a tentative requirement for an endurance of 2000 miles at 16kts and 24 hours at two-thirds power but this implied a very large ship and, eventually, they were designed for 1600nm at 16kts and 12 hours at full power despite all the wartime problems due to poor endurance.

In 1927 Asdic was still under development and the 'A' class were fitted 'for but not with'. They mounted two depth charge throwers and four chutes but carried only eight depth charges – despite the lessons of the war. Twin-speed destroyer minesweeping gear was fitted. Some improvements to habitability were introduced – a cold room, heating in living spaces, better washrooms and an oil-fired galley – costing 33 tons, £40,000 and ¼kt in speed. A 30kw diesel generator was fitted for harbour use which permitted electric lighting.[8] The required speed was 31¼kts at full load (about 35kts on trial). It should be noted that the Washington Treaty imposed no limits on size or numbers of destroyers but

The best features were combined in the 'A' class, ordered in 1928 and the 'B' class, 1929, such as *Boadicea*. (Wright & Logan)

1 D K Brown, *The Grand Fleet*, Ch 8.

2 4.7in Mk I, BL, 50lb shell. Short shield.

3 As usual, Yarrow had gone for light weight in *Amazon*. The Thornycroft ship was much bigger and more powerful.

4 J English, *Amazon to Ivanhoe* (Kendal 1993), Gives individual histories of these ships and details of alternative designs not built.

5 D K Brown, 'Torpedoes at Jutland', *Warship World* Vol 5/2. Torpedoes had also proved ineffective in the Russo-Japanese War.

6 There was even a proposal to fit a third quad tube in the 'B' class in place of the Y gun.

7 Tests with a magnetic pistol had been successful and the Duplex (contact or magnetic) pistol was available but only on 18in torpedoes. It proved unreliable and was withdrawn.

8 It is said that there were objections to this as better lighting would enable sailors to read on the mess deck and they might get hold of subversive literature!

Express was one of the 'A'-'I' class which was equipped to lay 60 mines, landing A and Y guns. Note the whaler is moved to the forecastle and the after mast is a tripod (see also Chapter 10). (Wright & Logan)

Flotillas consisted of eight destroyers and a bigger leader. Most leaders mounted five 4.7in as in *Inglefield*. (Wright & Logan)

the 1930 London Treaty limited size to 1500 tons (15 per cent could be of 1850 tons as leaders) and a total RN tonnage of 150,000 tons. The 1936 Treaty, which was not ratified, removed the limit on individual size and total tonnage. These ships were designed for a 16-year life with galvanised plating to delay corrosion and a stability margin to allow for 16 years' growth.[9]

Stanley Goodall was head of the destroyer design section and wanted a smaller ship with only two boilers and a single funnel. He also suggested a 'streamlined' bridge, possible in response to complaints from *Ambuscade* of excessive wind resistance at full speed but more likely to improve appearance.

The 'Tribal' class

By 1934 the Board recognised that the standard gun armament of the British destroyer was inadequate to fight the heavily-armed destroyers of Japan, with six 5in. A 'V' leader was planned, initially with ten 4.7in and owing something to the Fleet Scout of 1934 (see Chapter 4). In most aspects other than that of armament, the 'Tribals' were enlarged versions of the 'A'–'I' classes with similar machinery, enlarged to 44,000shp and giving the bigger ships an extra knot of speed,[10] and with a generally similar structure. During the development of the design, the main armament was reduced to

Somali of the big 'Tribal' class as completed. She was torpedoed off Iceland in 1942. (Author's collection)

eight 4.7in and the light AA armament increased to a 4-barrel pompom and two quadruple machine guns, the best weapons available at that date. The reduction of the torpedo armament to one quadruple mount inevitably attracted criticism. The twin 4.7in mount had hydraulic training and elevation but elevation was still limited to 40°. It was well designed and each barrel could fire nearly as fast as that in a single mount in fine weather and, with power ramming of the ammunition, much faster in rough seas. The weight of the twin mount was 28 tons which compares quite favourably with the 10-11 tons for a manually-worked single.

The 'Tribals' had a magnificent fighting record in the war and, since their heavy armament often led to their use in hazardous actions, their losses were heavy with three-quarters of the sixteen British ships (excluding Canadian and Australian) being sunk. The cost of a 'Tribal' was about £340,000 compared with £240,000 for the earlier ships, leading to the stark equation three 'Tribals' equals four 'Is'. Despite their record, it was far from clear that three 'Tribals' were more capable than four 'Is'.[11] The 1936 London Treaty removed the limits on the size of individual destroyers and on total tonnage which was just as well as additions during building brought their displacement up to about 1950 tons. As discussed later, the 'Tribals' were prone to be over-driven which, with relatively shallow draught, led to slamming and consequential leaking feed tanks; a serious problem but one which was easily cured.

The *Javelin* class (1936 Programme)

The introduction of the 'Tribals' led to the usual complaints that they were too big, coupled with demands for more torpedo tubes and for a heavier AA armament. There followed a lengthy and apparently sensible debate on how these aims might be satisfied. A dual-purpose, single mount with the new 4.7in Mk XI firing

a 62lb shell was favoured but would not be ready in time. The twin 4in was also considered but was rejected because of its poor capability at low angles and small shell. The *Javelin*s ended up with three twin 4.7in as used in the 'Tribals', a 4-barrel pompom and ten torpedo tubes.

The proposal to go to a two-boiler design caused prolonged debate. A paper was prepared summarising previous discussions going back as far as 1928.[12] DNC gave the following advantages of a two-boiler ship:

Reduces weight, space, cost and personnel for machinery.
Increased safety owing to reduced flooded length if ER and adjacent BR are bilged.
Extra space on upper and lower deck immediately under bridge where signal, asdic and accommodation spaces are all very congested.
'A vessel with two boilers would be smaller and cheaper than a similar vessel with 3 boilers and the same military qualities *or* a 2 boiler vessel of the same size as the 3 boiler vessel could be given superior military qualities.'

The E-in-C agreed with DNC's list of advantages but listed the disadvantages:

The use of two boilers would mean all boilers.
Peacetime boiler cleaning routine would be more difficult since each boiler would have to be shut down for 7 days cleaning after 21 days steaming and it would not be safe for a ship to be at sea with only one boiler available.
Lower economy at cruising speed
Reduction of power by ½ in the event of damage

In discussion a point well made by ACNS was that the final 20 per cent of speed demanded 50 per cent of total power. A two-boiler ship could make 24-25kts on one

Tartar post-war. X twin 4.7in has been replaced by a twin 4in HA, the light AA has been enhanced and she has a lattice mast–but still looks beautiful. (Author's collection)

9 The initial coating of paint weighed 17½ tons. The exterior would be repainted frequently and this was a major cause of weight growth. During the modernisation of the *Leander* class frigates up to 80 coats of paint weighing 45 tons were removed.

10 The fastest trial speeds were faster than those of the famous *Abdiel* class minelayers.

11 D J Lyon, 'The British 'Tribals'', in Antony Preston (ed), *Super Destroyers* (London 1978).

12 ADM 229 8.

boiler; a three-boiler ship would make 18kts on one and 26-27kts on two. Cs-in-C were consulted (1929) and generally felt that the advantages were considerable and that they could live with the problems. A big diesel generator would be needed to provide harbour power.

In 1936 E-in-C though the previous objections were valid but was willing to have a trial in one flotilla only. In fact, it was decided that both the 'J' and 'K' should have two boilers. There is a drawing in the file of 'JD3', a two-funnel, three-boiler *Javelin*. In 1938 the three-boiler ships *Imogen* and *Icarus* ran trials working as two-boiler ships, the two boilers being more highly forced to simulate a two-boiler ship. In the 1930s boiler cleaning was at 500 hours though during the First World War 750 hours was common. It was proposed to try 1000 hours in *Imogen* and *Icarus*. Lord Mountbatten was able to influence[13] the decision to adopt two boilers.[14]

Coles had adopted a conservative approach in the detail of this design, wise in the light of the comparative novelty of the approach. It is unfortunate that, for production reasons, it was unchanged through the wartime Emergency classes.

	Hogging	Sagging
Displacement (tons)	2244	2190
Maximum bending moment (ton.ft)	36,000	31,100
Stress in upper deck (ton/in²)	8.23	6.01
Stress in Keel (ton/in²)	6.28	6.34

These stresses are marginally lower than in earlier classes but the structure was better arranged to withstand them, particularly in compression which could lead to buckling failure.

As discussed later, shipbuilders were strongly opposed to longitudinal framing and this was reflected in higher tender prices, about £390,000 per ship. This

was probably the result of stronger price fixing as shown in the rising profits for Denny-built destroyers.[15]

Denny-built destroyers

Class	Price (£) (Two ships)	% to overheads and profit
'E'	495,433	7.9
'H'	508,616	14.2
'Tribal'	718,340	20.9
'J' and 'K'	802,598	31.5 (!)

Lightning class (1937 Programme)

The ships of the 1937 Programme were still seen as fleet destroyers required to have a heavy gun armament in weatherproof mounts and, after some debate, a heavy torpedo armament as well. Initial proposals were for much higher speed, up to 40kts standard but this was soon abandoned in the light of the very high cost. Technically, they were similar to the *Javelin*s but with more beam to offset the much heavier armament weight.

This class introduced the 4.7in Mk XI in the weatherproof Mk XX twin mount. It had an elevation of 50°, too small for a true AA mount and the gun was on the heavy side for rapid elevation and training. The shell weighed 62lbs and was brought up on a powered hoist on the centre line.[16] The weight of the mounting had gone up to 38 tons leading to some very big design studies.[17] The final design was still a big ship for its day at 2661 tons deep – a knot faster than the *Javelin*s, six of the new guns and eight torpedo tubes. The cost had risen from about £390,000 for a *Javelin* to £460,000 for a *Lightning*. Delays in production of the new gun mounting led to four of the 'Ls' completing with a high-angle armament of four twin 4in.[18]

13 Personal letter via A Payne.

14 Goodall, 10 March 1939. 'At sea in *Jersey*. Ship did well l "tho I ses it as shouldn't" [*sic*] she's a little beauty, spoilt by the galley funnel which I hope we can be put right. Absence of vibration impressed me and I thought ship looked small owing to one funnel. Heeled very little in turning'. And 1 June. '*Juno* with galley funnel inside main [funnel], a great improvement.'

15 H B Peebles, *Warship Building on the Clyde* (Edinburgh 1987).

16 The shell was of more modern design with a long nose, 5-10 calibre.

17 Design L70 was 3265 tons (deep), 40kts with a cost of £905,000. See E J March, *British Destroyers* (London 1966), p360.

18 There were problems in that the 4in at high elevation delivered a heavier blow on the deck than the 4.7in at lesser elevation.

19 It was suggested that national servicemen might have to be hand-picked for these ships as many would not be able to lift a 62lb shell in a seaway.

20 See discussion on prices in Chapter 11.

21 The 'O' and 'P' classes were the 1st and 2nd Emergency flotillas but were known as Intermediate classes. The 'Q' and later classes were often referred to as Emergency classes and were 3rd–14th Emergency flotillas.

22 After some renaming, these became the 'P' class.

Production of the twin Mk XX 4.7in mount was delayed and four of the 'L' class including *Legion*, completed with four twin 4in HA mounts (Author's collection)

Intermediate destroyers, 'O' and 'P' classes

In August 1938 the First Sea Lord expressed interest in a destroyer intermediate between the 'I' class and the larger classes of recent years. There was a prolonged discussion with general agreement that a fully HA armament was unsuitable for an unstabilised destroyer and that a true dual-purpose armament did not exist. Most of the early suggestions would have been very expensive but eventually a moderate design was accepted with four single 4.7in Mk XI (62lb shell) and 38,000shp.[19] As war approached, it was realised that there was not even a design for a single 62lb gun and the older, 50lb mount was accepted. The machinery was made identical to *Javelin*, saving time and cost. They cost about £410,000.[20] The 1st Emergency flotilla was ordered on 3 September 1939 and the second a month later.[21]

By the end of 1940 it was realised that the air threat to destroyers was much greater than had previously been thought and consideration was given to increasing their HA armament. Twin 4in mounts were not available and eventually, in February 1941 approval was given for eight ships to complete with five single 4in HA.[22] The figures on which this decision was based do not seem entirely convincing. During the first year of the war losses were as follows.

Air attacks on destroyers

Type of Attack	Number	Sunk	Serious damage	Slight damage
High level	50	2	2	7
Dive bomber	89	9	16	20

Onslaught in 1942. She is still quite close to design configuration except for early radars. (Author's collection)

Raider, third Emergency flotilla with four 4.7in on 40° mounts. Note the numerous Bofors carried by the end of the war. (World Ship Society)

23 See *Design and Construction*, p133-5 and March, *British Destroyers*, p390 for more detail.

24 It is doubtful if this change made any difference.

25 A very large drawing was kept on which every split in plating or framing in every ship was marked. This was to be invaluable in the 1950s in validating new structural design methods.

26 Goodall, 14 May 1943. 'White's welded destroyers are going to be late. *Contest* was launched by Mrs Lillicrap.' On 29 May 1944 Goodall noted – 'Sir John Thornycroft called, complained about welding.' Goodall responded 'If you decide to stick to riveting or to riveting combined with 50% welding, my view is that Thornycroft's day as a builder of light fast craft is over.'

27 This rammer had been developed by Vickers for a single 4.5in AA, intended for the RN but adopted by the Army and now finally returning to naval use.

28 *Savage* had the prototype twin BD 4.5in forward and, for consistency, had a single 4.5in aft.

29 If the author's memory of *Chivalrous* is accurate, we could fire 18 rounds from each barrel in the first minute.

30 Most ships in the Pacific had the Oerlikons replaced by single Bofors.

31 ADM 138 662 summarising discussion on TSD 575/41.

32 Goodall, 18 Aug 1941 (of one meeting, seven admirals present) '. . . almost as many opinions as Admirals'.

33 Goodall, 18 Nov 1941. 'Discussed body of high angle destroyer with Bessant. Can see no cure for wetness except more freeboard.'

34 Goodall, 16 April 1942. 'I wasn't happy over omitting stabilisers in 1942 destroyers.'

35 Viscount Cunningham, *A Sailor's Odyssey* (London 1951), p660; 'These Battles fulfil my worst expectations . . . we must get back to destroyers of reasonable size and well gunned'.

36 PREM 3 322.2.

37 ADM 116 5150 originally FB(42) Meeting of 5 Oct 1942.

38 I am not sure he was right. The three US destroyers lost in the Pacific typhoon of December 1945 had the poorest stability of the US ships present but their GZ curves were still better than many older RN ships.

The 4in was ineffective against dive bombers and it would have been better to fit good close-range weapons. In March 1941 it was decided to fit four of the 'O' class for minelaying and they received a main armament of four 4in. Only four 'Os' received the original four 4.7in.

'Q' and later Emergency class ships (3rd to 14th Emergency flotillas)

Soon after war broke out, it was realised that the threat of submarine attack would lead to higher fleet cruising speeds, typically 20kts instead of 15kts, which would leave most destroyers very short of fuel. It was quickly decided that putting the 'Intermediate' armament in a *Javelin* hull would allow an extra 125 tons of fuel to be carried, increasing endurance by 25 per cent. There was little new hull technology involved and there were no changes in machinery. Changes in armament and electronics were frequent. These changes are summarised below.[23]

Hull changes

All classes had a transom stern reducing resistance by 3 per cent at full speed (¼kt increase) and 1½ per cent at 20kts (70 miles more endurance). Without computers, it was not possible to consider trim following severe flooding but it is almost certain that the transom added greatly to their ability to withstand such damage. A deeper, V-type bilge keel was fitted and the bow shape was altered as in the 'Tribal' class in the 'S' and later classes.[24]

The structural design of *Javelin* was conservative and, though heavy, it was strong overall. Some early ships experienced cracking of the plating forward and this was stiffened in later classes and the RFW tanks were moved away from the ship's side.[25] J S White's Cowes yard was severely damaged by bombing and was rebuilt for all-welded, prefabricated construction. The first ship built in this way was *Contest*.[26] The wardroom was forward and accommodation for both officers and men was divided fore and aft. The cost of the 'C' class (excluding guns) averaged £627,000.

Machinery

Though there were no changes in main machinery (300lbs/in², 650°F) there were numerous changes in the auxiliaries. Three 50kW diesel generators were added in addition to the two 155kW steam generators, and two 20-ton electric pumps were added to the 40-ton steam pump and two 70-ton portable pumps were shipped. Cable runs were lowered and telemotor pipes to the steering gear were both lowered and duplicated.

Armament

The intended armament, installed in the first two flotillas, was four 4.7in 40° elevation mountings. Starting with the 5th flotilla, the mount was altered to give 55° elevation which involved fitting a spring-operated rammer.[27] The weight of the single mount had risen to 13.3 tons compared with the 7.9 tons of that in the 'V' and 'W' classes. From the 10th flotilla, the gun was the 4.5in in the same mount.[28] In the 12th-14th flotilla these mounts were given remote power control controlled by a Mk VI director, one set of torpedo tubes being sacrificed as weight compensation.[29]

Close-range AA armament varied somewhat from ship to ship depending on availability. The pompom was replaced by a twin Bofors from the 5th flotilla and four twin Oerlikons were fitted from the 4th flotilla[30]. Most had 10-pattern depth charge equipment. The increasing weight of antennae caused vibration and lattice masts, weighing 4½ tons, were introduced.

The DNC history claims that these changes were 'made in each case with due regard to the progress of construction.' There were 96 ships from the 3rd to 14th flotillas. When favourable reports came in from sea on the early ships, Bessant (head of destroyer section) commented ' . . . we all know that we can do much better and it is not sufficient to merely sustain our present pace for the concluding stages of the war.'

The 'Battle' class (1942 Programme)

By early 1941 it was clear that air attack, particularly dive bombing, was a much greater hazard to destroyers than had been anticipated and an 'all HA' armament was proposed. There was lengthy discussion with DNC and DNO favouring a 'Tribal' type with three twin 4.7in TA (50lb shell), one twin 4in (80° elevation) and a powerful light AA armament (others favoured the 4.7in (62lb shell)) whilst there was strong support for four twin 4in.[31] There was fairly general agreement that four big guns should fire forward and that there should be a 'four-cornered' light AA. Despite warnings from DNC, few seemed to realise the size of the likely ship.[32] It seems to have been DNC who proposed the between deck (BD) mount, initially with 4.7in (50lb shell) barrels. Goodall was insistent on the need for stabilisers in such a ship. DNC's design C had two twin Bofors forward of the bridge and two more aft and had a long forecastle as in *Black Swan*. It would have cost £890,000.[33] This led to draft staff requirements in July 1941 with two twin 4.7in BD forward. (See later section on armament.)

The close-range armament was to be four twin Bofors on triaxial Hazemeyer mountings based on the design used in the Dutch minelayer *Willem van de Zaan*. There were also four Oerlikons and a 4in gun for star shell. It was intended that the class should have Denny fin stabilisers but it was decided that the space was better used for 60 tons of oil fuel and only two ships, *Camperdown* and *Finisterre*, received stabilisers.[34] There was some argument about the torpedo fit, ACNS thinking that the ships were too big for torpedo attack and commenting that such attacks from destroyers had rarely been successful(!). However, they were given two quadruple sets and a heavy depth charge armament.

The machinery was based on the 'L' class but with steam pressure raised from 300 to 400lbs/in² and shp increased to 50,000. The layout was two boiler rooms, engine room, gearing room. The structure was similar to that of the Emergency classes. There was a transom stern giving 4-5 per cent reduction in resistance at top speed and 6 per cent at 20kts. A bulbous bow was considered but found to give no benefit. It seems strange that such a novel style of ship should have such conventional hull and machinery but the destroyer section was over-worked and could not spare the effort for novelty (Conversation with A J Vosper.)

The 'Battle' class was criticised by many senior officers, notably Cunningham,[35] as too big but they were the smallest ships which could carry the armament – and later classes were bigger! Churchill, now Prime Minister, was also concerned over their size but was answered on 2 September 1942 by the First Lord, Alexander, who pointed out that fleet destroyers need a gun whose shells were of the same weight as the enemy 5in, ie the 4.5in 55lb shell.[36] Experience showed the need for these guns to be fully capable of AA fire, meaning 80° elevation. Adding a powerful close-range armament and the power for a higher speed meant the 'Battles' were the smallest fleet destroyer for the future. In fact, they were smaller than contemporary USN, Japanese and German destroyers. They were well-liked in service but the rate of fire of the 4.5in at c12 rounds/minute was rather slow and the Hazemeyer Bofors mounting required much maintenance and was unreliable. It was replaced in the third flotilla by the STAAG which, though a better weapon, was also unreliable. The 4in gun was replaced by two single Bofors. The Mk VI director was late in production and some 4½ tons overweight.

At a meeting of the Future Building Committee in October 1942, Goodall compared USN destroyer practice with British.[37] The US DD445 (*Fletcher*) saved weight and space, particularly fuel space, by the use of high-pressure, double reduction machinery. A corresponding British ship would be about 700 tons more displacement. E-In-C was working in that direction but was unwilling to make the transition in the middle of the war. He thought the USN took risks with stability and fire which we would not accept.[38] The US ships had poor freeboard and no fin stabiliser and they carried fuel tanks to the upper deck. Strength and the position of the after gun 'were not such as DNC could recommend'.

Saintes, 1942 'Battle' class. The unreliability of the Hazemeyer twin Bofors mount and late delivery of STAAG and the Mk 5 twin meant that many completed without any twin Bofors. (Author's collection)

Dunkirk of the 1943 'Battle' class. Note the US Mk 37 director, single 4.5in abaft the funnel and the two STAAG mountings aft. (Author's collection)

The 1943 Programme and later 'Battles'

At first, it had been intended that twenty-six ships of the 1943 Programme should be repeats of the 1942 design but a number of changes were made. All ships were to have the US Mk 37 director and computer with British 275 radar. The 3rd and 4th flotillas would have had the 4in replaced by a single 4.5in whilst the remainder would have had four 4.5in twin upper deck (UD) mounts with a rate of fire of 20 rounds per minute. The close-range armament consisted of the STAAG Mk II which grew in weight so that the first sixteen ships had only two mounts and the later ships with increased beam would have had three. All but eight ships were cancelled at the end of the war though two of the later design with UD mounts were built in Australia. A Squid A/S mortar was fitted on the quarterdeck.

There was an interesting discussion on possible changes to the last five of the 1943 Programme and the 1944 ships at Controller's meeting of 18 August 1943.[39]

E-in-C said that economisers would add 25 tons and give 7 per cent better economy. If boiler trials in the 'Weapon' class were satisfactory he could re-design the machinery and, for no increase in weight, improve economy by 12 per cent. Unit machinery would increase length by 3ft 6in, weight by 20 tons and complement by 6 men. There was fairly general support for four guns forward and two twin UD mounts were seen as better than the five gun ships with BD mounts. It was thought that the later ships should have three twin UD mounts and unit machinery

The 'Weapon' class, 1943

The 'Battle' class were too big to be built on some of the slips used for earlier destroyers and it was decided to build a class of 'intermediate' destroyers to use this capacity. Displacement would have to be limited to about 1800-1900 tons standard. Armaments considered were

Scorpion of the 'Weapon' class. Note A J Vosper's funnel up the mast design to reduce upper deck length. She mounts an A/S mortar Mk 10 in X position. (Author's collection)

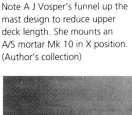

4 – 4.5in single, 55° elevation
3 – 4in twins, 80° elevation
3 – 4.5in single, 80° elevation

but it soon became clear that the only suitable guns for this size of ship were the twin 4in. The baseline armament became three twin 4in, two STAAG, two quad (later changed to quintuple) torpedo tubes and two twin Oerlikon with fifty depth charges (5 pattern). Various alternative schemes were considered with increased depth charges, A/S mortars or more light AA.

It was decided to install machinery on the unit system with alternating boiler and engine rooms.[40] The units were separated by a fuel tank 10ft long and a 2ft coffer dam to the after boiler room. The units were cross connected so that either turbine could work off either boiler. The two boilers were Foster-Wheeler working at 400 lbs/in² and 750°F driving Parsons single reduction turbines. It is said that the unit arrangement added 65 tons to the displacement but consumption at 20kts was 20 per cent less than in the 'Emergency' classes.[41]

Upper deck length was critical. The earliest drawings show a tripod mast and two conventional funnels. The mast was changed to a lattice and then the constructor, A J Vosper, had a novel idea and put the fore funnel inside a wide lattice mast.[42] Wind tunnel tests showed that this arrangement reduced the problem of smoke interference on the bridge.

The design was approved in June 1943 and nineteen ships were ordered at an estimated cost of £710,000. At the end of the war, all but four were cancelled. They completed after the war with two twin 4in guns and two Squid A/S mortars (*Scorpion*[43] had one Limbo). *Broadsword* also had the Flyplane 5 predictor for AA control, a triumph of thermionic valve technology, which was very effective for its day.

A modified 'Weapon' class, the 'G' class, was designed in 1944. It had the same hull with 14ins more beam and the same machinery. The main gun armament was two twin 4.5in UD and there would have been three twin Bofors. It was said to be very congested, and there was general relief when the class of eight ships was cancelled at the end of the war.

The 'Daring' class

At the same time as the 'Battles' were being criticised for being too big, the staff were thinking of an even bigger ship.[44] The first study came out at 4800 tons (deep), length 420ft. After various weight saving measures, DNC came up with 3360 tons (deep), 2594 tons (light). The design was approved on 9 February 1945 and sixteen ships were ordered but eight were cancelled and the other proceeded very slowly once the war ended.[45] They were to have three twin 4.5in UD mounts, three twin Bofors, two pentad tubes and, later, a single Squid.

The 'Darings' were the first destroyers designed for all-welded, prefabricated construction.[46] But due to lack of experience the standard of welding was generally poor, and the DNC radiography team found many cracks and serious slag inclusions.[47] There was extensive use of aluminium in minor structure such as minor bulkheads, superstructure decks and sides clear of gun blast etc. A strong box structure was built into the break of forecastle carrying the load down from the forecastle deck to the upper deck.[48] Welded fabrications were used as shaft brackets instead of forgings reducing manufacturing time by 50 per cent and cost by 40 per cent, though there was a small increase in weight. A fabricated stern frame for a larger ship achieved the same reductions in time and cost together with a weight reduction of 20 per cent.[49]

The machinery was on the unit system and was of far more up-to-date design than any previous destroyer.

39 ADM 229 30.

40 This decision was strongly influenced by the survival of USS *Kearny* after a torpedo hit in the forward fire room on 17 Oct 1941.

41 It is probable that there would have been an increase in complement.

42 Phone conversation author/Vosper 25 Oct 1999. He was talking to his chief, Bessant, at the time and the idea grew up in discussion, not uncommon in novel design.

43 White's ships were all welded, the rest mixed.

44 Goodall, 9 Aug 1943. 'Naval Staff are the limit, having decided that the Battles are too big, they draw up requirements for a ship which is bound to be much bigger. Controller thinks two twin 4.5, DFSL says three. I have to see what I can do on 2750 tons'. Later 16 Aug, Controller 'was not going to have a 2750 ton destroyer.'

45 The cost was estimated at £1,450,000 in 1947. The final price was c£2,280,000 due to delay and inflation.

46 Three ships had riveted longitudinals, beams and girders.

47 Goodall, 12 Oct 1943. 'In new Battles I am not prepared to go to US stresses yet. Must wait till welding is a uniform practice in our yards'. (In fact, the stresses were just slightly higher than those accepted for *Javelin*.) DNC's non destructive test group were leaders in the field for many years. Much later, when industry had caught up, it was my painful duty to disband this group.

48 This structure was very heavy and the forecastle could have been extended to X gun for the same weight.

49 Sir S V Goodall. 'Some Recent Technical Developments in Naval Construction', *Trans NECI* (1944) 13th Andrew Laing Lecture.

An unidentified *Daring* in October 1954. Even big ships take it green. (Author's collection)

Various designs of boiler and turbine were mixed to gain experience. The E-in-C preferred the Foster Wheeler design but four ships had Babcock and Wilcox; both worked at 650lbs/in² and 850°F.[50] Most had Pametrada turbines but two ships had Yarrow–English Electric and one John Brown BTH all developing 54,000 shp on two shafts with double reduction gearing.[51] They had an endurance of 4440 miles at 20kts from 590 tons of oil (7.5 miles per ton) compared with 4400 miles from 700 tons in the smaller 'Battles' (6.2 miles/ton).[52] The propulsive coefficient was some 10 per cent better than previous ships, attributed to the smoother welded hull. Twin rudders gave a turning circle of 525yds at full speed (as against the 665yds of the 'Battles').

Four ships of the class had an AC electrical system which it was hoped would be lighter and less demanding in space than the traditional DC system. These hopes were not entirely realised due to lack of experience in industry. Lead-covered cables were generally replaced by braided cables. Each compartment was planned on drawings at 1in = 1ft with every item of equipment shown instead of the old scheme of the man in the yard fitting the bits in wherever he could find space.

At last the RN had a modern destroyer with a longitudinally framed, welded hull, efficient and compact machinery, AC electrics and an effective dual-purpose armament. These 'innovations' were introduced a decade later than in the USN.

Armament

General considerations of medium-calibre guns are contained in Appendix 8. This section deals with topics specific to destroyers. The main gun armament for these ships was constrained by a requirement that the mount should be hand-worked. This was not perverse, power operation added considerably to weight and cost and, perhaps more important, the mounting could be put out of action by a power failure. Hand-worked guns could continue to fire whilst there was a man alive to put ammunition into the breech. However, hand working limited the maximum weight of any round of ammunition to about 50-60lbs.[53] Two experimental 5.1in guns[54] were made, one being used for shore trials, while the other went to sea in *Kempenfelt* where it was found that the 70lb shell was too heavy (fixed ammunition weighed 108lbs in total).

Even with a 50lb shell the maximum trunnion height for easy hand-loading at low angles was about 55ins and this limited the elevation of the CP Mk XIV mount in the 'A'-'D' classes to 30°. In the 'E'-'G' classes with the Mk XVII mount, elevation was increased to 40° by raising the trunnions 4½ins and dropping the mount into a pit of that depth with flaps which could be closed to give a 55in height for low-angle fire. This was not a very satisfactory arrangement and in the Mk XVIII mount, used in the 'H' and 'I' classes (and later in the 'Qs' and 'Rs') the balance weight was moved to the top of the gun and 40° could be achieved without pits. Higher elevation for at least one gun was recognised as desirable and a Mk XIII mount with 60° had been tried in *Mackay* and *Bulldog* but with a 68in trunnion height it was unsatisfactory at low angles. Recoil length posed a further problem. The shorter the recoil length the more severe was the blow on the structure and for this reason destroyer guns usually had a long recoil. For example, the recoil length of the 4.7in Mk XIX mount was 26.5ins compared with 18ins in the 'big ship' 4.5in Mk II.

British destroyers were often criticised for mounting the 4.7in gun rather than the 5in of many foreign navies. However, the 50lb shell of the British gun was not much lighter than most of the others. The inter-war concept of AAW is explained in Appendix 16. In brief, it was thought that a rapidly manoeuvring destroyer was an impossible target for a bomber. Little defence against air attack was needed but destroyer guns could contribute to the long-range air defence of the capital

50 At one stage, E-in-C offered a 50-ton reduction in fuel at the cost of 25 tons increase in machinery weight.

51 Vice-Admiral Sir Louis le Bailly, *From Fisher to the Falklands* (London 1991), pp74-5.

52 16 tons/hour at full speed, 1½ tons/hr at 10kts.

53 A belated recognition–small cruisers had mounted the 6in with 100lb shell. This gun had been tried in destroyers but had been a failure and was removed.

54 One wonders why the 5.2in used in the submarine *X 1* was not fitted. As a gun it was quite successful.

55 Capt (E) G C de Jersey, 'The Development of Destroyer Main Armament 1941-1945', *Journal of Naval Engineering* (Oct 1953).

56 A study of the 4.5in Mk II BD mount with 4.7in 62lb shells was known as the '4.6in bastard'. The long recoil for which the gun was designed was incompatible with the short space available for recoil within the mount.

57 The weight of these frames is included in the hull group. Simplistic 'payload' comparisons forget that much of the weight of other groups is only there to support the armament.

58 There seems to have been some thought of a 4-barrel pompom but this was not available.

Lookout just post-war with three twin Mk XX 4.7in. The gun was the Mk XI firing a 62lb shell–one of far too many different medium-calibre guns. (Author's collection)

Savage carried the prototype twin 4.5in MkIV turret forward with 80° elevation. The single guns aft were 4.5in in converted 4.7in mounts with 55° elevation. (Author's collection)

ships. For this role 30-40° elevation was quite sufficient.

The design history of the 'Battle' class mounting is interesting.[55] It was fairly quickly agreed that there should be two twin BD mountings, both forward, with elevation of 80-85°. There was a lengthy debate on which size of gun should be fitted, initial support for the 4.7in, 62lb shell,[56] waned over ammunition supply world-wide and the 4.7in, 50lb shell, was chosen before the final choice was made of the 4.5in with 80° elevation and 55lb shell with separate ammunition.

The 4.5in shell was heavier than most 4.7in projectiles and had better ballistic properties and these advantages were seen as outweighing the logistical problem of stocking the new shells. The 4.5in had been designed as an AA gun for big ships with 85lb fixed ammunition, then thought the largest which could be man-handled. Experience in the *Dido* class cruisers *Scylla* and *Charybdis* showed that this was too heavy in bad weather, even in a 5000-ton ship, and the 'Battles' had separate ammunition.

It was decided to try a pilot mounting forward in *Savage* (due to complete in April 1943) with two single 4.5in guns aft. A wooden mock-up was built at Barrow in October 1941 and after several inspections, approval was given in February 1942. Luckily, there was a spare mount for the aircraft carrier *Illustrious* under construction at Barrow and this was modified for *Savage*. There were numerous development problems but none serious and the prototype in *Savage* worked quite well. The twin mount was put into production for the 'Battles' and the single 4.5in for the 'Z' and 'C' classes.

The 'Battle' class mount was always seen as an interim fit as its rate of fire was too low, as was its speed of training and elevation. In late 1942 some tentative requirements were prepared and an elaborate mock-up was built at Newcastle with fixed ammunition and power loading. The rate of fire (12 rpm) was too low and new requirements asked for 18 rounds per minute. This led to separate ammunition and hand transfer from hoist to loading tray. A requirement for the type of shell

to be changed quickly led to two hoists per gun, and it was also that the Mk VI destroyer mount should use as many components as possible in common with the Mk VII for the *Malta* class aircraft carriers.

The loading bay was large and circular which caused DNC to complain about the weight of the numerous large cantilever frames need to support the mount itself.[57] The gun itself was modified considerably. The effect of RPC (Remote Power Control) was re-assessed and it was found that the rapid cross-level corrections needed in a rolling ship at high elevation was very considerable. The power per mount went up to 117hp compared with 80hp in the 'Battles'. This was a major factor in the introduction of AC electrics in four of the *Darings* as the AC motor was lighter and thought to be more reliable. Initial firings took place at Ridsdale in March 1945 and were reasonably satisfactory. A prototype mount went to sea in B position of *Saintes*. The Mk VI 4.5in proved very successful and was used in numerous post-war classes.

The early classes mounted two single pompoms for close-range AA defence,[58] while the 'Ds' had a single 12pdr, soon replaced by pompoms. Later ships had two quadruple 0.5in machine guns, which were thought to be a most effective weapon against aircraft.

Saintes in 1947 with the prototype 4.5in Mk VI mount in B position. It had a much faster rate of fire than the Mk IV and would have been fitted in later 'Battles' (as in the RAN ships). (Author's collection)

Hull design

The 'V' and 'W' classes were superior to earlier ships in stability, seakeeping, strength and other aspects of naval architecture. The 'A'–'I' classes were their equal or better and were seen as very satisfactory up to the outbreak of war. However, with hindsight, it is possible to see a number of aspects in which their technology fell behind the times.

Stability[59]

In peacetime there were no indications of stability problems with undamaged ships. From the outbreak of the war many additional items–AA guns, crows' nests, splinter protection and, later, radar–were added, with considerable weight growth, mainly high up–and many years of generous painting. By 1941 such increases amounted to about 150 tons in a typical pre-war destroyer. Some reduction in top weight was made by reducing the height of the funnels and masts and by removing half the torpedo tubes–the original *raison d'etre* but more often referred to as the 'main ornament'! Some permanent ballast was fitted in the oldest ships and most pre war destroyers were instructed to flood empty fuel tanks if oil carried dropped below 40 tons. No British destroyer capsized due to bad weather and accounts suggest that few, if any, were in danger (see table below).

Stability after damage is considered later but it is worth noting that the design intention was that they should float upright with the engine room and adjoining boiler room flooded. This was not a very demanding standard but, since capsize after damage was not very common, it may be argued that it was good enough. Of thirty-seven destroyers hit and sunk by one torpedo, only six capsized, while twenty-two broke in half, seven plunged by the bow or stern and one sank bodily.

Speed and hull form

The hull form was optimised for high speed, without any compromise, and the forms used were very good indeed for this purpose. At the very highest speed, *Ambuscade* is still one of the best forms ever tested at the Haslar ship tanks (AEW). Modern designers would incorporate a transom, with flap or wedge, but would not change anything else *if top speed were the only consideration*. However, the prismatic coefficient, which defines the longitudinal distribution of buoyancy, has little effect on top speed but a major effect on resistance and hence fuel consumption on speeds around 18kts (for these destroyers). Thus a very high price was paid on endurance (of the order of 15 per cent) for an increase in top speed which would not be measurable on trial.

Typical form characteristics (*Greyhound*)

Circ M–Length/(displaced volume)$^{1/3}$	8.04
C_P–Immersed volume/length x mid section area	0.67
LCB–Longitudinal Centre of Buoyancy from bow.	0.52L
B/T–Beam/Draught ratio	3.32
i_e–Half angle of entrance	12.2°
C_X–Mid section area cft	0.854

The propellers were constant in pitch from root to tip with sections at constant radius having a straight face (pressure side–facing aft) with the back (forward side!) forming an arc of a circle. Such propellers are cheap, very efficient at the speeds then in use and were only abandoned when cavitation noise became important. At higher speeds all propellers cavitate, that is the water 'boils' in the low pressure areas. The bubbles so formed collapse with great violence (say 100 tons/in^2) and excavate pits in the solid bronze of the propeller. Pits $^1/_8$in deep were seen as normal after a six-hour full power trial. During the 1930s aerofoil theory began to be applied to ships' propellers but the theory was then inadequate and experimental propellers suffered worse damage than the standard ones.[60] All propellers had three blades which, together with a rather small tip clearance from the hull, meant that vibration was a fact of life to such an extent that training of Y gun was difficult.[61]

Propeller particulars–'A' class

Diameter	9ft 6in
Pitch	13ft 0in
Developed area	53sq ft
Full speed rpm	350

Seakeeping

The general aspects of seakeeping are discussed in Appendix 19 and only specific applications to destroyers will be discussed here. Overall, destroyers with the length of the 'V'-'I' classes would lose the equivalent of 15 per cent of their operational time at sea in the North Atlantic, averaged over the year, due to motions. Only part of this loss was due to sickness; a recent trial on a destroyer with a modern power-operated gun mounting showed a 40 per cent hit probability in a calm, reduced to under 10 per cent if the mounting had a vertical velocity of 10ft/sec.

Motions at the bridge are reduced considerably as its distance from the bow is increased. The destroyers dis-

Weight increases and stability decreases

Class	1936		1940-1	
	Light dspt (tons)	*GM (ft)*	*Light dspt (tons)*	*GM (ft)*
Faulknor	1442	2.5	1558	2.17
Duncan	1403	2.48	1553	2.2
'F' class	1356	2.48	1522	2.18

cussed had the bridge in much the same position except for the 'Tribals' where it was relatively further aft, which led the captains of the 'Tribals' to drive them harder with bottom damage, often leading to leaking feed tanks. A rough guide to freeboard at the bow was that it should equal 1.1 √Lft, a criterion satisfied by most classes, but the 'Tribals' fell short and were wet. The low upper deck abaft the forecastle in all classes was frequently swept by heavy seas and many men were lost or injured. Only at the end of the war were walkways installed above the torpedo tubes.[62] RN destroyers were generally better as regards freeboard and wetness than those of other navies except the USN.

Wetness is related to both freeboard and pitching and there is often confusion between the contributions of the latter. For example, it is often said that the wetness of the German 'Narvik' class (*Z23*) destroyers was due to increased pitching when the heavy twin 5.9in turret was fitted. Dr Lloyd[63] has shown that this weight on a large ship had a negligible effect on pitching, increasing the average (significant) pitch in Sea State 5 from 2.60° to 2.62°. However, the freeboard was reduced from 19.685ft to 18.963ft and this would increase the chance of a single wave coming on board from 0.76 to 1.2 per cent. Sailors would notice this difference in wetness and blame it, incorrectly, on heavier pitching.

One of the 'Narviks', *Z38*, was briefly commissioned after the war as HMS *Nonsuch* and her RN captain's views are of interest.[64] Summarised, they were that in a gale wind Force 8 there was no sign of 'bumping' in head seas at 21kts.[65] It would take a great deal to make it necessary to ease down in a head sea owing mainly to the very fine bow sections but the design did not have the space for modern Asdics. The spray deflectors were very effective in reducing spray coming inboard as were the deck edge anchor stowages.[66] His final comment was that *Nonsuch* was overcrowded with an RN complement of 174 but her wartime complement (as *Z38*) was 364!

The table compares the actual freeboard of some RN and foreign ships with the value suggested by the rule of thumb = 1.1√L, ft.

Freeboard ratios and bridge abaft bow (fraction of length)

Ship	Length (ft)	Freeboard (ft)	1.1√L (ft)	Bridge
'V'&'W'	300	18.8	17.3	0.29
'I' class	320	16.8	17.9	0.29
'Tribal'	364.7	18.2	19.1	0.34
Javelin	348	19.7	18.6	0.29
Fubuki	378	20.8	19.4	0.23
Z23 (5.9in guns)	400	21.5	22	0.24
Fletcher	376	19.5	19.4	0.28
Le Triomphant	420	22.9	20.5	0.25

Slamming can damage ships and their equipment, particularly asdic (sonar) domes. For ships of generally similar form, as were those under discussion in this chapter, the probability of slamming in a given sea state depends mainly on speed and draught. Limited, recent data suggests that slamming would occur at about 16kts for the 'A' – 'Tribals' in Sea State 6 (16.3ft waves) which is consistent with contemporary accounts. The 'Js' and 'Ls' were deeper draught and on the same basis could reach 19 and 20kts respectively in the same sea state. This was better than most foreign destroyers, the Japanese ships being of particularly shallow draught, a contributory factor in the number of their bows which fell off. Once again, the USN were better than British ships in this respect.

Rolling affects manual tasks such as loading guns and depth charge throwers through the sideways force on men and their loads due to transverse accelerations. Up to the late 1930s, bilge keels were the only effective way of reducing roll, but by today's standards the 18in-deep keels of British destroyers were inadequate. This was about the largest keel for which a single plate was strong enough. The only foreign destroyer which was significantly different for which data can be found was the Dutch *Isaac Sweers* with double plate keels, 36ins deep. There is plenty of evidence that rolling caused a considerable loss of operational capability which could easily and cheaply have been reduced. There seems almost to have been a degree of masochism – sailors are tough – whilst the failure to exercise in peacetime in rough seas led to the false assumption that well-trained and well-motivated men would be unaffected by rolling.

All these destroyers had single rudders with an area about ¼₅th of the underwater profile area which gave them a turning circle of some 500yds at full speed and 200yds at low speed with full (35°) rudder angle. The turning circle at higher speed could be reduced to about 400yds by using a *smaller* rudder angle (30°).[67] The flow over the rudder at high speed and large angles was unstable and performance was unpredictable particularly as regards angle of heel. Turning circle was very important in depth charge attacks and could have been reduced considerably by fitting twin rudders but there was no requirement. Destroyers' presumed immunity from air attack depended on their manoeuvrability but again no one thought to improve this aspect.

Strength

The 'V' class was built of HT (High Tensile) steel, riveted and with transverse frames. Such a structure was easy and cheap to build and fairly light in weight. There were no serious structural failures in British destroyers during or between the two wars going some way to justify their conservative structural design though leaking seams were far too frequent. The 1924 experimental destroyers introduced the even stronger D quality steel (Appendix 15) in primary structure which was difficult

59 D K Brown, 'Stability of RN Destroyers during World War II', *Warship Technology 10* (London 1989).

60 *Garland* had propellers by Manganese Bronze; erosion up to 1⅜in in six hours. *Griffin* by Stones ⅞in in six hours.

61 HRH The Duke of Edinburgh. Discussion at NEC 100, page D1-4.

62 Based on my experience in *Chivalrous*, these were safe but you still got wet.

63 D K Brown and A R J M Lloyd, 'Seakeeping and added weight', *Warship 1993*.

64 Letter of 27 October 1948 now in the National Maritime Museum.

65 Over a long time wind of this speed – about 35mph – would produce waves some 5m high. In a short time, in confined waters, the height would be less.

66 As a result of this report, a spray deflector was fitted in the Type 15 frigate, *Rocket*, where it was ineffective.

67 A P Cole, 'Destroyer turning circles', *Trans INA* (1938). Analysis of 126 turning circles of the 'I' class. Note contributions by Earl Mountbatten and S V Goodall.

to weld in shipyard conditions. D quality steel offered a small saving in weight – for example 13 tons in the 'Hunt' class – but at considerably higher cost. It is likely that an all-welded mild steel structure would have been lighter as well as cheaper and stronger.

There was some justification for British conservatism in the introduction of welding, since both Germany and Japan had early and serious failures in welding unsuitable materials. Thus the bows of *Hatsuyki* and *Yugiri* fell off in a storm and several German ships, including *Bismarck*, lost their sterns after damage. The USN adopted welding for all their post-war destroyers with as far as is known no problems, reflecting the advanced state of their engineering industries. It would seem that they developed high strength steels which could be welded.

Longitudinal framing considerably increases the resistance to buckling,[68] of particular importance against under-bottom explosions, such as ground mines, and was also slightly lighter in weight than transverse framing. Longitudinal framing had been tried in the *Ardent* of 1910 at the suggestion of Denny[69] who do not seem to have had any serious difficulty in building it at much the same price as its transversely framed half-sisters. The First World War broke out soon after her completion and she was obsolete by the time the war was over. For some unknown reason the idea was not pursued.

Longitudinal framing was re-introduced by A P Cole, head of the destroyer section, in the *Javelin* class of 1936 programme against intense opposition from the shipbuilders who saw it as making erection far more difficult.[70] The Clyde builders even sent a delegation to the Controller seeking Coles' dismissal, but both he and DNC supported Coles and all future destroyers had longitudinal framing. Coles' structure for the *Javelin*s was a cautious design[71] with only a slight advantage over the older style.[72] They had eleven longitudinals each side of the keel and five on each side of the deck. The longitudinals were riveted channel bars. Tender prices for these ships were high probably reflecting excess profits rather than production difficulties. Building time from laying down to launch was a little longer in the early ships but, once the technique was mastered, the repeat 'N' class was quicker in build-

ing. The 'K' class had some problems forward where the plating panels were too big to resist slamming loads.[73] Leaking was mainly associated with single-riveted seams in the forecastle deck where they caused misery to the occupants of the mess deck below; also in the reserve feed water tanks where leaks were seen as more serious. Double riveting or welding cured such problems.

In structural design, naval architects used a nominal stress calculated for the ship[74] on a wave of its own length and a height of ¹⁄₂₀th the length with stresses calculated both for a wave crest amidships (hogging) and at both ends (sagging). Under these artificial but comparative conditions the maximum stress was usually just over 8 tons/in² in the upper deck under tension. This would now be regarded as rather high but was lower than adopted in other navies, the French accepting over 10 tons/in² in some classes which, together with the stress concentration at the break of forecastle, was the main reason for *Branlebas* breaking in half in a moderate gale off Dartmouth in December 1940. The Dutch *Isaac Sweers* had a tensile stress in the upper deck of 11 tons/in² and 8.2 tons/in² compressive in the keel.

Stresses are always increased considerably when there is a sudden change in the depth of section and the traditional break of forecastle close to amidships was a bad feature of British and most foreign destroyers – breaking in half was by far the most common cause of loss in action. In post-war trials, the ex-German Z38 (HMS *Nonsuch*) was exposed to an underwater explosion which her advanced welded, longitudinally framed hull with a double bottom was expected to withstand but she broke in half at the poorly designed structure at the break of forecastle. USN destroyers were longitudinally framed and the later ones were flush decked – no break of forecastle.

Battleworthiness – resistance to action damage

At the start of the war there were 136 destroyers in commission and in the first year of war 124 were sunk or damaged. In each of the following two years there was the same picture of the number hit only slightly less than the number in commission during that year. Even in the last three years of the war there was still about a one in three chance of sustaining damage in a 12-month period.

Bombs and torpedoes were the principal causes of damage or sinking. Pre-war studies had suggested that the chance of a hit on a fast, manoeuvring destroyer by a high level bomber was remote and this estimate proved correct, but the threat posed by the dive bomber had not been appreciated.

Destroyer strength – 'H' class

	Hogging	Sagging
Displacement (tons)	1828	1424 Deep =1864
Stress, Keel (tons/in²)	6.23C	6.1T
Stress, Deck (tons/in²)	8.33T	5.47C
Bending Moment BM (tons.ft) =WL/K where K =	21.9	21.9
Shearing Force SF (tons) = W/K₁ where K₁ = 5.0		5.34

Cause of damage or sinking for destroyers

Weapon	Sunk	Serious Damage	Slight Damage
Shell	13	40	74
Bomb	44	81	118
Mine	18	35	4
Torpedo	52	15	2
TOTAL	127	171	198

There were two specific problems; the stress concentration at the break of forecastle led to many ships breaking their back, and the length of the machinery spaces – more than half the ship – meant that the chance of being disabled was high.

Back breaking

Weapon	Sunk	Broken	% broken
Bomb	44	15	32
Mine	18	11	61
Torpedo	52	25	48
TOTAL	114	50	44

The USN lost a higher proportion to back breaking, 70 per cent of those suffering underwater damage, but this may be chance – or the enormous warheads of Japanese torpedoes. Ships such as sloops and frigates in which normal stresses were lower, more depth of structure and with no break of forecastle close to amidships were less prone to break their back (see Chapter 7).

From the 'Vs' to the 'D' class, British destroyers had three boilers in two rooms with the short room next to the engine room (except *Duncan*). From the 'E' class onward there were three separate boiler rooms which reduced the chance of the ship sinking but did little to reduce the chance of the ship losing all power from a single hit. In 1937, the USN adopted the 'unit' system of machinery arrangement with engine and boiler rooms alternating – BR, ER, BR, ER – so that there was a good chance that an engine room and a boiler would survive one hit. In 1930 there was a proposal for the leader, *Exmouth*, to have three boiler rooms and two engine rooms which was rejected as the ship would have been 10ft longer, cost an extra £15,000 and would have needed six more men.[75] The question of two boiler designs has been discussed earlier. At least five destroyers were sunk by our own forces or sank in tow due to loss of power and these, and possibly others, could possibly have been saved if they had unitised machinery.

It should be noted that a single cause of sinking is often meaningless since a badly damaged ship may be burning furiously and on the point of capsizing when it breaks in half. Fire, however, was not a serious problem; of 496 destroyers hit, there were 24 major fires and 36 minor fires. Of the major fires, sixteen involved oil fuel. The older destroyers were half the size of a modern frigate and lightly built so it should not be a surprise that they sank easily and quickly. Of forty-four sinkings where details are known, twenty-eight sank in under 10 minutes.

Small ships would sink quickly; the table below shows the time to sink for the forty-two ships where figures are known.

Under 10 minutes	28
10–20	12
20–30	1
30–60	1

Machinery

The 1924 experimental ships introduced superheated steam, a considerable advance, which led to improved economy and some reduction in space and weight. They also had a number of less obvious improvements, mainly in materials for turbine blades and gear boxes whilst the air supply was pre-heated. The 'A' class was generally similar with steam at 300lbs/in² and 625°F with the exception of *Acheron* which had an experimental plant working at 500lbs/in² and 700°F. Her fuel consumption was 0.608lbs/shp/hr compared with 0.81 lbs/shp/hr for her sisters but there were vibration problems with the impulse stage blades of her turbines[76] which were not cured before she left with her sisters for the Mediterranean. Her boilers and condensers gave no problems but this development was not pursued.

There were many developments in shore-based steam plants and five experimental boilers were purchased and tried for the RN. All were said to have had problems and none were pursued. In 1928 Yarrows claimed that a two-boiler arrangement would save 20 tons in weight, reduce the length of the machinery by 10ft and enable an extra 100 tons of fuel to be carried. There were many objections; with three boilers 26-27kts could be made with two alight and one down for maintenance.

The question of maintenance needs examination in conjunction with the frequent claim that RN machinery was more reliable than that of other navies. It is true that RN ships suffered no major breakdowns but there were innumerable minor problems, mainly steam leaks, which were used to justify the third boiler. British boilers needed frequent cleaning since additives in the feed water were not permitted[77] and cleaning occupied 25 per cent of operational time. RN boilers had to be cleaned every 750 hours instead of 2000 hours in the USN. It was argued that this did not matter as it fitted in well with peacetime leave arrangements but this is a circular argument and led to a serious lack of availability in wartime. The difference was almost entirely due to the use by the USN of a chemical additive in the feed

68 In the post-war explosion trials, shear buckling in the side was quite common in the transversely framed ships but did not lead to overall failure (Chapter 10 – see also *Albuera*).

69 D K Brown, *The Grand Fleet*, pp70-1.

70 Even Goodall wrote 11 Mar 1938 '. . . little uneasy of J framing, it looks such a big change of practice.'

71 It is unfortunate that all the wartime 'Emergency' classes used this structural design. The full advantage was only seen with the all-welded *Darings*.

72 There is some evidence that the longitudinally-framed ships were less likely to break in half following a torpedo hit but there were too few examples to be sure (see Chapter 10).

73 Goodall 1 Mar 1940 and 5 Apr 1940, also personal letter Viscount Caldecote on *Kingston*.

74 Based on a theory by Rankine, applied by Edward Reed and William White c1870. See D K Brown, *Warrior to Dreadnought*, Appendix 6.

75 Allowing for the changing value of money, these figures are very similar to the cost of an extra bulkhead in the post-war 'Tribals' and the 'Castle' class OPV but in both these the extra bulkhead was fitted.

76 Apparently not uncommon in Parsons designs of that time.

77 Le Bailly, *Fisher to the Falklands*.

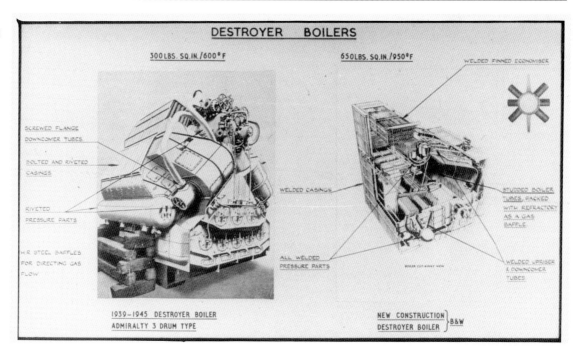

water which kept boilers clean. Though similar additives were used in UK power stations, their use was forbidden by the E-in-C department except in US-built ships. After an unofficial trial in *Victorious*, these additives were used in the Pacific Fleet against orders.[78] Le Bailley has drawn attention to the inter-war Board's lack of understanding of engineering and their denigration of engineer officers. The marine engineering industry was badly hit by the slump and was very old fashioned–it has been said that Parsons relied on good workmanship to make up for poor design.

The old-fashioned machinery fitted to British destroyers led to poor endurance, particularly when installed in hulls optimised for top speed and with outdated anti-fouling paint. British machinery was also rather heavy and took up considerably more space than that of most other navies. German designs went to extremes of both temperature and pressure and problems, mainly leaks, were never solved particularly since the layout was so cramped that maintenance was almost impossible. French machinery, too, was very cramped. For example, the *Mogador* had 0.67shp for each square foot of engine room floor whilst the figure for *Javelin* was 0.45shp. See Appendix 17 for US destroyer machinery.

Le Bailley mentions several other failings which may sound almost trivial but had serious consequences.[79] The nozzles which sprayed oil into the furnace were optimised to use Gulf oil and, when during the war Caribbean oil was used it was very difficult to avoid making smoke. The sealing material used for joints of steam pipes was poor; even the tired ex-USN 'Flushdeckers' had fewer leaks.

USN destroyer costs

It was, and remains, very difficult to compare costs between different countries as aspects such as local rates, tax credits etc, all have to be equated. The definition of cost may differ, but making all possible allowances, US warship building costs were very high.[80] The figures below are prices from Jane's 1939 edition.

Class	Cost ($M)
Farragut	3.4–3.75
Mahan	3.4–3.75
Porter	4.0
Somers	5.0
Gridley	3.4–3.75
Sims	5.5

Compared with British costs, these are very high indeed. However, the *Farragut*s were not all that advanced in technology[81] and there is no sudden increase as the more advanced machinery was introduced. Man days are available for a few ships–*Mahan* 150,000, *Benson* 165,000 and *Fletcher* 185,000. A British 'M' class is given as 4991 man months, a 'Hunt' as 2944.

Habitability[82]

The main problem in traditional destroyers lay in the lack of covered access to living spaces aft, mainly for officers. In later ships both officers and men were divided fore and aft and, in the later 'Emergency' classes, gangways above the torpedo tubes made access reasonably safe, even if still wet. At the other end of the ship, the forward messes were in a high-motion zone and leaking, single-riveted seams made life miserable. Men who were tired, wet and cold could not operate effectively. One can only be impressed with the number of thoughtful improvements in USN ships to laundry machines, ice cream plants, adequate illumination and ventilation, detailed in a series of papers to SNAME and ASNE, improvements not copied elsewhere (see Chapter 7, 'Colony'–'River' comparison).[83]

Stability and stress of weather.

During the war the RN operated some 370 destroyers which may be roughly grouped as:[84]

First World War survivors	80
Ex USN 'Towns'	50
Inter-war 'A'–'I'	90
'Tribals' and later	150

Not one of these was lost due to bad weather despite problems such as icing in the Arctic and the inexperience of many officers and men. This was no mean achievement; from 1934-44 the world's leading navies lost nine destroyers due to the effects of weather.[85]

In the RN there were few problems with the 'Tribal' and later classes but earlier ships were a source of increasing concern. By July 1940 there had been a serious increase in top weight due to the additional topweight, discussed earlier. Instructions were issued requiring older ships to ballast fuel tanks with water if the fuel load fell below a specified level. By June 1941 destroyers had typically lost 10 per cent of their metacentric height and Stansfield and Coles of the destroyer section put a paper to the DNC seeking his agreement to various simple limiting criteria.[86] They proposed a minimum value of GM of 1.25ft in the light condition and that the maximum GZ in the light condition should not be less than 0.7ft. These criteria were chosen for ease of calculation in the pre-computer age. There was to be a sliding scale of ballasting for those failing.[87] At a meeting on 22 June Goodall accepted the main points, emphasising that he would take risks on strength rather than stability and that additional armament was more important than meeting damaged stability criteria as the armament might prevent the damage.[88] In 1943 consideration was given to lowering the standards but this was rejected. The damaged stability criteria was only that with the engine room and adjacent boiler room flooded, the GM should be just positive. This seems to have been about right as of thirty-seven destroyers sunk by a single torpedo, only six capsized.

It is possible to set standards so high that safety is assured but at a high cost in other features. Studies of RN ships in bad weather, such as Gretton's account of

Losses to stress of weather

Ship	Country	Date	Cause
*Tomozuro**	Japan	16 Mar 34	Capsized
Branlebas	France	14 Dec 40	Broke in half
Lanciere	Italy	23 Mar 42	Lost power and foundered
Scirocco	Italy	23 Mar 42	Unknown
*Sokrushitelnyi***	Soviet	22 Nov 42	Pooped, lost power and later broke in half
Warrington	USA	13 Sep 44	Lost power and foundered
Hull	USA	18 Dec 44	Capsized
Monaghan	USA	18 Dec 44	Capsized
Spence	USA	18 Dec 44	Capsized

* E Lacroix and L Wells, *Japanese Cruisers of the Pacific War* (London 1997), p719.
** P Kemp, *Convoy* (London 1993), p114.

Duncan, show that the margin of safety was very small.[89] The loss of three USN destroyers in the typhoon of December 1944 showed that the assumptions made in conventional stability calculations were generally valid.[90] The safety criteria were reworked and the new ones formed the basis for post-war standards in most NATO navies.[91] It should be noted that *Duncan* at the time described by Gretton was well below the standards reached by the USN ships which were lost.[92]

Naval architects distinguish between seakeeping which describes the motions of a ship in pitch, heave, roll etc and seaworthiness which included seakeeping but also considers integrity of hatches, doors and air intakes. Finally, one must recognise the magnificent seamanship of RN officers and men (including reservists).

The 'Hunt' class

The design of this class is described in some detail both as representative of the design practice of the day and to clarify what went wrong in the biggest error ever made

78 The officer responsible was threatened with court martial for disobedience but finally promoted. le Bailly, *Fisher to the Falklands*, pp71-3.

79 le Bailly, *From Fisher to the Falklands*.

80 Goodall 27 Sept 1933. 'Mariner (British Corporation) called after visit to USA. Their prices for warships are terrific even allowing for higher cost of living.'

81 One might almost use an exchange rate of $10 = £1 instead of the official rate, then $3.4 = £1.

82 Covered in more detail under 'Escorts' in Chapter 7.

83 There were even quite serious proposals to remove such fittings from Lend-Lease ships as they might make our sailors 'soft'!

84 D K Brown, 'Stability of RN Destroyers during World War II', p107.

85 Amgiraglio di Squadra G Polltri and D K Brown, 'The loss of the destroyer *Lanciere* 23 March 1942', *WARSHIP* 1994.

86 They even added a simple *pro forma* inviting Goodall to tick in yes/no boxes. Goodall was usually seen as an autocrat but he seems to have been ready to approve initiatives from trusted staff.

87 These were to be estimated in simplified conditions to reduce the work load in this age before computers. See D K Brown, 'Stability of RN Destroyers during World War II'. There is evidence that this instruction was ignored. Cleaning tanks after filling with water was laborious. It seems that the US destroyers lost in the

typhoon on 18 December 1944 would have satisfied these criteria.

88 Goodall, 22 June 1941. '. . . accepting strength and stability margins which I do not like but extra topweight essential to win the war'.

89 Sir Peter Gretton, *Convoy Escort Commander* (London 1964).

90 D K Brown, 'The Great Pacific Typhoon', *The Naval Architect* (Sept 1985); Capt C R Calhoun, *Typhoon, the other Enemy* (Annapolis 1981).

91 T H Sarchin and L L Goldberg, 'Stability and Buoyancy Criteria for US Navy Surface Ships', *Trans SNAME* (1962).

92 See letter by E W K Walton, former Lt (E), RN of HMS *Duncan* on stability to *Warship Technology* No 12 (1990), p46.

in a British design.[93] During 1938 the naval staff[94] realised that there was a need for escort vessels which were small and cheap enough to be built in quantity and yet were much faster than the *Black Swan* sloops.[95] The head of the destroyer design section, A P Cole, pointed out that such ships would not be cheap, the supply of gun mountings would be difficult and it would take 30 months from approval of the sketch design to get the first ship to sea.

In September 1938 two design studies were carried out in parallel, one with a speed of 25kts and the other with 30kts, the faster needing double the power. Both designs had two twin 4in mounts and two quadruple 0.5in machine guns with a quadruple torpedo tube in the 30kt version. Both designs were to be 'strong and seaworthy' and were to have Denny fin stabilisers to make them steady gun platforms. This led to the first major design dilemma: the heavy armament required good stability (high metacentric height – GM) whilst the fin stabilisers worked best if the roll period was fairly long, implying a small GM. Roll period and stability are closely linked and the designer chose to work to a GM of 2ft corresponding to a roll period of about 7-8 seconds.

At a meeting on 28 September the First Sea Lord decided on a fast design with three twin 4in and no torpedoes. The design was then developed in detail with a form based on previous ships so that a power-speed curve could be scaled. Further attention was given to rolling and it was found possible to improve the stability and still retain an 8-second roll period.[96] The weights were re-calculated and estimates made of the height of the centre of gravity of each weight group. Once these calculations were complete, the design was reviewed by the DNC, Goodall.[97] His first reaction was that the design was too big but was persuaded that a length of 272ft was necessary. The corresponding cost was estimated as £390,000. He asked for the effect on size and cost of various options:

Change	Effect on –	
	Displacement (tons)	Cost (£)
Reduce speed by 2kts	-25	- 6,000
Reduce armt to 4-4in	-90	-40,000
Increase endurance from 3000 to 4000 miles	+200	+50,000

The 'Hunts' have often been criticised for poor endurance but these figures show that improvement would have been costly. As the design developed a number of changes were incorporated, all adding to weight and cost. Thirty more depth charges were to be carried, together with an asdic, more ammunition and more men, the cost reaching £400,000 despite savings elsewhere.

The lines had been drawn out and sent for testing at the Admiralty Experiment Works, Haslar. Altogether, seven models were run leading to a marked reduction in power required and hence in fuel consumption.

Reduction in power from model testing (%)

Speed	Displacement (tons)	
	Standard	Deep
20kts	6	9
Full	2	5

These are impressive, though not unusual, results, particularly since great care had been taken over the original lines plan. No wonder that the designer Bessant wrote with pride in his work book 'Better than any destroyer hull form'. With accurate data on speed and power it was possible to design the propeller and refine

Fernie, a Mk I 'Hunt', in as-completed condition. (Author's collection)

the endurance figures. The stresses on the hull in waves were calculated and found acceptable.[98]

By January 1939 consideration was being given to fitting a 4-barrel pompom in place of the machine guns at a cost of £20,000, a 4in loss of metacentric height, an increase in stresses and space per man reduced from 23 to 21ft².[99]

Goodall then asked for some trade-off studies between speed, endurance and armament. It was found that if all the armament weight was put into more powerful machinery the speed would go up to 38.8kts (standard) whilst if it were used for fuel the endurance would go up from 2500 to 6080 miles. If the top speed were reduced to 20kts and the weight saved in machinery put into guns the armament could be thirteen 4in. These studies were not intended to be realistic but they led to a good talking point in the equation-

1 twin 4in = ⅔ knot = 340 miles at 20kts.

The hull weights had been scaled from earlier classes, mainly the 'Tribals', using an ingenious formula of Bessant's:

$$(\triangle^{0.35}.L.B^{0.35}.T^{0.35})/(82.5D^{0.175}.f^{0.175})$$

Before computers, it was common to use complicated expressions to avoid repeated calculations. Today, one would use a simpler expression with many, almost instantaneous iterations. Note also the inclusion of the acceptable stress 'f' so that comparison could be made between mild and high tensile steel. As a check, Bessant then used the 'Hunt' class estimates as the basis for scaling up to the *Javelin* and got good agreement.[100]

The building drawings were forwarded for Board Approval on 8 February 1939 and at the same time to five shipbuilders. The shipbuilders thought that the Engineer-in-Chief's estimate of 270 tons for the machinery was about 20 tons light. They also wanted to increase the estimated hull weight from 450 to 475 tons.

This was a tricky point as the DNC estimate was actually 487 tons. However, the steel mills were required to roll under the nominal thickness and it was certain that the actual weight would be less[101] and a figure of 460 tons was agreed. The discrepancy on hull cost was more worrying with an average tender of £138,000 compared with the estimated £100,000. At a long conference in January 1939[102] the builders attributed the increased cost[103] to the effect of a short machinery space, the installation of fin stabilisers, higher costs measured in the 'L' class, ready-use ammunition stowages, and the rise in wages since the 'L' class due to expansion in the aircraft industry

They made the interesting point that in a small ship 'cost per ton rises at about half the rate at which displacement falls'. The builders said that building in all mild steel and omitting galvanising saved only £3000 but, when pressed, they agreed to use D quality which saved 13 tons of weight and to galvanise without extra cost. Reduced costs elsewhere brought the total tender price down to £397,000.

The orders had been placed before the detailed weight calculations were complete. These calculations were, and are, tedious. Each item on the drawing is mea-

Cattistock, a Mk I 'Hunt', fairly late in the war. Note the pompom in the eyes fitted for East Coast convoy work. (Author's collection)

93 This section forms the basis for a seminar which the author still gives (1999) to the postgraduate warship design class at University College, London, warning them of the possibility of error. 'To err is human, really to foul it up you need a computer.'

94 Viscount Cunningham, *A Sailor's Odyssey*, pp194. As DCNS in August-September 1938 he suggested a small destroyer based on the First World War 'S' class.

95 The position of these ships under the Treaties was slightly dubious. Warships over 30kts were destroyers and the 1930 London Treaty imposed a limit of 150,000 tons on the RN. However, this limit

was removed by the 1936 Treaty which was not ratified. They were declared as 'fast escorts' and were not known as destroyers until after the outbreak of war.

96 Estimated using the formula Period = $2\pi\sqrt{(k^2/g.GM)}$ where k is the radius of gyration in roll.

97 Diary, 10 Nov. 'Went thro' escort design, ship too big, Gave — (who has no initiative) notes'. 18 Nov. 'Altered yesterday's decision and put 7ft on length to give margin.'

98 The highest stress was 6.25 tons/sq in (tensile) in the deck when hogging, other stresses were around 4½.

99 It was said that hammocks were compressible!

100 Slightly surprising as *Javelin* was longitudinally framed but, as discussed earlier, full advantage was not taken.

101 This is a bit doubtful as scaling from the weighed weights of an earlier class would take in rolling tolerance. Perhaps they used estimated weights.

102 Unusually for the day, Goodall did not allow smoking in his meetings. However, if the meeting went on beyond 6pm, smoking was permitted and sherry was served.

103 See Chapter 11. It was mostly excess profit.

104 Scaling is very accurate and I would have launched a major investigation into this discrepancy.

105 Almost unheard of.

106 Diary 7 Feb 40. 'Cole came in with *Atherstone* inclining results, GM 1ft less than calculated, bad error in calculation, shall have to do something drastic.'

107 8 Feb. '. . . Came in having simmered down over fast escorts. . . . Think Cole's paper too pessimistic.'

108 Diary 9 Feb 'Phoned Controller who said go to bed and stay there. I love him.' (Fraser) 'I still think these ships could have been built; their hull weight seems excessive, their machinery and ammunition weight have gone up a lot.'

109 Diary 10 Feb. 'Cole and Pattison brought in Hunt modifications which were ridiculous altering ships unnecessarily.' 11 Feb. (Sunday) Design team '. . . came to hotel with Hunt modifications and GZ curves. Altered them and agreed to actions which they promised to have by tomorrow midday.' These were explained to Controller next day and agreed.

110 A very similar error occurred quite recently but it was large enough to be spotted easily.

111 Goodall, 31 July 1942. 'Denny Brown stabiliser is not popular, maintenance, upkeep and the fact that we have not trained people in its peculiarities.'

112 J English, *The Hunts* (Kendal 1987).

113 Goodall, 31 July 1940. 'Barnaby called (Thornycroft's chief naval architect, grandson of Sir Nathaniel). Told him not to run our Hunt at NPL. He bet me 2/6 that their form was worse than ours. He has a weird form for dry forecastle. We should be howled down for costly ships if we took it in'.

114 With a building time of about 18 months a constructor during a 3-year appointment would attend the trials of his predecessor's last ships and design two classes of his own.

sured, its weight and the position of its centre of gravity are recorded and then the whole set is summed to give the weight and centre of gravity of the ship. It is easy to make a mistake or to omit something so the calculations were carried out by two men working independently; by custom one would be an assistant constructor and the other a senior draughtsman. Their results would only be compared at the end. Due to pressure of work during re-armament, both calculators for the 'Hunts' were senior draughtsmen.

The results were surprising and disconcerting. The centre of gravity was now calculated to be 10ins lower than that estimated by Bessant.[104] Even so, weights had gone up and it was necessary to increase the beam, an unwanted change since John Brown's mould loft had already begun to lay off the lines. At a meeting on 9 February, Goodall agreed to a 6in increase but, having slept on it, he decided on a 9in increase of beam. The extra beam increased the hull weight by 5 tons and added 7 tons to the fuel load since the tanks got bigger, leading to a loss of ¼kt in the deep condition. Bessant had to complete some detailed calculations on the strength of decks and bulkheads but these were soon finished and he moved to a new section.

He was back on the old section in time for the inclining experiment on *Atherstone* on 4 February 1940. Even before the experiment a serious error had been found in the detailed calculations and the Assistant Director[105] joined Bessant for the inclining. The results were indeed disastrous (see table opposite).[106]

Bessant investigated what had gone wrong and found that there was an error in the detailed calculations which was found a year later, also that the ships had grown some 60-70 tons during build. Bessant's original estimates were much closer to the final figure.

For the first twenty ships (later three more) it was necessary to land one twin 4in, cut down the superstructure and add 50 tons of ballast.[107] Goodall's problems were compounded by a very bad cold.[108] Later ships would have the beam increased to 31ft 6in.[109] Some ships, including *Goathland* and *Haydon*, were 'kippered' on the slip to give increased beam whilst *Berkely* and *Hambledon* completed with two quadruple machine guns in place of the pompom.

Departmental tradition has it that the original error was to take the upper deck as 7ft above the keel rather than the actual 17ft. No proof has been found but this is consistent with the figures and probably correct. Mistakes are easily made when under pressure which is why there were two 'independent' calculators. In this case, one man almost certainly copied the other's figures. Computers make mistakes in arithmetic almost impossible but it is still possible to type 7 instead of 17![110] However, the *Black Swan* class were being designed in the same section with the same armament and 10ft more beam. Though of very different style, the difference in beam should have raised suspicion as

should the very heavy armament. The table compares the weights of the 'Hunt' (detail calculation) with those of the First World War Admiralty 'R' class of much the same size.

Comparison of Admiralty 'R' with 'Hunt' class

	Admiralty 'R'		*'Hunt'*	
	Weight (tons)	*%*	*Weight (tons)*	*%*
Hull	408	46	470	51
Equipment	48	6	60	7
Armament	40	4	88	10
Machinery	395	44	285	31
Stabiliser			15	2
TOTAL	891		918	

The armament weight of the 'Hunts' is more than double that of the earlier class and is high up, balanced by a reduction in machinery weight low down. It should have been obvious that the centre of gravity would be high.

Type 2 'Hunts'

Thirty-six more 'Hunts' were ordered under the 1939 Emergency War programme. Of these, three completed as Type 1 but the others had the beam increased to 31ft 6in with a lower bridge, further aft, and a shorter funnel. With stability restored, they were able to carry the original armament of six 4in, one 4-barrel pompom and two Oerlikons. The deep displacement had risen to 1430 tons and the speed dropped to 25¾kts, deep.

Type 3 'Hunts'

In discussion of the 1940 Programme, it was thought desirable that the next batch of 'Hunts' should have torpedo tubes. Eventually, it was decided that hull and machinery should be as similar as possible to the Type 2 with twin 21in torpedo tubes fitted and one twin 4in removed and twenty-eight such ships were built.

It was found that the fin stabilisers were rarely used and fourteen of the Type 3 and four of Type 2 were either not fitted or had the fins removed, the space being used for oil with about a 22 per cent increase in endurance. As mentioned elsewhere, control theory was in its infancy and the performance of the fins was disappointing, giving a jerky roll which made AA fire control more difficult than in an unstabilised ship.[111] There were a number of problems with the bridge. The short funnels allowed smoke to reach the bridge in a following sea which was partially cured by deflectors and restrictors in the funnel. As completed, the bridge was very windy. Goodall returned from Scapa in *Wilton* on 11 March 1942 noting 'Bridge is really draughty. Must stir up Coles '(Head of destroyer section). This was followed by a hastener on 23 March. The Type 3 cost about £352,000 and all three hatches were well liked and seen as good value for money.

Type 4 'Hunt'

Sir John Thornycroft proposed a design of small destroyer to Controller (Henderson) in October 1938, which was rejected for many reasons.[112] Thornycroft tried again in March 1940 and after discussions and further studies a design was accepted in May 1940 and two ships ordered.[113] The main advantage was its long forecastle, improving stability at large angles and providing safe and comfortable access fore and aft. There was also a novel bridge layout and funnel design intended to keep the bridge free of draughts and smoke – it appears to have been successful. There were a number of detailed changes taking account of criticisms. A knuckle was fitted in an attempt to keep the forecastle dry. They had six 4in guns and three torpedo tubes. The displacement rose from the 1430 tons of the Type 3 to 1561 tons (Thornycroft estimate 1480 tons). The detailed design took much longer than expected. They were well liked in service but had a number of structural problems.

Regardless of the real merits of this design, it is very hard to justify the decision to devote so much design effort for only two ships. It should also be remembered that they were very expensive whilst the essence of the 'Hunt' class was cheapness, and the long forecastle, their biggest virtue, was turned down for Admiralty designs, even for the 'Battles'. Thornycroft later suggested an armoured 'Hunt' (2440 tons deep) with 500 tons of protection, 2½ins thick over machinery. It did not stand up to scrutiny. There was a proposal in the 1941 Programme to build thirty more 'Hunts' but the staff preferred to use the effort on fleet destroyers.

Critique – Excellence to Obsolescence

The 'V' and 'W' classes were world leaders; continual small improvements led to the 'I' class which had fallen well behind other contemporary designs. British destroyers between the wars were designed for a fleet action in the North Sea or Mediterranean. This led to requirements for a heavy torpedo armament, low silhouette (freeboard), small size and short endurance. Anti-aircraft armament was not seen as of primary importance (at least up to the 'Tribals') since it was believed that the battlefleet could defend itself with its own guns and that destroyers were too difficult a target for bombers. Almost all these postulates proved wrong and war found them inadequate in endurance, anti-aircraft and anti-submarine armament and resistance to damage. Some improvement in AA armament was possible by removing half the torpedo armament, their principal *raison d'etre*.

Since the 'V' and 'W' classes were quite suitable for short-range fleet actions it was natural that post-war

	DEEP		LIGHT	
	Displacement (tons)	*GM* (ft)	*Displacement* (tons)	*GM* (ft)
Original calculations	1243	2.3	934	2.16
Corrected calculations	1316	1.22	992	0.95
From inclining	1314	1.16	995	0.74

designs should follow their general style. Evolutionary design, in which each class is a small improvement on its predecessor, is an almost foolproof method of avoiding serious problems but, if continued too long, will inevitably lead to mediocrity or worse.[114] Failure to adopt modern machinery, longitudinal framing, welding etc, can only partly be blamed on the designers as all were opposed by an obsolete and run-down industry. Considerable efforts were made to develop a dual-purpose gun but as discussed, this was virtually impossible with a hand-worked mounting. The USN's 5in/38 gun with 85° elevation, 20 rounds per minute and rapid elevation and training showed what could be done. It is almost unbelievable that compared with the USN's one medium-calibre gun the RN had the 4in, two very different 4.7in, the 4.5in and the 5.25in. No wonder that there was a bottleneck in gun mountings. The USN had also developed the most successful director system in the tachymetric Mk 37. The British Army had successfully developed the tachymetric system but the naval system was abandoned in 1928. Admiral Chatfield was to call this the worse decision between the wars though Pugh has shown that the benefit was only slight (see Appendix 16).

Pre-war British naval writers generally compared RN destroyers – to their disadvantage – with Japanese, French, German and Italian ships. Few noted that those of the USN were superior in every aspect but, it might appear, very costly. In war the British ships did well, better than many much vaunted foreign designs. As always, there was an insoluble debate between quality and quantity; expensive ships meant fewer ships. However, many advanced features were not expensive, and indeed welding would actually have been cheaper.

Brissenden, a Thornycroft designed Mk IV 'Hunt'. Capable but expensive. (Author's collection)

Six | Submarines

BRITISH SUBMARINE POLICY immediately after the end of the First World War seems confused.[1] On the one hand there were many who hoped that submarines could be outlawed by international agreement, despite the failure to get any such agreement at Versailles. A fallback for those who wished to neutralise the submarine was to agree such strict rules of warfare that attacks on trade would be impractical. On the other hand, Japan was a potential enemy and the RN would probably be an inferior power in a war in the China Sea and might welcome a strong submarine force. In view of these disputes it is surprising that one of the few ships ordered in the immediate aftermath of war was a submarine, *X 1*.[2]

The first part of this chapter contains an account, class by class, of the development of British submarines of the era. The second part considers some specific topics in more detail.

PART I: THE SUBMARINES

Overseas patrol submarines

A conference was held in May 1922 to consider proposals for future submarines as a result of which it was decided to go ahead with the design of an Overseas

Patrol submarine. This vessel, *Oberon*, was ordered under the 1923-4 Programme and completed in August 1927. The main changes from the 'L' class were much increased endurance (11,400 miles at 8kts) and a deeper diving depth of 500ft.[3] While the requirements and, indeed, the basic design were sound and repeated in several later classes, *Oberon* herself was flawed. Her intended speed on the surface was 15kts but the best achieved was 13.74kts, and while submerged she made about 7kts instead of the 9kts required. The main problem seems to have been too many external fittings, many badly designed or aligned.[4] The effect of surface roughness and, in particular, fouling was probably not fully appreciated until a series of trials with *Olympus*.

Olympus trials

Days out of dock	Speed (kts)	bhp	rpm
6	17.5	5800	396
72	16.2	6108	390
275	14.6	6239	381

Vickers then modified the *Oberon* design in two boats for Australia, lengthening them by 4ft 6in and reducing the drag of appendages. *Oberon* had two Admiralty

Oswald was one of the second group of the 'O' class. With better designed and aligned appendages and more power they were faster. The 'O' class was an updated version of the 'L' class with all wartime lessons incorporated and was a good design for its day. (World Ship Society)

Thames was an attempt at a
fleet submarine using the best
diesels available. Diving depth
was reduced to save weight.
(Author's collection)

(AEL) design diesels, built at Chatham, giving 1350bhp each (later uprated to 1475bhp). Vickers redesigned this engine, increasing bore and stroke and obtained 1500bhp and with this power and the improved form slightly exceeded 15kts on the surface and claimed 8.5kts submerged.[5]

Experiments had been carried out with an experimental Asdic set in *H 32* in 1923 and a set was fitted in *Oberon*. A much improved installation was fitted in the *Odin* class. It was originally intended for use as an active set, for attacking enemy submarines submerged. However, use in the active mode disclosed the position of the submarine and it was usually used as a passive, listening set as which it worked unexpectedly well. Another concealed advantage of these submarines was a low frequency radio receiver. It was found that Rugby radio (1500m) could be received submerged in the Sea of Japan at a depth of 50ft.[6]

The six boats of the *Odin* class (1925-6), six of the *Parthian* class (1927) and four of the *Rainbow* class (1928) were generally similar. They had eight-cylinder engines rated at 4400bhp for a surface speed of 17½kts (this varied slightly between boats). The diving depth was kept at 500ft but the test depth was now 300ft. *Otus* went to 360ft, suffering some distortion, and they were all stiffened aft. All these submarines carried most of their fuel in the external tanks and the 'O' and 'P' class boats had riveted tanks which leaked, leaving a trail of oil on the surface. The 'Rs' were built with welded tanks and the earlier boats were welded later.[7]

Power loading was introduced for the bow tubes and a second salvo could be fired 7 minutes after the first.[8] Overall, they were a quite successful design once the original problems had been overcome, shown by the way in which repeat classes were ordered.[9] By the outbreak of war they were ageing and it is said that there were still oil leaks. Some were used as cargo submarines, supplying Malta.

Fleet submarines

Post-war exercises with the steam driven 'K' class convinced Rear-Admiral (Submarines) (RA(S)), that there was a role for the fast submarine, operating with the battlefleet, and this view seems to have had strong, though not universal, support from submariners. A diesel-engined submarine was designed and approved in June 1929, merging the features of the overseas patrol and fleet submarine.[10] They were given two ten-cylinder diesels which could be supercharged, the blowers being driven by auxiliary engines. The quoted design speed was 21kts or 21.75kts supercharged. Considerable care was taken to reduce the drag of external equipment and this speed was exceeded on trial, *Thames* reaching 22.6kts, less than a knot slower than *K 26*. The design submerged speed of 10kts was also slightly exceeded by 0.6kts.

There was a price to pay for this performance. The cost had risen to £500,000, most unwelcome at a time of financial crisis. The standard displacement was 1830 tons which would be an embarrassment when the 1930 London Treaty imposed an overall limit on submarine tonnage. To save weight the pressure hull thickness was reduced from 35lb in the 'Os' to 25lbs in the *Thames* with a corresponding reduction in diving depth from 500ft to 300ft. Submarine COs seem to have agreed that there was no requirement to dive deeper than 300ft.[11] The stern torpedo tubes were omitted. Stability was poor as completed, particularly on surfacing (see 'S' class). Luckily a change in policy on submarine guns led to the 4.7in being replaced by a 4in, saving 6 tons high up. A change in the specific gravity of oil saved another 8 tons.

There had been an intention to build twenty of these boats but the cost and the Treaty limits were against this whilst it was becoming clear that the next generation of battleships would have speeds approaching 30kts,

1 D Henry, 'British Submarine Policy 1918–1939', *Technical Change and British Naval Policy 1860–1939* (Sevenoaks 1977), p80. Hereafter referenced as Henry.

2 D K Brown, *The Grand Fleet*, pp185-6.

3 D K Brown (ed), *The Design and Construction of British Warships 1939–1945* Vol II (London 1996), p14. Hereafter referenced as *British Warships*. The test depth was 200ft, see full note on diving depth.

4 A N Harrison, *The Development of HM Submarines from Holland No 1 to Porpoise* (BR 3043) (Bath 1977), p14. Hereafter referenced as Harrison.

5 The measurement of submerged speed was very difficult until well after the Second World War.

6 A Mars, *British Submarines at War* (London 1971), Ch 3. Mars concludes this book with a fictitious but realistic account of a Japanese invasion force being destroyed by British 'O', 'P' and 'R' class submarines off Formosa.

7 It is said that this did not entirely stop the trail of oil. The pressure hull was riveted and there were oil leaks through these rivets. This was probably the largest welded fabrication to date in the RN.

8 Mars, *British Submarines at War*, Ch 3.

9 It is sometimes said that their underwater manoeuvrability was poor (eg E Bagnaso, *Submarines of World War Two* (London 1977)). This seems unlikely; see Mars above who seems very pleased with the handling of *Regulus*. There was then a belief that big submarines could not be manoeuvrable; a generation used to SSN and SS(B)N would not agree.

10 *Thames* 1929 Programme, *Severn* 1931, *Clyde* 1932.

11 Ships cover 483.

virtually impossible for a submarine of the 1930s. In general, they did what was expected of them.

Goodall was then an Assistant Director with a strong ambition to follow Sir Arthur Johns as DNC. Realising that his experience of submarines was negligible he asked Johns to put him in charge of submarines. Johns (a very experienced submarine designer) agreed, 'DNC gave me a solemn little lecture on submarines to wit stability and care thereof. Unlike surface craft the lives of men are in jeopardy all the time. He said after an accident I [Johns] have not been able to sleep for 2 or 3 nights wondering if anything I had forgotten was the cause.'[12] Goodall soon had good cause for worry; on 1 March he noted that *Severn* had leaked aft on her deep dive and had buckled a pillar between the top and bottom of the elliptical stern sections. 'DNC very peeved with 8ft by 3in diameter solid pillar. Told me to keep an eye on these details.'[13] The buckling strength of such a long and thin pillar is negligible and should never have been considered. A few days later he wondered why it had not buckled in the earlier boats of the class and was horrified to find that the pillar did not even run across the hull but stopped on a light flat making it useless!

Smaller submarines: *Swordfish* and *Shark*

In 1929, RA(S) asked for a smaller submarine to be used in shallow and confined areas – the Baltic was specifically mentioned. After discussion, the principal requirement were laid down as an endurance corresponding to 600 miles transit at not less than 9kts, each way, with 8 days on station. There were to be at least four bow tubes, six if possible, a W/T range of 500-600 miles and a surface speed of at least 12kts. DNC produced two design studies for consideration, one of 600 tons standard, the other of 760 tons. The smaller was chosen as the basis for development.

Swordfish and *Sturgeon* were ordered under the 1929 Programme (two more the next year) with the following legend characteristics; 640 tons, six bow tubes, surface speed of 14.2kts and an endurance of 5750 miles at 8kts. Too much had been attempted on the size and they grew in weight during building. Excessively heavy bronze castings for the conning tower seem to have been a particular problem.[14] The fittings were said to be complicated and unreliable. Stability was insufficient, the submerged BG was 4.9ins and the low buoyancy GM only 2.9ins.[15] Various factors combined to make this problem worse; they had a permanent list of 3° in the normal surface condition which was much increased as stability reduced. This list caused air to occupy the higher tank when blowing to the surface, further increasing the list while the bridge and casing drained too slowly, trapping water high up. There was a large free surface in the compensating tanks. It was not uncommon for a boat to list 20° when surfacing in good conditions and surfacing in beam seas was to be avoid-

ed. Extra holes were cut in the bridge and casing and it was found that rapid surfacing reduced the problem. The first two boats had their 3in gun on a disappearing mounting but it was found that the exposed gun caused very little drag; removal of the disappearing mounting saved 6 tons of top weight.

The design was unsatisfactory but the concept was liked and a redesign led to the eight boats of the *Shark* class from the 1931 Programme onwards to 1935, though the poor reputation of the earlier boats was carried forward, unjustly. The fittings were simplified, length was increased by 6ft and displacement by 30 tons. These modified boats were very successful but in 1935 it was decided to concentrate on the 'T' and 'U' classes. The *Shark*s were so successful in the early months of the war that many further boats were built from 1940 onwards.

Minelayers

In 1927 the 'M' class submarine, *M 3*, was converted as a minelayer, carrying 100 mines in an extended casing. The trials showed that the scheme was basically sound but the jigger gear used to move the mines demanded excessive maintenance and the casing was slow to flood, increasing diving time. The longitudinal distribution of buoyancy was also poor. A prototype minelayer, *Porpoise*, was included in the 1930 Programme, laid down in 1931 and completed in March 1933.

Porpoise was closely based on *Parthian* but, to save weight for the 50 mines and their gear (54 tons), the diving depth was reduced to 300ft and speed was reduced with lower-power engines. The design speed was 15kts but, on trial, *Porpoise* achieved 16.2kts.

Five more minelayers of the *Grampus* class were ordered in the programmes for 1933-6. Externally, they looked similar to *Porpoise* but they were, in fact, a very different design. The saddle tanks were extended round the bottom making a double hull except within the casing. The pressure hull was circular up to about 2-3ft either side of the keel where it joined the top of tanks in the outer hull built to pressure hull standards for the carriage of oil fuel. *Porpoise* had carried her fuel in external tanks but, though it had been shown that welded tanks did not leak in peacetime, there was a fear that they might split under depth charge attack and internal stowage was desired. This change increased the main ballast capacity by 100 tons and improved stability. Much attention had been paid to quick flooding and their diving time of 1 minute 14 seconds (with the use of the quick-diving tank, Q) was remarkably good for such big vessels. They were quite successful, being able to lay mines as close as 120ft apart.

There were a number of later designs for minelayers, none of which were built. Four were included in the 1939 programme.[16] They were similar to *Grampus* but with a circular pressure hull and 'T' class engines (pos-

12 Goodall, 4 Feb 1935.

13 Goodall, 1 Mar 1935.

14 Bronze was needed to avoid interference with the magnetic compass.

15 Goodall, 12 March 1935. 'Went to sea in *Swordfish* and turned when submerged. Surprised the ship was so tender; she broke surface. I must look into this.'

16 Legend in ADM 1 2419.

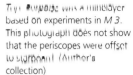

The *Porpoise* was a minelayer based on experiments in *M 3*. This photograph does not show that the periscopes were offset to starboard. (Author's collection)

Second: *Olympus* was a very different design from *Porpoise* with a near-circular pressure hull and all oil stowed internally. (Author's collection)

Third: *Sturgeon*, an early 'S' class. Note the housing for the gun which proved unnecessary. (Author's collection)

Fourth: *Starfish* was similar to *Sturgeon* but the gun was not housing and the conning tower was lowered, improving stability. (Author's collection)

Triton, an early 'T' class in 1939. Note that the external tubes amidships fire forward giving the exceptional bow salvo of ten tubes. (Vicary)

sibly Sulzer). It was emphasised that the lessons of the trial of Job 81 against depth charge attack had been incorporated. They were cancelled and a smaller minelayer based on the 'S' class was designed for operation in shallow waters. These, too, were cancelled and an order was placed in January 1941 with Scotts for three of the modified *Grampus* but the need for more patrol submarines led to their cancellation. By this date, ground mines could be laid from torpedo tubes, two replacing each torpedo, and the need for specialist minelayers was reduced.

The 'T' class

A number of factors came together in setting the requirements for this class. The London Treaty of 1930 had set an overall limit of 52,700 tons for the submarine forces of Britain, the USA and Japan. There was also an individual limit of 2000 tons on individual boats. The financial crisis made it difficult to build enough submarines to reach the overall total.[17] The successful development of Asdic and the expectation that other navies would make a similar development was also important and small size – about 1100 tons – was seen as advantageous in avoiding detection. It was also thought likely enemy anti-submarine action would mean attacking at long range, possibly on Asdic information alone, without exposing the periscope. This suggested that a numerous bow salvo of at least eight tubes was needed in order to score hits by 'shotgun' effect.

This concept was expanded into the *Triton* ('T') class with a displacement of 1090 tons, six internal bow tubes,[18] two more external at the bow and two more amidships, angled to fire forward giving an exceptional bow salvo of ten torpedoes. They had one 4in gun. By the outbreak of war fifteen of these boats had been completed or were still building (1935-8 Programmes). Their increased size gave them much greater endurance than the 'S' class. The majority of these early and later 'Ts' had two six-cylinder Vickers engines, Dockyard

boats having Chatham-built engines of Admiralty (AEL) design.[19] The total bhp was only 2500 giving a design speed of 15¼kts (16.2kts on trial).[20]

The diving depth was 300ft. In the three boats of the 1938 programme (and later) the riveted Z bar frames were replaced by welded T bars. These three were designed with vertical wells in the ballast tanks carrying six mines each side. Trials in *Tetrach* showed that the surface speed was reduced by 1½kts and the equipment was removed from her and not fitted in the other two. The cost of the early boats was about £300,000, rising to £460,000 with wartime inflation and additions.

The 'U' class

By 1936 the wartime 'H' class boats were nearing the end of their life and there was a requirement for a simple boat to replace them in the training role. Original studies had no armament but it was eventually decided that they should have four internal tubes (with reloads) and two external tubes. A 12pdr gun could be fitted in place of two reload torpedoes. Three were ordered under the 1936 Programme.

They were of single hull design with the ballast carried inside the hull. This arrangement has the disadvantage that, if the valves are open, the flat bulkheads of the ballast tanks are exposed to full sea water pressure or the shock of depth charges. They were designed for 200ft diving depth.

The bluff bow associated with the external torpedo tubes caused a big bow wave and loss of speed in a seaway and affected handling under water so these tubes were omitted in the wartime boats. By the time this class was designed, the importance of quiet operation had been appreciated and a number of measures were introduced to quieten submarines. Until the *Unity*, submarine propellers had been designed for optimum surface performance. The *Unity* was optimised for submerged running and it was hoped that this would reduce propeller noise.[21]

17 Henry, p98.

18 In a submarine of this size it was not possible to fit six tubes into a circular hull so the fore end had to be oval (like earlier boats). With an oval bow, there seemed no reason why a similar section should not be used aft.

19 Scotts built three with MAN diesels built under licence which were very unreliable. Cammell Laird built two with Sulzer engines which were liked at first but gave trouble later.

20 Mars complains of their speed but on the displacement no more could be done.

21 As we found after the war, the design of a quiet propeller is very difficult and I doubt if this change had any effect.

22 The success of these classes is attributed to L C Williamson and G W Pamplin.

23 *British Warships*, p19.

24 Baillie had led the design of most submarines from *Thames* onwards, Hill was an experienced overseer. The Admiralty lent constructors and draughtsmen to Cammell Laird to help them.

25 *British Warships*, p19.

26 In the 'T' class design, it was accepted that they could only operate in the Baltic or Black Sea if they reduced the fuel carried by 26 tons.

Urwin, an early 'T' class in January 1939. The external bow tubes caused high drag and a big bow wave and were omitted in later boats. (Author's collection)

Submarines at the outbreak of war

In 1939 there were three satisfactory but ageing designs of submarines; 'Ts' the largest, 'S' medium and 'U' very small. Most wartime building was of these three types.[22] There is a revealing passage in the DNC history which says that because submarines had low priority, design, building and maintenance staff were kept to a minimum and 'in consequence the British submarine fleet at the opening of hostilities in September 1939 consisted largely of out-of-date types.'[23] The writer of that passage probably had two specific points in mind, the development of a suitable steel for welding and the structural design of the hull, particularly the framing in which significant developments had been made in Germany. (Both these points will be treated in detail later in the chapter.) The need for submarines was so great in the early years that the delays caused by introducing a new design were unacceptable. Only when the RN moved back into the Pacific was it essential to build a new design. There was a serious setback when the *Thetis* sank on trials in June 1939, the 99 men lost

including two constructors and many of Cammell Lairds' submarine team.[24] The loss of experienced designers and builders caused major problems.

Wartime changes

The changes to boats of the 'S', 'T' and 'U' classes, both general and class specific, are described in some detail in the DNC history and are only noted briefly here.[25] There is one general point which is little understood; addition of weight anywhere in a submarine will cause the centre of gravity to rise. This is because the submerged weight of the submarine must always be equal to the buoyancy so that the addition of any weight has to be offset by the removal of a corresponding amount of ballast. Since the ballast is in the very bottom of the boat, its removal will lead to a higher centre of gravity. There is a further complication in that the buoyancy depends on the density of the water in which the boat is floating. Pre-war submarines were designed to operate over a wide range of densities from fresh water upwards.[26] (See later section on density.) Changes in

Splendid, a '1940 S', seen in August 1942. (Author's collection)

Tabard in 1946; note the
external tubes, two bow, three
firing aft. The author joined her
early in 1951 by which time she
had a Snort and was the
champion gunnery submarine.
(Wright & Logan)

buoyancy were allowed for by varying the internal
water ballast in special compensating tanks. Some
weight additions were accepted, without change of permanent ballast, leading to a reduction in the range of
density in which the boat could operate.[27]

General changes

Guns. The 'S' and 'T' classes had a 20mm Oerlikon fitted at the rear of the conning tower.
Radar. The type 286W, 1½-metre set was fitted from
1941. Later, a hybrid 267QW was fitted with both 1½-
metre and 3cm aerials and masts and a common dis-
play.[28]
Asdic. All boats had the 129 set at the fore end of the
ballast keel but this was blind above and astern. In 1943
the 138 was fitted on the after casing despite difficulties
in squeezing the gear into the engine room.
Habitability. The dehumidifiers fitted in some 'S' and
'T' boats were insufficient and full air conditioning was
introduced into most of these boats (and some 'Us').[29]
This was very successful; crews often preferred to sleep
in their air conditioned submarine rather than in the
depot ship in a tropical harbour.[30] A system of air
purification was developed and proved in *Thule* just

before the war ended. Fresh water capacity was
increased in some 'S' and 'T' boats either by converting
compensating tanks or by installing new tanks.
Distillers were also fitted. New equipments such as
radar reduced the crew space and, at the same time,
needed more men. All that could be done was to fit
portable bunks in the torpedo space.
Oil Fuel. In the 'S' and 'T' classes some of the main ballast tanks were converted to carry oil in an emergency
increasing endurance by 16 per cent and 40 per cent
respectively.
Noise Reduction. Very considerable efforts were made
from about 1937 to reduce the amount of noise radiated
into the sea by machinery. The first step was to fit simple, flexible mounts consisting of a steel and rubber
sandwich. These were standardised by the Admiralty
Research Laboratory (ARL) by early 1944, the mounts
also providing shock insulation. No reliable flexible
piping was produced during the war. Every submarine
was checked on the noise range at Loch Goil which
could identify any noisy machine for further treatment.
The 'A' class were designed with noise performance in
mind and there was a target of 500yds beyond which
machines should not be heard. As far as was possible,
the 'S' and 'T' class were brought up to a similar standard. It is probable that even in the Second World War
British submarines were the quietest.
Batteries. Early in the war it was found that batteries
were at serious risk of damage in a depth charge attack.
Numerous trials in a test section, Job 9, led to interim
fitting of rubber pads under the battery and a rubber
sheath round each cell. Later types of cell container
were stronger and the sheath was not needed.
Bridges. Several 'S' and 'T' class boats building in 1940
were given partially enclosed 'cab' bridges. These were
not liked and in February 1942 it was decided that these
should be replaced by an open bridge with improved
wind deflectors.

27 This could lead to problems off
major rivers where the water was
nearly fresh.

28 When the author served in
Tabard this
1½-metre set very useful as no radar
detectors were working in this
obsolete frequency.

29 It is said that one submarine
reporting temperature and humidity
readings was told that the figures
reported would not support human
life!

30 A J Sims. 'The Habitability of
Naval Vessels under Wartime
Conditions', *Trans INA* (1945), p50.
Thirty hours was about the

maximum submerged time possible
with wartime air treatments. The
author was submerged for 32 hours
in *Tabard* and felt very ill.

31 The last two had thicker, welded
plating and a diving depth of 350ft.

32 A third boat had a welded hull
and the early armament.

33 Seven surviving earlier boats were
modified to this configuration.

34 Two of the early boats had their
external bow tubes removed.

35 The first to complete was dived
to 400ft having previously been air
tested.

36 The causes of propeller singing
are complicated. Roughly, eddies are
shed from the trailing edge of the
propeller blade, alternately from the
back and face. If the eddy shedding
rate coincides with one of the
natural frequencies of the propeller
blade, it will be put into resonant
vibration, emitting an audible, clear
note which can be heard and
recognised at very long distances. As
well as the alteration to the stern
lines, a thinner trailing edge was
specified and manufacturing
tolerances reduced. In the author's
opinion, changes to the blade were
more likely to have cured the
trouble than changes to the hull.

Wartime building of the 'S', 'T' and 'U' classes

As mentioned earlier, it was decided in 1940 that more 'S' class boats should be built and thirty-three were ordered in the 1940 and 1941 Programmes. They had welded frames and riveted plating with a diving depth of 300ft.[31] After the first six boats, a single, external tube was fitted aft. Seventeen more were ordered under the 1942 and 1943 programmes. The first two were similar to the riveted, 1941 boats with a 3in gun and a stern tube.[32] Later boats were all-welded with a diving depth of 350ft and the stern tube was omitted to allow for the weight of a 4in gun. Both groups incorporated improved shock protection following trials in Job 81 and some noise reduction measures were incorporated. The cost was about £318,000.

Sixteen more 'T' class boats were ordered under the War and 1940 programmes and twenty-two more in 1941 and 1942. The main change was that the midships external tubes were moved to fire aft and another external tube added at the stern giving a stern salvo of three and a bow salvo of eight.[33] The bow external tubes in the original design made the bow very bluff, causing a big bow wave on the surface and impairing depth keeping submerged, and in the later wartime boats these tubes were moved 7ft aft to allow a finer bow.[34] The last twelve boats had all-welded hulls with 30lb S quality steel plating allowing a safe diving depth of 350ft.[35]

A total of seventy-one more boats based on *Undine* were ordered under the War 1940, 1941 and 1942 Programmes. The external bow tubes were omitted in all of them to improve the form. The shape of the bow and hence the length varied in the earlier boats, depending on how far building had advanced when the change was made. The earlier boats had a 12pdr gun, changed to a 3in (17pdr) in the later boats. The later boats from *Venturer* were altered more substantially. The bow shape was fined further and the stern lines were altered to improve the flow into the propellers. Several early boats suffered from 'singing' propellers and it was

Vulpine, a 'V' class submarine. She has been fitted with a dummy 'Snort' for A/S training. (Imperial War Museum: A25976)

though that poor inflow contributed.[36] This later group had an all-welded pressure hull with 25lb plating which increased their diving depth to 300ft.

Wartime design – the 'A' class

There were a number of proposals for new design submarines in 1941, mainly aimed at quicker production. However, it was thought that any gains would be offset by the time lost in changing. By October 1942 it was clear that a bigger submarine was needed for the Pacific and staff requirements were agreed in October 1942. Improvements were needed in surface speed and endurance, habitability and diving depth. A safe depth of 500ft was required and it was thought that this could only be met if the pressure hull was circular throughout the length. This meant that only four internal bow tubes could be fitted, together with two external. At the stern there were two internal and two external tubes.

Though the later boats of earlier classes were all welded, their design precluded full advantage being taken of this. The 'A' class were designed for welding from the start and this contributed to their much greater diving depth as well as easing production. They were designed for 19kts with either Admiralty or Vickers supercharged eight-cylinder diesels with a total of 4300bhp (18.5kts on trial). These were based on the 'T' class engines but E-in-C warned in November 1942 that

Amphion in 1954. Note the raised bow to improve seakeeping. (Wright & Logan)

Statesman streamlined as a high-speed target. Streamlining reduced the underwater drag by 55 per cent and with uprated motors they could reach 12½kts submerged. (Author's collection)

37 The design team was L C Williamson (ADNC), G Pamplin followed by A J Sims (Chief Constr), J F Starks followed by R N Newton (Constr) and F H J Yearling (Asst Constr). In 1944 Newton was Constr Cdr on FOSM staff and at the end of the year he and Starks exchanged jobs. The trials of *Amphion* were carried out by Newton and Yearling and there were no problems on the surface as the weather was calm.

38 Hydrodynamically, the cause was eddy shedding as described above for singing propellers.

39 Shades of the First World War 'J' and 'K' classes. Designers should read history!

40 This passage is adapted from a letter of 12 June 1999 to the author from F H C Yearling. A few words have been added to explain technical terms and one or two passages omitted.

41 The risk was increased as each builder had a different arrangement. Knowing how to operate the heads in one 'T' class boat did not guarantee safe operation of another.

42 This note is based on the notes of two meetings contained in ADM 1 19027, the first chaired by DDNC on 21 Nov 45, the second by Controller on 13 Mar 46 (Per G Moore).

43 ADM 1 18604 of 19 Jan 1945.

44 Chief Constructor G Pamplin followed by A J Sims, constructor Starks, assistant F H 'C Yearling.

45 Many people consider that the air purification equipment in SSNs was a greater feat of engineering than the nuclear power plant.

46 HTP was known in Germany as Ingolin, Aurol or T-Stoff.

a change of engine design would delay the whole programme unless planned with great care. Normal endurance was 12,200 miles at 10kts but with an extra 48 tons of fuel in No 4 tank this was increased to 15,200 miles. They were designed so that Snort could be fitted easily if required.

A full scale mock-up of most of the boat was produced and all builders would work to the same drawings. An elaborate scheme to use subcontractors as much as possible was devised. There was friendly rivalry between Chatham Dockyard and Vickers in devising the best scheme for pre-fabrication–after the war both British builders visited Germany and were satisfied that their methods were well in advance of German work on the Type XXI U-boat. The man-hours needed to build an 'A' class were considerably fewer than the requirement for a 'T' class, reflected in a slightly lower price of £450,000.

The first to complete, *Amphion*, was dived to 600ft with no problems and the design was generally satisfactory.[37] There were two annoying problems which will be mentioned as both are technically interesting. The periscopes vibrated badly at speeds above 2½kts.[38] The cure was to fit taller periscope standards and stiffen their supports. Seakeeping was poor in two respects. The bow was too low and a buoyancy tank had to be fitted.[39] The 'A' class also had a very uncomfortable rolling motion with a number of contributory causes; these were revealed during the trials in rough weather of the first Cammell Laird boat (*Affray*) under H Tabb when she rolled to about 30° and hung there for half a minute. The problem was an interesting one and is described below in some detail.[40]

The metacentric height of the 'A' class was very similar to that of the 'T' class and it was expected that their stability at large angles (GZ curves) would also be similar. Because of the overload of work the GZ curves had not been calculated. When the rolling problem was recognised, Assistant Constructor F H J Yearling was set to work to calculate these curves. There were no computers and it was all done, laboriously, with a mechanical integrator. The calculation was tedious as there were numerous buoyant appendages and non-

buoyant free flooding spaces to take into account. The normal submarine GZ curve has a maximum at about 40-50° and a vanishing angle over 90°. That of the 'A' class had a maximum at about 20° and vanished about 40°. The requirement for a high surface speed, low silhouette and a good GM in the low buoyancy condition had led to a midship section similar to a deeply immersed surface ship. As the submarine heeled the sharp top corner of the ballast tanks was soon immersed causing a loss of stability. The deep trough between the tops of the saddle tanks trapped water and made things worse. The external fuel tanks and ballast tanks were interchanged to lower the centre of gravity and the port and starboard tanks were separated. Once these minor, but important, changes had been made, they were excellent submarines.

A feature which was warmly welcomed was the installation of a sewage tank. Previously the heads had to be flushed each time they were used, the contents of the pan drained into a pressure pot which was then blown into the sea by compressed air. This had two hazards; the bubble might give away the position of the submarine (permission always had to be sought to use the heads), the other was that maloperation of the complicated system of valves and levers might lead to the user suffering the fate known as 'getting your own back'.[41]

High speed targets

Early in 1944 reports were received of a streamlined German submarine with a submerged speed of 16kts. There was an urgent requirement for a target submarine with as high a speed as possible to train ASW forces to operate against this new threat. *Seraph* was in refit at Devonport and it was decided to alter her. The hull was cleaned up by removing the gun and the external tube, fitting a smaller streamlined bridge (removing one periscope and the radar masts), and blanking the torpedo tube apertures. Freeing ports in the casing were much reduced–they are surprisingly resistful–and reshaped at the expense of much increased diving time. These changes reduced the submerged resistance by 55 per cent. The motors were uprated by 13 per cent, a bigger battery was installed and 'T' class propellers of higher pitch were fitted. On trials in September 1944 under J F Starks she reached 12.5kts at periscope depth (1647bhp) compared with 8.8kts (1460 bhp) for an unconverted sister. *Seraph* handled as well or better than standard boats.

Improved 'A' class, 'B' class and Experimental Submarine

Three 'Improved A class' submarines were included in the 1944 Estimates and one experimental boat in the 1945 Estimates but it is far from clear what form these submarines would have taken–indeed a final decision was probably not made.[42] The original proposal for the improved 'A' was for a streamlined 'A' with the most up-to-date equipment and optimised for submerged performance. They would have had an improved Snort, a bigger control room and more space for torpedo loading. A design on these lines was started but following a paper of January 1945 and a meeting in July 1945 Admiral (S) asked for a more radical change.[43] DNC then prepared a new sketch design with novel Snort arrangements and a high-capacity battery.[44] DNC favoured a fairly conventional boat with a much larger battery giving a submerged speed of about 13–14kts on a form displacement of about 1800 tons. All were agreed that twin shafts were preferred to a single shaft. Stern tubes must be omitted in the interest of propulsive efficiency. This design could be started almost at once and would provide valuable experience in air purification equipment.[45]

This design had not got very far before Admiral (S) called for a high-power, submerged propulsion unit. News of the Japanese surrender came at the same time providing the opportunity for a re-think. Most favoured the use of Walter turbines as used in the German Type XVII U-boats, running on High Test Peroxide (HTP).[46] The carriage of HTP as an oxidant rendered the power plant independent of atmospheric air and allowed them to operate submerged at high speed for considerable periods. DNC prepared a design known as B1 which would have a nominal 6000shp per shaft. With a displacement of 1770 tons it should have a speed of about 21kts for 6 hours provided appendages were kept to a minimum. It was noted that the power of these engines fell off quite rapidly with depth because the exhaust—carbon dioxide—was discharged against the back pressure of the sea. For example, the output of two 7500shp units would be 12,500shp at shallow depth and 9500shp at 330ft. The E-in-C hoped to reduce this loss with developments of exhaust compressors or scrubbers.

A possible programme was:

Complete drawings and specification	Late 1946
Lay down	Early 1947
Complete on Walter units	Early 1948
Complete with Walter units	Early 1950

E-in-C wanted diesel-electric drive as it reduced the problems of clutching in the turbines and reduced underwater noise with flexibly mounted machinery. However, the weight and bulk of the DC motors then available at these powers was unacceptable For a given endurance (miles) a submarine with a good submerged form would need 50 per cent more fuel snorting than would an older type of submarine on the surface (neglecting the effect of zigzagging). For the older type of submarine, endurance on the surface would be about four times that snorting. A hull designed for fully submerged performance would have lower resistance than one designed for snorting but the endurance would only be a fraction of that snorting or on the surface owing to the necessity to carry oxidant as well as fuel.

There was considerable debate on the production of HTP. FOSM thought that a wartime flotilla of ten boats, each of 12,000shp and carrying 150 tons of HTP would use about 12,000 tons of HTP at £120 per ton. This was double the total output of the two Bad Lauterberg plants. It was hoped to bring these German plants to this country and build two more. In the event,

Explorer in 1957. She and her sister were intended to help train A/S forces in hunting very fast submarines. On trial they reached 27kts submerged and their surface escort was unable to keep up.
(Author's collection)

the HTP requirements of both the RN and rockets (Blue Steel, Black Knight, Sceptre etc) were met by Messrs Laporte from their plant at Warrington. The bags to hold the HTP gave many problems as did storage and transport.

There was further discussion of the 1945 experimental submarine. The favoured option was two 6000shp units as in the 'B' class which, in a smaller submarine, omitting all military equipment, would reach about 25kts.[47] Alternative schemes were to build two replicas of the 2500shp units in *Meteorite* (ex *U 1407*) possibly geared to a single shaft or to use a Type XVIII X plant of 7500shp. *Meteorite* was then expected to be restored by the end of 1946 and was thought to be 75 per cent safe! She was expected to reach between 17½ and 19kts. One 'S' class boat was to be rebuilt to give a speed of 16kts.

Experience with *Meteorite* led to the development of the experimental submarines *Explorer* and *Excalibur* (776 tons, two-shaft HTP turbines, 15,000shp) with a speed of 27kts.[48] On completion in 1956 and 1958 they were briefly the fastest submarines in the world. As such, they played a very important part in developing tactics against fast submarines such as the nuclear boats coming into service.

It is said that drawings for the 'B' class were complete by 1951, and some material had been ordered but the design of the *Porpoise* class was underway and this was preferred.[49]

PART II: SOME TECHNICAL ASPECTS

Diving depth and pressure hull strength[50]

In the early days of submarines the term diving depth was used quite loosely and could mean several considerably different things. One may recognise three different and important figures, though terminology varied.

Operational Depth. This was the maximum depth which could be used safely in normal operation. It included margins for error in the design calculation or in building and for an inadvertent overshoot in manoeuvring etc.

Test Depth. A new submarine would carry out a test dive, usually to the operational depth. Many captains would go 10 per cent deeper to give confidence to their crew.[51]

Collapse Depth. The depth calculated by the designer at which the pressure hull would collapse under water pressure. It seems that by about 1930 it was British practice (and that of most navies) to take operational depth as half the collapse depth. Note that in the *Oberon* 'diving depth' was quoted as 500ft, operational depth as 300ft and test depth as 200ft. It is probable that 500ft was the expected collapse depth.

The way in which a pressure hull fails may be consid-

An 'X' class midget submarine after depth charge trials. The dimpled plating between the frames is similar to that caused by exceeding the safe diving depth. (Author's collection)

cred under three headings. The whole of a compartment can buckle, often initiated by frame tripping, the plating between frames can buckle in a large number of nodes or the plating can yield between the frames. Prior to the war, there was general awareness of these failure modes but there was no very sound procedure for calculating the first two.

The strength of plating between the frames could be assessed with surprising accuracy by a very simple formula intended for use in cylindrical boilers.

Stress = (Pressure x Hull Radius)/Plating thickness

This was used on a comparative basis using details of a submarine which had involuntarily dived very deep (*L 2*'s dive to 300ft was usually used). The formula does assume circular sections but all the boats described in this chapter prior to the 'A' class had oval sections at the ends. The size of frames was based on experience and caution led to very heavy framing[52]. When *U 570* was captured, Goodall visited her and noted in his diary 'Why such a thick pressure hull in association with comparatively flimsy frames?'[53] In fact, work in Germany on land-based pressure vessels had led to an improved method for sizing frames.[54] This work was published but seen in the UK too late to be used in the 'S', 'T' or 'U' classes.

The table (top right) lists the 'Formula' depth in feet (as above), the operational depth as used in service and the greatest depth recorded. At the end of the war several submarines, including an uncompleted 'A' class, were lowered until they collapsed and these figures have been included.

Note that the earlier ones fell well short of achieving the formula depth due to their section shape and, possibly, inadequate framing. The advantages of deep diving were an Ability to rest on the bottom in deeper water, the reduced risk of Asdic detection by hiding under a density layer and the increased time for a depth charge to drop leading to reduced chance of it exploding close.[55] Prior to the war, the value of a strong pressure hull was seen as increasing its resistance to an explosion. Submarines rarely dived deep.

Diving times

Since submarines spent most of their time on the surface, and dived only to attack or to evade detection, the time to dive from surface trim to periscope depth was very important. From *Oberon*, boats had a quick diving tank, Q, which would be full when cruising on the surface. This tank made the boat heavy and it would be blown as the boat went under, bringing it back to submerged trim. There was some opposition to the use of Q as blowing usually allowed the release of an air bubble but, if it was done quickly, any bubble would be mixed with the disturbance due to diving.

Formula depths (ft)

Class	Operational	Formula	Max	Trial, depth and boat
'L'	150	320	300	
'O', 'P', 'R'	300	880	400	
Clyde	200	550	300 (Some distortion)	
Porpoise	200	598		
'T'	300	626	400	
'U'	200	500	400	
'S'	200	407		
1940 'S'	300	534	510	527–537 *Stoic*
1942 'S'	350	700		647 *Supreme*
'V'	300	616	380	576 *Varne*
'A'	500	840		877 *Achates*

Time from full buoyancy to periscope depth (mins–secs)

Class	Time	
Odin	1-00	
Parthian	1-06	
Rainbow	1-19	
Thames	1-34	
Starfish	1-06	
Porpoise	1-16	No mines
	1-12	With 50 mines

In wartime, boats would operate on the surface in a low buoyancy condition and could reach periscope depth in just under a minute. These figures are at least as good as other navies and probably better.[56]

Density

The buoyancy of a submarine depends on the density of the water in which it is floating, least in fresh water, increasing with the salinity. From the *Odin* onwards, it was decided that submarines should be able to dive in water of specific gravity (sg) 1.00 to 1.030. The difference in buoyancy in *Odin* amounted to 53 tons which had to be compensated for with internal water ballast. Added weights during the war reduced this range first to 1.005–1.03, then 1.01–1.03 and finally 1.015–1.03.

Torpedoes

British submarines relied almost entirely on the Mk VIII weapon with some variants. It used compressed air and a heater obtaining a range of 5000yds at its maximum speed of 45.5kts. The warhead was initially 722lbs TNT, increased in later models to 805lbs Torpex. It was a simple and reliable weapon and did not have an angling setting meaning that the submarine had to steer along the predicted path for the torpedo.

During the war, 5121 Mk VIIIs were fired by sub-

47 It seems later to have been decided that this boat should have two torpedo tubes. She would have had a small battery but no recharging equipment.

48 Nicknamed *'Exploder'* and *'Exciter'*.

49 My thanks are due to George Moore for research into these boats and to Mr F H C Yearling and Miss E MacNair for their memories of working on the design of these boats and their novel machinery.

50 For a more detailed account see: D K Brown, 'Submarine Pressure Hull Design and Diving Depth Between the Wars', *Warship International* 3/87, p279. This article is based very largely on a detailed study made by J H B Chapman, later DNC, in the design of *Sunfish* in 1929. His work book is now held in the National Maritime Museum. His summary of this work is in ships cover 483.

51 Since this habit was well known the 10 per cent was added to the factor of safety in setting operational depth.

52 The heavy frames did ensure that fabrication errors leading to 'out of circularity' were not a problem. Heavy frames were inevitable at the oval end sections.

53 Goodall, 11 Oct 1941.

54 The early German work was for vessels with internal pressure and could have been misleading for externally loaded sections. However, it did form the valid basis for post-war work by Windenberg and Trilling in the USA and then by Wilson and Kendrick in the UK.

55 The standard depth charge fell at about 10ft/sec.

56 In the USN and other navies, the *last* man to leave the bridge would press the diving hooter – in the RN the *first* man pressed the hooter.

marines for 1040 certain and 95 probable hits, a success rate of 22.2 per cent.[57] The early magnetic pistol (Duplex) was not used in submarine torpedoes, but from late 1943 some 250 torpedoes were fired with the CCR magnetic pistol with a success rate of 35.7 per cent. The Mk VIII came into service about 1930 and remained in use until the mid-1980s, sinking the Argentinean cruiser *General Belgrano* during the Falklands War.

Submarines could carry only a limited number of torpedoes and the gun was frequently used against smaller targets. The tactic was to surface close astern of the enemy and disable his stern gun with the first round. This was the basis of the post-war submarine gunnery competition. (*Tabard* was the champion at the time I served in her.) It was a time trial with the watch started on the umpire's 'Go' at periscope depth and stopped when the first shell went through the target. The trick was to anticipate the 'go' by starting to blow ballast, holding her down with planes. At 'go' the planes were put to rise and the lightened boat would very surface rapidly. Two very strong men would push on the hatches which they could open just before surfacing–it was reckoned that about 1½ tons of water came down! If the attack had been correctly judged, the submarine would be about 300yds on the quarter of the target and a first round hit would follow.

Comparisons

Some comparisons will be drawn with British submarines of the First World War and also with contemporary submarines of other navies. The submarine of the Second World War was still a surface ship which would dive to evade and, sometimes, to attack. It would spend most of its time on the surface for transit and battery charging and would frequently attack on the surface with gun or with torpedo. Even the German Type XXI paid attention to surface performance and mounted anti-aircraft guns. Until the general introduction of radar, the chance of sighting a low-lying submarine on the surface at night was low. In consequence, submarines of the Second World War did not differ all that much in overall characteristics from their ancestors (see tables below).

In both tables the biggest change is in complement, reflecting the additional, more complicated equipment such as radio and Asdic (radar was still to come).

The hurried conversion of *Seraph* to a high speed target shows the potential for dramatic improvements to underwater performance had it been required. The penalty of loss of surface performance, lack of a gun, slow diving and lengthy diving time were thought to be unacceptable. Goodall compared U-boats with British submarines in 1941.[58] He said that German boats saved weight by lighter, short-lived batteries, by running the engines at higher load and by greater use of welding. British diesel engines were considerably heavier and less reliable, while German crews had to put up with poor habitability. After the war, when surrendered U-boats had been inspected and tried, Starks commented on their low reserve of buoyancy, poor accommodation, unreliable hydroplane gear and dangerous battery ventilation.[59] All these points are consistent with design for a short life.

The USN, faced with Pacific operations, wanted high surface speed and long endurance, implying big submarines. Later, they were given a heavy gun armament and would fight surface actions at night. In co-operation with the railway industry, compact diesels were developed which were powerful, reliable (after some teething troubles) and easily maintained. These engines improved surface speed by about 3kts. Great attention was paid to habitability with an evaporator which made fresh water available to an extent undreamed of in other navies. From the mid-1930s, air conditioning supplied another 100 gallons a day for the laundry![60]

57 The USN fired 14,748 torpedoes, sinking 1314 ships–9 per cent. The German percentage was much higher being against numerous slow targets at close range.

58 Goodall, 23 Jun 1941.

59 J F Starks, 'German U Boat Design and Production', *Trans INA* (1948), p248. Starks, an experienced submarine constructor, was serving at submarine headquarters.

60 Japan did not see any need for good living conditions and one may wonder if exhaustion contributed to the poor performance of their boats.

British submarines

Boat	Date	Dspt (tons)	L (ft)	Speed surface (kts)	Speed sub (kts)	Gun	Torp	Tube dia (in)	Crew	Range (miles @ kts)
'L'	1916	891	231	17	10½	1-4in	6	18	35	3800/10
'S'	1942	814	217	14¾	9	1-4in	6	21	48	N/A

Perhaps surprisingly, German submarines showed the same overall similarity.

German submarines

Boat	Date	Dspt (tons)	L (ft)	Speed surface (kts)	Speed sub (kts)	Gun	Torp	Tube dia (in)	Crew	Range (miles @ kts)
U 161	1918	820	239	16.8	8.6	4.1	6	19.7	39	8500/10
U 69	1939	749	223	17	7.6	3.5	5	21	44	8500/8

Escorts | *Seven*

Early sloops

B Y THE LATE 1920s the wartime-built sloops of the 'Flower' class and the 'Hunt' class minesweepers were showing signs of their age and of arduous service. A replacement was envisaged with the dual role of peacetime colonial policeman and wartime minesweeper.[1] It was intended that they should mount two 4in HA but, to save money, one was replaced by a LA gun, available from store. Asdic was to be fitted when available. It was hoped to build one ship with diesels (but no suitable engine could be found), more than one screw was essential and draught was not to exceed 8ft 6in. The bridge was to be as far aft as possible to protect it from a mine exploding at the bow.[2] The first design was thought to be too big and expensive.

	Diesel	Turbine	Reciprocating
Displacement (tons)	1330	1190	1475

A cheaper ship was designed with a speed of 16kts instead of 18kts and with only one gun. This came out at 945 tons. Two ships of the *Bridgewater* class were ordered under the 1927 Estimates. During the detailed design and building much of the equipment removed to save cost was put back, *eg* a second gun was supposed to

be an alternative to the minesweeping winch but they completed with both. The complement went up from 76 to 96 with corresponding increases in stores, water etc.

They were designed with a short forecastle with low freeboard and an open shelter deck extending aft. They came out overweight and seriously deficient in stability at large angles as the centre of gravity had risen whilst the freeboard had reduced. The shelter deck sides had to be plated in making a long forecastle and ballast was added.[3] This gave them a maximum GZ of 1.1ft in the light and 2.35ft in the deep condition which was just about adequate. Once put right, they were well liked in service. They had bilge keels 16ins deep, quite good for the day. They carried out a quarterly sweeping exercise and their A/S equipment was readily available when needed. Four more generally similar ships were ordered in each of the next three years, together with one for the Royal Indian Marine.

The *Grimsby* class changed the principal wartime role to escort and had a heavier armament. It was again hoped that they would mount two twin 4in HA but these were still scarce and only *Fleetwood* completed with this outfit, most having two 4.7in LA and one 3in AA as completed.[4] Two ships were ordered each year from 1931 to 1934 together with one for India and four similar ships built in Australia.

1 A Hague, *Sloops 1926–1946* World Ship Society (Kendal 1993). A general reference for this chapter.

2 Ships cover 440.

3 D K Brown, 'Sir Rowland Baker' *Warship 1995*, p152. Quoting Baker's views on sloops. Baker's original letter is held in the RCNC Centenary collection at the National Maritime Museum.

4 Many of these ships were used in subsidiary roles – dispatch vessels, survey ships – with reduced armament or none.

Bridgewater, the first post-war sloop. Weights were allowed to grow during building and stability was inadequate. As part of the remedial measures the openings below the forecastle deck were plated-in after which the design was very satisfactory. (Courtesy John Roberts)

Shoreham, very similar to
Bridgewater with all problems
cured. (Author's collection)

Transitional ships

The first of the *Bittern* class was renamed *Enchantress* as the Admiralty yacht, retaining a (reduced) 4.7in armament but the second, which took the name *Bittern*, completed with three twin 4in HA.[5] The role was now clearly escort and they were not fitted for minesweep-

ing. A new, smaller class of minesweepers was built. *Bittern* was very successful and served as the prototype for the numerous wartime classes.[6] *Bittern* had the first RN installation of the Denny-Brown fin stabiliser, largely at Goodall's insistence.[7] They were followed by three *Egret* class with four twin 4in and then the *Black Swans*, covered later.

5 *Stork* completed as an unarmed survey ship but mounted three twin 4in guns in wartime. Four modified *Bitterns* were built for India.

6 Baker attributes the design to V G Shepheard and I King who would rise to DNC as Sir Victor and Director of Dockyards respectively.

7 Goodall, 1 June 1938. '[Australian liaison officer] I was of the opinion that they were wasting their money building an *unstabilised* sloop'. Also 7 July. 'Mountbatten called. Asked if Royal Family were good sailors. HM wanted stabilisers.'

8 Two of the nineteen completed as survey vessels and were brought back to the minesweeper role during the war. Two more had a much more elaborate conversion and remained in the survey role.

9 It would still have been seen as an advanced design after the war, ten years later.

10 This section is based on A Nicholls, 'The All-welded Hull Construction of HMS *Seagull*', *Trans INA* (1939), p242. Nicholls was Manager of Devonport Dockyard at the time). Also letters from R Baker. (Sir Rowland)

Wellington showing the
minesweeping gear carried in
the earlier sloops. (Author's
collection)

Fleet minesweepers

From 1931 onwards, nineteen specialist minesweepers of the *Halcyon* class were built in parallel with the sloops, which were getting too big to be satisfactory sweepers and certainly too expensive.[8] The *Halcyons* cost on average £100,000, *Grimsby* upwards of £160,000 and *Bittern* £224,000. The *Halcyons* were similar in style to the early sloops and, indeed, spent most of the war on escort duties. The first five had three-cylinder compound engines with poppet valves worked by cams, two had conventional triple expansion and the remainder geared turbines. They had two single 4in, originally LA, changed to HA. Later one was removed and as escorts they had one 4in HA, four 20mm and forty depth charges, together with radar and magnetic sweeping gear.

Seagull – the first welded ship in the RN

Seagull is usually listed as a ship of the *Halcyon* class but her hull was entirely different. She was designed in 1936 by R Baker as an all-welded ship with longitudinal framing and a flush welded skin.[9] Industry was generally opposed to welding so *Seagull* was built in Devonport Dockyard alongside the *Leda*, a riveted half-sister, so that a comparison of the cost and value of the two systems could be made.[10]

The number of welders employed averaged twenty with a peak of forty-one. Great attention was paid to the selection and training of the welders and, even more important, their supervisors, and careful records were kept of each individual's performance. To maximise welding in the downhand position the bottom units were fabricated upside down. The maximum size of the

Bittern, the first of the new generation of sloops with a heavy AA armament. She had the prototype Denny fin stabiliser to aid AA fire control. (Author's collection)

Halcyon, lead ship of the specialist minesweepers, much cheaper than the bigger sloops. (Perkins)

Blackpool was one of the few *Bangor*s to be built to Baker's original design with diesel engines. An excellent design as conceived for wire sweeping only but became grossly cramped with wartime additions. (Author's collection)

11 Baker letters quoted in D K Brown, *A Century of Naval Construction*, p172. Also Goodall, 20 Mar 1939. 'Looked through MS drawing and dictated note. Woolard rather inclined to let Baker run away with him'. (Baker saw this as proper delegation!)

12 Scaling down was often unsatisfactory.

13 Goodall, 25 Oct 1938. 'With Baker discussed small minesweeper 1939 programme. He is floundering a bit over diesels and not getting much help from E-in-C'.

14 The mixture of engine types caused problem in station keeping when operating in a mixed flotilla. P Lund and H Ludlam, *Out Sweeps!* (London 1978), pp 115 (paperback edition).

15 1.1(sq rt L).

16 The *Algerine*s also had bow trim. When, after the war, some were used for fishery protection, the heavy minesweeping winch was removed from aft, and the bow trim was so great that they could not be steered.

17 A Payne, '*Bathurst* class minesweepers', *Naval Historical Review* (June 1980), p19, Garden Island, NSW.

18 Capt S W Roskill, *The War at Sea* (London 1956), Vol II, p271, and Peter Elphick, *Life Line* (London 1999), pp152-6.

19 ADM 229 24.

Rowland Baker (later knighted) as a Commodore while serving in Canada. He designed the *Seagull, Bangor*s, *Algerine*s and most landing ships and craft. Later he successfully directed the nuclear submarine and Polaris programmes. (*Journal of Naval Engineering*)

weldments was limited to 2½ tons by the derricks on the slip but even this was quite big for the 1930s.

From the start it was realised that distortion due to contraction of the weld metal as it cooled could be a major problem and great care was taken to control it. An allowance of ½in was made for a 30ft bulkhead. The measures were successful and at launch when the structure was complete (313 tons) she was only ¼in shorter than design and the forefoot had lifted 1¾ inches.

	Seagull	Leda
Time building to launch (weeks)	37	30
Weight of structure (tons)	311	345*
Direct labour cost (£)	13,998	14,248
Cost per ton (£)	45	41

* *Leda*'s bulkheads were welded, reducing the advantage of *Seagull*.

The advantages of welding showed clearly even in this first example and lessons had been learnt which promised even bigger savings in future welded work. A particular advantage of the welded construction lay in a 45 per cent reduction in the cost of water testing and rectification. Her first commanding officer commented on the lack of the minor leaks which plagued riveted ships. More important, her smooth skin and 3ins less draught made her slightly faster and much more economical than the riveted ships. She was also quieter and had lower vibration levels than her half sisters. *Seagull* spent much time in the Arctic and was trouble-free – unlike several other navies' first ventures into welded construction.

Fleet minesweepers – *Bangor* and *Algerine* classes

The *Halcyon*s are clearly descended from the earlier sloops and fit here. The *Bangor*s were different but the *Algerine*s derive from the *Halcyon*s. The origin of the *Bangor* class has been described by their designer, (Sir) Rowland Baker.[11] A staff appreciation suggested that the *Grimsby* class were far too big and even the *Halcyon*s too big for minesweepers. Something more like the First World War 'Hunts', perhaps with diesel engines, with a wire sweep, was needed. Baker scaled the design down from the *Halcyon*, the size depending on the complement.[12] Suitable diesels were hard to find and only four were built in the UK and ten in Canada.[13] Four more were ordered with steam turbines and were 12ft longer. It was soon found that the supply of turbines was also limited, and two variants with differing types of reciprocating engine were produced, a further 6ft longer.[14] The diesel-engined ships had a complement of forty-seven, the others fifty-four, but both much increased in service. In all, 45 ships were built in the UK with others in Canada, India and Hong Kong for a total of 109.

Had they been used as intended they might have been seen as a great success but, with the addition of more sweeps, Asdic, radar and depth charges, they were overloaded and certainly overcrowded – up to eighty-seven men. As built, the diesel ships had a freeboard of about 15.3ft compared with a rule of thumb of 14ft but they were described as wet.[15] Such wetness may have been associated with the design which had them trimming by the bow, in order to ensure that if they hit a contact mine, the explosion would be right forward.[16] The *Bangor*s were often criticised by those who did not understand their intended role. This led Lobnitz to propose a design of their own but by then the *Algerine* design was complete. Lobnitz then complained of that design in a letter to Goodall. Baker demolished almost all Lobnitz's points (a few good suggestions were adopted) and Goodall responded in a firm letter of 30 July 1943.

The Australian *Bathurst* class has a somewhat similar appearance to the *Bangor*s and is often said to be a derivative of that design. However, both Baker and Australian sources are clear that they were completely

independent designs [17] The Australian ship was slower
because it was intended that their engines should be
small enough to be manufactured by railway engine
builders. Twenty were ordered for the RN but were
lent to the RAN. The *Bathursts* were more dual purpose A/S-M/S than the simple minesweeper of *Bangor*
type. One cannot leave the *Bathurst* class without mention of one of the most remarkable escort battles of all
time when the Indian *Bengal* with the Dutch tanker
Ondina beat off two Japanese armed merchant cruisers,
sinking one of them, *Hokoku Maru*.[18]

By September 1940 it was realised that the *Bangors*
were too small to carry the complex gear needed to
sweep influence mines and the *Algerines* were designed
by Baker, roughly the same size as the *Halcyon*, a little
shorter, a little wider and somewhat slower. Goodall
answered some criticisms in a note of 27 November
1940.[19] Their length was as great as any minesweepers
except the *Halcyon*s which had accommodation for

Above: *Seaham* was a *Bangor*
with triple expansion engines.
She is seen were with towing
gear to pull an 'eggcrate', an
early – and unsuccessful –
pressure mine sweep. (Vicary)

Upper left: HMAS *Geraldton*, a
minesweeper designed and
built in Australia. Though very
similar to the *Bangor*s they
were completely independent
designs. (Author's collection)

Lower left: *Hare* of the *Algerine*
class post-war. Note the
'cocooned' gun. (Author's
collection)

20 H T Lenton, *British and Empire Warships of the Second World War* (London 1998), p265 for the rather complicated changes to the original order for 32 BAM.

21 S Roskill, *Naval Policy between the Wars* (London 1976), Vol II, p165.

22 D K Brown, 'Sir Rowland Baker' *Warship 1995*.

23 Watson was the Assistant Director dealing with escorts – in the First World War he had been responsible for the P boat design.

24 Goodall, 25 March 1939. 'I spoke against *Guillemot* and for whalecatcher'.

25 G D Franklin, 'Asdic's Capabilities in the 1930s, *Mariner's Mirror* Vol 84 No 2 (May 1998), p204. This is a most important paper, disproving many myths of Admiralty lack of interest in ASW while still showing that the problem was not understood at high level.

26 Goodall, 11 Mar 1936.

27 S Roskill, *Naval Policy between the Wars*, Vol I, p294.

28 S Roskill, *Naval Policy between the Wars*, Vol II, p336.

29 Most of the remainder of this chapter is based on a paper which I read to a conference in Liverpool in 1993. I am indebted to the organisers, the Society for Nautical Research, and the publishers, Lionel Leventhal, for permission to reproduce this material. D K Brown, 'Atlantic Escorts 1939–1945', *The Battle of the Atlantic 1939–1945* (London 1994), p452.

30 J P M Showell, *U Boat Command and the Battle of the Atlantic* (London,1989).

31 It was found that French workers could refit a submarine more quickly than German workers!

32 W Glover, 'Manning and Training the Allied navies', *The Battle of the Atlantic 1939–1945* (London 1994), pp 188 and J Goldrick, 'Work Up', *The Battle of the Atlantic 1939–1945* (London 1994), p220.

33 Only very brief treatment of weapons and sensors here. An excellent account is contained in W Hackmann, '*Seek and Strike*' (London 1984).

VIPs in the Gulf. More length would mean less draft and inferior seakeeping. He apologised for an off-the-cuff remark in which he had expressed doubts over the transom stern and admitted he was over-conservative in this respect. They were required to sweep all types of mine in weather up to Sea State 5 and were also to be capable of AS duties.

The original design featured turbine machinery but a later batch had reciprocating engines and, later still, Lobnitz-built ships had their own design of high speed reciprocating engines. They cost about £210,000. The structure was to warship style and, though simplified, they were more difficult to build than corvettes. A total of 107 *Algerines* were built for the RN, 51 in the UK and 56 in Canada; a further 12 were built for the RCN (9 others were cancelled).

The *Algerines* were very similar in performance – though not in appearance – to the US-built *Catherine* class of which twenty-two served in the RN.[20] They had diesel-electric propulsion so that current would be available for magnetic sweeping, and their greater power gave them a speed of 18kts compared with 16kts for the *Algerines*. Both classes were well liked but the ocean minesweeper of the early 1950s was closely based on the *Algerine* design.

Coastal sloops

A major review of the RN's ASW capability was carried out in 1930.[21] It was considered that the sloops, building at two to three a year, together with older destroyers, to be fitted with Asdic, would be available in sufficient numbers to protect against the limited threat perceived on the oceans. There was a weakness in coastal escorts and a class of coastal sloops (later re-classified as corvettes) was designed. They were beautiful, expensive and could not be built in large numbers.

The weight estimates for the first six, *Kingfisher* class, were pessimistic in the light of the problems with *Bridgewater* and they completed with a draught 1ft less than intended which made them poor Asdic platforms.[22] The hull structure was increased in the three ships of the *Shearwater* class and the form altered.

Corvettes

The 1930 review of ASW also suggested that more trawlers were required as escorts on the east coast. Some commercial vessels were purchased and experimental conversions carried out (see Chapter 8). Though such vessels were seen as valuable it was also appreciated that something better was needed. The use of whalecatchers was considered but the subdivision of existing designs was thought to be inadequate. Mr William Reed of Smiths Dock then suggested an enlarged version of their *Southern Pride* catcher would be satisfactory. The design was developed by Smiths Dock under the guidance of A W Watson, still as a coastal escort, better than a trawler.[23] Sixty were ordered in July and August 1939 and more later to a total of 151 in British yards while a further 107 were built in Canada.[24]

ASW between the wars

It is clear from many Admiralty papers that the surface raider was seen as the main threat whilst, increasingly, aircraft came second, at least on the east coast. There seems to have been a conviction that the submarine had been defeated in the previous war without Asdic and that, with this wonderful device, the submarine should no longer be a threat. Quite frequent exercises were held which seemed to support this view.[25] Many of these exercises were held off Portland where the shallow water failed to show the difficulty in finding the depth of the target submarine. The strong currents also made it unlikely that density layers would occur. Exercises would also involve several hunters to each target and no thought was given to surface attack even though this had been used frequently in 1918, particularly in the Mediterranean where Doenitz had served. The capability of German submarines was underrated; even Goodall, reading an intelligence report in 1936 that Germany could build 87 submarines a year noted 'Don't worry; they're rotten subs.'[26] He was referring to the Type I U-boat but, even so, he should have realised that improved boats would follow. (See comparison of First and Second World War designs in Chapter 6.)

Mallard, originally classified as a coastal sloop; they were later known as corvettes. They were too expensive to be built in numbers. (Author's collection)

Kistna, typical of wartime sloops of the *Black Swan* class. (Author's collection)

As early as 1921 the Admiralty recognised that numerous escorts would be needed if ever there was a further war on trade.[27] In February 1937 the Admiralty set up the Shipping Defence Advisory Committee which initiated work on defensive armaments, training and convoy organisation.[28] By 1938 the convoy organisation was in place and could be implemented when unrestricted submarine warfare began. It may well be true that the pre-war Admiralty under-estimated the submarine threat; it is not true that this threat was ignored.

War 1939-40

Though the Admiralty may have been somewhat complacent, the course of the submarine war prior to the fall of France suggests that they were not far out.[29] Up to March 1940, when the U-boats were diverted to support the Norwegian campaign, they had sunk 854,719 tons of shipping for a loss of seventeen U-boats, a ratio of tonnage sunk per loss of 16.6, not very different from 1918. The U-boat offensive was handicapped by unreliable torpedoes, teething problems with the new submarines and slow refits. The German objective was unclear; they do not seem to have intended unrestricted attacks but were driven to it by over-enthusiastic commanding officers and the impossibility of observing the Prize Rules.[30] At the outbreak of war there were fifty-seven U-boats in commission of which thirty-nine were available for operations; too few for Wolf Pack attacks. A big building programme was started but would take some time to get new boats to sea.

U-boats began using French bases from August 1940 which increased their time in operational areas by 25 per cent.[31] This was partially offset by the need to allocate more boats to train the new crews coming forward. Overall, the balance swung in favour of the submarine and the RN identified the following problems.

Inadequate number of effective ships
Weapons and sensors with inadequate capability against submarines either running deep or on the surface.
Poor endurance.
Speed.
Seakeeping.

In addition, the need was seen for improvement in the training of individuals, of crews in their ship and of escort groups. This aspect will not be dealt with here but it may well have proved decisive in winning the Battle of the Atlantic.[32]

Sensors and weapons

The range of sensors and the characteristics of the weapons had a major effect on the number of ships required and on their attributes.[33] In the early years the Asdics of the 121-128 type had a range of about 1300yds in average conditions with 2500yds in ideal conditions. This short range meant that large numbers of escorts were needed to guard the perimeter of a convoy. There was a big advance in 1942 when the advantage of big convoys was realised in that the length of the perimeter and hence the number of escorts needed increased only as the square root of the number of ships in the convoy.

Initially, the only sensor which could detect a surfaced submarine was the human eye and even after the

Torrid was used for trials of an ahead-firing weapon in the 1930s. Mounted in A position it fired a stick bomb to 800yds. It was abandoned for unknown reasons. (Author's collection)

Clematis on completion in the original 'Flower' class configuration. Note the short forecastle which meant a walk across the open well deck to get to the bridge or bring food from the galley. (Author's collection)

introduction of early radars, the eye remained the best sensor until the end of 1942. Radar began to enter service in escorts early in 1941 with the Type 286 with a fixed aerial which could detect objects within about 50° either side of the bow. It is claimed that it could detect a surfaced submarine at 6000yds.[34] The first centimetric set, Type 271, entered service in *Orchis* in March 1941 and by the end of the year there were fifty sets at sea. The early radars were, perhaps, of greater value in helping escorts to keep station while zigzagging on a dark night than in detecting submarines. The introduction of voice radio in early 1941 also eased the problems of the escort commander and made group action more effective.

Forcing a submarine to submerge was, in itself, an important achievement, reducing its speed from 17kts on the surface to a usual 3-4kts submerged (9kts maximum but the battery would be exhausted in one hour). If an escort could be spared it could maintain contact with the submarine for hours until air or the battery ran out.

In 1939 the only weapon which could be used by surface ships against a submerged submarine was the depth charge, little changed since 1917. The 1939 Mark VII had a charge of 290lbs of Amatol and was thought to have a lethal radius of 30ft, but in service, the lethal radius against the tough, welded hull of a U-boat was more like 20ft though damage at 40ft might force the submarine to surface.[35] The combination of early Asdic and depth charges was not very effective; in the first 6 months of the war there were 4000 attacks resulting in 33 sinkings.

There were two related problems. The shape of the sound beam from an Asdic set meant that contact was lost as the attacking ship got close, enabling the submarine to change course, speed or depth undetected. The Mark VII depth charge sank at 7-10ft/sec adding considerably to the dead time. In late 1940 the Mark VII 'heavy' was introduced which sank at 16ft/sec and its

Giffard, a modified 'Flower', note the increased sheer and bow rake together with the taller bridge. She was built in Aberdeen as *Buddleia* and transferred to the RCN as *Giffard*. (Author's collection)

Minol charge was lethal at 26ft. Dropped in patterns of ten, effectiveness increased considerably. In December 1942 the 'One Ton' depth charge was introduced with a 2000lb charge which was fired from a torpedo tube, sank at 21ft/sec and was said to be as lethal as pattern of ten Mark VIIs. A further improvement came in 1943 with the Q attachment, fitted to earlier Asdics, which could hold contact to much closer range. The 144 set entered service in 1943 and was a much more capable set with better detection and classification properties. Many of its features were retro-fitted to earlier sets.

The true answer lay in the ahead-throwing weapon which would fire whilst the submarine was in the Asdic beam. Such a weapon had been tested in the early 1930s in *Torrid* but had been abandoned in 1934.[36] Hedgehog was the first such weapon to enter service. It fired twenty-four contact-fused bombs, each weighing 65lbs, forming a circular pattern, 40yds in diameter, centred 200yds ahead of the ship. The charge weight had led to a lengthy and heated argument; the inventor thought a 5lb charge would be sufficient but, in the end, DNC prevailed and a 30lb charge adopted – and that was barely sufficient. Hedgehog was not very successful at first as both installation and maintenance had problems, not surprising since few ships had handbooks. With contact fuses there was no bang without a hit which led to criticism, but in time it became a most successful weapon.

The Squid was a three-barrelled mortar firing depth-fused bombs with a charge of 200lbs Minol to a range of 275yds where they formed a triangle with a side of 40yds. They sank at 44ft/sec to a maximum depth of 900ft. If two Squids were fitted, the bombs were set to explode 60ft apart in depth. Twin Squids were fitted in the 'Loch' class and a few destroyers, and a single Squid in the 'Castle' class. The Squid was designed as a com-plete system with Asdic 147 which had a true depth measuring capability and automatically set the depth on the bomb till the moment of firing. In the last two years of the war, a single depth charge attack had about 6 per cent chance of success, Hedgehog 25-30 per cent, double Squid 40 per cent and single Squid 25 per cent.[37]

It proved very difficult to sink a surfaced submarine as the shells would usually bounce off the rounded pressure hull. Ramming was more certain and by May 1943 some twenty-four U-boats had been sunk in this way. Howver, damage to the escort would typically mean 7-8 weeks in dock and ramming was discouraged as shallow-setting depth charges became available. A special shell for attacking surfaced U-boats, 'Shark', was entering service as the war ended. It weighed 96lbs and could be fired from a 4in gun.

The ships

The Allied objective in the Battle of the Atlantic was the safe arrival of cargoes; sinking U-boats was merely an important means to that end. Keeping a U-boat down until the convoy had passed was a successful tactic and this, together with the short range of the early Asdic led to an emphasis on numbers of ships. The only design which was available and which could be built in numbers was the 'Flower' class and, though they had been designed as coastal escorts, they had to be used on ocean convoys. They were seaworthy in that they were safe in any weather but the loss of operational capability in bad weather was considerable (see Appendix 19).

Building time varied greatly with Smith's Dock (the designer) having the best average building time of 6½ months – the worst yard averaged 19 months. Variations within a yard and, to some extent between yards, were

34 This claim seems unlikely since the much superior 271 could only detect a submarine at 5000yds.

35 A submarine at full speed would cover a distance equal to the lethal radius in under 3 seconds.

36 It fired a 3.5in stick bomb with a range of 800yds.

37 Detailed figures are given in Hackmann, repeated in Brown.

Towy, a typical 'River' class frigate built by Smiths Dock. Note Hedgehog in A position and the 4in gun in B position. (Author's collection)

usually the result of bombing. It is interesting that later ships took longer to build than the earlier ones, contrary to the usual effect of the learning curve, reflecting the combined effect of bombing, shortages of labour and materials and war-weariness.

The design of a 'twin screw corvette', later known as the 'River' class frigate was started late in 1940 and the ships began to enter service from mid-1942. Their structure was a little more refined than the 'Flowers' but still to commercial standards. Most of them used two sets of reciprocating engines, similar to the single set of the 'Flowers'. They had similar Asdics to the earlier ships and the weapon was initially the depth charge though they carried up to 150 of them. Hedgehog was added as it became available.

In 1942, a large programme of 'Lochs' and 'Castles' was started, carrying the Squid/Asdic 147 system.[38] The 'Loch' was seen as the more desirable ship but the smaller vessel could be built on slips too short for a frigate. The original programme envisaged some 120-145 'Lochs' and 70-80 'Castles' in service by the end of 1944. Detailed plans, matching hulls to slips came up with 133 'Lochs' and 69 'Castles' and 226 sets of machinery were ordered in December 1942. Thanks to an improved hull form from AEW Haslar, the 'Castles' were ½kt faster than the smaller 'Flowers' with the same machinery.[39]

The 'Castles' were built using traditional methods but the 'Lochs' were to be built 'on American methods', *ie* prefabricated. The first of the class, *Loch Fada*, was

Loch More. The author was serving in her at the time this photo was taken. The 'Lochs' were the most deadly U-boat killers of the war and were effective well into the 1950s. (Author's collection)

built by John Brown[40] and drawings were prepared from her which enabled structural engineers – mainly bridgebuilders – to produce prefabricated weldments weighing up to 2½ tons.[41] It was found that building time for the hull was considerably reduced though the number of man hours needed increased. Goodall (1 Jan 1943) '. . . [shipbuilders] don't want bridge builders in the job. I got depressed; it looks as though the builders steady opposition to pre fab is gaining ground.'

The design was simplified as far as possible to help contractors not experienced or equipped for shipbuilding. For example, the form was designed with minimum curvature in waterlines and framelines and the sheer line was made up of three straight lines. The majority of structural engineers had no bending slab and could only undertake cold bending. A drawing office was set up in Glasgow by the Shipbuilding Corporation under the direction of WPS Scotland and with about half the draughtsmen from structural engineers. The number of drawings prepared was about four times the number which would have been used in a contemporary shipyard. Henry Robb laid off the lines and prepared all the moulds. It was estimated that the cost of a 'Loch' was about 50 per cent more than if built using normal methods.

There were thirteen shipyards which assembled 'Lochs' and five which acted as specialist outfitters. The number of structural engineers involved was very considerable and can only be summarised in the incomplete table below.

Item	No of firms involved
Keel	8
Shell longitudinals	1
Web frames	2
Plating	5
Stringer and sheer	4
Lower deck	6
Upper deck	7

This table omits about fifty headings, with their sub-

contractors. In addition, six shipbuilders supplied from other bilge and superstructures.

Most of the problems in the programme were correctly identified but few were solved. The electrical work was much more extensive than in earlier classes so that it was estimated that 400 extra electrical fitters would be needed but few were found and many lost to the Army.[42] Installed electric power is a good measure of the complexity of the ship and hence of its cost.

Installed electrical power

Class	Cost (£1000)	Power (KW)
'Flower'	90	15 (15 added later)
'River'	240	180
'Castle'	190	105
'Loch'	300	180
Black Swan	360	190-360

Centralised outfitting yards were set up at Dalmuir for Clyde built ships and at Hendon Dock for the North East coast, but mainly due to shortage of skilled labour, they could not keep up with the delivery of hulls. By 1945, the yards were full of ships whose fitting out was delayed but, since the Battle of the Atlantic was almost over, such delay was not serious.

It is not easy to compare US and British production but, in general, US building times were much shorter but took many more man hours and cost more.[43] Comparing these aspects for British-built 'Rivers' with US-built 'Colonies' (based on the Rivers) and US 'Captains':

Escort costs and building times

Class	'River'	'Colony'	'Captain'
Fastest building time (months/days)	7/5	5/0	1/23
Man hours (1000)	350-400		600-700
Cost (£1000)	240	560	

38 Goodall, 6 May 1943. He attended the Board meeting to approve the 'Loch' class and was horrified that the First Lord, Alexander, wanted to replace the Squids with a 4in gun!

39 Goodall, 3 Sept 1942. 'At Smiths Dock. Told Reed to give plenty of beam to new single screw corvette and good bilge keels but not a bar keel.' A variant of the 'Flower' class was tested at Haslar with a straight line form to ease production. It was 14½ per cent more resistful at 16kts and 6½ per cent more at 10kts. Other straight line forms had smaller penalties and it is probable that this 'Flower' form could have been improved.

40 Laid down 8 June 1943, completed 29 March 1944.

41 Goodall, 9 July 1943. 'Controller re Clydebank frigate; he agreed that this must be built as a prototype and this may mean ship more slowly built than if Clydebank did more work.'

42 Wartime propaganda made much of the work of women in shipyards. In fact, few were attracted and the value of these few was limited by trade union opposition.

43 I L Buxton, *Warship Building and Repair During the Second World War* (Glasgow 1998). Note that similar ratios applied to merchant ships; a Liberty ship cost £450,000 and took 500-650,000 man-hours compared with £180,000 and 350,000 for a similar British Empire vessel.

Carisbrooke Castle. A clever design for a ship to be built on slips too short to build 'Lochs'. Though bigger than the 'Flowers', they were faster with the same machinery due to a better hull form, developed at Haslar. (World Ship Society)

Rupert, a steam version of the US-built 'Captain' class. (World Ship Society)

US-built ships, 'Captains' and 'Colonies'

The 'Captain' classes (USN 'DE') derived from BuShip's studies from 1939 onwards for small destroyers which could be built quickly and cheaply.[44] These ideas had begun to crystallise when, in 1941, the RN asked for 100 escort vessels with a dual-purpose armament. As the 5in/38 was scarce, they were armed with three 3in/50, even though their shells would be unlikely to penetrate a submarine pressure hull. The RN asked for 112 depth charges, later increased to 180, with eight throwers and a Hedgehog. A tall open bridge of British style was also required.

Engine supply was a problem and the first class (USN *Evarts*) were fitted with four 1500bhp diesels, driving twin shafts through DC generators and motors for a speed of 21kts (DE). The next class (USN *Buckley*) had turbo-electric machinery giving 24kts (TE).[45] They had twin rudders which gave a 25 per cent reduction in turning circle compared with a single rudder. Both the 'Captain' classes were flush deck with considerable sheer forward to reduce wetness. They were unduly stiff which led to heavy rolling (see Seakeeping appendix). They entered RN service from the first quarter of 1943, missing the worst of the battle, but scoring many successes. The 'Colony' class were adapted by the US Maritime Commission from the 'Rivers'.[46] They had three single 3in guns. Their reciprocating engines were Skinner 'Uniflow', supposedly more efficient but unreliable in service.

The ten ex-US Coast Guard cutters are generally understood to have poor stability. However, a letter from Mr R F Linsell (Lt Cdr RNR retd), who served as engineer officer in *Gorleston* gives a rather different story.[47] The stability statement was based on a Coast Guard inclining in February 1941 which showed a negative GM in the light condition, so the RN imposed a limit of fuel not to drop below 50 tons. In August 1942 she was refitted in Immingham and a Hedgehog added.

A new inclining gave quite respectable stability and Linsell re-checked the USCG figures finding an arithmetical error. Their stability was satisfactory but their subdivision was poor.

There were discussions in 1943 over a proposed Anglo/US joint design.[48] It seems to have started about May and died in August 1943.[49] The principal features included a simple rugged hull with good seakeeping, a speed of 24kts and endurance of 6000 miles at 15kts (12½ per cent allowed for fouling). Fitted for Arctic and tropical service, they had a complement of 9 officers and 180 men. Officers accommodation was under the bridge, with the men split fore and aft. The armament consisted of two 5in single with director, two twin 40mm, 5-6 Oerlikon, a triple 21in torpedo tubes, two DC racks, 4 throwers each side, 100 DC, 10 reloads for Hedgehog and 20 for Squid. It was hoped all this could be done on 1700 tons.

Marine engineering

During the Depression, when many shipyards closed, supporting industries suffered as badly or worse. Marine engineering firms capable of building turbine plants and their gearing were fully occupied with major warships and there seemed no alternative to the steam reciprocating engine.[50] It was also believed, probably wrongly, that the reservists manning these ships could not cope with more advanced machinery. Later, it took only six weeks to convert such men to the advanced machinery of the 'Captains'.

Resources, particularly labour, were limited, even for reciprocating engine production. The marine engineering work force did rise from 58,000 in 1939 to 85,000 in March 1942 but the increase was mainly in unskilled men. Between September 1939 and December 1945 942 sets of reciprocating engines were produced totalling 1,800,700ihp.

44 N Friedman, *US Destroyers* (Annapolis 1982), Ch 7.

45 B H Franklin, *The Buckley Class Destroyer Escorts* (London 1999).

46 Goodall, 12 Jan 1944. 'Inspected drawing of Maritime Commission frigate; told DDNC to see first to arrive is carefully inspected.'

47 Responding to my chapter in *Atlantic Escorts.*

48 ADM 1 13479 24 June 1943.

49 Goodall, 5 April 1943.' McGloghrie re start to standardised US & RN escort.'

50 I am not convinced that turbine builders were fully involved.

51 Even allowing for some evasive action, convoy routes did not depart greatly from a great circle route.

Availability

Averaged over the whole war, at any time 22 per cent of escort vessels were unavailable for operations. The worst time was late 1940 when so many were repairing damage from Dunkirk, and winter was notably worse than summer due to storm damage. Some specific class problems may be recognised. The early corvettes often completed with poorly aligned crankshafts which caused early bearing failure. The older British destroyers had no intrinsic problems but old age led to leaking rivets causing misery for the crews and contaminated fuel and feed water. The ex USN 'Town' class suffered from incurable 'condensenitis' as the tube plates were weak and not parallel, from bearing problems due to corrosion of the cast iron housing as well as leaky rivets and bridges too weak to withstand the impact of heavy seas.

The 'Captain' classes, with either machinery fit, had few problems but the reciprocating engines of the 'Colony' class were troublesome showing the fallacy of believing that simple machinery is necessarily reliable.

Endurance

The North Atlantic is a big ocean: Halifax to Liverpool was 2485 miles on the most direct route.[51] A typical convoy would travel some 3000 miles taking 14-19 days but escorts would cover many more miles, zigzagging and prosecuting contacts and might also use high speed at times. Refuelling at sea was only introduced in 1942 and was a slow and unreliable operation. The older destroyers were unable to cross the Atlantic without refuelling and other classes had only a marginal capabil-

Endurance

(The figures which follow are nominal and the true figure in service was almost certainly less, but they are comparable)

Destroyers	Class	Miles/kts	Oil (tons)	(Long range versions)	
	'V' & 'W'	3180/14	450	2680/14	450
	'B'	2440/14	390		
	'E'	3550/14	480		
	'H'	4000/14	329		
	'Town'	2000/14	284	2780/14	390
Sloops					
	Fowey	4000/14	329		
	Black Swan	4710/14	425		
Frigates and Corvettes					
	'Flower'	3850/12	233	(5650 with WT boilers)	
	'Castle'	7800/12	480	(6200 @ 15)	
	'River' Trpl ex	4630/14	470	6600	
	'River' Turbine	4920/14	470	7000	
	'Loch'	4670/14	730		
	'Captain' DE	4670/14	197		
	'Captain' TE	3870/14	335		

ity. The Long Range Escorts (mainly 'V' and 'W' class destroyer conversions) lost a boiler room and a little speed to get increased fuel stowage.

Speed

The submerged speed of a submarine was 3-4kts and the speed of the escort was irrelevant while hunting. The

Lawson, one of the diesel version of the 'Captains'. (Author's collection)

Somaliland, a US-built (Maritime Commission) frigate of the 'Colony' class. They were based very closely on the 'River' class but were much more expensive. Their machinery was unreliable. (Author's collection)

maximum speed at which Asdic could be used was about 15kts. On the surface the U-boat could make about 17kts which set a minimum requirement for escorts; one missed by the 'Flowers'. The real need for speed was in rejoining the convoy after a prolonged hunt astern, and the staff wanted 25kts, satisfied only by destroyers and the turbine 'Captains'. For this reason, the faster ships were usually left to prosecute a contact.

When dropping depth charges over the stern, a small turning circle was useful. The 'Flowers' were outstanding because they were short, the 'Captains' with twin rudders far better than British frigates and destroyers and the 'Towns' awful.

Turning circles

	Diameter (yds)	Speed (kts)
'Flowers'	136	
'Rivers' & 'Lochs'	330-400	12
'Captain' DE	280	16
'Captain' ET	359	18
RN Destroyer	370	10
	404	15
	600	30
'Towns'	770	15

Human factors

North Atlantic escort duty was inevitably exhausting, particularly in winter. Today, it is recognised that the combat efficiency of the crew is increased if they are well fed and can rest properly when off duty but this was not recognised during the war and British ships fell well short of what was possible and desirable. There was an impression that sailors were tough and almost revelled in discomfort; in particular, it was thought that discomfort was necessary to keep men awake when on duty. It was also claimed that hammocks were more comfortable than bunks in rough weather, though there

was no obvious desire amongst officers, most of whom had used hammocks, to give up their bunks. The traditional RN messing was unlikely to provide a balanced diet.

The early, short-forecastle 'Flowers' were the worst. They had bunks in the forecastle where the motion was worst and to reach the bridge or engine room meant crossing the open well deck, inevitably getting soaked in rough weather. Worse still, the galley was aft and food had to be brought along the open deck to the mess, getting cold, if not spilt on the way. As more equipment was added, overcrowding got worse. The following quotation sums up conditions very well.[52]

> It was sheer unmitigated hell. She was a short fo'c'sle corvette and even getting hot food from galley to fo'c'sle was a tremendous job. The mess decks were usually a shambles and the wear and tear on bodies and tempers was something I shall never forget. But we were young and tough and, in a sense, we gloried in our misery and made light of it all. What possible connection it had with defeating Hitler none of us bothered to ask. It was enough to find ourselves more or less afloat the next day and the hope of duff for pudding and a boiler clean when we reached port.

Ventilation was grossly inadequate, contributing to the high incidence of tuberculosis, and, in the first fifty-six ships the side was unlined. From 1940 onwards, the side was sprayed with asbestos which would cause the death of many who worked in shipyards. Washing and toilet facilities were crude and insufficient.

The frigates were a little better as they were bigger, reducing vertical accelerations and hence seasickness, they had covered access fore and aft and their later design remedied some of the defects of the 'Flowers'. With only a little thought and a slight increase in cost much of this unnecessary discomfort could have been avoided. Monserrat compares two ships which he commanded, the US 'Colony' class and the 'River' on which it was based.[53] The American ship had a laundry,[54] ice

52 J B Lamb, *The Corvette Navy* (London 1979) – and he was describing a Canadian corvette whose galley was further forward than in British ships.

53 N Monserrat, HM *Frigate* (London 1946).

54 So did *Warrior* in 1860!

55 The author served in the unmodernised submarine *Tabard* in early 1951 and the 'Lochs' were the only escort vessels we feared in exercises. I then transferred to *Loch More* which confirmed my views on their excellence.

Catherine. The US equivalent of the *Algerines*. (World Ship Society)

water in each mess, a dishwasher, potato peeler, cafeteria messing, good insulation and ventilation, an internal communication system and was still built more quickly – and no one can suggest that USN sailors were soft.

One cannot leave the topic of human factors without emphasising the importance of the 'ace' on both sides. Men such as Walker, Gretton and others and on the other side, Kretschmer, Prien etc, were good enough to distort all statistics. The difference was that escort commanders lived to improve their skills, and to pass them on while U-boat commanders had a short life.

Some miscellaneous topics

Bridges. The layout of bridges was – and is – an emotional subject but RN opinion was unanimous in advocating open bridges and, with 30-50 per cent of first contacts made visually (up to the end of 1942) they were surely right. There was, however, an unrecognised price to pay in exhaustion leading to impaired decision-making. The USN favoured enclosed bridges and gun houses.

Life saving. The question of escape is closely related to habitability. Though losses of escort vessels were not unduly high, many of their crews found sleeping difficult in the lower mess decks and cabins with a long and tortuous route to the upper deck and preferred to rest, if possible, close to the upper deck. Adequate escape routes add greatly to peace of mind, when sinking may be very rapid, and men will stay at their posts longer when they know that escape is easy.

Very little thought had been given to lifesaving gear before the war. Boats could not be lowered in time and neither they nor the Carley float gave protection from exposure. The inflatable lifebelt was shown to be dangerous in tests just before the war but was put into production without change. A very high proportion of deaths of naval personnel occurred in the water after successful escape from the ship. The task of rescuing survivors from the water was all too frequent and, once again, little thought had been given to it before the war.

How good were they?

It is quite easy to draw attention to good points and bad points in the various classes of escorts but, it is less easy to draw an overall conclusion. The double Squid and associated Asdic was by far the most effective weapon system and gave the 'Lochs' pride of place as U-boat killers.[55] Single Squid probably came second but not far ahead of Hedgehog once experience had been gained with that weapon.

Destroyers were fast and able to catch up after a hunt. Many had inadequate endurance and the 'V' and 'W' long range escorts lost a boiler but could still make 25kts with a very respectable endurance and more living space. The combination of high speed and shallow draught meant that destroyers were very prone to slam-

Hedgehog was unpopular when it entered service for a number of reasons (see text), one of which was an accidental explosion which demolished the bridge of the *Escapade*. (World Ship Society)

A W Watson, who was responsible for escort vessels during the Second World War. (Author's collection)

56 The author led the design of the current 'Castle' class OPV. There was little in their hull design which could not have been used in 1939 but they would have been steam engined.

57 The use of kills/ship in service is an interesting statistic but not overriding. I used it in my Battle of the Atlantic paper and a more refined approach is due to D J Collingwood, 'WWII Antisubmarine Vessels', *Warship World* 5/11 (1997), p14

58 D K Brown, 'The 1945 Sloops', *Warship World* 3/3 (1989), p15.

ming, the effects accentuated by light structure. They were also wet and could have done with more freeboard. Turning circles were wide, but this became less important once Hedgehog was fitted.

The early pre-war sloops seem to have been generally satisfactory. The heavy AA armament of the later sloops from *Bittern* to the *Black Swan*s enabled them to operate in the Bay of Biscay where targets were plentiful. Even though their fire control was poor, the volume of fire would put most bombers off their aim. Their success rate is due to a considerable extent to the genius of Captain 'Johnny' Walker and it seems that appointment to a *Black Swan* was sometimes the reward for a successful officer.

The 'Flowers' were intended for coastal work and had many drawbacks for ocean work. They were so short that pitch and heave motions were very severe, which led to a high incidence of sea sickness and, probably, impaired decision-making, whilst their habitability was poor in every aspect. Their bilge keels were inadequate in size which led to heavy rolling and they were too slow to keep up with a surfaced submarine. On the other hand, they were cheap and could be built quickly, in large numbers, so important in the days of short-range Asdics. The concept of a cheap escort was valid in 1939 but the 'Flowers' were not a good design. Something on the lines of the 'Castle' class even with a depth charge armament would have been better.[56] As Goodall wrote 'moral is don't try and force cheap ships on the Navy which, as Winston says "always travel first class"'.

The 'Rivers', originally known as twin screw corvettes, were bigger and faster but with the same Asdic and depth charge fit. Hedgehog was fitted to both classes later. The table below compares the number of successes of 'Flowers' and 'Rivers' in the Atlantic, related to the number operational. A kill is credited if a ship of that class participated in the sinking. Figures are shown as 'Flower'/'River'.

There are clear indications that the bigger and faster 'River' were more effective in killing U-boats than the 'Flowers' but they were twice as expensive, used two sets of the scarce engines and do not seem to have been twice as effective. There is a more fundamental point; the Allied objective during the Battle of the Atlantic was the safe arrival of cargoes and sinking U-boats was only an important means to that end. It is probable that the more numerous 'Flowers' were better than the

'Rivers' at keeping U-boats down and out of reach.[57]

The 'Castles' were a little longer than the 'Flowers', making them better seaboats and their long forecastle gave covered access over most of the length. Even in a single mounting, Squid was a very effective weapon. The 'Colonies' were US versions of the 'Rivers' with the usual excellent living standards but handicapped by unreliable engines. The 'Captains' were expensive ships but their advanced machinery was very reliable and easy to operate. Once the initial rolling problems had been overcome, they were good seaboats and the turbine ships were fast.

Contemporary lessons

Lessons as perceived at the time were summarised in the requirements for the '1945 Sloops'.[58]

25kts in rough weather.
Double Squid; later Limbo (A/S mortar Mk 10)
Good turning circle.
Twin 4.5in gun.
Easy to build.

After many changes, these ships entered service as the *Whitby*, *Leopard* and *Salisbury* classes. They were all good designs, the *Whitby*s outstanding, and one can only agree with the committee which drafted the 1945 requirement – though they were hardly easy to build.

Hindsight

It is interesting to speculate on what should have been built before the war. The 'Flowers' were seen as superior to trawlers for coastal work but a larger ship such as the 'Castle' (or, even better, similar to the current 'Castle' class OPV) would have been more effective and little more expensive. The Vickers diesels for the 'T' class submarine could have been fitted, though additional manufacturing facilities would have been needed.

Since the fall of France was unexpected, the need for open-ocean escorts did not seem pressing in comparison with other urgent needs but it would have been wise to design and build a prototype or two of a more capable ship with turbine machinery, perhaps re-using the machinery from 'S' class destroyers when they were scrapped. A ship of 1500-2000 tons would have reached 26-27kts and carried 450 tons of oil. In the late 1930s such a ship would have had a 'River' class armament but a big growth margin would have been wise. It should have had a long forecastle and high freeboard, twin rudders, deep bilge keels and as deep a draught as possible. It might have looked like a two-funnelled *Black Swan*. However, hindsight is easy and the staff and constructors did the best they could with very limited resources, and the progress of the war until France fell seemed to justify their plans.

U-boat kills ('Flower'/'River')

Year	1940	1941	1942	1943	1944	1945
Average No in Atlantic	18/0	50/0	74/8	65/17	47/20	31/19
Kills	1/0	7/0	6/1	16/7	2/5	1/1
Kills/ship (%)	5/-	14/-	8/12	25/41	4/25	3/5

Miscellaneous Vessels | *Eight*

A S WELL AS the principal warship types described in Chapters 1 to 7, numerous ships and craft of many different types were designed and built or converted. In this chapter the problems of some of these vessels will be outlined without any attempt to describe every individual category.

Light coastal craft[1]

Only two of the 116 First World War coastal motor boats (CMB) remained in the Navy.[2] The ambitious building programme of 1923 (see Introduction) did envisage one experimental CMB each year from 1924. Although this came to nothing, it shows that there was still interest in fast motor boats.[3] By the mid-1930s a considerable number of fast, hard chine motor boats were in service as ships' boats and between the wars Thornycroft had built over forty motor torpedo boats for other navies, based on the 55ft CMB. In 1935 Scott-Paine of the British Power Boat Company (BPB) proposed a 60ft torpedo boat with a service speed of about 33kts.[4] They carried two 18in torpedoes, launched

through the transom. The initial order was for six boats, later increased to 18,[5] the first entering service in mid-1936. Goodall went on trials, writing;

> With Controller at Scott-Paine.[6] He met us in MTB and took us down Southampton Water; ship behaved well but should think would be easily picked up on hydrophones. I don't see they are of much military value but as ships I was impressed . . . offered help of Haslar.[7]

MTB 34, a Vosper MTB. (Author's collection)

1 D K Brown (ed), *Design and Construction of British Warships 1939-45* (London, 1996) Vol 2 Light Coastal Craft, p78. This is a general reference for the chapter. This chapter of that book was written by W J Holt and was modified slightly as W J Holt, 'Coastal Force Design' *Trans INA* (1947), p186. The former is referenced as *Design and Construction*, the latter as Holt *INA*. Much of the data has been supplied by Geoffrey Hudson, a friend from schooldays and historian of the Coastal Forces Veterans Association.

2 Even today one First World War ML survives as a houseboat. The 70ft *CMB 103*, designed to lay magnetic mines, is in Chatham Dockyard. The similar *104* is a houseboat. Both were recommissioned 1942-4. *CMB 4* is to be seen in the Imperial War Museum, Duxford.

3 On 11 August 1918 a force of six CMBs were attacked by German seaplanes which sank three and drove the others into internment in Holland. In the author's view, this should have marked the beginning

of the end of fast motor boats for naval work, at least in daylight.

4 Up to 37kts at light trials displacement.

5 Also *MTB 100* ex-*MMS51*.

6 The controller was Henderson who was very keen on these craft. See Holt *INA*, p205, discussion by Goodall– 'I did not see eye to eye with him in details.'

7 Goodall, 26 April 1937. The military value of these craft will be discussed later.

MGB 65, an early British Power Boat Design. (Imperial War Museum: A7630)

ative seakeeping trials off the Isle of Wight in Sea State 4 the Scott-Paine boat was much drier than the Vosper one but the latter was thought to have the stronger bottom. There were also a few other experimental craft such as the White hydrofoil *MTB 101* which was a failure – Goodall; 'I was not impressed . . .'.[12]

Engines

It was recognised from the start that availability of engines would be a limiting factor in any serious MTB building programme. At a meeting in February 1938 various possibilities were considered. The Napier Sea Lion was available and now reliable in the 60ft boats but at 500bhp would only be suitable for MASB. The only currently available 1000bhp engine was the Italian Isotta Fraschini which of course ceased to be available in June 1940.[13] A marine version of the Merlin would be available in 6 months from a go-ahead.[14] Similarly, the Napier Sabre could be adapted to a 1700bhp marine engine in 2 years. All these were petrol engines and a lightweight 1000bhp diesel was highly desirable but development would take at least 3 years with no certainty of success. None of these options was followed up and as a result twelve short MTB completed with 900bhp Hall-Scott engines giving a top speed of 25kts. These under-powered engines gave our boats a bad reputation, until the American Packard became available.[15] In all, 4686 of these engines came to Britain, initially at a cost of $21,500 plus a 10 per cent commission to British Power Boats. In this desperate situation, a very advanced steam plant was designed for the steam gunboats. It was quite reliable but very vulnerable even to machine gun bullets and was not repeated.[16] The machinery and the lightweight hull meant that they could only be built at the expense of destroyers and only seven of the planned sixty were built.[17]

There were no suitable weapons available either and a variety of guns such as the 2pdr Rolls and various machine-guns were fitted. Gradually, the Oerlikon, pompom and the 6pdr followed. The 4.5in 8 cwt gun was just too late for the war.

These 60ft MTB along with a MASB version and two Vosper MTB were the only boats in service at the outbreak of war. It therefore follows that there were very few officers with experience of this type of craft and none of them of senior rank.[8]

In 1935-6, Vosper's built a bigger (68ft) and much faster craft as a private venture which was purchased as *MTB 102*.[9] This had a speed of 35.5kts at 31 tons, 43.7kts on trial. Goodall wrote;

> At sea in Vosper MTB. Sea very smooth. Speed [about 17 tons displacement] 43.9. Vibration small [I suspect he means motions] similar to Scott-Paine ie small amplitude, small period. Turning good but not as good as SP, control not so good. But other people besides SP can build this type and if we were permitted we'd beat them all.[10]

In early 1938 Scott-Paine also built a bigger and faster boat with a speed of 40.5kts, 44.4kts trials.[11] In compar-

Grey Goose, a steam gunboat, commanded by Peter Scott. After the war she was used for trials of gas turbines and at the time of writing she is still afloat as a houseboat. (Author's collection)

Hull form

All the pre-war boats (except *101*) were of hard chine form as were almost all the wartime short boats (about 70ft long). For fast boats this form is superior at speeds of V/√L >3 (Knots, feet–25kts for a 70ft boat), but is considerably more resistful at lower speeds. Before the war, the Admiralty (W J Holt) developed two forms for longer boats which were tested at Haslar between August and November 1939. That later used for the Fairmile Type 'D' was described by Holt as '. . . grafting a destroyer type bow onto a fast motor boat stern in an attempt to obtain less pounding when driven at high speed into a head sea and also to produce a dry boat forward' The other form was used for Camper and Nicholsons boats from *501* onwards and was a round bilge form. From *511* they had a knuckle carried well aft.[18] These craft were thought by their crews to be more comfortable than the 'D' types.[19] *501* was designed by Holt starting in 1938 as an anti-submarine boat.[20] She would have carried a 3in gun, two twin 0.5in MG and either twelve depth charges or two torpedo tubes. Engine fit was altered frequently. The original intention was four 1000bhp Paxman diesels which would have given 31kts. Lack of availability changed this to three Paxmans and 27kts. Later still, three Isotta Fraschini were chosen although when this craft was destroyed, her replacement, which later became *MGB 501*, completed with three Packards.[21]

A little-recognised characteristic of fast craft is the loss of stability at high speed due to the different waterplane and pressure distribution. A 110ft boat which has good stability at 30kts might lose 2-3ft of metacentric height at 40kts. At 50kts stability would depend almost entirely on dynamic forces and would probably be satisfactory. DNC's memo submitting the steam gunboat drew attention to this problem. These changes in stability were very difficult to predict and would still cause problems after the war.

The environment

Levels of noise, vibration and motions (pitch, heave, roll etc), were very high in these craft and must have affected the performance of their crews.[22] The effect on physical performance is well documented, the effect on judgement is less clear. In the author's view judgement would certainly have been impaired and accounts for some of the things which went wrong in action.[23]

Weight growth

The original 'D' types had a displacement of 91 tons and made 31kts with four Packards. This was increased to 32½kts at 98 tons in later boats with reduction gearing. By the end of the war the displacement of the heavily-armed combined torpedo/gun boat had reached 120 tons and the speed had fallen to 29kts. A similar trend may be seen in short MTBs where between 1939 and

1942 the displacement rose from 41 tons to 45 tons while the continuous speed fell from 40kts to 34.2kts. By 1944 military load had increased in Vosper boats by 70 per cent over the 1938 version.[24] Clearly, armament (including radar) was valued more highly than speed. DNC pointed out that adding torpedoes to the steam gunboat cost ½kt in speed whilst 30 tons of overload fuel would cost 3kts and risk overstraining the structure.

This weight increase exacerbated the problem of matching propeller and engine characteristics. High power petrol engines could only develop full power over a very limited range of rpm and if the torque required caused a drop in rpm, there would be a very serious loss of power and a risk of damage to the engine. This was made still worse at speeds around V/√L = 1 where the resistance increased suddenly and at higher speeds when propeller performance was affected by cavitation. The problem was alleviated, though not completely solved, when the cavitation tunnel was opened at Haslar in 1942.[25] Up to 4kts extra speed was obtained following tests.[26] This enabled the development of cavitation on a scale model propeller to be observed under controlled conditions and the most suitable propeller selected.

Strength

Driving a small craft at speed through waves imposes very severe loads on the structure and there were a number of failures, particularly in BPB 70ft craft and in early 'D' types. The former was cured when they were redesigned as 71ft 6in boats with help from Holt whilst steel reinforcement largely cured the 'D' type's problem.[27] On the other hand, there were many cases of boats surviving the most severe action damage.

---

8 Captain A Agar VC was probably the senior officer with fast boat experience.

9 *MTB 102* has not only survived until 1999 but still goes to sea. Her designer was Peter Du Cane. Her CO at Dunkirk, Commander Christopher Dreyer DSO DSC, hopes to rejoin her for the 60th anniversary in 2000.

10 Goodall 31 May 1937.

11 Usually referred to as the PV70. Design by George Selman, but at Scott-Paine's insistence it was given a hollow deck line which proved a source of weakness.

12 Goodall 1 October 1936. He thought the drag of the foils was too great.

13 A suggestion that Vosper should build these under licence was not pursued. The Italian price was £5250 each and thought excessive.

14 Scott-Paine held the sole rights to this engine which went to sea in PV70 in October 1938.

15 J Lambert and A Ross, *Allied Coastal Forces of World War II*

(London 1993), Vol II, p180. It was not the same engine as the aircraft Merlin built by Packard under licence.

16 G Moore, 'Steam Gunboats', *Warship 1999*. Also Goodall, 21 Mar 1942. 'Holt back [in office] . . . form of SGB good [Holt used it for the post-war 'Ford' class], ship depends on one boiler, one feed pump. To move in harbour she is towed to save raising steam in big boiler.' Cdr H A K Lay and Cdr L Baker, 'Steam Gunboat Machinery – A Light-weight Steam Plant', *Trans INA* (1949), p108.

17 Admiralty papers generally refer to fifty SGB but Cabinet approval for sixty was obtained.

18 Goodall, 14 March 1941. 'Lost *ML 501* in blitz last Monday, a sad thing for me personally, this was my pet.' The later boats were classified as MGB then MTB but the original *501* was always an ML.

19 D K Brown. 'Fast Warships and their Crews', Small craft Supplement, *The Naval Architect* No 6 (1984). This is based on numerous letters from those who

served in Coastal Forces via Geoffrey Hudson.

20 Ships cover 650.

21 Two from *MTB 101* when she was seen to have failed and the other a spare for *102*.

22 There is an arbitrary distinction between noise and vibration at 1 Hz.

23 This view was strengthened by reading Captain Peter Dickens, *Night Action* (London 1974). In subsequent correspondence, partially reported in my Fast Warships article, Capt Dickens seemed prepared to accept my view whilst hardly any other correspondent did so.

24 Holt *INA*, discussion by Du Cane, p209.

25 Goodall himself had fought a hard battle to get this built.

26 Holt *INA*, discussion by Gawn, p206.

27 Cynics believed that reinforcement made little difference as the boats were then driven faster until they broke again.

MTB 775, a 'Fairmile D' - Dog Boat. She mounts two 6pdrs, a twin Oerlikon, two twin 0.5in machine guns and four torpedo tubes. (Author's collection)

Production

For most of the war, short MTBs were mainly built by various builders to the Vosper 71ft design whilst short gunboats were designed and built by BPB.[28] Long boats were overwhelmingly of the 115ft Fairmile 'D' type. At the outbreak of war the Fairmile organisation under Sir Noel Macklin proposed a design of motor launch designed around sawn plywood frames which could be cut by furniture makers and assembled quickly. A number of these were built as the 'A' class ML and they were followed by the 'B' class to an outline design by Holt adapted for production by Fairmile. The 'D' class MTBs were built on the same principle.[29] Total numbers built were:[30]

Steam Gunboats	7
Short MTB	287
Short MGB	67 (+ 19 MASB)
Fairmile 'D'	209*
Long MTB other	43

*Plus 19 RAF rescue craft

In addition, eighty-three MTBs and forty-one MGBs (including six MASBs) were received from the USA,

ML 100, a 'Fairmile A' class ML. The Fairmile system of building offered great advantages in production (see photo in Chapter 11) but the 'A' class hull was not very successful. (Author's collection)

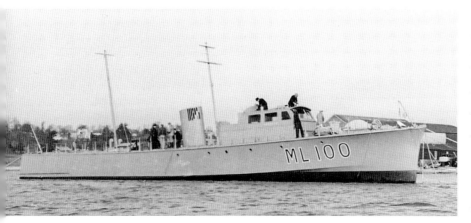

eleven MTB from Canada, and two ex-French short MGB were also acquired. Note also that two 70ft CMB recommissioned and twenty-six short boats were completed before the war.

Motor launches

The first motor launch of the Fairmile 'A' class was started just before the war. They introduced the Fairmile system of prefabricated hulls using many sub-contractors, mainly furniture makers. Widely spaced transverse frames were cut from large sheets of plywood and slotted to receive the longitudinals. These and the other parts were assembled by yacht builders.[31] The 'A' type eventually had three Hall-Scott engines of 600bhp each giving a continuous speed of 22kts (25kts maximum) though some completed with only two engines. Their relatively high speed made them suitable for conversion to minelayers. Twelve were built.

The 110ft 'A' class had very poor endurance due to limited fuel stowage and the high resistance of the hard chine form which also made them poor seaboats. A much more suitable round-bilge form had been designed by W J Holt and tested at Haslar. Holt also produced an outline general arrangement and this was handed over to Fairmile to adapt to their successful building procedures. This design, the 112ft 'B' class of 67 tons, was intended to have three Hall Scott engines but supply was limited and it was decided to fit two only, accepting the loss of speed to get more launches at sea. They were very successful and 388 were built in the UK and a further 266 in the Commonwealth (including 80 for the RCN).[32]

Holt also designed a smaller, 72ft launch for harbour defence which was built by smaller yards using conventional techniques. It displaced 54 tons and had a speed of 11-12kts. These smaller launches were Holt's favourites of which he wrote; 'In a seaway they seemed to possess an unusual harmony of weight, buoyancy and shape forward, in relation to pitching and speed, which enabled them to move in rhythm with the seas to make the best of prevailing conditions.' Three hundred were built in the UK, seventy in the Commonwealth[33] and seventy-four in the USA under Lend-Lease.

W J (Bill) Holt quietly dominated the design of light coastal forces during the war and for some years after. He and his brother (Neville[34]) were enthusiastic yachtsmen and tried to use their knowledge of the sea to design sea-kindly craft. Bill even made a voyage before the mast in a Finnish windjammer when the RN was proposing to build a non-magnetic research ship.

Success?

Light coastal craft claimed to have sunk 574 enemy ships including 49 E Boat/MTB, 26 destroyers, 'M' class minesweepers, corvettes and larger warships and 2 submarines during the war. They fired 1328 torpedoes for 355 probable or certain hits, a 26.7 per cent hit rate, better than that for any other category of ship. The direct cost was 1 steam gunboat, 144 MTBs, 39 MGBs, 80 MLs and 52 HDMLs. It is believed that coastal forces laid 7714 mines in 1373 sorties; nearly double the number of sorties carried out by naval minelayers (*ie* excluding aircraft). Known casualties were 60 warships, 25 auxiliaries and 14 supply ships.

Support of these craft involved setting up numerous bases for training, maintenance and operations and a few depot ships and, it may be argued that the results did not match the effort put in. Personnel peaked at 25,000 in 1944 (compared with *c*300 pre-war). On the other hand, the Axis navies had to devote corresponding efforts to counter that of the Allies.

Motor minesweepers etc

The large-scale use of magnetic mines by the Germans led, in late 1939, to a requirement for a wooden minesweeper of robust construction, about 90ft long and with a draught of less than 8ft. After development by Holt's team, a rather larger motor minesweeper of 105ft length and a draught aft of 12ft 6in was approved. The total weight of ferrous materials, including the engine, was kept down to 50-60 tons to maintain a safe magnetic signature. They were intended to operate the double L sweep for magnetic mines but an acoustic sweep was added soon after the first completed. The double L reel was hand operated and getting in the sweep was an 'all hands' task.

In most aspects they were very successful; Holt wrote that they '. . . were good sea boats and were dry' but were prone to rolling.[35] The problems experienced were mainly associated with the shortage of seasoned timber for the heavy scantlings required. The use of green timber caused their shape to alter, affecting shaft alignment. The shaft was very long and any wooden hull will change shape.[36] They were responsible for the majority of non-contact sweeping in coastal waters. Average building time was 9 months and a total of 278 were built including some in Canada and India.

In late 1941 it was decided to build a class of larger sweepers for use in more exposed waters and more suitable for ocean passages. Holt designed a 126ft craft with acoustic and magnetic sweeps; a few boats were given a wire sweep as well.[37] The structure was stronger and they did not suffer from alignment problems. Holt sees them as even better sea boats than the earlier class, noting that they were particularly dry. The average building time had gone up to 14 months and 85 were built. Both classes were rather slow; 10kts free running, 8-9kts sweeping.

There were also 150 US-built BYMS, 130ft long with a speed (free) of 14.6kts which were equipped for wire, magnetic and acoustic sweeping. Compared with the British MMS the US-built ships were luxuriously equipped though the mess deck, with three high bunks,

was cramped. Holt says they were extremely lively in a seaway though this improved when bilge keels were added. A number of coasters were converted for sweeping magnetic mines using a very large electric magnet to explode the mine at a safe distance.[38] There was even a proposal to use the non-magnetic ship *Research*.[39]

The potential hazard from pressure mines was recognised well before their actual deployment. AEW at Haslar identified the pressure signature of most classes of major warship from which safe speeds in different

Top: HDML 1040. Bill Holt, who was responsible for light coastal force design, wrote that the HDML was his favourite. (Author's collection)

Lower: MMS 32, one of the early 105ft design. They were a little short for open sea work but were invaluable for estuary sweeping. (Vicary)

28 The later 71ft 6in BPB craft were very much stronger than their 70ft private venture design. Holt was involved in the structural design.

29 Holt was an enthusiast yachtsman and loved going to sea in his naval designs. He was never seasick.

30 The figures which follow (including weapon firing) are simplified from a very detailed schedule prepared by Geff Hudson. Some boats were transferred to or from other roles or for other services. Others completed but not taken into service. The figures given do give an indication of the success of the building programme.

31 For a more detailed account see: *British Warships*, p80 and J Lambert and A Ross, *Allied Coastal Forces of World War II*, Vol I, p9.

32 For Holt's account of the Board approval see D K Brown, *A Century of Naval Construction*, p173. There were also two for the Australian army and an uncertain number (about twenty) for the US army. About thirty were cancelled.

33 About fifty cancelled.

34 Who designed the first post-war frigates.

35 The author would agree having experienced a *gregale* off Malta in one of these craft. The bilge keels seem to have been rather small. Also

Goodall, 1 Nov 1941. 'Went to St Monance [now spelled St Monans] to see MMS. Very interesting and looks good solid job.'

36 See *British Warships* for a fuller explanation.

37 Holt was also responsible for the outline design of four classes of motor fishing vessel (MFV). Fifteen of the 75ft vessels were converted for sweeping in rivers and canals.

38 Goodall, 9 Jan 1940. '*Borde* [the first magnet ship] has just blown up four more mines and retired hurt.'

39 Goodall 7 Dec 1939. 'Controller wants *Research* for magnetic [sweeping] a war crime to use that lovely ship for mine sweeping.'

40 Details of these are obscure. See P Elliott, *Allied Minesweeping in World War 2* (Cambridge 1979), p88 (photo). Also Goodall, 9 Mar 1943. 'Controller is worried over clash between Stirling and MAC at Denny.'

41 On the other hand, Goodall, 19 Sept 1942. 'Stirling craft explosion did little damage and my forecast was wrong.'

42 The author directed the ERMISS project in later years, another gallant failure.

43 L E H Maund, *Assault from the Sea* (London 1949).

44 Goodall, 24 April 1939. 'Worked on Fleming design for landing craft; don't like it'.

45 R Baker, 'Notes on the Development of Landing Craft', *Trans INA* (London 1947).

46 Baker's own version is given in full in D K Brown. 'Sir Rowland Baker RCNC' *Warship 1995*.

47 I L Buxton, 'Landing Craft Tank, Mks 1 & 2', *WARSHIPS* 119 (London 1994) In fact, the prototype Mk III was built up from sections of LST 137 and LST 143 after the remaining sections had been lost in November 1941.

48 In 1944 there was a shortage of Paxman engines and seventy-one were built by shipbuilders with Sterling Admiral engines.

49 Baker tells that the steel tank deck would gently undulate as it went through waves.

50 Plus two modified Mk VI for trial.

51 It is remarkable that almost all the Allied landing ships and craft were designed by three men, Baker, Barnaby and Higgins of whom the first and last were very colourful characters. (Brown on Baker, above)

52 A D Baker III (ed), *Allied Landing Craft of World War II* (London 1985); also J D Ladd, *Assault from the Sea* (Newton Abbott 1976).

53 R Baker, 'Ships of the Invasion Fleet', *Trans INA* (London 1957).

54 Design by McMurray, Bartlett, Mitchell.

55 B Macdermott, *Ships without Names* (London 1992).

56 The original request for seven *Boxer*s was changed to LS Dock.

57 One hundred and fifteen were lent to the RN.

58 There was considerable opposition to the LST (3) programme, notably from Lord Leathers, Minister of Transport. ADM 205/32. He was reminded that the programme, both in the UK and in Canada was at the expense of escort vessels and not merchant ships.

59 Goodall, 16 & 19 Dec 1943.

depths were deduced. Two special sweeping devices were built, *Cyrus* and *Cybele* (known as Stirling craft).[40] They were unpowered, 4000 tons, 361ft long, 65ft beam and 25ft draught. They were intended to generate a strong pressure signature and survive an explosion underneath. *Cyrus* completed in 1943 and was badly damaged when a mine was exploded under her stern.[41] She was laid up. *Cybele* completed in January 1944 and was tested to destruction. A number of 'Egg Crates' were built in the USA and some were used by the RN. Details are obscure but they were 3710 tons, 331ft x 64ft x 21ft. Eight *Bangor* class minesweepers were converted to tow them, two of these being able to tow an 'Egg Crate' at 6¼kts. The swept path was very narrow and they were not seen as a success–one mine is claimed! The Stirling craft and the 'Egg Crates' were unsuccessful but they were a sensible first attempt; later ideas have proved little more successful.[42]

Landing ships and craft

Military thinking before the war was dominated by thoughts of static warfare based on the Maginot and Siegfried lines and there seemed little prospect of amphibious operations. In these circumstances, it is surprising how much was achieved.[43] The early landing craft were slow, unseaworthy and expensive but by 1939 a prototype of a good design for personnel (which became the LCA) was available and a prototype for the Landing Craft Mechanised (LCM) was under construction.[44] These two craft were designed by Ken Barnaby of Thornycroft and were built in large numbers. The LCA weighed about 9 tons–it grew to 13½ tons by the end of the war–and could be hoisted in normal lifeboat davits; the LCM could be hoisted but needed special davits for its all-up weight of 36 tons which included a 1-ton tank. By the time of Dunkirk the prototype LCM was the only RN vessel capable of carrying a tank.[45]

Though some thought had been given to a Tank Landing Craft in 1937, no design had been prepared. In June 1940 Churchill started pressing for a shore-to-shore tank carrier. It should carry three of the largest tanks then envisaged (40 tons) at 10kts and land them in 2ft 6in water on a 1-in-35 beach. The designer, Rowland Baker, added some requirements of his own as he was quite convinced that bow doors would always leak. He arranged a sump behind the door to collect minor leakage. In the event of the whole vehicle deck flooding, the side walls provided enough buoyancy and stability to keep the craft afloat and upright.[46]

Thirty of these LCT Mk I were built by shipbuilders, being delivered between November 1940 and April 1941. Though the Mk I was a very good first shot it was soon realised that by increasing the beam by 2ft a second row of tanks could be accommodated. This led to the improved Mk II of which seventy-three were built; the first sixteen by shipbuilders and the remainder by

structural engineers with deliveries from June 1941. They had three shafts driven by Napier Lion engines. Later ones had two or three Paxman diesels. A Mk II was lengthened 32ft and became the prototype Mk III of which 235 were built.[47] They had Paxman diesels on two shafts.[48] A later requirement for landing in very shallow water led to the Mk IV which carried 300 tons of tanks with a draught of 3ft 8in forward and 4ft 2in aft. It was originally intended to be expendable, making a single, one-way channel crossing and was very lightly built.[49] However, with some stiffening, many sailed out to the Far East. Some 787 were built.

The Mk V was built in very large numbers in the USA and 400 were lent to the RN.[50] It was designed to carry tanks from the bigger landing ships to the shore and was based on a sketch by Barnaby. The bigger and much more elaborate Mk VIII was just completing when the war ended. These tank landing craft proved very versatile and were converted to mount 4.7in guns as LCG (monitors) or numerous AA guns as LCF. Others carried large numbers of bombardment rockets (LCT(R)), were adapted as repair craft (LCT (E)) or salvage vessels. At least one was fitted to carry railway engines and there are even rumours of a mobile detention quarters! The LCI was a shore-to-shore personnel carrier to carry 200 fully equipped soldiers, mainly built in the USA, of which nearly 200 served in the RN. Some were converted into headquarters or administration vessels.

The LCA had protection for its passengers against rifle fire while the equivalent USN craft, the LCP, was unprotected but faster. The LCP was designed by Higgins and served in large numbers in both the USN and RN.[51] It was developed into the LCP(R) with a bow ramp and then into the LCV(P) which could carry a small vehicle. This brief account cannot mention every type of landing craft–the author's records lists thirty-six types plus eight types of Landing Barge–nor the problems of design and production involved.[52]

Landing ships

There were three main types of landing ship with many variants. The Landing Ship Infantry were converted merchant ships which at the upper end of the scale ('Glens') carried over 1000 troops, 240 landing craft crews and a ship's complement of 300.[53] Many more were converted cross-channel vessels with six or eight landing craft and up to 600 troops and crew. Though seemingly simple, all presented problems of strength and stability with the heavy weight of landing craft and their davits high up. It was soon realised that combined operations needed a joint headquarters ship and several small merchant ships were so converted.

The first RN tank landing ships were converted tankers with a shallow draught built to operate in Lake Maracaibo.[54] They were quite successful and took part in many landings but were clearly not the answer.[55] The next design originated from Churchill who wanted an enormous vessel; design studies were known as 'Winstons'. This soon proved impractical and a smaller version was designed – 'Winettes' – and three were built. The requirements were very demanding – it will be argued too demanding – 13 Churchill tanks, 27 vehicles and 193 men in addition to a crew of 169. Speed was to be 18kts at beaching draught, 16½kts deep which precluded a shallow draught. In consequence, the three *Boxers* had an enormous bow ramp with a total length of 140ft taking up much of the tank deck when stowed. They, too, proved valuable in several Mediterranean landings.

There were schemes to build seven more *Boxers* in the USA and Baker went to discuss this and other designs.[56] One scheme was for a much simpler LST which was developed in the USA from Baker's study into the LST(2), a war-winning design. Welded hull construction and powerful, lightweight diesels helped to attain a beaching draught forward of only 3ft and a slope of 1-in-30. It could carry 18 Churchill tanks, 27 trucks, 8 jeeps and 177 soldiers (ship's crew of 86) at a speed of 10kts. Even though they were built in very large numbers, there were never enough.[57] The date of several invasions, and the cancellation of others, depended on availability of LSTs.

This shortage led to the LST (3), built in the UK and Canada.[58] The first order was stopped by the Cabinet because of the cost quoted by MF Branch at £550,000. They had not consulted DNC whose estimate was £425,000![59] The only engines available were triple-expansion type from cancelled frigates. These were heavy as was the largely riveted hull and, even though more powerful than the diesels of the Mk (2), they were only a little faster – 13kts instead of 10kts. The LST(2) and (3) had Baker's floating dock section so that they

Glenearn, a Landing Ship Infantry (Large). (Imperial War Museum: A25033)

Upper left: Breconshire, supply ship, sister to *Glenearn*, more or less as converted for Operation Catherine. (Imperial War Museum: A6926)

Lower left: There were many 'one-off' modifications of standard landing craft, too numerous to describe in the text. *LCT 582* is a Mk IV with an upper deck added using Bailey bridge components. (Author's collection)

would float upright with the vehicle deck flooded.[60] A small number of LSTs were converted for other roles such as emergency repair, headquarters, and fighter direction.[61] There was a design for a bigger and faster (14½kt) British LST with turbines on two shafts but it does not seem to have got very far.

Large numbers of small landing craft were needed in the invasion area and special ships were needed to carry them. The first attempt was to use two train ferries which could launch small craft down a chute at the stern – Landing Ship Stern Chute.[62] They could carry thirteen LCM. Three RFA tankers were fitted with large transporter cranes to lift landing craft from deck to sea – Landing Ship Gantry. They carried fifteen LCM which could all be launched in 35 minutes.

The best solution was the Landing Ship Dock, a self-propelled floating dock which could carry thirty-six LCM at 16kts.[63] The original design study was Baker's and it was ordered in the USA. The design was developed in the USA and built for both navies. The dock could be flooded down in 1½ hours and pumped out in 2½ hours at 18,400 gallons per minute. Inevitably, they were also used as floating docks for repair work on small craft.

Both landing craft and landing ships had design features which conflicted to some extent – simplicity, ease of building and of maintenance, light weight (for shallow draught), reliability and seaworthiness. The first landing craft between the wars were propelled by jet units as it was feared that propeller damage would be frequent in beaching. The available units were inefficient, reducing speed and were expensive. It was much cheaper to replace propellers. The *Boxer* class LST had a high speed requirement which led to steam turbine propulsion and a deep draught hull which in turn, required a long ramp taking up much of the vehicle deck.

The design of these ships demands restraint and mutual understanding between staff and designer. Much later, I was to design an LSL of 11,500 tons, 630ft long. This led to the expected dialogue – Staff 'That's not what we wanted' and my riposte 'But it is what you asked for!'

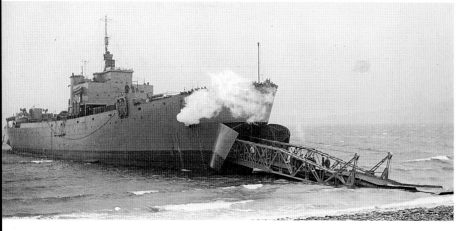

LST 3010, a British built Mk III. They had steam engines ordered for the frigate/corvette programme. (Author's collection)

60 One LST was deliberately flooded as a trial. Would that RO-RO ferries had the same feature.

61 The fighter direction tenders had ballast on the upper deck to *reduce* stability – a rare feature!

62 Baker noted that these commercial ferries would capsize if the train deck was flooded and recommended that the side structures be made watertight in future ferries!

63 Alternative loads: two LCT (3) or (4) or three LCT (5), and 263 army personnel and 36 landing craft crew were also carried.

64 Designed by M K Purvis.

65 Information from G Moore.

66 Goodall, 20 Feb 1943. '6 inch monitor. Controller was horrified at size and cost. He had a little sketch of enemy coasters but they apparently all guns, no endurance and low speed instead of our 15 knots.'

67 This section is based on D K Brown, 'Armed Merchant Ships – A Historical Review', *RINA Conference Merchant Ships to War* (London 1987). See also Dr R H Osborne, *Conversion for War* (World Ship Society 1993).

68 Too seriously in the author's opinion – see conclusions, Chapter 12.

In 1942 the Staff asked for a small monitor mounting two 6in guns with a speed of 15kts. They were surprised at the cost estimated at £285,000 and the delay to frigate and landing craft programmes. Various alternatives were considered, including one of composite construction by Fairmile before the converted LCT was accepted. The table compares the final monitor[64] with various LCG.[65]

1942 Monitor vs LCG

	Monitor	LCG(L)3	LCG(L)4	LCG(M)
Guns	2-6in	2-4.7in	2-4.7in	2-25pdr
Speed (kts)	15½	10	10	11¾
Dspt (tons)	1250	491	570	380
Draught (ft)	6	6	6	5-6

The high cost of speed is notable as is the concept of purpose-built craft. One is reminded of the old adage 'The best is the enemy of the good enough'.[66] These problems can be seen in the LCG (M), originally intended for 15kts and a very elaborate flooding system so that it could sit on the bottom to fire its army-type guns – 25pdr or 17pdr anti-tank.

Conversions[67]

Armed merchant cruisers

The threat of the surface raider was taken very seriously between the wars.[68] In 1920 it was decided that owners would be paid to fit stiffening for guns in fifty suitable ships for conversion into armed merchant cruisers in wartime. In 1936 detailed plans were prepared for a typical liner, the P&O *Carthage*, which could be implemented in three refit phases taking 3, 5 and 10 weeks respectively. Fifty-one British merchant ships were chosen together with two Australian and three Canadian ships and these were allocated to specific dockyards at home or abroad. Each yard would use the *Carthage* plans as guidance for the work on their vessels. This preparatory work was well organised and the actual conversions went smoothly.

The first step was to fit six or eight 6in guns and two 3in AA with stiffening and their magazines. Accommodation was provided for 230 naval personnel in addition to the Merchant Navy engine room crew. Between 1500 and 3000 tons of ballast was installed. Some 1in protection was installed in the second phase. As they became available, more modern guns were installed with director firing in nine ships. A few ships had a cat-

Cilicia, typical of an armed merchant cruiser with Phase 3 modifications including hangar, catapult, radar and modern guns. (Author's collection)

Grain, an Admiralty design trawler. (Author's collection)

69 The *James Ludford* was built for the Admiralty during the First World War but was entirely typical of commercial craft of the period.

70 As late as 1949 Cochranes, one of the best trawler builders, 'measured' stability by balancing cardboard sections on a knife edge!

71 See table on p91 of D K Brown (ed), *Design and Construction of British Warships, 1939-45.* (London 1996), Vol III.

72 D K Brown (ed), *The Design and Construction of British Warships 1939-45*, Vol 3, p13.

73 Goodall, 11 Feb 1944. 'Controller re Fleet Train. I said all clear except for hull repair ships, aircraft maintenance and coastal force workshops. We must wait for LST . . . ', and 3 May 1945.' *Mullion Cove* bad . . . read riot act.'

74 MoD (Navy), *War with Japan* (London 1995), Vol VI, p281.

75 Facetiously known as the 'Fleet Despair Ship *Remorse*'.

A drifter, possibly *Silver Crest*, towing a Mk I skid (designed by W J Holt), an early magnetic mine sweep. (Author's collection)

apult and crane with one or two seaplanes. Later empty oil drums were packed in the 'tween decks around the damaged waterline to preserve buoyancy and stability. This device proved very successful as although fifteen AMCs were sunk, only one capsized (see Chapter 10).

By early 1942 the role of the armed merchant cruiser was over and they became troopships or LSI. *Canton* remained in use until April 1944 by which time she had:

Nine 6in guns on PVII* mounts with director control
Two twin 4in AA
Two 40mm and fourteen 20mm AA
One Kingfisher seaplane with catapult and crane
Two depth charge throwers and three radar sets

Trawlers

There was a major review of AS warfare capability in 1930 which identified a shortage of coastal escorts. It was concluded that much of this shortage could be made good by converted trawlers and in 1933 the *James Ludford* was fitted out as a prototype AS trawler.[69] She was given an Asdic set, twenty-five depth charges and a 4in gun. After experience with her, a number of other trawlers were converted. By 1939 thirty-five trawlers had been purchased and converted either as AS or M/S duties.

The main problem with these and later conversions was lack of stability and, in most cases, lack of informa-

tion on what the stability was.[70] Smith's Dock and a leading consultant were engaged to measure stability and local Warship Production Superintendents would ballast to give a GM of 12ins in the arrival condition (10 per cent fuel and stores). Unnecessary equipment and stores were removed and deteriorated structure – usually the wooden deck over the hold – made good or replaced. A minimum freeboard was laid down, 33ins for the biggest down to 27ins for the smaller ones (drifters 24ins). The capsize of the whaler *Shera* in March 1942 due to icing in bad weather was of particular concern to DNC. She was the only RN ship lost due to weather during the war (excluding landing craft). Damage resistance was negligible though Admiralty design trawlers had a bulkhead between the engine and boiler rooms which made them much safer than commercial vessels.

The magnitude of this programme was impressive; 1706 trawlers, whalers, drifters and yachts were converted for naval purposes.[71] The most numerous were minesweeping trawlers (510) and AS trawlers (209). Whalers were excellent seaboats and presented few problems except inadequate ventilation for hot climates! Trawlers accounted for a considerable proportion of the 126,000 mines swept but the cost was high; 251 trawlers, 107 drifters and 34 yachts were sunk.

The Fleet Train

A committee was set up in 1936 to consider the support of a fleet far from a shore base and by 1939 it was fairly clear what was needed. However, until the Japanese conquests of 1942 there were plenty of bases available and there were better uses for suitable merchant ships. A start was made in early 1942 when five liners were taken up for conversion to depot or repair ships. Planning for the Pacific fleet began in September 1943 and an enormous list was prepared of the ships needed.[72] It was soon clear that far fewer ships would be available as many were needed to feed and re-supply the newly liberated peoples of Western Europe – not to mention the UK.[73]

A considerable number of new ships were made available in Canada but, even so, many of the ships were barely suitable for their roles. There were seven repair ships, twenty-three maintenance ships, three accommodation ships, a seaward defence ship and an amenity ship (Appendix 20). Five more Fleet Train ships were cancelled. In addition, there were tankers, store carriers, tugs, harbour craft, hospital ships and floating docks. Comparatively few completed in time for service during the war.

In July-August 1945 the Fleet Train consisted of ten repair and maintenance ships, twenty-two tankers, twenty-four store carriers, four hospital ships, five tugs, eleven miscellaneous vessels and two floating docks together with six escort carriers and thirty-seven

Forth, submarine depot ship, October 1942. A 'T' class is alongside with a 1940 'S' outboard. The outboard submarine is uncertain but could be *Graph* (ex *U 570*). (Author's collection)

escorts.[74] The brief notes which follow can only outline a few of the numerous problems affecting the Fleet Train.

Repair ships

There was one fleet repair ship before the war, *Resource*.[75] In November 1940 the Cunard liner *Antonia* was taken in hand to become the fleet repair ship *Wayland*. To accommodate the large workshops it was necessary to cut away portions of A, D and F decks and fit additional strengthening in compensation. This involved much extra weight high up and 3000 tons of permanent ballast and 1000 tons of water ballast were added which would ensure that she would float upright

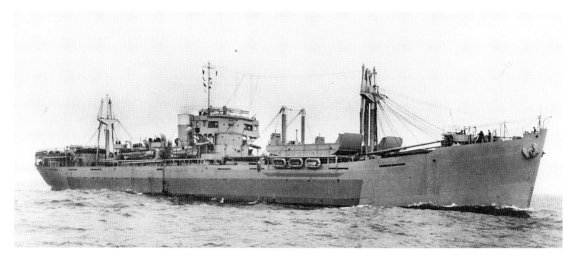

The hull repair ship *Mullion Cove*. (Author's collection)

76 Goodall, 25 March 1942. 'Saw *Antonia*, yard has a huge job to finish by time. I am still sure that this depot ship policy (Depot + warship + WT ship) is all wrong'.

77 *Mullion Cove* and *Dullisk Cove*.

78 Others became store ships retaining their 'Fort' names.

79 The author carried out design studies for such a ship in the late 1970s and would certainly agree that the problems are numerous.

80 Vice-Admiral Sir D B Fisher, 'The Fleet Train in the Pacific War', *Trans INA* (1953), p224.

81 A second ship, *Agamemnon*, was uncompleted when the war ended.

The repair ship *Alaunia*. (World Ship Society)

with any two main compartments flooded. She mounted four single 4in HA and their magazines were protected by 3in of mild steel.[76]

Two of her sisters were converted in 1941, *Artifex* and *Ausonia*. The design was changed to increase their capability for major repairs and they were referred to as base repair ships but, later, base facilities were omitted as well and they became repair ships. These change meant that they had armoured magazines for 4in guns which were no longer fitted. Even more structure was cut away for their big workshops with additional stiffening in lieu. Later *Alaunia* and the P&O liner *Ranpura* were converted on similar lines making four very capable repair ships. They were intended to work with floating docks and also required the support of accommodation ships which provided living quarters for the numerous Special Repair Ratings (Dockyard) needed and for whom there was no space in the repair ships. It was thought that the early repair ships, *Resource* and

Wayland, lacked capability for heavy structural repair work and two PF(C) type cargo ships were converted as hull repair ships to work as a unit.[77] They were still under construction and conversion posed few problems. They were ballasted to the usual 'two compartment standard'.

Maintenance ships for escorts, landing ships and craft, and coastal craft were all converted from 'Fort' type merchant ships building in Canada.[78] The conversions were extensive with extra decks and deckhouses but were not particularly difficult. Equipment varied depending on the type of craft to be serviced and was extensive. Several of these ships remained in service long after the war.

The Aircraft Group

The first requirement was for aircraft maintenance ships for major inspections, servicing and repair to airframes. A new design was prepared but it was too elaborate and,

in order to get them into service quickly, two *Colossus* class carriers were converted as *Perseus* and *Pioneer*. All flying arrangements were deleted, making space available for the new equipment and the men to use it. *Pioneer* just joined the Pacific fleet before the war ended. Aircraft were embarked by crane from lighters and an extra crane was fitted for that purpose (see Chapter 3).

One PF(C) cargo ship was fitted out as an engine repair ship and another as a component repair ship repairing fittings such as hydraulics and electrical equipment. In addition, a number of escort carriers were used as freighters carrying crated aircraft to the advanced base for assembly and checking whence they would be ferried to the operating area in further escort carriers.

Tankers, store ships etc

Before the war the RN relied on numerous fuelling depots world-wide, within the British Commonwealth and little attention was given to refuelling at sea. Early attempts to refuel at sea used the over-the-stern method which was slow and unreliable. The tankers were also slow and could only pump slowly whilst the fighting ships lacked experience. All these problems were tackled but the RN during the war was always well behind USN practice. Two 15kt tankers building by Harland and Wolff were taken up in 1943 and became the start of the 'Wave' class which marked a big advance in capability but only four reached the Pacific before the war ended. They had a pair of derricks over the after tanks which gave some capability for refuelling abeam.

During 1942-3 thought was given to a fast tanker which could accompany an assault force and supply stores and ammunition as well as fuel. It was then decided that such a valuable ship should be protected by fighter aircraft carried on board. There were no resources available for such a complex design and the project was abandoned.[79] Two 17kt tankers under construction were taken over as an interim solution and *Olna* served in the Pacific at the end of the war. An ex-German ship was taken over as *Northmark* (later *Bulawayo*) but she did not complete until December 1945. Post-war, she was used for numerous trials of refuelling equipment and procedures.

The supply of fresh water was a major problem and the Fleet Train was eventually joined by a distilling ship but, as Admiral Fisher describes, this did not end the problem.[80] The distilling ship was the only coal-burning ship in the fleet so the collier was moored alongside but the collier's boiler leaked badly so that she took almost all the output of the distilling ship! Another problem was when the only big tug proved so unreliable that she had to be towed home from her only visit to the operational area.

One cannot omit the uniquely British contribution to the Fleet Train concept, the amenity ship *Menestheus*.[81]

The amenity ship – and floating brewery – *Menestheus*. (Author's collection)

She had a theatre seating 350, quiet rooms, a large NAAFI, a chapel and bars. The latter needed a brewery and one was designed which could brew 250 barrels a week. She reached the Pacific as the war ended but worked successfully for a year until more permanent amenities were available to British forces in the area.

There were many problems in setting up and running the Fleet Train but they were overcome sufficiently for an RN task force to participate in the final defeat of Japan. Thanks are due to Canada for the big programme of maintenance ships and store ships and to the USN for the help given in the Pacific, so much greater than had been promised.

Other types

There is no space to discuss all the numerous types of ship built or converted during the war. These included nine big merchant ships converted into minelayers, laying the Northern Barrage, carrying up to 550 mines each. There were monitors, boom defence vessels, salvage ships, hospital ships, tugs, dummy battleships etc, etc.

The monitor *Roberts*, with two 15in guns removed from *Marshal Soult*. See I L Buxton, *Big Gun Monitors* for the problems involved in moving the turret from Portsmouth to Glasgow. (Author's collection)

Nine | Modernisations, Updates and Scrapping

DURING THE NINETEENTH CENTURY, and even earlier, modernisation of older ships was common practice involving new armament, machinery etc. But in the twentieth century, up to the end of the First World War, there were no such modernisations mainly because the *Dreadnought* revolution had made the older ships so outdated that modernisation was not feasible, and during the 1920s and early 1930s the existing ships in service were fairly modern and there seemed little point in spending substantial sums from the scarce funds available on them.

By the mid-1930s the situation had changed; ships dating from the First World War were deficient in protection and anti-aircraft armament while their out-of-date machinery was tired and inefficient. Ideally, they should have been replaced by new ships but this was not possible due to Treaty limits (prior to 1936), shortage of funds and, most important, lack of shipbuilding capacity. The Japanese, Italian and, to some extent, the US navies were spending large sums rebuilding their older ships and a programme for similar action in the RN was drawn up.

Of the battlefleet, *Warspite*, *Queen Elizabeth*, *Valiant* and *Renown* received full modernisation while *Malaya* and *Repulse* received limited treatment. Many of the 'C' class cruisers and *Delhi* became anti-aircraft

ships along with a number of 'V' and 'W' class destroyers. The *Kent*s were very substantially updated and *London* even more so. Many other older ships had their AA armament much enhanced and some had extra armour fitted. Those not updated were of little value in the war to come. This chapter will examine what was done, what the process absorbed in the way of resources and what proved of value in war.

Capital ships

The trials of shells against *Emperor of India* and of bombs against *Marlborough* in 1931 showed the weakness of the deck protection of the older ships and action was taken to improve matters.[1] A meeting of the Sea Lords in October 1933 was told by the Director of Naval Intelligence that the USN had spent some £16 million on modernising their battleships, Japan had allocated £9 million and would probably spend more whilst the UK had spent only £3 million.[2] It was decided that extra deck protection should be fitted to the magazines and engine rooms of older ships at their next major refit, provided their expected life made it worthwhile.

Barham had come in for a major refit in 1931 and a decision had already been made to improve her deck

Barham had a limited update in 1931-4 during which she was given 500 tons of deck armour. Note here in 1938 the blue white and red stripes on B turret as identification during the Spanish Civil War. (Courtesy John Roberts)

protection. She was given 500 tons of 4in non-cemented (NC) plates laid over the original 1in plates over the magazines and for a few feet beyond, either end. The extra plates fitted after Jutland were removed. She was also fitted with bulges. Her AA armament was augmented with two HACS Mk I directors, four 4in (replaced in 1938 by four twin mounts) and two 8-barrel pompoms.[3] The cost of the refit was £424,000 compared with £195,000 for an earlier refit of *Warspite*, similar except for the armour. She was in hand at Portsmouth from January 1931 until January 1934.

Malaya came in for refit from October 1934 till December 1936. The original intention was for the same treatment as *Barham* but in 1933 it was decided to fit 2½in NC over the engine rooms and a cross-deck catapult with hangars, altering her profile considerably.[4] The original conning tower was replaced by a smaller and lighter one, saving 220 tons – roughly equivalent to the weight of aircraft equipment installed. It was expected that she would float 5ins deeper than *Barham*. She received four twin 4in AA guns. The cost of her refit was £976,963.

Repulse was refitted on similar lines to *Malaya* at Portsmouth between April 1933 and May 1936. Her deck protection over the magazines and engine rooms prior to 1933 consisted of three thicknesses of 1in HT steel. The new scheme was complicated but the main features were; over the magazines, one thickness of the HT was removed and replaced by 3¾in NC. Over the engine rooms two thicknesses of HT were replaced by 2½in NC. She had a cross-deck catapult, eight 4in AA and two pompoms. The refit cost £1,377,748.[5]

Royal Oak had a two-year refit starting in June 1934 in which she was given 900 tons of armour, 4in NC over the magazines and 2½in over the engine rooms; in both cases over existing 1in plate. She had the usual package

of four twin 4in AA and pompoms with a catapult on X turret. The other four *Royal Sovereigns* had enhanced AA armament but no extra armour before the war.[6]

Reconstruction of Warspite

The modernisation of the earlier ships was not entirely satisfactory as they were left with tired and inefficient machinery and had sunk deeper in the water than desirable. It was decided to make much more dramatic changes to *Warspite* while she was in hand at Portsmouth from March 1934 to March 1937. She was given new machinery which was lighter, took up less space and was much more efficient. These savings made it possible to modernise the main armament, greatly increase the protection, fit a cross-deck catapult and hangars for four aircraft and she was given a modern tower bridge and superstructure as well as all the usual AA improvements.[7]

The 15in turrets were removed and altered so that the guns could be elevated to 30° increasing the maximum range from 23,400 to 29,000yds with the older 4crh shell, or 32,200yds with 6crh shells. The revolving weight went up from 785 to 815 tons. The forward and aftermost 6in guns on each side were removed which enabled the forecastle to be widened, helping to make the remaining battery less wet. She was given four twin 4in AA and four 8-barrel pompoms.[8]

The deck armour was much as in *Malaya* except that it covered the boiler rooms as well with a total weight of 1104 tons. The protection to the 6in battery was reduced to 2in NC, saving 445 tons. Removing the conning tower saved some 230 tons.

The twenty-four Yarrow large tube boilers were replaced by six Admiralty three-drum boilers each in its own boiler room. The direct-drive turbines were replaced by Parsons single reduction geared turbines.

Malaya in 1937. She was to have had similar treatment to *Barham* but a late decision to give her a cross-deck catapult and hangar altered her profile considerably. *Repulse* was given similar treatment. (Courtesy John Roberts)

1 It is interesting that the protection of *Hood* was seen as the best of the wartime ships.

2 American costs were so high that their figure can be divided by 2-3 in comparison with UK figures.

3 See Raven and Roberts, *British Cruisers of WWII* (London 1980) for complete package.

4 It was thought that the greater subdivision of the boiler rooms made protection less essential.

5 Goodall, 13 July 1935. 'Asked DNC if £650 to save 11½ tons on aluminium kit lockers in *Repulse* was too much – he said "Yes"'.

6 Goodall, 14 Mar 1939. '1st Sea Lord sent for me re *Royal Sovereigns*. I said to send them to fight up to date capital ships would be murder. He agreed.'

7 There was a proposal to try her bridge on *Iron Duke*. Goodall, 4 Jan 1935.

8 Goodall, 20 Sep 1933. 'As a result of *Centurion* bombing DNC wants all M pompom to fire right forward in old capital ships.'

The original three engine rooms were divided by a new longitudinal and a transverse bulkhead giving four engine rooms and four gearing rooms.

Machinery changes to *Warspite*

	Before	After
shp at full power	75,000	80,000
Shaft rpm	300	300
Fuel consumption at full speed		
(lbs/shp/hr)	1.22	0.75
(tons/hr)	41	26.8
Endurance at 10kts (nm)	8400	14,300
Fuel stowage (tons)	3425	3735
Engine room weights (tons)	1737	967
Boiler room weights (tons)	1461	900
Total machinery weight (tons)	3691	2300
Deep displacement (tons)	35,557	36,096

The displacement did not breach Treaty rules as existing ships were allowed to grow by 3000 tons.

The new machinery performed well and she made 23.8kts on trial. There was an embarrassing problem when the new steering gear jammed with the rudders hard over. It was eventually decided that the new gear had been designed to produce the same torque as the design figure for the older gear, but the older unit in fact gave much more torque than the design figure. There was also heavy vibration when turning as the slip stream of the outer propellers impinged on the inner screws. The problem was alleviated, but not cured, by slowing the outer shaft on the outboard side of a turn.

Warspite's modernisation cost £2,362,000. Goodall (22 Mar 1939) was still critical (summarised); 'The protection of *Warspite* will be much below desirable standard. The boiler rooms will have no modern deck protection . . . side armour not sufficiently deep will not compare with modern capital ship against B bomb and non contact torpedoes'.

Queen Elizabeth and Valiant

Queen Elizabeth and *Valiant* were modernised on similar lines to *Warspite*; *Valiant* was taken in hand at Devonport on 1 March 1937 and *Queen Elizabeth* at Portsmouth on 11 August of the same year. *Valiant* presented particular problems as the work was carried out in a floating dock. With the decks stripped out to

Page opposite: Warspite in 1938. She was given a major modernisation in 1934-7 with new machinery. (Author's collection)

Below: Valiant on completion of modernisation in November 1939. Note the five twin 4.5in mounts either side. This was a much more effective AA armament than the 5.25in fit of the *King George V*. (Imperial War Museum: FL3963)

Renown received new machinery and a secondary battery of 4.5in mounts. (Imperial War Museum: A18655)

replace the machinery, the hull had very little strength and a floating dock, unlike a graving dock, is flexible. Frequent checks on deflection and changes to ballast in the dock ensured that all was well.[9] These two ships were fitted with a dual purpose secondary armament of ten twin 4.5in in between-deck mountings. There was the usual concern as to the effectiveness of the 56lb shell against destroyers.

There were eight boilers in four rooms arranged along the centre line with big wing spaces for auxiliary machinery etc. *Valiant* completed in November 1939; *Queen Elizabeth* was much slower and, late in 1940, when Portsmouth was suffering heavy air raids, she was moved to Rosyth where she completed at the end of January 1941. No costs have been found but they must have been somewhat more expensive than *Warspite* and a little less than *Renown*.

Renown

Renown was taken in hand at Portsmouth in September 1936 for modernisation on similar lines to *Valiant* and completed on 2 September 1939. She had been given additional deck protection during 1923-6 so the new protection generally incorporated the old. She was given 4in NC on 1in D quality structure over the new 4.5in magazines and 2in NC over the engine rooms. The new machinery consisted of eight Admiralty boilers in four rooms with geared turbines in four engine and four gearing rooms which saved 2,800 tons. At average action displacement she could make 30kts on trial, making her a most valuable ship. She was inclined on 1 July 1939 and the results showed a deep displacement of 36,080 tons, just over 2000 tons less than estimated.[10] Her modernisation cost £3,088,008.

Other plans

Hood was due to follow *Queen Elizabeth*.[11] In December 1938 the main features were decided as new machinery, secondary armament to be eight twin 5.25in mounts with six 8-barrel pompoms, and a cross-deck catapult. The conning tower and torpedo tubes were to have been removed.[12]

Some thought had been given to *Nelson* and *Rodney* coming in about 1940 but the final scheme had not been agreed.[13] It was thought to be urgent to deepen the belt and to armour the lower deck forward. It was hoped to carry out this work at a cost of £330,000 during their 1937-8 refit but Dockyard effort was not available. *Nelson* alone got 2¾-3in armour forward. There were three schemes for modernisation; in all the 6in and 4.7in AA would have gone and been replaced by either:

London was the only 'County' class to be fully modernised – perhaps just as well as the extra weight overstressed her. This caused leaks in both deck and bottom which took some time to remedy. (Author's collection)

(a) Eight twin 5.25in, two pompoms, catapult on X turret;

(b) ten twin 4.5in, two pompoms, catapult and hangars on the shelter deck; or

(c) six twin 5.25in, two pompoms, catapult on X turret.

There was a proposal to refit and modernise the *Iron Duke*, and even to purchase the *Almirante Latorre* (ex-*Canada*) from Chile!

At the end of the war, a considerable amount of precious dockyard effort was applied to refitting old battleships etc. Goodall was furious (6 July 1943): 'Discussed C & D class cruisers – what should be done with the old crocks?'. (7 July 1943). 'Rearm *Nelson* and *Rodney*.' (13 March 1945) 'Doing a lot of work in Royal Dockyards on old junk eg *Renown*'. (15 May 1945) 'Horrified to hear *Cardiff* to go to Stephen for repair'. Repairs meeting'. (22 August 1945) 'Junk *Renown*, *Valiant*.'

Operation 'Catherine'

Operation 'Catherine' was a scheme devised by Churchill to take a fleet into the Baltic in 1940.[14] The plan involved increasing the AA armament and deck protection of the ships taking part, with the *Royal Sovereign*s planned to undergo the most dramatic changes. The proposals varied from time to time but the final version involved the following. Enormous bulges would be fitted increasing the beam to 140ft, which would reduce their draught by 9ft so that they could navigate a 26ft channel. The bulges – codenamed 'galoshes' – were in two sections, the inner could be fitted in dock and the outer section attached afloat. In deeper water, some of the bulges would be filled with water to bring the bottom of the belt back into the water. The extra buoyancy would enable 4-5in deck armour to be added. It was originally hoped to retain all eight 15in guns but later schemes had only four with 30° elevation. Their speed would have been about 16kts at light draught, 13-14kts at 'fighting draught'. Even when Operation 'Catherine' was cancelled, Churchill directed that design work on the *Royal Sovereign* should continue as a convoy escort, but even that died soon when it was realised that there was no effort available to carry out the work.

Was it worth it?
One may draw up a price list:

	Cost x £1000
Ordinary refit with bulging (*Warspite*)	200
Barham	400
Malaya	1000
Warspite	2300
Renown	3000
New ship	c7000

There can be little doubt that the fully modernised ships were valued much more highly by Commanders-in-Chief. All four such ships had a very active war, playing a major part in numerous actions. It is less clear that the changes made to them were significant. *Warspite* had probably the most active life of any battleship, old or new. The action off Calabria in 1940 when she hit the *Cesare* at 26,000yds was a justification for the increased elevation of the main armament and led Cunningham to ask for another such ship.[15] *Warspite* was twice badly damaged by bombs, firstly off Crete by a 550lb SAP bomb which exploded on the upper deck in the 6in battery. Her increased deck armour was not involved. The second hit by a 3000lb FX1400 off Salerno penetrated the deck over the boilers, and no conceivable thickness of armour would have protected her.

It is tempting to think that modernisation played a part in *Renown*'s spirited action against *Scharnhorst* and *Gneisenau*, but she opened fire at 19,000yds, well within the range of unmodernised turrets. It is unlikely that *Renown* would have done much better than *Repulse* against Japanese torpedo bombers. It is probable that the new machinery was more reliable and better able to maintain high speed, but it is not possible to prove this statement.

Cruisers – the 'C' and 'D' class AA ships

By the mid-1930s the older cruisers from the First World War were an embarrassment. Their anti-aircraft armament was negligible, prohibiting their use in the North Sea or Mediterranean, whilst their endurance was too small for use on the trade routes. Their poor stability made change difficult. Finally, in 1934, it was decided to give them an all-AA armament and the first two, *Coventry* and *Curlew*, were taken in hand during 1935-6.

Their original armament was replaced by ten single 4in Mk V on Mk III mounts and two 8-barrel pompoms with two HACS Mk III. The conversion was planned for minimum cost: even the 4in guns were removed from other ships as they received twin 4in. About 100 tons of ballast was installed, improving their stability.[16] They were seen as reasonably successful, though the armament was reduced to eight 4in soon after the out-

9 It is surprising that the officer responsible for the success of this refit was held to blame when the floating dock at Trincomalee collapsed under *Valiant*.

10 I do wonder if the inclining result was correct. By 1944 she had 'grown' 2315 tons of which only 694 tons could be accounted for.

11 Goodall, 5 Oct 1932. '*Hood* protection. Really she is poor against bomb attack over engine rooms.'

12 This would have been a very difficult modernisation. *Hood*'s structure was overloaded and it would have been difficult to keep the stresses down. Trunks for the 5.25in turrets through the strength deck would have been a problem. Goodall, 3 Mar 1939. 'First Sea Lord talking about *Hood*. Believes Japan building 12 inch battlecruisers. I said that was an argument against laying up *Hood*.'

13 Goodall, 24 Oct 1938. '*Nelson* new machinery and armour, athwartships catapult.'

14 D K Brown, 'Operation Catherine', *Warship* 40 (October 1986), p232.

15 26,000yds is the greatest range at which any battleship scored a hit in action. Cunningham was soon joined by *Valiant*.

16 Raven & Roberts *British Cruisers of WWII*, pp212-21.

Curlew refitted as an AA cruiser. The conversion was cheap and these ships were useful but they required a large crew to support an armament little better than that of a sloop. (Author's collection)

17 G C Connell, *Valiant Quartet* (London 1979), p41.

18 Most people would see this as a better armament than the earlier ships. However, Connell, who served in *Coventry*, preferred the singles as they could engage more targets and, without shields, visibility was better (p28).

19 Two sets of the 4.5in twins eventually went into *Scylla* and *Charybdis*.

20 Three had been sunk in action, five had been scrapped and one had run aground, subsequently scrapped.

21 A Raven & J Roberts, 'V and W Class Destroyers', *Man o' War* 2 (London 1979). Also A Preston, *V and W Class Destroyers 1917-1945* (London 1971).

22 D K Brown, 'V & W conversions, two that were not built', *Warship Supplement 101* (Kendal 1990).

23 Unofficially known as the Five Wide Virgins.

24 D K Brown, 'V & W conversions, two that were not built', (Quoting S G Hopkins' work books, now in the National Maritime Museum).

25 I am in good company in making this comment. Goodall, 3 Sep 1938. 'To First Sea Lord "I said I should like to see *Furious* and the *Royal Sovereigns* scrapped before war came"'.

26 P Gretton, *Convoy Escort Commander* (London 1964), p58; D A Rayner, *Escort* (London 1955), p131.

Curaçoa, a later AA cruiser with a more effective armament. (Imperial War Museum: A10645)

break of war since the waist guns had very limited arcs of fire and their blast was troublesome to the shelter deck guns.[17] One of the pompoms was also removed as they were scarce and it was thought other ships had greater need.

It was decided to go ahead with the remaining eleven ships between June 1936 and March 1940, but effort was not available until 1938. Two were re-armed in 1938-9 and two more in 1939-40. These four ships were given four twin Mk XIX mounts and a quadruple pompom with two HACS Mk III.[18] No more were converted till *Colombo* in 1942-3 who received three twin 4in, two twin Bofors (on Hazemeyer mounts) and fourteen Oerlikons. The last ship, *Caledon,* was generally similar. In 1943 it was decided that it was not worth converting the remainder. These conversions were cheap and most of the equipment was fairly readily available. However, their capability was little more than that of a sloop, and they were expensive in manpower (*c*440) and required much maintenance.

In 1936 it was decided that the 'D' class should be re-armed with four twin, upper deck 4.5in Mk III and a quadruple pompom. Approval to start work on the first three was given in 1938 and the guns were ordered, but effort was not available for the conversion.[19] The RN received very enthusiastic reports on the performance of the US 5in/38 gun during 1940, and eventually the US agreed to fit five single 5in/38 with two Mk 37 directors, two quadruple pompoms and eight Oerlikons in *Delhi*. They also agreed to refit the ageing hull and machinery. The work was carried out from May to December 1941 at New York. Trials in February 1942 were very successful with 25 rpg per minute on ready-use ammunition and 15 rpg per minute with supply by

hoist. Agreement had been reached for more ships to be converted, but once the USA was at war they had better use for their guns than converting elderly cruisers to the armament of a destroyer. (The 'County' class have been covered in Chapter 4.)

'V' and 'W' class destroyers

At the outbreak of war, there were fifty-eight ships of the 'V' and 'W' classes surviving.[20] Of these, twenty had been allocated for conversion to WAIR–AA escorts.[21] Three had completed conversion when war broke out and eventually fifteen completed, the last early in 1941. The conversion, all in Royal Dockyards, was a big job, 7-10 months being typical. The superstructure was removed and all existing armament replaced with two twin 4in AA, two quadruple 0.5in machine-guns and a new bridge carrying a HA director. These destroyers were employed almost entirely on the East Coast convoy routes and were seen as successful. The leader *Wallace* was given a similar conversion but, being bigger, she also received a quadruple pompom.

During the war, twenty-one more of these classes were converted to long-range escorts, eleven in Royal Dockyards, the rest in commercial yards. Conversions started from January 1941 to April 1943 and finished from June 1941 to August 1943, 5-6 months being typical. The forward boiler was removed and the lower part of the boiler room converted to a fuel tank with space for accommodation and equipment above. Speed dropped to 24½kts but endurance went up to 2930 miles at 12kts so that they could cross the Atlantic without refuelling. They retained B and X gun, some had a triple torpedo tube for 1-ton depth charges and a

Hedgehog and up to 150 depth charges. An improved design was started in 1943 but not proceeded with.[22] There are indications that a version fitted with Squid was also considered but no details are known. The leaders, *Broke* and *Keppel* had similar conversions.

Whitehall, in 1941, was given an experimental fit of five big mortars in A position which could fire standard depth charges ahead of the ship.[23] This appears to have been unsuccessful, probably because the shape of the charge gave an unpredictable flight in the air. *Westcott* carried out the first trials of Hedgehog in mid-1941. A fast replenishment version was also sketched with 711 tons of fuel and 200 depth charges. It would have had two Atlas diesels of 1600bhp giving 15-17kts at 2031 tons and a draught 12ins greater than designed.[24]

The older destroyers of the 'S' and 'R' classes were fitted with more depth charges, AA guns etc, but they were too small for any major modernisation.

Scrapping

Ships scrapped post-Washington up to the outbreak of war were (older vessels omitted):

	Class	No. scrapped
Battleships	Orion	2
	K George V	3 (*Centurion* survived as a disarmed target ship)
	Iron Duke	4 (*Iron Duke* demilitarised as training ship)*
	Tiger	1
Cruisers	Caroline	5
	Calliope	6
	Centaur	2
Destroyers	Late 'M'	6
	Adm 'R'	33
	Thny 'R'	4
	Mod 'R'	8
	Adm 'S'	43
	Thny 'S'	3
	Yar 'S'	6
	Leaders	3**
	'V' & 'W'	5

* There was even a proposal to re-arm and modernise her!
** Includes *Bruce*, expended in torpedo magnetic pistol trials.

It is often claimed that many, even most, of these ships would have been invaluable in the war to come. The evidence does not support this view. The *Royal Sovereigns* were more of a liability than an asset and the older battleships would have been even worse.[25] One might think of modernising *Tiger* (although her retention would not have been allowed by the Treaties) but she would have needed new machinery and surely *Hood* was more important. The unmodernised 'C' and 'D'

class cruisers were useless and more would not have been worthwhile. Amongst destroyers, the big leaders and the 'V' and 'W's were useful but one may assume that the few that were scrapped were those in poorest condition. The older destroyers from the 'S' class backward were of little value.[26] As discussed in Chapter 7, serious thought should have been given to re-using some fifty low-mileage, geared turbine sets.

Conclusions

In view of the shortage of resources and Treaty restrictions on new building, the major modernisations of battleships represented good value. Half measures (*Malaya*) were expensive and not very useful. In general, however, it must be said that not enough ships were scrapped before the war.

From top to bottom:

Vanity, an AA conversion, often referred to as a WAIR. (Author's collection)

Whitehall with five experimental A/S mortars in A position – known as the 'Five Wide Virgins'. (Imperial War Museum: A4671)

She later became a long-range escort. (*Journal of Naval Engineering*)

$\mathcal{Ten}$ | Wartime Damage

Suffolk was bombed off Stavanger on 17 April 1940. The damage was not severe but it proved difficult to stop the spread of flooding. The incident was subsequently made into a training film. (Author's collection)

DETAILED RECORDS were kept in DNC department of every incident involving damage or loss and these have survived.[1] These were summarised soon after the war[2] and it is possible to produce soundly-based statistical analysis for many topics.[3] The study of vulnerability was taken very seriously and Goodall himself would frequently interview survivors. US reports were also made available and studied. This chapter will consider important topics in general terms with a very few incidents described in more detail to add a touch of reality to bare statistics. A few comparisons will be made with ships of other navies (mainly the USN because of the availability of data), where relevant.

The chance of being hit

During the early years of the war the chance of being hit was very high indeed. The upper table shows that, for each of the first three years, the number of incidents involving damage to destroyers was nearly equal to the number in commission.

It is not generally recognised that the probability of damage was so high, yet much the same is true of the Falklands War when out of the twenty-three frigates and destroyers which went out sixteen were hit (most of those which were not hit had only just arrived when the war ended).

The upper table shows the chance of being hit; the next table shows the type of weapon and a crude indication of the extent of damage.

Most of the conclusions are obvious; torpedoes rarely caused slight damage, damage from shells was rare–2-3 per cent hits and usually not serious. The relatively small number of incidents to escort vessels show that the Battle of the Atlantic was waged primarily against the merchant ships whose casualties were horrific. Bombs took a heavy toll of the smaller ships; of 243 destroyers hit by bombs, 44 sank. Unfortunately, the size and type of bomb is rarely recorded.

Effect of weapons

The diagram shows the range of weapons which could be used against ships in the war. However, their effects on the ship may be divided into Flooding, Fire, Magazine Explosion, Structural Failure, Shock, Impact (Splinters), and Blast.

Torpedo

Naval architects are always taught that, to sink a ship, one must let the water in. Typically, torpedoes from German ships or submarines had a warhead of 300kg, enough to make a big hole. The effects of underwater explosions are notoriously variable and the diagram below shows the probability of rupturing a bulkhead at

Proportion of ships in commission damaged each year (no. in commission/ no. sunk or damaged)

	1939-40	40-41	41-42	42-43	43-44	44-45
Capital Ships	11/11	13/12	9/10	9/2	8/4	6/0
Carriers	5/3	6/7	5/6	8/4	16/2	27/7
Cruisers	44/20	46/53	42/45	35/14	36/22	29/9
Destroyers	136/124	154/108	170/106	185/60	197/79	147/20
Sloops, etc	55/24	135/43	253/32	340/31	450/57	494/41

Note: Numbers in commission could vary considerably in the course of any one year and are only approximate.

Warships sunk or damaged by category and type of weapon (sunk/serious damage/slight damage)

Ship type	Shell	Bomb	Mine	Torpedo	TOTAL	% sunk
Capital ships	1/2/3	-/6/11	-/5/-	4/5/-	5/18/14	13.5
A/Carriers	1/-/-	1/10/7	-/1/-	5/3/-	7/14/7	25
Cruisers	3/9/22	10/42/45	1/8/2	13/24/-	27/83/69	15.1
Destroyers	13/40/74	44/81/118	18/35/4	52/15/2	127/171/198	25.6
Sloops etc	2/2/10	16/28/33	17/39/10	50/19/2	85/88/53	37.6
GRAND TOTAL					251/374/341	26.0

different distances from the explosion. The length of the hole in the outer bottom would be about half the distance over which such damage would occur. There is strong evidence that the hole in *Ark Royal* was about 120ft long.

The damage to *Indomitable* when she was hit by an Italian air-launched torpedo in the Mediterranean (charge equivalent to 700lb TNT) on 16 July 1943 is particularly interesting. She was hit on the bottom of her 4in cemented side armour which is brittle under explosive loading. Pieces of armour broke off and were thrown through the torpedo protection into the port boiler room. She made her way to the USA where repairs took 8½ months.

Of 134 ships hit by one torpedo, 99 sank, and of the 35 which reached port, 17 were not repaired (*ie* constructive total loss). The smaller ships, corvettes and frigates, had little chance of surviving and, in fact, only 2 out of 34 got home. Destroyers did a little better with 11 out of 48 surviving and if the smaller, older ships are omitted, these figures improve to 11 out of 39. However, of the 10 repaired, none rejoined in less than 8 months. Of 15 destroyers hit by two torpedoes, two survived while, not surprisingly, both those hit by three torpedoes sank. The sloops and frigates did even better with nearly half surviving (22 out of 47) and three of those lost were scuttled for immediate tactical reasons. That sixteen were not repaired was due to the ready availability of replacements.

The *Prince of Wales*[4] was sunk by five Japanese air-launched torpedoes each with a charge of 330lbs.[5] Her protection was designed to withstand 1000lb charges of TNT and had been tested, full size, on Job 74 (see Introduction). There are various partial explanations for this difference.[6] The main damage was due to hits on the propeller shafts; in the first attack there was a hit on the port outer shaft bracket which bent the shaft and the flailing shaft ripped the ship open on that side up to

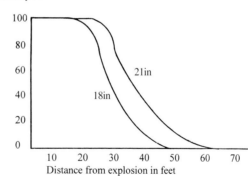

Probability %

Distance from explosion in feet

A comparison of the weapons and ships of the Second World War with those of today

Low capacity, contact

1 cannon shell, HE and AP

High capacity, contact

2 HE shell
3 HE bomb
4 HE bomb, near miss
5 contact torpedo or mine

Medium capacity, contact

6 missile, sea skimming, and SAP shell
7 missile, high level
8 medium case bomb

High capacity, non-contact

9   magnetic-fused torpedo
10 ground mine
11 Proximity-fused missile

Left: Probability of rupturing a bulkhead from a torpedo hit. This diagram was produced from a limited number of examples, all mainly rivetted construction, and is only a rough guide.

1 This author was able to release the contents of two large cupboards to the PRO with the help of Dr N A M Rodger.

2 BR 1886 (2) now in PRO.

3 This chapter is based on a paper written jointly by the author and J D Brown, Naval Historical Branch, and circulated privately. My thanks are due to the 'other' David Brown for his help and for his agreement to using the material here. Note that the original records are not entirely consistent on the number of incidents etc, and some of this inconsistency has entered this chapter.

4 W H Garzke, *Battleships* (Annapolis 1980).

5 60 per cent TNT, 40 per cent hexanitrodiphenylamine. The 'Nells' had this torpedo, and it is possible that 'Betty' carried Mod 2 with a 450lb charge.

6 D K Brown, 'A Note on the Torpedo Protection of the *King George V* and Job 74', *Warship* 1994.

Liverpool was torpedoed in the Mediterranean in 1941. A leaking petrol tank led to a secondary explosion which blew her bow off. (Author's collection)

Lagan was hit by a German acoustic homing torpedo in September 1943. It homed on the propellers, wrecking the stern and shafts. Although not obvious in this photograph, the whipping caused by such torpedoes usually buckled the deck amidships making repair almost impossible. (Author's collection)

Express was mined. (Imperial War Museum: A534)

records of the Job 74 trial have come to light; it could be that the charge was insufficiently confined. One weakness in *Prince of Wales* was that the protection was not deep enough so that the deck above was ruptured allowing flooding to spread. This was remedied in *Vanguard*.

The Government set up an enquiry under Mr Justice Bucknill into the loss of the *Prince of Wales* which opened on 12 March 1942 and reported on 25 April.[7] Goodall thought that this enquiry had been set up to make him, personally, the scapegoat for the loss. He objected strongly to the terms of reference which allowed the enquiry to consider other losses but not cases of survival after heavy damage.[8] Admiral Wake Walker was on the committee as an expert on explosions so Goodall thought he ought to have been a member as an expert on ships.[9] He complained forcibly about errors of fact in the draft report and was furious when this was circulated without correction.[10] When the wreck of the *Prince of Wales* was inspected by divers, long after the war, it was discovered that the actual damage was very different from that deduced by Bucknill.[11]

The effect of homing torpedoes is shown in the illustration of *Lagan* (left) hit by the first German homing torpedo, south-west of Iceland by *U 270* on 10 September 1943.[12] She was hit near the propellers and some 30ft of the stern was blown off. The next 30ft was wrecked and blown upwards. There were two serious buckles in the upper deck due to whipping, one just forward of the main damage, the other amidships. She had lost rudder, steering gear, propellers and tail shafts and all her depth charge gear while the after gun was dismounted. She was towed home but not repaired.

Both Britain and Germany had successfully tested pistols actuated by the magnetic field of the ship before the war[13] but the early versions were very unreliable and soon withdrawn. From about the end of 1943 both countries had reliable versions though it is probable that most attacks used contact pistols. If the magnetic pistol worked it was far more damaging as there was no real protection against under-bottom explosions and whipping would be very damaging.

B boiler room which flooded within 18 minutes. In the second attack a torpedo hit the starboard shaft bracket causing similar damage though less extensive flooding. There were three hits on the protection system. In the first attack there was a hit on the port side close to frame 206 which may have caused flooding in the auxiliary machinery space though this could have entered as a result of the shaft damage.

In the second attack the protection at frame 236 worked well. The void spaces near frame 109 (starboard) had been filled as counter-flooding and could not – and did not – prevent flooding following the hit. It seems clear that the Job 74 tests over-valued the protection. More recent tests would not indicate that the protection of this class would resist 1000lb charges though they should easily have resisted 330lb. No detailed

Mines

Minesweepers were, of course, more exposed than other types and, with corvettes frequently used for sweeping,[14] suffered 51 of the 112 mining casualties. Despite their small size, 57 per cent were repaired and put back in service. Ground mines caused damage which was very difficult to repair and 22.5 per cent of ships which remained afloat were not repaired. Only 45 per cent of destroyers which were mined returned to service with sloops a bit better at 55 per cent.

The serious mine damage suffered by HMS *Belfast* came as a shock.[15] She was mined in the Firth of Forth in November 1939.[16] There were nineteen casualties

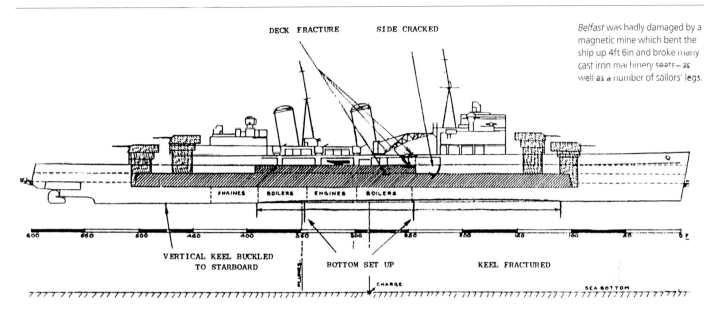

DECK FRACTURE   SIDE CRACKED

FNAINES | BOILERS | ENGINES | BOILERS

VERTICAL KEEL BUCKLED
TO STARBOARD

BOTTOM SET UP

KEEL FRACTURED

CHARGE

SEA BOTTOM

Belfast was badly damaged by a magnetic mine which bent the ship up 4ft 6in and broke many cast iron machinery seats – as well as a number of sailors' legs.

with broken bones – mostly legs – due to the violent whipping caused by the explosion. The direct damage was not unduly severe, centring on the starboard side of the forward boiler room where the outer bottom was badly dished over a length of 20ft, but the effects of whipping were far more serious. Towards the ends of the ship, heavy weights were thrown up with such violence that they hit the deck above.[17] The outer bottom failed in compression, the flat keel being fractured. There was a severe buckle, 14in deep, in the upper deck and there were several fractured plates in the deck. Altogether the ship was bent upwards by some 4ft 6in. This was, in part, due to a failing in structural design which led to problems in *Edinburgh* and some of the *Southamptons*.[18] There was a break of forecastle amidships and, nearby, the armour deck and side armour

Belfast was docked for lengthy repairs. (Author's collection)

7 Bucknill had previously led the enquiry into the loss of the *Thetis* and, later, into the escape of the *Scharnhorst* and *Gneisenau*.

8 Goodall papers, ADM 52793-4. These papers were sealed for many years at Sir Stanley's request. They contain little technical information not available elsewhere but demonstrate Goodall's bitterness at the treatment he received.

9 Goodall, 2 March 1942.

10 There is a long diary entry on 19 August 1942 in which Goodall told Controller (Wake Walker) that Bucknill was 'an insult to me'. Wake Walker revealed that the enquiry had been asked if DNC could be changed.

11 Goodall was wrong too. He thought seven, possibly eight torpedo hits (30 Jan 1942). He gave evidence on 31 March and 7 April.

12 The US anti-submarine homing torpedo, the Mk 24 'mine' or FIDO, sank its first victim, *U 266*, on 15 May 1943. It is often claimed that the homing torpedo was a German first but that is not so.

13 *Cavour* and *Duilio* were sunk by RN magnetic pistols; *Littorio* by contact pistols.

14 Two lost, two damaged while sweeping.

15 *Warship Supplement 87* (World Ship Society, 1986).

16 Either a submarine-laid TMB ground mine with a charge of 420-560kg or, possibly, an air-laid LMA of 300kg.

17 The torpedo tubes were thrown off their turntables which is interesting, as when *Edinburgh* was torpedoed she whipped violently but the tubes remained in place.

18 Goodall 28 Jan 1941. '. . . these *Southamptons* are a groggy lot.'

stepped down a deck. The surviving ships were strengthened.[19]

Damage to the machinery was even more serious. The cast iron discharge pipes of all the fuel pumps were shattered, oil was spurting out and it was fortunate that there was no fire. The stools of all the turbines in the forward engine room were destroyed as was at least one in the after space. All three dynamos tripped and the ship was in darkness for about 10 minutes (there were only twelve lanterns in the ship).

Belfast was patched up at Rosyth and towed to Devonport, arriving in June 1940 and completing in November 1942. Shock effects had been studied on Job 74 (see Introduction) but there was no whipping on this short, box-shaped pontoon. Immediate measures were put in hand to reduce the severity of shock damage but it was not possible to replace all cast iron overnight.[20] The RN was no worse than other navies and, thanks to *Belfast*, quicker to realise the magnitude of the problem – nearly 5 years later *Tirpitz* was immobilised by shock damage from midget submarine charges.

Bombs

Direct hits

Destroyers suffered heavily with twenty-eight out of forty-eight hit being lost. Surprisingly, at least at first sight, the larger, more modern types lost disproportionately with nine out of twelve sinking compared with ten out of twenty-two of the smaller 1300-1600-ton types. It is possible that the losses of the modern ships were due to their being used in areas where the enemy was strong. Even though the 'Hunts' and sloops were frequently attacked from the air there were only nineteen hits, of which six sank (including three scuttled). These ships carried a very heavy anti-aircraft armament and though they destroyed few aircraft, there is evidence that powerful AA fire is a deterrent to accurate bomb aiming. The pre-war view that high level bombing was

not a serious threat to smaller ships proved correct but, of course, the idea that dive bombers would not be used was tragically wrong. The bombing of *Illustrious* is mentioned in Appendix 13, but it should be noted that the only bomb which hit her armoured deck penetrated and burst in the hangar.

Near misses

The most common damage was from splinters which did little damage to the ship but killed or wounded exposed crew. Zarebas of protective plate were a partial answer but at the expense of more topweight. Large capacity bombs bursting close under water could cause flooding which accounted for 8 losses amongst 110 recorded incidents. Seven of these were destroyers.

Shells

Canberra was a cruiser of the *Kent* class, much derided between the wars as 'Tinclads', a label apparently justified when an Australian enquiry found that she was sunk by about twenty-five hits from 5.5in and 5in shells. However, a recent book reaches a very different conclusion.[21] The principal author was a midshipman on board at the time of her sinking. Use of USN track charts showed that the ships firing on her were 8in cruisers and about twenty-seven shells hit. The final sinking was probably due to two torpedo hits.[22] Indeed, she took some sinking.

The most infamous loss of a British warship to shellfire was the destruction of HMS *Hood* by the *Bismarck* in 1941. There were two inquiries into her loss. The first was criticised (by Goodall and others) because they did not call all witnesses and failed to record the statements made. The second inquiry under Rear-Admiral H J C Walker had D E J Offord as a member and he had run DNC's damage section for nearly a decade. By far the most reliable account of the sinking of *Hood* is that of Jurens.[23] By and large he agrees with the verdict of the second inquiry, that the after magazines exploded, very probably following the explosion of the 4in magazine[24] aft of the engine room. One of the main difficulties is that some witnesses saw the plume as forward of the main mast while a significant minority place it abaft the mast. Captain Leach of the *Prince of Wales* stated that one shell hit from *Bismarck*'s final salvo whilst his Commander, standing beside him, saw two hits.[25] There are several routes by which a 15in shell from *Bismarck* could have reached a magazine.[26] Initial explosion of the 4in magazine would account for the plume being seen forward of the mainmast by the majority of the few eyewitnesses.[27]

Goodall and Offord both thought that the explosion was due to torpedo warheads and this view must be considered carefully since Offord had been in charge of the damage section since 1931 and had seen far more explosions than anyone else involved in the inquiry.[28]

Cornwall was sunk by Japanese dive bombers on 5 April 1942. (Imperial War Museum: HU 1838)

His successor in the post re-examined the evidence and accepted the inquiry view. The worst case would be two 500lb warheads exploding which would be sufficient to destroy a large part of the strength deck amidships. *Hood* was highly stressed and the sea was quite rough and such damage could cause her to break in half immediately. However, the reported nature of the explosion is more consistent with a propellant explosion. Offord had warned Goodall (then Assistant Director) of the hazard from *Hood's* above-water torpedoes before the war and, when she blew up, I suspect they jumped to a previous conclusion.

It is often suggested that *Bismarck* was much more resistant to damage than RN ships, but examination of the wreck[29] shows that this was not so. There were probably 300-400 hits from the 2871 shells fired at her but, as Garzke puts it, the later hits merely re-arranged the debris. Fire was opened at 0847hrs and by 0900hrs B turret was out of action when a shell (probably 14in) went through the 340mm barbette armour and burst, blowing the back plate off, and A turret seems to have been out of action by then. D turret went about 0921hrs and C at 0931hrs. She was no longer a fighting ship after this – no discredit to her crew as she could not steer and was almost immobilised following damage by *Ark Royal's* torpedo.

The belt is largely buried in silt but several penetrations can be seen. There were two known penetrations of the deck, both probably by 16in shells, one bursting in the port engine room, the other in the starboard boiler room. Post-war tests on armour removed from *Tirpitz* show it to be almost as good as British material.[30] The arrangement was old-fashioned as in *Baden* but in a largely close range action it did as well as could be expected – but it was not magical. The stern fell off during the sinking as a result of the torpedo hit from *Ark Royal*; one of several German ships which lost their stern after damage due to discontinuities and poor welding.

Back breaking

Thinking of warships sinking normally brings up pictures of capsize, foundering or magazine explosion. In fact, the most common cause of sinking for unarmoured warships was structural collapse – back breaking. The table (overleaf) shows the number of ships which broke their back/number hit and the percentage of back breaking.

Not surprisingly, there is an indication that the more highly-stressed ships were more likely to break their back. The most vulnerable ships were destroyers, highly stressed and with a break of forecastle amidships which would much increase the stress locally. They were also shallow, keel to deck, which meant that a hit would destroy a higher proportion of the hull girder than in a deeper ship. The converse of this is seen in the

Hood had a big fire in the ready-use ammunition for the rocket launcher (centre right) early in the last encounter with *Bismarck*. The fatal explosion took place near the twin 4in a little further aft. (Author's collection)

sloops with low stress and a deep hull. USN experience is somewhat similar; of thirty sunk by above-water attack six broke their back (37 per cent) whilst of twenty-seven sunk by underwater weapons, nineteen (70 per cent) broke their back. There were few hits on modern, longitudinally-framed destroyers but *Kelly* would probably have broken her back had she been transversely framed.

Machinery arrangement, the unit system

The unit system of machinery involves grouping together all the components needed to drive one shaft line (two shafts of a four-shaft ship). A 'Unit' for a steam ship would usually consist of one boiler room and an engine room though there might be a separate gearing room. Many Second World War ships had two units and it would be possible to cross-connect either boiler room to either engine room. It was very important to ensure that the autonomy of a unit was not comprised by a common auxiliary system such as the lubricating line. Ideally, the two units should have another, non-machinery space between them.

The object is to minimise the amount of flooding or damage from a single hit by any weapon and to ensure,

19 *Warship Supplement 87* (World Ship Society 1986).

20 Goodall's diaries had many references to the problems with cast iron, eg 16 Dec 1940. 'Cast iron with Offord. He was very reasonable but E-in-C should have taken strenuous measures to eliminate cast iron years ago and DNC should have kept him up to it.' Also 5 May 1941. '*Erne* shows machinery cast iron again'.

21 B Loxton and C Coulthard-Clark, *The Shame of Savo – Anatomy of a Naval Disaster* (St Leonards NSW 1994).

22 The authors suggest that the most likely firing ship was USS *Bagley* though this cannot be confirmed.

23 W J Jurens, 'The Loss of HMS *Hood* – a Re-examination', *Warship International* 2/87.

24 A more recent study showed that 4in magazines were much more likely to explode than was realised in 1941 (an article on this subject is with *Warship International*).

25 Jurens estimates the chance of two hits from a four-gun salvo as between 5-9 per cent. 1 in 20 chances do come up!

26 Goodall wrote that *Hood* v *Bismarck* was like the *Majestics* turning up at Jutland! His dates were right.

27 It is unlikely that a more conclusive answer will be found. Even if the wreck is visited it is unlikely that it will be possible to tell where the massive explosion originated.

28 Offord wrote to me in 1980 that he still believed that torpedoes were to blame. Goodall, 9 Jan 1935. 'Controller approved upper deck torpedoes for *Malaya* and *Royal Oak*. Very much concerned over torpedo tubes above armour. *Hood* and *Repulse* as carriers possible'. 14 Dec 1935. 'DNC signed paper on *Hood* tubes. Coming out before big repair in 1940 [They did not].'

29 W H Garzke, R O Dulin and D K Brown, 'The sinking of the *Bismarck*'. *Warship* 1994. Based on: W H Garzke and R O Dulin, 'The Bismarck Encounter', *Marine Technology*, SNAME (Jersey City 1993). See also: J Roberts, 'The final action', *Warship* (London 1983). The 1994 article was written as a sequel to that of 1983 giving information not available at the earlier date.

30 US cemented armour of the Second World War was about 25 per cent inferior to British and German armour.

Back breaking (no./no.hit %)

Type	Bombs	Mines	Torpedoes	TOTAL
Destroyers	14/243 6%	11/57 25%	25/69 36%	50/369 14%
Sloops etc[31]	2/77 3%	5/66 8%	10/71 14%	17/241 8%

This information can be presented in slightly more detail. The table shows Number breaking back/number sunk = %

Type	Typical stress*	Bomb	Mine	Torpedo	All
Destroyers	6.0	14/44 32%	11/18 61%	25/52 48%	50/114 44%
Frigates	5.0	0/0 -	0/0 -	4/10 40%	4/10 40%
Sloops	3.0	1/5 20%	0/1 -	2/8 25%	3/14 21%
Sweepers	3.0	1/6 17%	5/9 56%	4/11 36%	10/26 38%
TOTAL		16/55 29%	16/28 57%	35/81 43%	67/164 41%

* Typical design stress in the upper deck, sagging (deck in compression), tons/in²

as far as is possible, that the ship retains some mobility. Theses objectives are not quite the same and neither is easy or cheap. Dividing the machinery into numerous compartments will increase the size of the ship quite considerably as access is needed on both sides of a bulkhead. Testing for watertightness and subsequent rectification was expensive, particularly in riveted ships where leaky seams were all too common. The engine room complement will also increase.

A typical Second World War torpedo would make a hole some 35ft long and 15ft high, rendering bulkheads non-watertight over twice that length. A torpedo would flood at least two compartments and probably three along the length. If the machinery is unitised, it is essential that there are no common systems which can put both units out if disabled.[32] The diagrams show machinery subdivision in ships of different types and ages.

Battleships

Most British battleships of the First World War had a layout as shown for *Royal Sovereign* and *Malaya*'s modernisation did not alter her layout. The large spaces would admit a lot of water and it was all too likely that a single hit would flood all three boiler rooms or the three engine rooms. The fully-modernised ships were much more closely sub-divided, made possible because the new machinery was more compact. Even though the spaces were small, they still had all the boilers and all the engines, together and a single hit could still bring the ship to rest as happened when *Warspite* lost all six boiler rooms off Salerno.[33]

Nelson and *Rodney* were no better but the *King George V* class was far superior. Alternating boiler and engine rooms made it very unlikely that all power

31 Includes corvettes which often sank so quickly that the actual cause of loss is uncertain.

32 There are stories that some early unit systems had a common lubricating oil system but I have been unable to confirm this.

33 Sir Andrew Cunningham, Remarks in *Trans INA* (1949), p99.

would be lost from a single hit. They would have been even better if another space had been worked between the forward engine rooms and the after boiler rooms. *Prince of Wales* has been discussed earlier in this chapter.

Aircraft carriers

Carriers were particularly difficult as there was very little height below the hangar floor in which to run uptakes, and longitudinal separation of the boiler rooms was difficult since it was desirable to keep the island, with funnel(s), as short as possible. *Ark Royal* (1934) was similar to the sketch of *Illustrious* but with only one space between the boiler (B) and engine rooms (E). The four-shaft *Implacables* were only marginally better. The bigger American *Essex* class had an arrangement with BBEBBE which gave more protection at the expense of very long ducts from the after boiler rooms.

The later British carriers were bigger and incorporated the lessons of the loss of the *Ark Royal*. The five-shaft *Malta* was particularly impressive though the later Design X benefited from more compact machinery. The *Colossus* class light fleets had an ingenious arrangement of two combined machinery spaces, widely separated, each containing two boilers and a turbine.

Cruisers

The *Enterprise* of the First World War was the first British cruiser with separated machinery units. Post-war ships did not have proper units until the *Amphion* though it was possible to cross connect. From the *Amphion* onwards, British cruisers had alternating boiler and engine rooms. The forward boiler room had two boilers side by side, occupying the full width of the ship. The after room had the boilers fore and aft with wing compartments outboard. As discussed in Chapter 4, these contributed to the capsize of several ships, particularly amongst the smaller *Dido*s. The two 1944 designs are much better subdivided but the amount of longitudinal division in the small (8050-ton) 'N2' is worrying.

The table below indicates some typical cruiser arrangements (Forward compartment on the left)

B Boiler Room
E Engine Room
V Other space *eg* magazine
M Combined engine/boiler space

Ship	Machinery	
Enterprise	BBVEBVE	
'County'	BBVEVE	
York	BBEE	
Leander	BBBEVE	
Amphion	BEBE	and later ships

Machinery Layouts

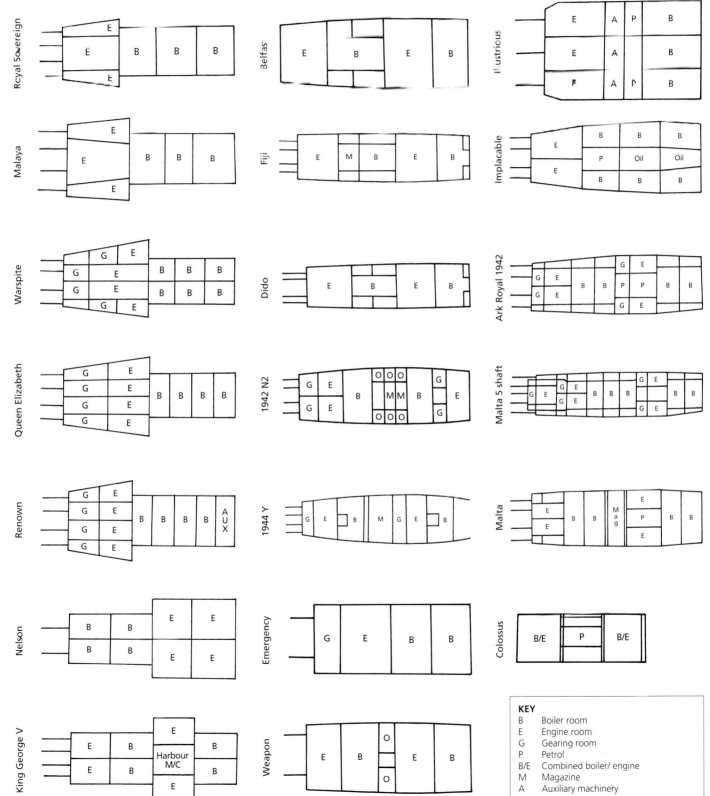

KEY

B	Boiler room
E	Engine room
G	Gearing room
P	Petrol
B/E	Combined boiler/ engine
M	Magazine
A	Auxiliary machinery

The *Amphion* arrangement was used in all later cruisers of the war. Though it was basically sound, there was a serious flaw, discussed in a later section. About seventeen incidents can be identified in which units were involved. Seven capsized rapidly but in the other ten they retained some mobility and got home

Destroyers

From the *Javelin* to the 'Battles' all RN destroyers had two boilers, each in a separate room, then a single engine room and, lastly, a gear room. The 'Weapons' and *Daring*s were much superior with boiler room, engine, fuel and then a second unit. They completed too late for the war but USN experience shows the greater survivability of destroyers with unitised machinery.

US ships and experience

The USN introduced the unit system at about the same time as the RN in the *Detroit* class and all later cruisers had some form of unit arrangement. Some typical arrangements were:

Ship	Arrangement
Detroit	BBEBBE
Chicago	BBEBBE
Atlanta	BEBE
Baltimore, Cleveland	BBEBBE
Des Moines	MMVMM

A BuShips paper summarised the results of torpedo hits:

Torpedoed	31
Of which sunk	7
Hit in machinery	11
Immobilised	2

A very fine performance, particularly against the massive Japanese torpedoes.

From about 1937 USN destroyers had machinery in units (BEBE) and there are many examples in the war of destroyers remaining in action at 18–20kts with one unit immobilised.[34] No British destroyer in the war had unit machinery which was introduced in the 'Weapon' and 'Daring' classes.

Longitudinal subdivision and wing compartments

The problem with the BEBE arrangement in RN cruisers lay in the wing spaces alongside the after boiler room (see sketch in Chapter 4). The heel produced by flooding one of these spaces was very small and thought acceptable. However, a torpedo explosion in this area would flood three main spaces and the nearer wing compartment. This would greatly reduce the stability of

the ship and the heel from the buoyancy of the intact wing opposite would probably capsize the ship. Five cruisers torpedoed in this area and *Spartan* hit by a large guided bomb all capsized, mostly very quickly. *Cleopatra* was torpedoed and went to a large angle but was saved because there were standing orders to counterflood without further instruction if the heel exceeded a certain angle.[35]

Longitudinal subdivision has no place in any but the largest warship.[36] The Japanese cruisers had centreline bulkheads in their cruisers in the engine rooms and all but the foremost boiler room. No wonder that ten of the twelve ships damaged in this area capsized. On the other hand, when *Fiji* was torpedoed on 1 September 1940 the forward boiler room was flooded but she was able to steam home on the after boiler and engine room.

Shaft damage

It is sometimes suggested that separated machinery spaces increase the danger of being immobilised since the forward shaft is very long and may be damaged. Wartime experience does not support this view. In fifty-six non-contact explosions, causing whipping, there were fifteen cases of shaft damage. Of these, five were due to fractured plummer blocks, probably of cast iron, and two to fractured shaft brackets. Only in eight cases was bending of the shaft reported. The flexible bulkhead glands tried in *Penn* would probably have made damage to the shaftline unlikely (discussed later in this chapter).

Kamikazes and guided weapons

The Japanese suicide bomber attacks are of interest as they foreshadow the guided missile. The bare statistics are:

Sorties	2314
Expended	1228
Sunk	2 escort carriers, 13 destroyers and 20 small vessels
Damaged	16 fleet carriers, 3 light fleet carriers, 17 escort carriers, 15 battleships, 15 cruisers 111 destroyers and over 100 smaller ships.

Included within these totals are those inflicted by the Ohka ('Baka'), a purpose built, rocket-propelled missile with a speed of 620mph and a 4000lb warhead. Their score seems to have been well below average:

Expended	60
Sunk	2 destroyers, 1 minesweeper, 6 damaged.

They were probably too fast for human control.

There were some remarkable examples of survival, *eg* USS *Laffey* which endured twenty-two attacks with six

34 It is said that USS *Kearney*'s arrival at Iceland with the forward unit flooded convinced the RN of the need for machinery to be in units.

35 From memory it was 15°. While serving in *Euryalus* I tried to get permanent demolition charges fitted to these longitudinal bulkheads.

36 I would suggest not unless the beam is over 100ft.

37 The Naval Staff History suggests that they were attracted by her three big funnels! *War with Japan*, (HMSO 1995).

38 D K Brown. 'Attack and Defence, Part 4', *Warship 28* (October 1983).

39 Picked out by eye from a very complicated table.

40 Note that ships whose cause of sinking is some other cause may have been on fire at the time.

Kamikaze hits, four bomb hits and a near miss. She lost 31 killed and 72 wounded but her guns were firing in local control and she was repaired. Damage to RN armoured hangar carriers is dealt with separately in Appendix 13

The *Kent* class cruiser HMAS *Australia* seemed to have a special attraction for suicidal Japanese.[37] She was hit on 21 October 1944 when serious fires broke out in the bridge area from burning petrol. She was hit again on 5 January 1945 but remained in action with damage to her AA guns. She was hit again the next day with more damage and casualties to her AA guns and their crews. On 8 January she was hit by two more and a further one on the 9th, but was able to steam slowly back and was repaired in 6½ weeks.

There were a few guided bombs which scored heavily *Warspite*, *Spartan* and *Erne* being among the victims. *Spartan* was hit by an HS 293 glider bomb off Anzio on 29 January 1944. A large hole was blown in the upper deck and there was a serious fire in the after superstructure and in Y turret. The after engine room (and one wing space) and the after magazine flooded within 10 minutes. She was abandoned after an hour and capsized soon after.[38]

Armed merchant cruisers

As discussed in Chapter 9, considerable thought had been given to the conversion of passenger liners which, in service, were required to float with two main compartments flooded. Protection against underwater weapons included the installation of between 1500 and 3000 tons of ballast to improve stability after major damage. 'Tween decks, particularly around the waterline were packed with empty, sealed oil drums to preserve both buoyancy and stability (waterplane inertia). These measures proved very successful and were used in the *Colossus* class carriers. Of the AMCs hit, *Cheshire* had two main holds flooded quickly and a third flooding slowly but was able to make slow speed and was repaired in 6 weeks, while *Patroclus* was hit by four torpedoes and then two shells. Another torpedo hit but she was still afloat 2 hours later when she was hit by two more torpedoes (seven in all), finally sinking after another 2 hours. *Salopian* was hit by five torpedoes and was floating with four out of six holds flooded when her back was broken by a sixth hit.

Time to sink

The time to sink varied very considerably but the table gives some idea of the number sinking in various time bands.

It will be seen that these figures follow the so called 'bath tub curve' with peaks at the beginning and end. If a ship survived the first few minutes, it had a good chance of lasting an hour.

Time to repair

Repair times are even more variable since the opportunity would often be taken to install new equipment. Some of the very severely damaged ships (eg *Belfast*) were put to one side and only worked on when other work fell off. Very detailed charts are held by Naval Historical Branch from which the table below has been extracted. The figures are the most common time[39] (the mode) to repair in months.

Repair time (months)

Weapon	Modern destroyer	Escort DD, sloops, frigates	Corvettes & mine-sweepers
Shell	3	1	3
Torpedo	8	8	None
Bomb	6	6	3
Mines	12	12	12
Ramming U-Boat	2-3	2-3	2-3

Fire

Serious fires were not common in the Second World War;[40] taking destroyers as an example fires were reported in 60 cases out of 496 incidents of damage. Of these 60 cases 24 were said to be serious and 36 minor. The breakdown by cause was:

Shells	17
Bombs	25
Mines	5
Torpedoes	13

Of the twenty major fires, sixteen involved oil fuel (so did two minor fires).

It seems that fire was much less likely than in the later Falklands War. Possible explanations for the higher incidence in 1982 include the use of diesel oil with a lower flash point (though the difference was not great), much greater personal effects aboard and, in some cases, missile fuel.

Time to sink

Type	0 - 10 Min	10 - 20	20 - 30	30 - 60	> 60 Min
Battleships	2	1	-	-	2
Carriers	2	2	-	1	2
Cruisers	3	2	2	2	15
Destroyers	28	12	4	14	37
Frigates	3	-	1	1	2
Sloops	2	1	-	1	4
Corvettes	13	2	3	-	3
Minesweepers	8	1	1	2	5

Kelly. She was torpedoed amidships and nearly capsized due to loss of stability. Mountbatten saved her by jettisoning topweight. The aerial view shows how close she was to foundering whilst the view in dock shows the extent of the damage. (Author's collection)

Riveting

The majority of ships damaged were largely riveted. Distortion of the structure would lead to leaking seams which could let in a lot of water quickly.[41] A leaking seam was very difficult to stop; the only thing to do was to drive in softwood wedges but great care was needed as it was all too easy to open up the gap rather than stop it. Welded structure was, in those days, liable to be brittle and fail along the heat-affected zones either side of the seam. Better steel and procedures after the war made welded structures which were far superior.

Damage control

It is clear that insufficient attention had been paid to damage control between the wars by both designers and operators. A damage control school was set up only after the loss of *Ark Royal* and training prior to that was very limited and sometimes even wrong. There were too few items such as diesel generators,[42] portable pumps, emergency lighting and supply leads and breathing apparatus, nor were the crew adequately trained in their use.

Very many accounts of damage refer to shoring up the bulkhead as the first step. There are very few cases of bulkheads collapsing which is not surprising since they were tested to a head of water greater than that they were likely to be exposed to. It would seem that shoring was almost a religious rite taught, incorrectly, in pre-war training.

An exception to the usual poor damage control was HMS *Kelly* when under the command of Mountbatten. During the development of the 'J' class design, Lord Mountbatten was a frequent visitor to the design section under A P Cole. He has told how they discussed the likely effects of damage and what remedial action to take.[43] *Kelly* was torpedoed and very seriously damaged in May 1940.[44] The extensive flooding led to a complete loss of initial stability and she was lolling – not listing[45] – away from the hole. As a result of what he had learnt from Coles, Mountbatten realised that he had to jettison top weight and he had already a prepared list of items to ditch, beginning with the torpedoes. Coles' structure and Mountbatten's damage control – with a touch of luck – saved the *Kelly*.[46]

Conversely, *Ark Royal* fared much worse. She was torpedoed when she was turning fast and heeled well over. The explosion was on the turn of bilge, below the protection system. The damage was unusually extensive – when she turned over, the captain of a 115ft motor launch said that the hole was longer than his

boat.[47] One engine and boiler room flooded immediately and the centre line spaces followed. The main electrical switchboard room flooded so that the circuit-break-
ers on the ring main which had opened with the shock
of the explosion could not be operated by remote control as usual and the settings overrode early attempts to
reset them manually. All lighting failed and there were
only thirty-five battery-operated lamps for the whole
ship. She did not have any diesel generators.

As she heeled, water rose into the uptake space below
the lower hangar restricting the flow of smoke from the
remaining boiler room. This caused overheating leading
to a fire, and power was lost in the remaining machinery. Most of the crew had been taken off soon after she
was hit including the technical ratings who could have
restored electrical power.

As mentioned in Chapter 2, the mis-estimate of speed
and power led to the choice of three-shaft machinery. If
designed with only two shafts, the run of uptakes
would have been easier though still difficult in a double-
hangar ship of limited depth. The lack of emergency
power was a weak feature made worse by the over-
hasty evacuation. She could still have been saved. For
many years after there was a standard demonstration at
the damage control school showing that flooding the
remaining engine and boiler room would have brought
her upright allowing her to be towed into Gibraltar.

Magazine explosions in the Second World War[48]

It is widely believed that propellant charges contained
in brass cartridge cases are unlikely to explode and that
it is also unusual for a magazine explosion to be initiated by underwater weapons such as mines or torpedoes.
Nevertheless, study of RN records,[49] and those of the
USN,[50] show many examples of explosions in magazines containing cased propellant, mostly initiated by
torpedo hits.

Mechanism of a magazine explosion

An ammunition explosion, as opposed to a very rapid
fire, needs a rise in both temperature and pressure in the
compartment. A charge may be ignited by hot splinters,
by flash or by high temperature from a fire started outside the magazine and the fire can spread to neighbouring charges. Prompt operation of the magazine spray,
the use of a flooding system[51] or, best of all, very rapid
flooding from the sea through a hole made by the
incoming weapon can extinguish such a fire before it
builds up to an explosion.

If the fire is not extinguished quickly, temperature
and pressure will build up and an explosion is almost
inevitable. Venting through blow-off panels, doors and
hatches or damaged structure may prevent the pressure
building-up to a dangerous level but large venting areas
are needed. An explosion is more likely when the

Ark Royal. Everything went wrong. A poor quality photo but the last we will see of this famous ship. (Author's collection)

charges are tightly packed. It takes a little time for pressure to build up so reports nearly always speak of two
explosions, the first of the enemy weapon followed a
few seconds later by a much bigger explosion as the
magazine goes up.

A severe fire may raise the temperature of the magazine sufficiently to cause high explosive bombs or shells
to detonate and hot splinters will ignite further charges.
The USN identified 5in AA shells as a particular hazard. Thin-walled, high explosive munitions can also be
detonated directly by splinters.

RN experience

Examination of war damage records leads to the following breakdown of incidents involving magazines.

Major explosion in a magazine	6
Major explosion probably involving magazine	19
Magazines damaged but not exploding	23
Other incidents in which magazines were flooded	25

It is quite likely that this list is incomplete and there
could be errors but it is close enough to draw some general conclusions. The nature of the propellant is rarely
recorded.

Magazines certainly could and did explode, the list
above contains twenty-five probable magazine explosions, most of which involved fixed ammunition or separate ammunition with propellant in brass cases. These
explosions could be initiated by weapons hitting above
or below water.

Explosion initiated by:

Shell	Bomb	Torpedo	Mine
1	7	16	1

41 *Titanic* was sunk by leaking seams.

42 Goodall, personally, seems to have been hostile to the use of diesel generators though his reasons are not stated. Possibly he thought them big and heavy in relation to their output.

43 D K Brown, *A Century of Naval Construction*, p192 for letter from Earl Mountbatten on *Kelly*.

44 It is almost certain that she would have broken in half but for Cole's insistence on longitudinal framing.

45 An attempt to correct the heel by shifting weights to the high side would have been fatal.

46 The author had to recalculate *Kelly*'s damaged state as a check on our proposals for the subdivision of the post-war 'Tribal' class frigates.

47 It is almost certain that the outer bottom in this area was riveted.

48 Slight revision of 1992 paper.

49 *Damage to HM Ships*. BR 1886(2) Public Record Office.

50 *Summary of War Damage*, USN Navships, and *Striking Power of Airborne Weapons*, OPNAV July 1944.

51 It is very difficult to devise a system which will flood quickly enough as pressure rises in the magazine.

Javelin lost both bow and stern when hit by two torpedoes when under Mountbatten's command. She was repaired. (Author's collection)

In ships which survived, with one or more charges having burnt, the most usual cause of ignition was a hot splinter. It is likely, though not certain, that splinters were also the primary cause of magazine explosions. It is clear that in most cases the rise of pressure was extremely rapid and neither flooding nor venting was possible except through large holes caused by damage. Fire or explosion of one charge would usually, but not always, spread to neighbouring charges.

The number of incidents is too small for proper statistical analysis but the distribution by date is suggestive.

RN magazine incidents by date

	1939	40	41	42	43	44	45
Exploded	-	2	2	6	3	10	2
Did not explode	-	1	5	6	8	1	2

There is a slight suggestion that explosions were more likely in the later years of the war. Whilst too much should not be read into this, there could have been a more careless attitude with less-experienced crews.[52]

There were some trials in 1936 which showed the vulnerability of fixed ammunition. In the first trial a 4.7in CPC shell was fired into a number of charges which did not explode. When a 6in CPC, filled Shellite, was fired into 98 rounds rack-stowed there was a short pause followed by complete disintegration of the magazine. In the next trial, a 6in was fired into 94 rounds, box-stowed, resulting in a fire which destroyed the stowage in 48 minutes; it was thought that had the space been confined there would have been an explosion.[53]

USN experience

The USN concluded that only destroyers, in which the magazines were unprotected, were likely to suffer a magazine explosion from a torpedo hit. The risk was assessed at 50 per cent. The older, light cruisers of the *Omaha* class had unprotected magazines but their arrangement and the type of ammunition were thought to make an explosion unlikely. Escort carriers were very vulnerable and their bomb stowage was much reduced in order to provide better protection.

In smaller ships, such as cruisers and destroyers, an explosion following a bomb hit in the magazine was not inevitable, as almost always the damage would cause flooding through the side or bottom which would extinguish a burning charge and would vent the pressure build-up. Such ships did carry the 5in AA projectile which was vulnerable to splinters. In the case of larger ships, such as battleships and fleet carriers, it was less likely that a projectile would reach a magazine, but if it did, flooding and venting were less likely and an explosion was almost inevitable.

Propellants[51]

The most usual propellant in the RN was cordite SC (19.5 per cent nitrocellulose, 41.5 per cent nitroglycerine, 9 per cent Centralite[55]) though there may have been some of the older, less stable cordite MD. During the war a flashless material NF was introduced (55 per cent picrite [nitroguanidine], 21 per cent nitroglycerine, 7.5 per cent centralite, 0.3 per cent cryolite).

Until mid-1944 the USN used nitro-cellulose exclusively (0.5 per cent diphenylamine). After much discussion, a flashless material N, an army version of NF, was purchased from Canada and was issued in mid-1944. Other more complex propellants only came into service after the war. USN propellants seem to have had a good safety record, perhaps due to good quality control in manufacture. Jurens (p151) refers to US tests which show their propellant to be very much safer than RN cordite.

A magazine contains a vast amount of stored energy whose explosion will almost certainly destroy any ship. It does not seem that there were any accidental explosions during the Second World War, mainly due to greater care in manufacture. It was probably impossible to give total security against enemy attack but protection of ammunition in bulk or in transit where it might form a train was vital.

Post-war ship target trials

Though every effort had been made to learn the lessons from wartime damage, such incidents were uncontrolled. The size of the weapon was often unknown, the

52 One officer remembers being taught 'Cordite is safe as long as you remember it is dangerous'.

53 ADM 116/4352 quoted by Jurens WI 2/87.

54 J Campbell, *Naval Weapons of World War II* (London 1985).

55 Symmetrical diphenyl diethyl urea.

Orion with the second of two 1090lb charges going off underneath her. She broke right across the upper deck and part way down the sides showing that riveted joints would not always stop a crack from spreading. (Author's collection)

Underwater trials; cruisers and destroyers

Ship	Date	Charge weight (lbs)*	No of charges	
Emerald	1947	187	12	
		1080	21	
Orion		1080	2	Non-damaging 187 fired to calibrate
Ambuscade		187	23	
Anthony		1080	8	
Jervis		187	1	
Active	1944-9	50	9	
		1080	2	
Brilliant	Apr 47	1080	1	
Amazon	Sep 48	187	1	
Ashanti	Nov 48	6000	1	
		187	2	
Kelvin	Mar 49	187	1	
Javelin	Apr 49	1080	1	
Eskimo	May 49	6000	1	
Kimberley	Jun 49	187	1	
Racehorse	Sep 49	1080	2	
Nonsuch	Oct 49	1090	1	ex-German *Z38*
Z30	1948	1090	3	
Penn	49-50	187	2	
Oudenarde ex-*Jutland*				

* The charges were 187lb – a Squid projectile, 1080 Mine Mk IXA, 50lb probably half-filled Squid.

position at which it exploded was often difficult to determine (particularly in the case of non-contact weapons) and repairs to get the ship back into service had priority over detailed surveys of damage.[56] Early in 1945 it was proposed and agreed in principle to carry out a large number of tests on British ships coming up for disposal at the end of the war and on enemy ships which might be surrendered.

Even though the war in Europe was still continuing, a trials programme with some forty headings was prepared and in October 1945 the Ship Trials Committee was set up under DCNS with an officer from DNC as secretary. This steering committee worked through eight subcommittees, each dealing with a particular type of trial.[57] The principal operator was the Naval Construction Research Establishment (NCRE). During 1942, following the loss of *Ark Royal* and *Prince of Wales*, there had been a number of proposals for a test site for underwater explosions. It was thought that it should be well away from the south coast and close to a dockyard or shipyard. Goodall was insistent that it should be a structural research establishment under his control and run by a constructor while others wanted either nothing more than a test site or, at the other extreme, a pure science laboratory. Goodall's views are clear in his diary for 24 July 1942. 'I wanted an underwater protection laboratory at Portsmouth [later changed to Rosyth], DNC to provide the Superintendent, DTM the deputy, which could make their own structures other than full size, make up their own charges and have a hulk on which ⅓ scale models could be fixed and to carry the recording instruments'. After lengthy arguments he got his way and the establishment[58] opened on 10 June 1943 under Dudley Offord RCNC.[59]

The main objectives of the trials were:

1. The effect of non-contact, underwater explosions on surface ships, submarines and their equipment.
2. The effects of above water weapons on surface ships.
3. The structural strength of surface ships and submarines.
4. Magazine safety and venting.

By the time the war was over it was clear that funds were going to be very limited and that the desperate shortage of scrap steel meant that ships could only be held for a very short trials period and that very few could be sunk. The maintenance ship *Mull of Kintyre* was the headquarters ship and could carry out minor

Nonsuch (ex-German *Z38*) breaking in half after the explosion of a 1090lb charge. It was expected that a modern welded ship would survive but poor detailed design at the break of forecastle led to high stresses which caused her to break in half. (Author's collection)

Jervis with a 187lb charge exploding. (Author's collection)

56 A very limited number of shock trials had been carried out during the war on the *Cameron* and *Proteus*, later *Ambuscade*. In most of these trials non-damaging 50lb charges were used with the object of finding out what accelerations were experienced using different mountings for equipment.

57 These trials are discussed at much greater length in *Warship* 41-44 (1987). D K Brown, *Post War Trials*. Where necessary, these articles will be referenced as *Warship* number.

58 It was originally called the Admiralty Undex Works but unfortunate misinterpretations led to a rapid change of name!

59 He had been in charge of the damage section since 1931 and had immense experience, particularly on underwater explosions.

60 One early recommendation was that explosion trials against ships in commission should be carried out at distances at least 60 per cent more than the critical distance.

alterations and repairs. Most of the underwater trials were carried out in Loch Striven.

The two cruisers and *Nonsuch* had double bottoms and various trials were made with these partially filled. Not much was learnt, as the cruisers were too old and *Nonsuch* broke at the first shot.

The aim of many shots was to cause rupture of the hull without sinking. For a given orientation of the charge, rupture will depend on the value of $W/\sqrt{D}$ where W is charge weight in pounds and D the distance in feet. The first sign of damage was usually in the form of dimpling of the plating between frames, shear wrinkles in the side, straining of rivets and tearing of the plating at hard spots. Once this stage was reached, catastrophic failure was imminent.[60] At first sight, there was little difference in resistance to rupture of the shell plating between riveted and welded ships, longitudinally or transversely framed ships or British and German ships. More careful analysis suggested that the poor performance of the ex-German *Nonsuch* was due to bad detail design, steel not very suitable for welding and poor welding techniques. As a result, E W Gardner designed the *Whitby* class structure with thin plating and closely-spaced stiffeners based loosely on *Nonsuch*.

Under-bottom charges caused the ship to whip through several feet. The usual failure mode was tensile failure of the upper deck near a stress concentration, such as a break of forecastle, followed by failure of the bottom in compression. The trial with *Penn* was partic-

ularly interesting as two different designs of flexible bulkhead glands had been fitted to her port shaft. A 187lb Torpex charge was exploded under the keel, breaking her back. The bottom was pushed in, the upper deck buckled and there were shear wrinkles in the side. She whipped through ±10ins settling with a

Penn – a model representing the deflection of the hull due to whipping at 0.15-second intervals following the explosion of a 187lb charge. The maximum deflection was 10in either way with a 3in permanent set. (Author's collection)

An 'X' class midget submarine – tested to destruction. (Author's collection)

could be caused by deflections of the shell. Finally, the bulkhead could be damaged by shock loading on heavy items supported on it or by big pipes such as condenser outlets passing through it.

Trials against MTBs

Three British Power Boat 71ft 6in boats[61] and three Fairmile Ds[62] were allocated but *702* foundered in bad weather and was not replaced. The trials were carried out in Loch Striven between March and December 1947 using 187lb charges at varying distances and depths with six to eight shots per boat. Against the 71ft 6in boats rupture occurred at 41ft for 20ft depth, 60ft at 50ft depth. At the same depths, the Fairmiles failed in the petrol tank compartment at 28ft and 53ft respectively.

Trials against submarines

These trials were similar in aim to those against surface ships but depth of submergence added another variable and also made support and recovery, possibly severely damaged, more difficult. The first sixteen trials used nine 'midgets', roughly ⅓-scale models of the bigger submarines. The first two shots were against the Varley boats, *X 3* and *X 4* which were suspended from *Barfoot* and were to establish the trials procedure. The first serious trials began in Loch Fyne in March 1947 and used 8lb charges at different depths from 15ft to 450ft. Boats used were *X 3*, *X 4*, three of the *XT 1-4* class and one of the *X 5*[63] group.

permanent 3in deflection. Despite this the port shaft turned freely; the starboard shaft could also be turned though with difficulty as a plummer block had broken. The starboard shaft had damaged the bulkhead while the structure in way of the port shaft was undamaged.

Failure of bulkheads was frequent. The most usual cause was shock in a liquid-filled space causing the bulkhead to fail if air-backed on the other side. Wrinkling and tearing of the boundary connecting the bulkhead to the hull or of the bulkhead plating itself

The next sequence using the *XT 5* class involved constant charge weight and depth with explosions above, below and astern of the submarine. The last sequence used 187lb charges at constant depth. From these trials

Stygian following the explosion of a 200lb charge. (Author's collection)

a clearly defined graph was established relating charge weight, depth of submergence and the square root of the charge distance.[64]

Between October 1947 and October 1949 eleven submarines were expended in trials to determine the lethal distance of charges of different weight at different depths.

Submarine trials

Name	Depth (ft)	Charge weight (lbs)	Date
Seadog	Surface	100	Oct 47
Sybil	Surface	100	Dec 47
Sybil	Surface	187	Feb 48
Seanymph	Surface	620	Mar 48
Sceptre	325	200	Aug 49
Stygian	325	200	Aug 49
Spark	325	200	Sep 49
Proteus		187	1947
Job 9*		187	
Job 9		187	
Sea Rover	75	200	29 Sep 49
Surf	75	200	5 Oct 49
Upshot	75	200	Oct 49
Vivid	Shallow	200	Oct 49
Shalimar	75	200	May 49
Ace	6 Surface	187	Nov 48
Ace	2 @110	187	Nov 49
Ace	6 @ 70	187	
Ace	1 @ 35	187	

* Job 9 was a replica of the midships section of an 'A' class, built for shock trials

The first series of trials were carried out in Loch Striven and were on the surface since lifting craft were not available. Later trials were carried out in Loch Linnhe which was 430ft deep at the trial site. Two lifting craft were used, *LC 8* and *9* which could each lift 1200 tons. They were held apart by a Mulberry harbour pierhead and two smaller lifting craft, *LC 23* and *24*, were used to provide extra steam for the winding gear of their bigger sisters. Four 9in lifting slings were arranged round the target submarine with their ends buoyed to facilitate salvage. Several submarines were salvaged in under a week but *Shalimar* took 4 months. *Vivid* was intended for test at 325ft but accidentally sunk to the bottom. By the time she was salved the lifting craft had left so she was tested at shallow depth and sunk again!

It was found, as expected, the lethal distance D was given by $D = K.W/t$ where W is the charge weight and t is the thickness of the submarine plating. K varies with depth being 30 per cent greater at operational depth than at the surface. The results of the trials on the bigger submarines were consistent with the earlier results from the midgets.

Airborne weapons

The first trial was with cannon fire against two midget submarines surfaced in Aberlady Bay[65] to the south of the Firth of Forth. It was concluded that they were a difficult target but hits were possible and would be lethal. HE ammunition was slightly more effective than AP.

Though many ships had been hit by bombs during the war, the size and type of the bomb was often unknown, as was the precise point at which it detonated. A series of trials were held in Angle Bay, Milford

Surf after a trial. (Author's collection)

61 *454*, *472* and *484*.

62 (*702*), *745* and *774*.

63 This class had been built in three sections, bolted together, and tended to leak at the joint. Eventually, they were welded up.

64 See *Warship* 43 for particulars of these boats and partial identification.

65 Their remains are still on the beach.

Weston after the explosion of a 500lb bomb in the engine room. It was thought that she would have remained afloat with the loss of about twenty-five of her crew. (Author's collection)

Haven, in which 500lb bombs were detonated in or close to sloops and corvettes.[66] In the first in March 1947 a bomb was exploded in the gland space of *Bridgewater*. If at sea the after end would have fallen off but the fore end would have floated. An attempt was made to estimate the number of casualties with the crew at action stations. For this trial the estimate was ten. The next trial was in the forward boiler room of *Folkestone*. She would have floated, immobilised with thirty casualties. The third explosion was in the engine room of *Weston*. The ship floated, without power and suffered an estimated twenty-five casualties. The last of the series was with the corvette *La Malouine* with a bomb in the forward mess deck. She could have got home in good weather with twenty casualties.

The next series was on the Turbot Bank near Pembroke Dock and started in March 1947 with a 500lb bomb attached to the mast of *Balsam*. There would have been some fifteen casualties but the ship would not have been in danger. *La Malouine* was used again with a 1000lb bomb on the mast. Damage was slight but the bridge and Oerlikon crews would have been lost. In April, a 500lb bomb was detonated just above *Balsam's* forecastle at North Middle Ground in the Bristol Channel. The bridge was badly damaged and casualties would have been heavy but she could have proceeded under her own power. The last in this series involved a 1000lb bomb above the forecastle of *Campion*. The whole bridge was blown over and casualties would have been very heavy but she was still seaworthy. There were so many variables that it was difficult to draw general conclusions – except that bombs were dangerous.

In May 1947 a series of bombing trials were organised against *Hawkins* in Spithead. Phase 1 was to test the strength of the bomb case and the functioning of the fuse, Phase 2 involved dropping bombs with an inert

filling and a very small burster to see where detonation occurred, and Phase 3 would have involved exploding bombs at selected locations but was cancelled as her scrap metal was required so urgently. The bombers were Lincolns flying at 18,000ft and in 27 flying days they dropped 616 bombs scoring 29 hits – good accuracy from that height. In the first series there were seven hits with 500lb Mk VII and XIV of which five broke up. In the next series of fifteen hits, nine functioned (with partial detonation from two more). In the last series with 1000lb bombs five of seven hits functioned correctly. The trials party learnt a lot about damage control and the need for portable pumps, better torches and the difficulty in finding the way round a dark ship.

The most spectacular trial was that of bombs against the 6¼in deck of the *Nelson*. Both the 1000lb medium case and the very special 2000lb Mk IV were dropped between June and September 1948 from Barracuda Mk IIIs of a very experienced squadron at 55° to the horizontal and 280 knots. The trials were off Inchkeith in the Firth of Forth with cameras and a weather station on the island. In the first phase, 1000lb bombs were dropped from about 3000ft to give the pilots practice. The striking velocity was about 600ft/sec, hitting at 25° to the vertical. The release height was then increased to between 4000-5000ft giving a velocity of 700ft/sec and the first two bombs broke up on hitting thick armour. The third bomb hit the superstructure and passed through six decks before hitting the armour so that the bomb came to rest intact.

The release height was increased again to 8000ft for Phase 3 and one hit was scored with a 2000lb bomb. This sliced through 3¾in deck armour and broke up on the back of the side armour. For Phase 4 bombs with a very small bursting charge were used with a delay of 0.074 second and, initially, the release height was 8000ft. After thirty-nine very expensive bombs had missed[67] the release height was lowered to 6000ft. The first bomb hit B barbette and exploded on impact causing extensive damage. It was decided that the charge was too big and this phase was abandoned. Phase 3 was extended with a release height of 5500ft. Two hits were scored, the first hit the bridge and penetrated nine decks before hitting 3¾in armour which was dented but not penetrated. The second went through 6¼in deck and out through the bottom. Altogether 104 bombs were released for 12 hits on a large, stationary and undefended target.

On the other hand, had the bombs been filled, *Nelson* would have been put out of action very quickly and sunk soon after. The 1000lb bomb tended to break up if dropped from over 3000ft – would dive bombers have come as low as that in 1945 against a defended target? The 2000lb AP Mk IV bomb was something special. The nose was a very thick forging of special steel which would go through thick armour and continue on out through the bottom after explosion. The sides were very tough steel which would make large splinters, rupturing bulkheads either side of the explosion, allowing the floodwater caused by the nose's exit hole to spread. The bomb was designed 20 years after *Nelson* and it is no discredit to her designers that her protection failed. On the other hand, new *Lion* class ships would have had little better protection

Structural trials

In the first series, five submarines were lowered until their hulls collapsed under the pressure of water.[68] The first trial used a midget of the *XT 1-4* class which was lowered from *Barfoot* until she collapsed. She was fitted with forty-nine strain gauges which could be read until she collapsed in the battery compartment. It was also possible to move the rudders, hydroplanes and shaft to ensure these all functioned at extreme depth. Three more trials were then carried out on fairly modern submarines of different construction.

Varne	Partially welded
Stoic	Riveted shell, welded frames
Supreme	All welded

The final trial was of the uncompleted *Achates* in Gibraltar Bay. She was first lowered to 100ft to check instrumentation and then, on 19 June 1950, she was lowered to 600ft. She was then lowered in steps of 50ft until the estimated collapse depth was approached when the steps were reduced to 25ft; strain readings being taken at each step. At the last depth the readings became non-linear and after 5 minutes at that depth, she collapsed violently. The remains were brought close to the surface and examined by divers. The after end had fallen off and the fore end from the after bulkhead of the torpedo compartment was hanging down making it impossible to dock her or even to beach her. Collapse had initiated by failure of plating between the frames; water had then rushed in at enormous pressure and the trapped air bubble had oscillated wildly, tearing the boat apart. One of the internal welded T bar frames had torn loose and was found wrapped round the instrumentation cable.

The results of these tests was very encouraging as all five had collapsed very close to the predicted depth. True, failure often started at a detail such as the torpedo loading hatch but there was evidence that interframe plating collapse was close. The main guide to pressure hull plating strength was the 'boiler formula'.[69]

$$\text{Stress} = \frac{\text{Pressure x Radius of Hull}}{\text{Thickness (Pressure hull plating)}}$$

The table below compares the collapse depth predicted by this formula with the measured collapse depth.

	Formula Depth (ft)	Actual Depth (ft)
XT	702	565
Varne	860	877
*Stoic**	534	527-537
Supreme	700	647
Achates	860	877

*It is of interest that *Stubborn* had inadvertently dived to 540ft while evading attack. Her rumpled plating showed that she was very close to collapse.

There was one last trial on the strength of a surface ship. At that date the bending moment and hence the stresses were calculated for a stationary ship balanced on a wave of its own length and a height of ½0th the length, first with a crest amidships and then with a crest at bow and stern. This approach was comparative in that acceptable stresses could only be judged by experience; that it was safe was shown by the absence of major failures in British ships. The number of leaking riveted seams suggested that it was not over-cautious.

To test this approach, the uncompleted destroyer *Albuera* was loaded in dock until she broke.[70] She was connected to two supports, 70ft apart, either side of amidships, and the water level lowered until she snapped. The final failure was initiated by shear buckling in the side plating. There were a large number of strain gauges whose readings showed that the design approach was satisfactory.

There were a number of other trials of which no record has been found. *Furious* was used for trials on the stowage of rockets and other ammunition. There were tests of 6in, 4.5in and 4in shells against corvettes, LCTs and E-boats. Coastal force guns of 20mm, 40mm, 6pdr and 4.5in were tried against targets representing E- and R-boats, flak lighters and eastern junks. Only the 4.5in was effective.

Lessons

All the lessons were fed into the post-war frigates, the *Leopard*s and *Whitby*s. In some aspects, such as bulkhead design, the trials merely showed there was a problem and research at NCRE, followed by large scale tests were needed to find a solution. These trials were cheap; the ships were available, the staff involved were not numerous and there was no more urgent work for them. A little-known success story.

66 *Warship* 44 has a more detailed account.

67 For all its faults, the Barracuda was thought to be an excellent dive bomber. Only in the Mk I did the tail tend to fall off.

68 *Warship* 44.

69 D K Brown, 'Submarine Pressure Hull Design and Diving Depth between the Wars', *Warship International* 3/87.

70 D W Lang and W G Warren, 'Structural Strength Investigations on the Destroyer *Albuera*', *Trans INA* (1952).

Eleven | Production and Repair

THIS BOOK IS PRIMARILY about the design of British warships but freedom of design is constrained by the availability of resources – shipyards, engine works, armament and armour manufacturers and many other specialised suppliers. For this reason a brief treatment of production problems and achievements is included here.[1]

Pre-war orders

Orders placed before the war stretched the capacity of shipbuilding and associated industries to the limit and beyond. When the war broke out there were some 690,000 tons (standard) of warships under construction made up of:

9 battleships
6 aircraft carriers
19 cruisers
44 destroyers
11 fast minelayers, sloops and minesweepers
12 submarines

This overloaded programme was cut at the outbreak of war when the four *Lion* class battleships were suspended followed by five cruisers in early 1940.

The state of the industry

During the slumps between the wars some thirty shipyards had closed as had two of the three main armament firms and many engine builders. The number of slipways over 250ft in length had reduced from 459 to 266 of which it was expected that 134 would be available for warship building. There had been little investment in new plant. These visible reductions were not the most serious problems, which lay in skilled manpower. Few apprentices had been entered in the early 1930s and management was ageing and reluctant to take any risks. The cuts in the bad years had led to very poor industrial relationships leading to strange demarcation practices.[2]

On the bright side, the UK still had sixty shipyards and built more than twice as much merchant tonnage as each of its next largest competitors, Germany and Japan. From 1937 onwards, re-armament brought full employment and profitability to the industry though it

1 This section is very largely based on Dr I L Buxton, *Warship Building during the Second World War*, The Centre for Business History in Scotland, Research Monograph No 2 (1998). I am most grateful to Ian Buxton for permission to use his work. Other material is from unpublished research by George Moore and Phillip Pugh.

2 As an apprentice, I was told of one gun mounting which had three circular lightening holes. The two smaller ones were cut by drillers but the largest had to be cut by a caulker using an identical burner. Eventually the holes were drawn freehand and non-circular holes of any size were the task of a caulker!

3 H B Peebles, *Warship Building on the Clyde* (Edinburgh 1987).

4 Goodall, 30 July 1943.

5 Compared with 630 and 559 in January 1933!

6 See Chapter 7 for installed electrical power in frigates.

Arethusa under construction at Chatham in 1933. The use of welding was considerably extended in this class and Chatham was the leading yard of the day. (Author's collection)

would seem that little of these profits was invested in new tools.[3] The Admiralty funded new armour and armament plant and some heavy cranes.

Changes of plan

As the war developed, there were inevitable changes of plan though many thought that too many changes were made, Goodall writing 'It is heart rending that we cannot settle down to a building plan. No sooner do we key up a firm and get them busy than we have to butt in, stop them and get them busy on something else.'[4]

There was continual pressure, notably from Churchill, to concentrate on ships which could be completed quickly, before the war ended. Thus in March 1941 Churchill issued an instruction that work should only proceed on warships which could complete by the end of 1942 (and merchant ships by the end of 1941). Later, it was decided that the war with Japan would be over by the end of 1946. On the other hand, the Board were by no means convinced that the war would be over quickly and were worried over the shortage of modern battleships. They were undoubtedly concerned that the RN should emerge from the war as a powerful and balanced force.

Whilst some yards specialised in either merchant ships or warships there were others which could build either, and there was great debate as to where the emphasis should be placed. Initially, the aim was to keep merchant ship output about the same as that in a good peacetime year. In practice, the numbers engaged on both merchant ship and warship new construction and repair increased at much the same rate up to 1944. There was a similar conflict between new construction and repair work.

Employment

Employment figures in 1000s

	Jun 40	Sep 43	Jun 45
Naval Vessels			
Private Yards, new work	62.4	89.3	73.9
Repair and conversion	41.5	44.1	38.8
Dockyards	26.4	36.7	35.7
Total Naval	**130.3**	**170.1**	**148.4**
Merchant Vessels			
Private Yards, new work	28.8	42.9	42.5
Repair and conversion	44.0	59.5	61.4
Total merchant	**72.8**	**102.4**	**103.9**
Total new work	94.2	135.2	119.4
Total repair	*108.9*	*137.3*	*132.9*
Grand Total	**203.1**	**272.5**	**252.3**

Note: assumes 3000 of Dockyard on new work. Marine engineering not included.

MGB 601 under construction at Tough Brothers on the Thames. The Fairmile system used sawn plywood frames with longitudinals slotted through. *601* was laid down in May 1941, completed in January 1942 and lost in a fire in July of that year. (Author's collection)

The table shows that of the quarter million-strong workforce some 60 per cent were employed on naval work and just under 50 per cent on new construction. There were more than 950 firms involved in 1944-5, over half employing fewer than 100 people. By far the largest firm was Harland and Wolff with 16,328 in the shipyard and 8978 in the engine works in September 1943.[5] Employment of women peaked in 1944 at 27,500, making up about 10 per cent of the workforce and split 50:50 between operatives and administration. These figures may be compared with naval personnel six times the pre war figure at 756,000 men and 65,000 women. The total industrial workforce associated with Admiralty work was about 918,000 in December 1943, including the production of all forms of equipment and stores but excluding the manufacture of raw steel.

The balance of skill changed considerably during the war as more and more craftsmen, particularly electricians, were taken on. By 1944 there were 12,000 electricians of which only 1000 were working on merchant ships – and this was still insufficient (see Chapter 7).[6] It was estimated that the balance of unskilled to skilled was 10/18 for warship work and 10/13 for merchant ships. This reflects the increased complexity of warships with new or increased degaussing, radar, heating, ventilation, fire control, communications and air-conditioning.

The number of welders increased by about 80 per

cent over the two years 1943-4 in the twenty-seven warship yards. Goodall frequently claimed that progress in welding was too slow but, to some extent, progress was limited by availability of plant – welding gear itself, electrical supplies, cranes and suitable fabrication shops, which were all scarce in wartime Britain. Allowance has then to be made for the disruption which any large change would cause.

Marine engineering

Complete records of the output of marine engines have not been found but there was clearly a great achievement whilst output of engines still formed a constraint on new construction. Major warship building depended on the output of fourteen turbine builders so, with a few exceptions, turbines were only used at power levels above 4000shp. It is probable that gear cutting formed an even greater bottleneck.[7] The six biggest engine builders each built over sixty sets of more than 1 million horsepower.[8] Land builders of power station machinery built a few sets, including ten for frigates by C A Parsons.[9]

The pre-war diesel industry in the UK was not very strong. The diesel engine had only made slow progress in British merchant ships whilst railway engines were almost all coal-burning steamers. Even so, there were seven firms building submarine diesels and three build-

ing small engines for landing craft and MMS.[10] The problems of MTB engines are discussed in Chapter 8. The number of workers in the marine engineering industry rose from 58,000 before the war to 88,900 in June 1943 (of which 13,100 were women), falling slightly to 80,500 in June 1945.

Production problems

Bombing. It is said that only ½ per cent of production was lost due to damage from bombing.[11] This seems unlikely and probably omits loss of production associated with many sleepless nights and the effect of blackout. As the war dragged on there was a general weariness. There was also a strange philosophy that Churchill had assured the people of victory and it was not necessary to work too hard. This was associated with the idea that the 'Freedom' for which the war was being fought included the right to strike for better working conditions and the defence of demarcation etc.

Strikes etc. There were far too many strikes, over 1 million working days being lost in 1944. But even so, Goodall's frequent notes on visits to shipyards is inclined to put much of the blame on poor management. Average wages rose from about the equivalent of £3.50 per week in 1938 to nearly £7 by the end of the war. This compares with a petty officer receiving £2.50 in 1939 and £3.50 in 1946 – with no right to strike.

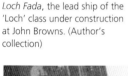

Loch Fada, the lead ship of the 'Loch' class under construction at John Browns. (Author's collection)

British warship building 1939-45
Number of vessels completed/standard displacement (tons x 1000)

	1939	1940	1941	1942	1943	1944	1945	Tot 1	Tot 2
Battleships, carriers, cruisers	3	10	11	8	10	6	7	50	55
	29.6	126.9	161.5	110.4	84.9	88.3	84.3	636.0	685.9
Destroyers	22	97	39	73	37	31	22	229	251
	38.6	31.3	50.6	99.5	61.6	53.7	41.9	337.3	337.2
Frigates, sloops, corvettes	5	49	74	30	57	73	28	311	316
	4.2	48.8	75.4	35.0	73.1	88.2	32.9	356.4	363.8
Submarines	7	15	20	33	39	39	17	164	170
	8.1	12.0	14.1	24.0	27.7	29.0	15.0	123.3	129.9
Minelayers, sweepers, trawlers, boom defence vessels etc	20	47	92	95	79	39	28	380	400
	13.2	27.3	63.0	58.1	56.4	28.8	18.4	251.8	265.2
Total warships	57	148	236	239	222	188	102	1134	1192
	93.7	246.3	364.6	327.0	303.7	288.0	198.7	1704.8	1822.0
MTB, ML, MMS etc	14	121	395	403	337	234	103	1575	1607
	0.3	6.9	37.7	46.1	44.4	24.5	12.0	169.7	171.9
Landing ships and craft	4	158	246	521	1462	1306	739	4324	4436
	0.1	4.6	19.5	60.6	151.2	152.7	138.9	507.6	528.6
Total craft	18	279	641	924	1799	1540	842	5899	6043
	0.4	12.5	57.2	106.7	195.6	177.2	150.9	677.3	700.5
Grand Total Numbers	75	427	877	1163	2021	1728	944	7033	7235
Displacement	94.1	258.8	421.8	433.7	499.3	465.2	349.6	2382.1	2522.5

Tot 1 is Sep 1939–Sep 1945, Tot 2 is all 1939 to end 1945

Steel shortage. Steel was short in all UK engineering work and had to be shared between warships and merchant ships and with tanks etc.

Comparison with the USA

During the war, US shipyards set up some incredible records for rapid building, but measured in man hours or in cost the superior performance of British yards is clear, despite the problems discussed above. The early US DE destroyer escorts took about 1 million manhours reducing to 600-700,000 with experience while the British-built 'River' class needed 350-400,000 manhours. The cost (including ASIs) of the 'River' was about £240,000 while the very similar 'Colony' class built by the US Maritime Commission cost $2.25 million (c£570,000).[12] In submarine construction it was said that the US worker produced 3.8 tons in a year compared with 8.8 tons per year for the British worker.

The average cost of a Liberty ship was $1.78 million (£450,000) whilst a similar Empire ship built in the UK would cost about £180,000. The US ship would need 500-650,000 man-hours, the British 350,000.

Contracts and costs

Warship production from DNC was headed by Superintendent Contract Work (SCW) who supervised work through a numerous overseeing force.[13] Contracts were placed by the Director of Naval Contracts. From 1941 onwards, firms were allowed 6½ per cent to 7½ per cent profit based on the average actual cost of the class which ensured that the best firms did well but the poorer ones were not driven out of business. Buxton has produced figures for the total cost of wartime building:

	£M
Hulls of ships building by contract	294.9
Propelling machinery	182.3
Auxiliary machinery	55.5
Fairmile boats	23.1
Hull and Machinery Total	**555.8**

To this figure one must add the items purchased directly by the Admiralty and supplied to the builder (Admiralty Supply Items – ASI). Multiply by about 30 to get today's value.

	£M
Armour	15.2
Gun mountings & air compressing plant	100.6
Guns and ordnance stores	43.9
Electrical and scientific apparatus	201.0
Admiralty Supply Items Total	**360.7**

7 I feel that there is something wrong here. In the First World War there were very many geared turbine plants built and only a few of these manufacturers had been lost. It may be that the early gear cutting machinery could not meet the standards required in the Second World War.

8 John Brown, Wallsend, Cammell Laird, Fairfield, Hawthorne-Leslie and Vickers (Barrow).

9 Surely these firms could have built more?

10 Most LCTs had Paxman diesels from a new plant intended to build engines for 'Nellie' the trench-digging machine. By July 1943 they had built 1000 engines.

11 Buxton quoting CAB102/539.

12 See Chapter 7 for comparison of their equipment – but this would not account for much of the price difference.

13 C Hannaford RCNC was SCW for most of the war. He was selected by Goodall but they do not seem to have got on well together.

Using a slightly different approach, Buxton gives the following spread of costs for the war years. The table below excludes ASI and auxiliary vessels which account for much of the difference from the first table above. In round figures, the value of wartime warship building was £500 million.

	£M	%
Battleships, carriers and cruisers	96	23
Destroyers	88	21
Escorts	53	13
Mine ships, trawlers, boom defence etc	38	9
Total major warships	302	73
Light coastal craft	51	12
Landing vessels	61	15
TOTAL	**414**	**100**

Building times[14]

Type	Time	Man-months
Battleship	54	46,000
Carrier	46	31,115
Fiji	28	15,017
Dido	28	8214
DD 'M'	28	4991
'Hunt'	15	2944
Corvette	10	922
Submarine	20	2700

Terrible, later *Sydney*, ready for launch at Devonport. She was the only carrier built in a dockyard. The slipway is now a Grade II listed historic building! (Author's collection)

Excess profits

During 1943 the Exchequer and Audit department carried out an investigation into the profits made on warships ordered during re-armament with horrifying results, 30 per cent or more profit[15] being common. It is certain that the cost of the *King George V* (and of many other ships of the period) was far less than the estimate which was used as a basis for the fixed price contract.[16] It was suggested by the Exchequer and Audit in 1943 that DNC's cost estimators (usually referred to as costers) had based their prices on Dockyard figures and not allowed for the greater efficiency of private yards, and this explanation was followed by the official history.[17]

Dockyard efficiency

It is fairly certain that before the First World War the Dockyards were considerably more efficient than commercial yards, as demonstrated by their much greater speed in building ships of the same class. The reasons were complicated but include better management at both senior and middle levels, better labour relations and greater capital investment in machinery. Perhaps most important, there was a determination to keep costs down, shown by Portsmouth's early introduction of electric lighting inside ships under construction, which very greatly improved productivity and the same yard's use of standardised plate sizes in *Dreadnought*.[18]

It is very probable that the much reduced building programmes of the 1920s and 1930s reduced the Dockyards' efficiency in new construction. This seems to have been recognised as the following table for costs of the *Kent* class (Table 1) shows higher costs for the

Dockyard ships.[19] This data makes two points–
Dockyards were then less efficient and the fact was
recognised and allowed for. It is also possible that work
which could not be fully identified was booked to new
construction, a long term item.

For the estimated hull cost for *Suffolk* (and *Cornwall*), the Dockyard-built ships is within the span of the
ships built in commercial yards but the 'Establishment
costs' – overheads including profit, is much higher. The
full table in Bate then adds on £60,000 to the commercial
costs on 'account of higher rates at the Dockyards'.
These figures date from about 1930 and it is possible that
the Dockyards deteriorated further by the time the *King
George V* was ordered, there is no evidence either way.

The cost of King George V

It seems almost certain that the estimated cost of the
King George V was based on the recorded price of
Nelson and *Rodney* as they were the only reasonably
recent battleships.[20]

Table 2 gives an estimated breakdown of cost which
seems to have been used as a basis for the contract. It is
taken from the work book of H S Pengelly, head of the
design section. He describes it as Vote 8 III, excluding
Dockyard charges, but it includes guns and ammunition
which were vote 9 as in *Nelson* above.

Table 2: Cost estimate for King George V [21]

	£ x 1000
Hull and electrical	2050
Main and auxiliary machinery.	825
Armour	1425
Guns[22]	550
Gun mounting and compressors	1514
Ammunition	805
Aircraft	34
+ Bombs and torpedoes	21
Boats	20
Incidentals	27
Dockyard labour and materials	25
TOTAL	7493

It is possible to compare some of these figures with
those of *Nelson*. Armour should vary with weight.[23]
Armour cost £1,431,000 and weighed 10,250 tons in
Nelson. One would expect that the 12,700 tons in *King
George V* would cost 12,700 x £1431/10,250 =
£1,773,000 instead of the £1,425,000 of the table above.
Similar reasoning gives a hull cost for *King George V* of
£1,027,000, about half that given by Pengelly. There is a
difficulty here in that hull group for the later ship
includes electrical equipment. However, even if there
was an error in *King George V* it does not explain the
errors in almost every other class of ship.[24]

Table 1: Comparison of Dockyard and commercial costs

Ship	Suffolk	Berwick	Cumberland	Australia	Shropshire	Sussex
Hull cost £1000	640	543	571	662	701	704
Establishment cost	165	34	35	40	42	42

Overheads and profits in commercial yards

In the 1920s and 1930s, even though naval work was
scarce, profitability was rising. For example, between
1928 and 1933, John Brown built three pairs of destroyers of the 'A', 'B' and 'F' classes. The table below shows
the average price per ship and breakdown.

Table 3: John Brown destroyer costs (costs etc in £ x 1000)[25]

Class	Date	Invoice price	Materials	Labour	Overheads & profit
'A'	1928	221	122	82	16
'B'	1929	219	123	69	27
'F'	1933	245	123	62	60

The first obvious point is that costs were falling while
the agreed invoice price in the contract rose. The fall in
costs was due to reduced labour costs which could be
due to increased efficiency (most unlikely at John
Brown) or falling wages, discussed later. Note that these
figures were not available to the Admiralty.

The increase in contract prices was most probably
due to the success of the Warshipbuilders' Committee.
This was initiated in November 1926 when, with
Admiralty assistance, a rota was established to share the
scarce orders equitably. This seems to have evolved into
a price-fixing ring whose deliberations were secret.
Peebles suggests that its existence was well known to
the Admiralty and was the main reason why competitive tendering was abandoned in 1935.

Prices and profits continued to rise shown in figures
for destroyers built at Denny's in the later 1930s.

Table 4: Denny destroyer costs (cost in £ x 1000)

Class	Date	Invoice	Overheads and profit
'E'	1934	247	20
'H'	1936	254	36
'Tribal'	1938	359	75
'J', 'K'	1939	401	126

The 'E' and 'H' classes were generally similar and the
'Tribals' much bigger but of similar style. The 'J' and
'Ks' were the first longitudinally-framed class of
destroyer and it seems likely that all shipbuilders added
a considerable sum to their tender because of imagined
difficulty with this system.

14 ADM 1 11968.

15 Profit as a percentage of the
shipbuilders' contract price, *ie*
excluding Admiralty supply items
such as weapons.

16 There are several entries in
Goodall's diaries early in 1943. He
was interviewed on 27 May and
wrote. 'High profits at PAC.
Atmosphere as trial of a convict
with Exchequer and Audit council
for the prosecution, the chairman as
judge, rest of them jury. Treasury
counsel for the defence on the
whole'.

17 W Ashworth, *Contracts and
Finance* (HMSO, London 1953).

18 H E Deadman, 'On the
Applications of Electricity in the
Royal Dockyards and the Navy',
Trans I Mech E (London 1892).

19 E R Bate's papers. Now in the
National Maritime Museum.

20 A detailed breakdown of the cost
of these ships is given in D K
Brown, *The Grand Fleet*, pp182-3

21 H S Pengelly. Work book.
National Maritime Museum.

22 Goodall, 29 Nov 1939. 'Money
kills. The recommencement of
capital ship construction and the
gun mounting and guns costing
more than half the total are the
nigger in the woodpile'. Also 30
Nov. 'Slept on INA paper (Cost of
warships) and decided "No" it
would show up the gun mounting
ramp and I funk offending Vickers'.

23 The allocation of protective
plating between hull and armour
groups may have varied.

24 Goodall, 19 Feb 1943. 'Craven
called, showed him my yarn on high
profits. He agreed with small mods
said KGV was the cheapest of the 5
ships. PoW made about ¾ profit of
KGV. DoY least profit, about half
that of KGV. Rewrote yarn.'

25 H B Peebles, *Warship Building
on the Clyde*, p131.

This diagram shows how building costs rose during the Second World War. Much of the increase is inflation but the greatly increased complexity was also significant. Trend curves like this are valuable but care is needed to insure that they are not self fulfilling when a forecast increase appears to justify a higher tender whereas improved procedures should lead to a decrease.

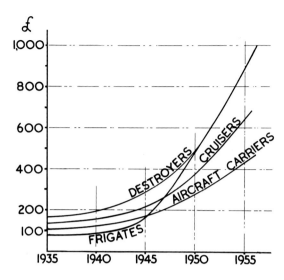

Table 5: National wage rates[26]

Year	Wages		Year	Wages	
	Money	Real		Money	Real
1927	101.5	95.8	1933	95.3	108.1
1928	100.1	95.2	1934	96.4	108.1
1929	100.4	96.7	1935	98.0	108.3
1930	100.0	100.0	1936	100.2	107.7
1931	98.2	105.1	1937	102.8	105.4
1932	96.3	105.7	1938	106.3	107.7

The figures above do not suggest low wages as an explanation of the reduction in labour costs shown in Table 3 but they may not fully represent shipyard wages.[27]

Some personal thoughts

Until about 1960, cost was not something which designers worried about unduly. A series of studies were produced, the costing department put a figure on them, and the Board decided what they could afford. The need to keep costs down was recognised and some quite trivial changes were vetoed as too expensive but such decisions were often made without any real idea of the sums involved.[28]

The costing group consisted almost entirely of draughtsmen who used available data to produce simple rules of thumb, almost always a cost/ton figure for different weight groups. These men tended to stay in the post for a very long time and had much knowledge in a very narrow band. The chief constructor in charge was not usually a high-flyer.

The figures they provided were self-justifying as it was easy, using trend curves, to show what the tender prices for the next class would be. The estimated costs were not seen as particularly confidential and it is quite likely that shipbuilders were aware of them and how they were produced so that in preparing a tender, they would know what would be expected and acceptable. The estimate started from a shaky base and extrapolated, getting further and further from reality.

The lack of other work and the shortage of naval orders meant that the overall profits of individual yards were small. A careful examination of company accounts should have revealed high profits on individual orders – there may even have been a blind eye turned since it was seen as in the Navy's interest to keep shipyards alive – this was the reason for the near-cessation of Dockyard building.[29]

Overheads and rising costs

A paper by Karamelli, Principal Accountant, Admiralty Contracts Department, contains some further information, notably on firm's Establishment Charges (Table 6).[30] Karamelli does not accept the PAC view that the costers estimates were wrong due to false comparison

All the Clyde yards discussed by Peebles found that warship building could make a major contribution to overheads and profit, *eg* Fairfields found that *Howe* contributed 29.9 per cent to overheads and profit. He also suggests that 'general charges were applied more selectively' with warship work paying much the larger part. It could be argued that there was some small degree of justice in this. Warships were more refined, certainly involved more white-collar input (draughtsmen) and probably used equipment not required for merchant ships.

The 'County' class cruisers (Table 1) were probably the last ships where a true comparison could be made between Dockyard and commercial costs. The reducing costs and rising profit margin do not seem to have been recognised. Shipbuilding wage rates have not been found; the table below gives average national wages for the period.

Table 6: Rates of Establishment Charges 1937 and 1941

Firm	Hull			Machinery		
	1937	1941	% of 1937	1937	1941	% of 1937
John Brown	43.2	22.25	52	39.6	36.5	92
Cammell Laird	46.6	32.25	69	40.4	37.5	93
Denny	47.5	40	34	60	65.5	109
Fairfield	75	30	40	63.5	45	71
Harland & Wolff	56	40	71	62.5	33.5	86
Hawthorn Leslie	59	38.25	65	102	54	53
Swan Hunter						
Neptune	45.3	41.5	92	50	56.5	113
Wallsend	45.8	34	74	-	-	-
Scotts	53	25	47*	41	44*	107
Vickers-Walker	58	32.5	56	-	-	-
Lithgow	40	15.5	39			

* 1940 rates – 1941 not available

with Dockyard costs and seeks, not altogether successfully, for other explanations.

The first point to note is that both the rates and their
change from 1937 to 1941 vary considerably. There was
little of no formal management training in those days
and the make up of Establishment Charges – overheads
most probably varied considerably from firm to firm.
(It seems that drawing office work was charged as
direct labour in some and as overheads in others.)

Karamelli then shows that a typical fall of 14 percentage points on overheads leads to a 7½ per cent fall in
cost with a corresponding increase in profit which is
much less than the discrepancy in profit. He then goes
on to suggest that the 7.5 per cent fall in steel prices was
important. (Pugh points out that this fall would only
give a 3.8 per cent reduction in cost. I think Karamelli is
comparing this small fall in cost with an expected large
rise for which allowance had been made in the tender.)
Karamelli also suggests that the tenders allowed for
increased labour costs which did not happen.

There is some confirmation of this in discussion of
the tenders for the 'Hunt' class. Bessant (head of the
design team) noted that the Admiralty estimate for the
hull cost was £100,000 whilst the average tender was
£138,000. The firms gave several reasons for this, most
specific to the 'Hunts', but including 'the rise in wages
since the 'L' class due to expansion in the aircraft industry'. This note also implies that the Admiralty estimate
was discussed with the contractors which would have
been of great value in setting their bid for the next
class.[31]

The *Daring*s were the first class
of destroyer designed for
welded construction. (Author's
collection)

26 C Cook and J Stevenson, *The
Longman Handbook of British
History* (London 1983).

27 Weekly time rates for skilled
workers (platers, plumbers) on the
Tyne in shillings per week were
1928 56, 1929 58, 1930 60, 1936 62,
1937 64, 1938 68, 1939 70, 1940 75.
Excludes bonuses, overtime. Some
bonuses were withdrawn in 1931
amounting to a pay cut.

28 Goodall 13 July 1935. 'Asked
DNC if £650 to save 11½ tons on
aluminium kit lockers in *Repulse*
was too much – he said "Yes"'.

29 Goodall, 7 June 1943. 'Secretary
meeting. All thought I was in for it
next Wednesday' and – 9 June. 'Got
badly mauled over submarine costs
and KGV as I expected. I think I
made a tactical error in finding
actual rise in costs 1937-40 and
saying what I assumed rise would
be. I got in no counter attack and
came away depressed. Trouble is I
had a bad case on submarines.'

30 ADM 229/28 of 3 March 1943.

31 See 'Hunt' class, Chapter 5.

Table 7: Some representative profits

Ship	Builder	Date (Tender)	Profit %	
King George V	Vickers	1937	41.6	Battleship
Formidable	H & Wolff	1937	9.1	Carrier
Nigeria	Vickers	1939	26.7	Cruiser
Phoebe	Fairfield	1937	25.1	
Kelly	Haw Leslie	1937	31.0	Destroyer
Truant	Vickers	1937	86.6	Submarine
Unbeaten	Vickers	1939	77.7	
Black Swan	Yarrow	1937	23.2	Sloop
Fernie	J Brown	1939	34.1	'Hunt'
Bangor	H & Wolff	1939	15.0	Minesweeper
Gladiolus	Smiths	1939	40.8	Corvette
Fandango	Cochrane	1940	25.7	Trawler

Karamelli's small changes do add up.

Actual cost	100
Error in overheads	7
Allowance for increase in steel	4
wages	5
Profit estimated	7

This would give a tender price of 123 (and the profit aimed at would probably be higher) and a profit achieved on real cost of 23 per cent. If the falls in steel price and wages are inserted the cost drops to 91 and the profit to 35 per cent, about what was observed.

Conclusions

The main reason was that engineers did not regard cost as part of their job and took little interest in the subject. The DNC himself, Sir Stanley Goodall, would check technical estimates with great care but his diaries suggest that he paid little attention to cost estimates. It is virtually certain that commercial engineers were of similar mind and that firms' internal estimates of cost were crude and inaccurate. (They certainly were in post-war years.)

This lack of interest led to several errors:

(1) The failure to notice that commercial costs were falling throughout the 1930s. This would have required some simple detective work in company accounts and some intelligent observation by overseers. This error was probably compounded by rising costs in the Dockyards due to their very limited new construction load.

(2) The misuse of trend curves. It was probably noted that tenders for similar ships (eg destroyers) were gradually rising and an even higher bid next time would be regarded as confirmation of the estimate rather than as grounds for suspicion.

(3) The failure to realise that overheads would fall as the number of orders increased.

I disagree with the Auditor General that the error was due to using Dockyard costs for estimates of commercial work. DNC was well aware of this. As suggested above, the costers may well have applied a trend of rising cost from the Dockyards to commercial work but they would not have applied costs directly (Table 1). This is not a blind defence of my old department; their real error – lack of interest in cost – was far more serious, even if fairly universal.

The 1945 building programme

The 1945 building programme changed frequently as the forecast date for the end of the war changed and as pressure grew to change the shipbuilding industry to merchant ships. The version shown below is roughly what the Admiralty thought necessary in January 1945 against a forecast that the war with Japan would finish by the end of 1946. It was pointed out that losses in the Pacific could be heavy and would be suffered amongst the most modern ships.

The principal cancellations were three destroyers, forty-two submarines and two sloops.

Lion and *Temeraire* were to complete in 1952, while *Conqueror* and *Thunderer* were suspended.
3 *Ark Royals* to continue; 4 *Maltas* deferred.
4 *Hermes* to continue, 4 deferred.
1 *Tiger* (1941 Prog) and 5 heavy cruisers to build in slow time completing not later than 1950
16 'Battles' (1944 Prog – 'Darings'), 4 'Weapons' (1943) and 6 (1944 'G') to complete 1947-9
Submarines; 8 'A', 1 improved 'A' and 1 experimental to be built in slow time.
In addition, 5 survey ships, 4 new escorts and 2 new fast oilers were included.

What is a Good Design? | *Twelve*

We apprehend that it is the object of our labours, as it is the business of science, to endeavour to produce the best effects with given means.

Chatham Committee of Naval Architects, 1842[1]

FEW WOULD DISPUTE the application of the Chatham Committee's words to warship design before, during and after the Second World War. However, all the attributes can be interpreted in different ways. A 'Good Design' will often be seen by some naval architects as one which meets the Staff Requirement at a reasonable price.[2] The sailor, proud of the ship in which he lives, will attach considerable importance to aesthetics and habitability. The historian will look back on the performance of the ship at the end of its life and may, looking through the wrong end of the telescope, attach undue importance to the way in which the ship operated in the last years of its life, nearly worn out and, perhaps, being used in a role very different from that for which it was designed. All these views are understandable, if incomplete, and represent different approaches to the whole problem, which are in turn compounded when an attempt is made to judge what makes a good fleet.

Foretelling the future

A warship's life is a long one and it may be seen as conceived long before the first ship is ordered. There will be discussions within the Staff and with DNC; usually such discussions have no clear starting point. The true starting point is the Staff's appreciation of the type of war which will be fought. For much of the inter-war era the emphasis was on a new 'Jutland' with an enemy battlefleet slowed by carrier aircraft and then sunk by the big guns of the RN battle line. Such thinking also led to the heavy torpedo armament and low freeboard of destroyers (and even torpedo tubes in cruisers). The threat to the trade routes was expected to come from surface raiders. The Staff were right in thinking that the submarine threat to shipping in mid-Atlantic was small in 1939 and also right in thinking that the threat from high-level bombing was not great. The view that dive bombers were unlikely to be a serious threat was based on RAF advice and was clearly wrong.[3]

The development of a requirement for a specific ship from a policy is lengthy. For example, it is usually said that the *King George V* derives from a Staff paper of 1933 leading to the first studies in April 1934. However, both the paper and the studies owe much to earlier work. It is wrong to think that the requirement and

design studies are separate, consecutive stages; as Sir Rowland Baker put it: 'As the chicken comes before the egg, so does the warship before the Staff Requirement'.[4] The studies for the new battleships led to approval of a sketch design in May 1936, orders for two ships in July and approval of the final design in October so that the ships could be laid down on the earliest date permitted by the treaty – 1 January 1937. They took 4 years to build and might have expected a 20-year life, scrapping 27 years after the first gleam in the eye.[5] Smaller classes took less time but it could still be considerable. The table gives an approximate idea of time for conception.[6]

	Cumulative years to		
	First study	*Approval*	*1st ship complete*
Battleship	1	3	7
Carrier	1	3½	7½
Cruiser	1	2	5
Destroyer	1	1½	4½

The lengthy lifespan of most warships means that they should be versatile as built and adaptable to changing roles as they age, a point which will recur. Almost inevitably, the initial, tentative requirement will be over ambitious leading to a ship which cannot be built within treaty limits or is too expensive.[7] Successive iterations will decide which features can be accommodated within

Anson in 1942. Often underrated, this class was well designed within the constraints of Treaties and the limits of industry. (Author's collection)

1 Read, Chatfield and Creuze, Chatham Committee of Naval Architects, 1842. See D K Brown, *Before the Ironclad*.

2 The author would regard this definition as far too narrow.

3 The trials of dive bombing against *Centurion* in 1933 do seem to have alerted both Staff and constructors to the problem. Though there was a big increase in the AA armament of the fleet, it was still inadequate. These trials probably influenced the decision to procure the Skua dive bomber.

4 Between the wars, the Staff and DNC department were close together, in the same building, and much of the discussion at this stage would be informal, face to face (see Goodall diaries). Surviving documents, *eg* Ships Covers, do not therefore give a complete picture of the extent of these discussions.

5 The phrase 'sperm to worm' is often used in preference to the shorter time scale of 'cradle to grave'.

6 Forward design group's motto was 'Conception is more fun than birth'.

7 It would seem that the Japanese Staff insisted on getting all they wanted, accounting both for their gross breaches of the Treaties and for stability and strength failures. E Lacroix and L Wells, *Japanese Cruisers of the Pacific War*.

Kent, in the author's view, the best of the early Washington cruisers. Seen with few wartime changes. (Imperial War Museum: A12592)

the constraints and which must be sacrificed. Quoting Baker again, '. . . our [DNC)] business is not to agree with the Staff, or argue with them, but control them (They can only have what "we" can offer).'[8]

Quality versus quantity

The problem of using the tonnage available under the Treaty and the money in tight budgets on a few 'super ships' or many lesser ones is eternal.[9] There can be no definitive solution to this problem. It was not important in battleships where, by 1937, there was no limit on fleet tonnage, and the naval architects just did the best they could on 35,000 tons per ship. The problem became acute in cruisers during the early 1930s when the RN decided on the *Leander/Amphion* with a few *Arethusas* as most suited for its needs but had to move to fewer, big *Southamptons* as a response to the Japanese *Mogami*. One may also recognise the problem in the 'Tribal' class destroyers in which the RN was driven to a bigger ship than they wanted and the converse in the 'T' class submarines where, to get the numbers, sacrifices, particularly in speed, had to be made.

A related topic is what has more recently been called 'Availability, Reliability, Maintainability'. As has been said in earlier chapters, British ships were reliable in the sense that they did not break down, break in half, cap-

size etc. On the other hand, their availability was not very good; for example, destroyers and escorts were operational about 75 per cent of the time allowing for boiler cleaning, refits etc. They were fairly easy to maintain but needed such work too often. In defence, it must be said that they were better than the ships of most navies other than the USN which were far superior. There was a misconception that 'simple' machinery was more reliable than advanced plants but the reliability and ease of operation of the US built 'Captains' showed that this was not necessarily true.

Summary of specific problems

The problems which afflicted ships of this era were mainly due to the constraints discussed in the Introduction. Shortage of funds meant few orders and this, in turn, meant that specialist industry was reluctant to develop equipment solely for naval use. Under tight financial pressure both Staff and constructors tended to a conventional view and were reluctant to pursue more advanced solutions.

Machinery. Compared with USN machinery, British machinery was heavy, bulky, leaky and, most important, uneconomical leading to poor endurance. This was mainly due to a backward industry but the Admiralty could and should have exerted more pressure (Chapter 5).

Medium calibre Guns. Guns and gun mountings were recognised as a potential bottleneck but the RN persisted in installing 4in in various forms, 4.5in, two very different types of 4.7in and the 5.25in gun for roles which the much larger USN satisfied with single or twin 5in/38 calibre.

Fire control. While surface fire control was as good or better than other navies, AA fire control was less effective than those navies which adopted the tachymetric system. Pugh has suggested that this was not as important as has been made out as AA gunfire was more effective in scaring rather than hitting prior to the adoption of the proximity fuse (Appendix 16).

Asdic. The problem here was over-confidence in the early versions, particularly due to the lack of depth

8 Private letter (now in National Maritime Museum) used in D K Brown, *A Century of Naval Construction*, p175.

9 A Soviet naval architect referred to the extremes as 'the superbattleship paradox' with one fantastic ship or, at the other extreme, 'the Chinese junk paradox' with a numerous fleet of tiddlers; L Y Khudyakov, *Analytical Design of Ships* (Leningrad 1980).

Newcastle early in the war. The *Southamptons* were bigger than the RN wanted but were a necessary counter to the *Mogami*. A generally successful design despite too many minor structural problems. (Author's collection)

information and knowledge of the effect of density layers. Combined with the lack of an ahead-throwing weapon this made the RN's ASW capability much less than had been assumed.

Ships. Attention has been drawn to the failure to build welded ships and submarines. It is clear that DNC Department would have liked to have moved faster but D quality steel was not suitable for reliable welding and resources were not available to develop a weldable, high tensile steel. Longitudinal framing for destroyers was stronger and lighter, shown by *Ardent* prior to the First World War. Its introduction was strongly opposed by shipbuilders but, when the Admiralty, belatedly, took a strong line, no serious problems were found. Unfortunately, the introduction was so late that the early *Javelin* structure, which was rightly conservative, was used for all wartime destroyers even though it failed to take full advantage of potential weight saving.

Submarine pressure hulls. Whilst the structural design of British pressure hulls was inferior to that of the Germans, it would seem that this was largely bad luck in that the designs of the 'S', 'T' and 'U' classes were frozen before better design methods were available. Again, lack of a weldable steel exacerbated the problem (Chapter 6).

Top speed. The 'Jutland' obsession focused all attention on top speed, particularly for destroyers. As a result, the hull form was optimised for top speed, with only a marginal benefit, but with a large penalty at cruising speed.

Habitability. During the Depression, with its massive unemployment, it was easy to recruit sailors and little attention was paid to their comfort. Exercises were planned for times and places where extremes of temperature or weather were not expected. Finally, extra equipment added in wartime usually reduced crew space whilst at the same time increasing the number of men. The basic mess deck was spartan, with hammocks, wooden benches and tables, often unlined and with poor ventilation, inadequate in hot weather and too draughty in cold. The food had to be brought from the galley and was often cold, sometimes spilt, with no attempt to provide a healthy diet. It was not recognised

that men need to eat and sleep well if they are to perform well. There was an avoidable loss of life from inadequate life saving gear. Life jackets were badly designed and the Carley float provided no shelter for the men resting on it. A closely related consideration was:

Seakeeping. (See Appendix 19.) Many classes rolled badly. The active fin stabiliser introduced in *Bittern* and fitted in *Black Swan*s, some 'Hunts' and a few 'Battles'

Alamein, a 1943 'Battle'. Note the fifth 4.5in gun behind the funnel. (World Ship Society)

10 Modern fin systems have a much better control system and are very much more effective. The author remains unconvinced of their value, a minority view.

Thrasher in 1943. The 'T' class were built under Treaty limits and were also designed just before improved methods for pressure hull strength became available. (Author's collection)

was an expensive and not entirely satisfactory way of reducing roll.[10] Bigger bilge keels were fitted to the 'Captains' and some 'Flowers', increasing their operational capability very considerably. Pitch and heave combined to produce severe vertical accelerations, particularly at the fore end. Mess decks were in the worst place, making rest difficult (or worse) whilst in some classes the bridge was too far forward with a marked loss of efficiency. Exercises must include bad weather. The criticisms above are severe but most other navies had far worse problems. RN ships did not break in half or capsize and their machinery was far more reliable than the Germans. However, the USN was better in almost all aspects except, perhaps, in seakeeping.

Good designs

Clearly this must be a subjective view and others may amuse themselves with alternative solutions. The bigger ships were dominated by Chatfield's views on the need for thick armour. The *King George V* class were good,

though not outstanding, and, in the author's opinion, more armament and less armour would have improved them. Even though a great deal of attention, including full-scale trials, had been paid to underwater protection it does not seem to have worked as well as it should.

The armoured hangar carriers were a magnificent technical achievement but an unarmoured hangar with more fighters would have been more capable. The *Ark Royal* was a good start, spoilt by her clumsy lifts, and an improved version would have been better. The *Kents* were possibly the best of the first generation of Washington cruisers. *Ajax/Amphion* were fine small cruisers whilst *Southampton* could have been a superb big ship had it not been for too many structural problems. The *Dido* class was very well suited for RN requirements – if only it had had a better armament (such as ten US 5in, or even ten 4.5in).

Poor machinery and guns prevented any destroyers meeting the highest standard though the Emergency classes were very good. The *Black Swans* were excellent escorts but pride of place must go to the 'Lochs', with a

very advanced weapon system and a clever but simple hull structure. The submarines were all good but not outstanding. The production methods for the 'A' class were very advanced for the day.

Fleet balance

With hindsight, the obvious question is whether new battleships were needed in 1937. Other navies, including Britain's potential enemies, were building such ships and in 1937 the RAF said that they could not guarantee to sink them in any weather. It is probable that the same answer might have been given in 1945 though the chance of a battleship surviving was much less. It is often said that the battleship died because it was vulnerable: this cannot be correct since the new capital ship, the carrier, was far more vulnerable. The battleship died because it had very little capability for damaging the enemy. Nevertheless, there can be little doubt that given the situation in 1936, the decision to build battleships

Wartime construction programmes

	39w	40	40s	41	41s	41sp	42	42m	43	43a	44
Battlecruiser		1									
Fleet Carrier		1					2			4	
Lt Fleet							4	12	8		
Heavy cruiser			4								
6in cruiser	2[1]			3		3	6	(3)[10]			
5.25in cruisers	6										
Monitors		1		1							
Fast M'Layer				2							
Fleet DD							16		26		14
Intermed DD	16[2]	16	16	40			26		17		8
Escort DD	36[3]	30									
Sloops		18[4]		11			3				2
'T' Submarines	7		9	17[7]			14				
'S'	5[5]	6	14[6]	15			13		3		
'U'	12	10	12	20			24		2		
'A'									46[8]		
Minelaying			3	2	(5)						
Turkish							4				
Steam GB			9[9]				10				
'River' Frigates		27		29			12				
'Loch'							6		105		
'Flower' Corvt	60[11]	31		22			5				
'Castle'							14		82		
LST				3[12]					80		36

Notes: Programmes (Column headings) are: 1939 war, 1940, 1940 supplementary, 1941, 1941 revised, 1941 supplementary, 1942, 1942 Additional, 1943, 1943 Amended, 1944.

1. Approved in 1939 Programme – orders brought forward from March 1940

2. Plus six requisitioned building from Brazil. Two Turkish requisitioned c1942.

3. 'Hunt' class, twenty already ordered in 1939. There is some confusion here. Twenty ordered 4 Sep 39, all in 39 war prog, sixteen ordered 20 Dec 39 (prog uncertain), thirty more ordered Jul-Aug 40, 40 programme. This programme gives thirty-four 'Hunts' to which six more ordered as *Black Swan* should be added. Total from Cabinet papers is eighty, including *Black Swan*.

4. *Black Swan*. Cabinet papers give fourteen in 140 sup and fourteen in 41, two in 42 and two in 44. Draft of 1939 as at 21 March 1940 gives ten *Black Swan* and twenty-four 'Hunts', then six *Black Swan* changed to 'Hunts'. (These *Black Swan* were given Job Numbers.) Figures from College.

5. 'S' class 39 war – not in original programme, ordered 23 Jan 1940

6. 'S' class, seven ordered 4 Nov 1940 but cancelled Jan 1941.

7. There is little agreement between figures for submarines in 1941 and 1942 between Cabinet papers and College. Latter used here. However he does not take into account Programme adjustments in 1941 – have only noted minelayer (*Cachalot*) cancellations.

8. Cabinet papers give thirty-eight 'As', ten 'Us', four 'Ss' and four 'Ts' cancelled and re-ordered as 'A', further six ordered later. The ten 'Us' were cancelled. The twenty 'As' for 1944 were not ordered.

9. The original programme was for fifty steam gunboats, 1941 shows reduction to nine!

10. Three cruisers cancelled when Light Fleet Carriers ordered. One more cruiser deleted in November 1942.

11. As College.

12. 1941 were LST (1) (*Boxer*). Later, 1943-44 were LST (3) (forty-five in UK in 1943, others in Canada).

was inevitable.[11] In particular, a shift to carriers in the late 1930s would have meant many more and better aircraft would have been needed which could not have been built in the light of RAF requirements.

When war broke out, the RN was building five battleships (four more planned) and six carriers, a not unreasonable balance. Cruisers and destroyers were being built on every suitable building slip. Even if more funds had been available, shortage of slips, guns and armour would have prevented any significant increase in the building programme.

It was thought that there were sufficient sloops and old destroyers to act as ocean escorts which seemed to be correct up to the fall of France. Had France not fallen, it is likely that the German building programme would have produced enough U-boats by the end of 1940 to pose a mid-ocean threat. A cheap ocean escort should have been designed and two prototypes built.

Conversions are not usually worthwhile but with the shortage of resources and the limits on new construction they could be justified in the late 1930s. The four fully modernised capital ships and the WAIRs were most valuable.

Envoi

Goodall noted on 15 August 1945 'Japan surrenders. Interesting to compare with meeting [drinks in the Board Room] on 3 September 1939, I am the only man to have been at both meetings'.

Sunset

During the long years of the Second World War the White Ensign flew night and day. On 2 September 1945, after the formal surrender of Japan in Tokyo Bay, Admiral Fraser ordered the resumption of peacetime routine and invited the senior officers of British Commonwealth ships and a token representation from the lower deck to the first 'Sunset' ceremony for 6 years aboard *Duke of York*.

Allied and Commonwealth flags were flying from the fore and main yardarms with the Commander-in-Chief's flag at the masthead and the White Ensign at the gaff. Every space on the after gun mounting and the superstructure was packed with men while, in the distance, the decks of US ships were also crowded as they had been told about this strange 'Limey' rite.

When Admiral Fraser came on deck the Quartermaster reported – 'Sunset, Sir'. The 'Still' was piped. The Royal Marine guard presented arms while the band played 'The Day Thou gavest Lord is Ended' together with 'Sunset' as only a Royal Marine bugler could sound it.

For the first time in six years the White Ensign came down; the war was over – and the vast crowds on the US ships were at attention and saluting too.

11 In post-war correspondence between Forbes and Roskill, both thought we should have built carriers rather than battleships.

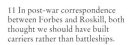

Duke of York returning from the Pacific. Her quarterdeck was the scene of the Sunset ceremony described in the text. (Author's collection)

Appendices

Appendix 1
The Goodall Diaries

In his will, Sir Stanley Goodall left his diaries and certain other private papers to the British Museum, later becoming part of the British Library. These are:

ADM 52785	Diary 1932
ADM 52786	Diary 1933
ADM 52787	Diary 1934
ADM 52788	Diary 1935
ADM 52789	Diary 1936
ADM 52790	Diary 1937-41*
ADM 52791	Diary 1942-46*
ADM 52792	Correspondence notably bombing trials
ADM 52793-95 sealed	Papers on Bucknill Committee,
	for many years, now open. Little of value
ADM 52796	F O Bamford. No value

*These have the same day for the five years, say 5 June, on a single page.

A particularly valuable feature is that every 6 months, Sir Stanley sets objectives for the next 6 months and reviews his own success or failure over the previous 6 months.[1]

Goodall's diaries were written each day, in the heat of the moment, and some of his criticisms would have been toned down on reflection. In general, I have not used his more critical passages unless they are repeated or otherwise justified. I have usually removed the names of those criticised. His handwriting is difficult to read, entries are often in note form, and he had his own abbreviations, so I have had to guess some passages and add words to clarify the meaning.[2] Where the exact words seem important, I have used double quotes. He usually sorted problems out over the drawing bench– entries almost always conclude with the words "gave decision". Another frequent phrase is "a thick (or very thick) day".

Appendix 2
Instructions for the Director of Naval Construction (1924 with amendments)

These instructions are very lengthy. Sections dealing with internal administration have been omitted.

1. The Director of Naval Construction will be responsible to the Board for the efficient performance of the duties of his Department.

2. He is the principal technical adviser to the Board of Admiralty, and the final authority on the design of warships and other vessels of H. M. Navy, and will be directly responsible to the Controller for all matters of design, stability, strength of construction, weight built into the hulls of ships, armour ['and other protection' inserted later], boats, masting and all other nautical apparatus for all ships whether building in H. M. Dockyards or by contract.

3. He will submit to the Controller all plans of importance affecting the ship and her control. No alteration in, or addition to, the original design of any ship as approved by the Board is to be made without the approval of the Controller, and if the plans affect in any way the qualities of the ship or entail any alteration in the design as approved by the Board, a clear statement as to the effect of such alteration is to be made when submitting them.

4. He will be jointly responsible with the Director of Naval Ordnance for the design of gun mountings and for the mechanical arrangements connected therewith, and will sign the principal drawings and specifications relating thereto. All proposals regarding changes in patterns of guns, gun mountings or torpedo mountings, &c., will be referred to him by the Director of Naval Ordnance and Director of Torpedoes and Mining for his concurrence before being decided on. ['He will be similarly responsible with the Engineer-in-Chief as regards catapults.' Inserted 1927]

5. Save as provided in paragraph 2 of the instructions for the Director of Dockyards, he will be responsible for the economical, expeditious, and correct construction of all Admiralty ships according to the approved designs, and for the inspection of materials and workmanship.

Sir Stanley Vernon Goodall. This painting was presented to Goodall by members of the RCNC and now hangs in the headquarters of RINA. (Author's collection)

1 Quoted in full in D K Brown, *A Century of Naval Construction*, pp178-80.

2 For example, engineers use the Greek letter η for 'efficiency' so Goodall writes in η for inefficiency.

Four heads of the RCNC: (from left to right) Shepheard, Goodall, Lillicrap, Sims. Shepheard followed Lillicrap and Sims later became the first DG Ships. (All were knighted). (Author's collection)

6. In the case of ships being built to standard displacement as defined in the Washington Naval Treaty of 1922, he will advise the Controller if any excess displacement appears likely to occur and as to the steps necessary to prevent the same: or, alternatively, as to any surplus displacement available for deferred additions to the design. He will also keep a list of all such proposed additions for the final consideration of the Board when the ship is nearing completion.

7. He will be responsible for the examination and survey of vessels proposed to be purchased for fleet purposes or to be employed as armed merchant cruisers, &c., and will make all the necessary calculations as to stability &c., and prepare the plans and instructions for alterations or conversion.

8. He will be consulted concerning inventions connected with diving and the design of diving material and submerged escape apparatus. He will be responsible for the provision of anti-gas portable fans and hose and for the design and application of purifiers and purifying systems to ships' ventilation. [Added 1932]

9. He will be consulted in all cases where large repairs are necessary to completed vessels and will give advice on alterations and additions to such vessels.

10. He will prepare such estimates of the cost of hulls of ships (except those built in H.M. Dockyards), armour, &c., as may be necessary for financial purposes. He will also prepare schedules of instalments and furnish certificates to enable payments to be made.

11. [11, 12, 13 inserted 1941[3]] He being responsible that the protection of warships meets Board requirements is to co-ordinate and keep in his records all the data obtained in collaboration with the Director of Naval Ordnance, the Director of Torpedoes and Mining and other Heads of Departments responsible for the design and production of weapons, which show the effects of such weapons on ships of all types. He will receive all requests for particulars of the damage effect on ships of weapons, including shells, bombs, torpedoes, mines, depth charges, bullets and splinters, and he will consult the Heads of Departments responsible for the weapons concerned.

12. He will undertake any experimental work required to provide data regarding the effect of weapons on ships and will consult all other Departments concerned before submitting proposals to the Board.

13. He will be consulted by all Departments or Divisions requiring data concerning the effect of weapons on targets other than ships, e.g., personnel or shoe establishments, before experiments are undertaken.

14. He will be responsible for target designs to meet requirements as formulated by the Director of Gunnery Division. He will consider and report regarding all alterations and additions regarding the stability, strength and seaworthiness of existing battle practice targets as for ordinary ships, new designs of targets being forwarded to the Director of Gunnery Division for concurrence or remarks.

15. [15, 16 Inserted 1925] He shall be consulted as regards the limiting dimensions and weights of aircraft of the Fleet Air Arm and all designs and specifications for such aircraft will be referred to him for consideration from the point of view of their suitability for service in H.M. Ships, built or projected.

16. He will be responsible for maintaining liaison with the Department of the Air Member for Supply and Research, Air Ministry, in matters of the design and construction of aircraft for the Fleet Air Arm which bear upon the construction and equipment of aircraft carriers or other ships in which aircraft may be embarked.

17. (Inserted, date unclear) He will be responsible for the provision of fire fighting appliances in H.M. Ships without prejudice to the [next line missing].

18. All questions arising under the Treaties of Washington Act, 1922, relating to applications for, and grants of, licences for building vessels of war, altering, arming, or equipping any ship so as to adapt her for use as a vessel of war, including the stiffening of merchant ships to carry guns, will be referred to him, and he shall be responsible for all such inspection of ships and shipyards as is necessary to ensure compliance with the obligations of the Treaty.

19. He will report to the Board of Admiralty, for transmission to the Powers concerned, the standard displace-

ment in tons and metric tons, the length at the water-line, and the mean draught at standard displacement of each new ship when laid down and when completed.

20. He is the Head of the Royal Corps of Naval Constructors and will deal with the appointments of all members of the Corps, consulting the Director of Dockyards when Dockyard appointments are concerned.

21. The Admiralty Experiment Works at Haslar will be under his direction.

22. He and his representatives will as requisite for the efficient performance of the duties assigned to him, visit H.M. Dockyards and other naval establishments and private establishments where work may be in hand for the Admiralty.

23. He will consult the Heads of other Admiralty Departments as necessary in all matters affecting their departments including appointments of staff, and will keep them fully informed of all matters relating to the work of his department with which they should be acquainted.

24. [Inserted 1933] When proposals dealing with materiel are under consideration which affect the interests or welfare of Naval personnel, he should consult the Director of Personal Services before the question is submitted to the Board.

[25-27 deal only with internal administration and are omitted]

Note: Nothing contained in these instructions shall modify the direct responsibility of the Director of Naval Construction that the vessel realises the intention of the design as approved by the Board, or the procedure which has been laid down by the Board with regards to the preparation of the designs of H.M. Ships. A copy of the Board Minute describing the procedure to be followed is attached to these instructions.

By Command of Their Lordships,
Oswyn Murray
Admiralty 29 September, 1924.

Appendix 3
DNC Office Procedures

During and even after the Second World War there was a large number of small departments under the Controller and consulting all of them could be time consuming.[4] DNC's title of Principal Technical Adviser to the Board conveyed, at best, moral authority. Many were tempted to short cut the official procedures which frequently led to disaster when some vital body had not been consulted or even informed of a change. Usually there was a compromise and quick discussion, possibly by phone, would obtain broad agreement so that the official paper could move quickly.[5]

Staff requirements

Staff views on requirements were co-ordinated by DTSD (Director of Tactical, Torpedo and Staff Duties) consulting numerous staff divisions.[6] In general, fairly informal discussions within the staff would lead to broad brush requirement known as 'Sketch Requirements'. DNC would then prepare a very quick design study (a day or two) or, if the requirements could not be met in full within available resources, several alternative studies.

After discussion, both informal and more formally on the New Construction Committee, DTSD would prepare Draft Staff Requirements from which DNC would prepare a slightly more detailed design study. The Draft Staff Requirements would be circulated within the Staff Divisions and amended as necessary. As amended, they would become Agreed Staff Requirements and forwarded through ACNS (Weapons) for Board Approval.

The Staff Requirement covered:

Function
Speed, Endurance
Armament, Protection,
Navigation and Manoeuvrability,
Radar, Asdic,
Signals & W/T,
Any special equipment, *eg* aircraft
Habitability

Handling of paperwork[7]

The Admiralty was a government ministry and its procedures, as with any other ministry, were geared to providing a secretariat for the Minister, the First Lord. It was also the operational headquarters of the navy and the First Sea Lord was the Chief of Naval Staff.[8] The procedures were not ideal to run the largest technical business in the country. Even in the First World War, d'Eyncourt complained that the Admiralty was the largest engineering business in the country and lacked an engineer on the board. The Controller (Third Sea Lord), head of the technical departments, was a seaman officer. The Secretary of the Admiralty (Permanent Secretary) was responsible for ensuring that correct procedures were followed and was also the formal link to the Treasury.

All incoming correspondence was addressed to 'The Secretary' whence it passed to a secretariat division (P Branch for DNC papers) who would register it with a number and enclose it in a docket marked to depart-

3 Presumably part of the build up to the creation of NCRE.

4 Instructions on handling staff requirements listed sixteen departments to be consulted by DNC, several being outside the Controllerate.

5 The Admiralty had its own phone service (manual exchange) which was very inefficient. It was often said that the old semaphore system which could get a message to Portsmouth in 20 minutes was quicker.

6 Up to twelve divisions are listed but many were only involved with vessels for their own speciality, *eg* combined operations. DTSD, D of P, DOD and DAWT were concerned with all ships.

7 This section is based on a paper 'Office Procedures in DNC Department', a guide to newcomers, written, I believe, by Rowland Baker. It is a world apart from today, much more formal. The section on office etiquette appears reactionary today but was probably seen as revolutionary when written. The author began work in 1953 when procedures were little different from those of wartime.

8 The Admiralty was much more of an operational headquarters than the War Office or Air Ministry.

ments concerned. After getting formal comments, DNC would draft a reply which would be sent to the initiator by P Branch, 'for Secretary'. This cumbersome system could work quite fast. In the early 1950s the rule was that if you could not reply fully within four working days, a printed postcard was sent giving the name and phone number of the individual handling the query. On Saturday mornings the section clerk would give the constructor a list of papers which had been in the room more than a fortnight.

Ships' Covers

The Ship's Cover was a hardback binder with stub pages to which all important papers were to be glued for permanent record. The majority of these covers, over 30 years old, are held in the National Maritime Museum and are an invaluable source for the technical historian. However, the quality varies considerably and some can even be misleading as when a decision was made and recorded but not the later change of plan. Often decisions would be made or changed in verbal discussion and not recorded.[9] Frequently, the reason for a decision is not given. In a busy office, the Cover was low priority and inserting documents was left to the next quiet period–if any. It was not uncommon for a slightly dubious decision to be omitted deliberately. So, 'The Truth, Nothing but the Truth but often far from the Whole Truth'. It was never clear when a design was firm enough to justify opening a Cover so that the early stages are often missing. (Sometimes they may be found at the back of the Cover for the preceding class.)[10]

Work books

Everyone in DNC dept was issued with a foolscap size work book with his individual number of the cover.[11] Every calculation had to be entered in the book and it was forbidden to alter a figure. If a mistake was found or a change needed for other reasons the alteration was to be made in red ink, crossing out the old figure and writing the new figure alongside. The date was to be inserted every day of use and all entries were to be indexed.

Instructions from senior officers[12] and assumptions made were to be recorded. Section heads were supposed to inspect work books each month to ensure that instructions were obeyed and advise junior staff as needed. If all these instructions had been obeyed, work books would be an invaluable source. Unfortunately, few people in a busy office devoted the time needed and most books are just a mass of figures which often cannot be related to a particular ship. (C S Lillicrap, later DNC, was almost perfect and his books, in the National Maritime Museum are most valuable.) A small selection of work books is held in the Museum.

Appendix 4

The Washington Treaty 1922 – Main Provisions

Main provisions affecting the Royal Navy

1. The total tonnage of capital ships was to be limited to 525,000 tons, the same as the USA. Japan was limited to 315,000 tons (5:5:3). France and Italy were each allowed 175,000 tons.

2. The RN was allowed to build two new 16in gun ships to match similar American and Japanese ships. No other new ships were to be built by any country for 10 years. Until the two new British ships were complete, four older ships could be retained.

3. No capital ship was to be replaced until it was 20 years old.

4. The maximum displacement and gun calibre for various categories was defined as:

Capital Ships	35,000 tons/16in
Aircraft Carriers	27,000 tons/8in (up to two conversions of 33,000 tons)
Cruisers	10,000 tons/8in

5. Existing capital ships could be given additional protection increasing displacement by up to 3000 tons. (Differing interpretations of this clause were to cause some ill feeling.)

6. The Anglo-Japanese alliance was to be disbanded. Over a considerable area of the Pacific, the building or extension of dockyards and fortifications was prohibited.

7. There were a number of clauses containing definitions. Of these, the most important was Standard Displacement–the ship fully equipped for war but excluding oil fuel, reserve feed water and other liquids.[13] There was also scope for varying interpretations of this definition; in particular, many ships were given magazines which could hold more rounds than allowed for in the declared standard displacement.

8. The Treaty was to remain in force until the end of 1936 and there after until the expiry of 2 years' notice by any of the contracting powers. Basic data on new construction was to be given promptly to other Treaty powers.

Appendix 5

The London Treaty, signed 22 April 1930

Main factors affecting the Royal Navy

1. Capital ships were not to be laid down until 1936. Three battleships and a battlecruiser were to be scrapped and another battleship demilitarised as a training ship (all 13.5in gun ships).

2. Aircraft carriers were redefined and carriers of under 10,000 tons with guns over 6.1in were forbidden.

3. Submarines over 2000 tons or with guns over 6.1in prohibited (three larger boats allowed in each navy).

4. Ships exempt from the Treaty included:
   (a) Surface vessels less than 600 tons.
   (b) Surface vessels between 600 and 2000 tons provided that they did not:
       (i)   mount guns larger than 6.1in;
       (ii) mount more than four guns greater than 3in;
       (iii) launch torpedoes;
       (iv) exceed 20kts speed.
   (c) Auxiliaries provided that they were not armoured, could not land aircraft, or operate more than three aircraft.[14]

The remaining part of the Treaty was signed by Britain, United States and Japan only.

(1) Cruisers were divided into two categories:
    (a) Guns over 6.1in (heavy cruisers);
    (b) Guns not greater than 6.1in (light cruisers).

Destroyers were defined as not greater than 1850 tons with guns not greater than 5.1in. Tonnage in service on 31 December 1936 was not to exceed

	USA	British Empire	Japan
Cruisers (a)	180,000	146,800	108,400
Cruisers (b)	143,000	192,200	100,450
Destroyers	150,000	150,000	105,500
Submarines	52,700	52,700	52,700

2. Not more than 16 per cent of destroyer tonnage was to consist of ships exceeding 1500 tons.
3. Not more than 25 per cent of cruisers were to have landing decks. 10 per cent of cruisers (b)/destroyer tonnage was interchangeable. Two old British cruisers (a), could be disposed of in 1936. Britain could build 91,000 tons of cruisers prior to 31 December 1936.

The Treaty was to remain in force until 31 December 1936.

Appendix 6

The London Treaty 1936 – Summary

This Treaty was not ratified.

No capital ship is to exceed 35,000 tons or carry a gun exceeding 14in calibre unless any of the signatories to the Washington Treaty fail to agree to the above provisions by 1 April 1937 when the calibre may be increased to 16in. No capital ship shall be less than 17,500 tons nor carry a gun smaller than 10in *

No aircraft carrier shall exceed 23,000 tons nor carry a gun over 6.1in. No more than ten guns of 5.25in or over is allowed.

No cruiser exceeding 8000 tons or with a gun larger than 6.1in shall be laid down or acquired.*

No submarine shall exceed 2000 tons nor carry a gun larger than 5.1in.

Destroyers were not mentioned but appear under Light Surface Warships which must not exceed 3000 tons with guns no larger than 6.1in. Note that limits on global tonnage are no longer imposed.

* These two clauses were seen as important by the Admiralty as they banned the 'Pocket Battleship', still the RN's nightmare.

Appendix 7

Underwater Explosions

On detonation, an explosive charge is converted, in some 40 milliseconds, into an incandescent ball of gas at a pressure of several hundreds of tons/in². The sudden formation of this gas bubble delivers an intense blow to the surrounding water setting up a compressive shock which travels through the water, initially supersonic, but soon at the speed of sound in water. This shock wave can shatter nearby structure and, at lesser force, will travel long distances. The peak pressure from a depth charge filled with 300lb of Amatol is about 2 tons/in² at 25ft, 1 ton/in² at 50ft. The development of instruments with which to measure these effects is outside the scope of this book but demanded the best efforts of bright scientists for many years.

The gas bubble will expand rapidly to a maximum radius which for the depth charge is of the order of 22ft. At its maximum size, the pressure inside the bubble will be much less than that in the surrounding sea and it will begin to collapse. In deep water there will be several cycles of expansion and contraction. This is particularly important in the case of ground mines when the bubble rises and the second expansion is closer to the target ship and may be more damaging than the first.

9 For example, neither the cover nor the drawings make it clear whether *Leander* was built with a bulbous bow. There was a clear intention to fit and indications that this decision may have been reversed.

10 In the 1950s, I wrote the early history of the Type 81 ('Tribal') specifically for the cover.

11 My number was the easily remembered 999.

12 Particularly important if you disagreed with the instruction!

13 Both the RN and USN thought they could conceal the use of water-filled spaces in torpedo protection using this clause.

14 *Unicorn*!

Underwater explosions. Plume of a mine explosion close to an MMS during post-war trials. (Author's collection)

previous bending, or may be grossly distorted until it fails. Different explosives may have greater effect in one aspect or the other.

Appendix 8
Anti-Destroyer Guns

During the 1920s and 1930s there was considerable debate as to the calibre of guns to be mounted in battleships against destroyer attack and whether these could be dual purpose for use in the AA role. During the war there was similar debate on the gun needed in small cruisers. All this time there was a parallel debate on the guns to be mounted in destroyers to fight similar ships.

Medium calibre guns

Gun	Weight proj (lbs)	Rate of fire (rpm)	Muzzle velocity (ft/sec)	AA capability
6in Mk XXIII	112	6	2758	None
5.25in Mk I	80	6-8	2672	Poor
4.7in Mk XI	62	10	2538	Poor
4.7in Mk IX	50	10	2650	Some (55° mounts)
4.5in Mk I	55	12[15]	2449	Good
4in Mk XVI	35	12	2660	Good
US 5in 38	55	18	2600	Good

The visible effects of an underwater explosion can be explained in terms of the shock wave and bubble expansion. When the shock wave hits the surface a dome of spray will be formed. For a 500lb charge of TNT, 50ft down, the dome is about 37ft high. Deep explosions do not form a dome; for a 300lb charge this depth is about 140ft. When the large mass of water set in motion by the bubble expansion reaches the surface, a tall plume will be thrown up

Structure may either be shattered, broken without

Muzzle velocity would appear to be important in AA fire as reducing the time of flight and hence minimising prediction difficulties. However, the differences shown above are not significant, indeed, the most successful

Meteor with the Mk XI 4.7in in Mk XX mounts, one of far too many medium.calibre guns in production. The gun was too heavy and the 50° elevation inadequate for AA fire. (Author's collection)

gun, the US 5in, has a relatively low muzzle velocity.

When mounted in a battleship, hits on a destroyer would be few over 10,000yds and the destroyer would probably launch torpedoes at 6000yds. The problem was to sink or at least disable a destroyer within this bracket; two minutes at 30kts. Destroyers could take quite a lot of damage if the machinery was not affected, eg *Glowworm* in April 1940 against *Hipper* was actually able to ram her enemy before sinking after a number of 8in hits. *Onslow* off North Cape remained in action after three 8in hits, also from *Hipper*. During a torpedo attack the destroyer would be nearly bows-on until turning to fire and any hits would probably be in the forecastle, causing casualties but little loss of capability. Between cruisers or destroyers action might be more on the broadside when damage to machinery would be much more likely. Even the smallest shell could break a steam pipe, disabling the ship.

The 4in gun in mounts then in use was not very suitable for low angle work due to their trunnion height. It would seem that the 4.5in (or, even better, the US 5in) was adequate for all purposes. Specific anti-destroyer guns were not needed in a battleship as enemy destroyers should be kept out of range by their own destroyers.[16] The arguments for cruiser armament are outlined in Chapter 4. The choice of the 5.25in seems well argued and the later change to 6in was a whim of the First Sea Lord (Cunningham).

Appendix 9
Docks

The size of dry and floating docks was a limitation on the size of the last battleships and on the biggest carriers. The list below gives brief particulars of those available to the RN. The figures for length, beam and displacement are for a ship of *King George V* form; if of *Nelson* form the beam could be increased about 4ft but with little change in displacement.

Admiralty graving docks

	Length (ft)	Beam (ft)	Displacement (tons)
Devonport	825	116	48,300
rebuilt 1939	830	124	
Portsmouth C&D Locks	860	103	44,700
Rosyth 1 & 3	854	109	45,200
Rosyth 2	864	109	45,500
Gibraltar 1	875	123	50,200
Singapore 1	1006	130	65,800

	Length (ft)	Beam (ft)	Displacement (tons)
Admiralty floating docks			
Malta	962	140	65,000
Singapore	855	130	50,000
Others			
Liverpool Gladstone	1050	120	61,000
Southampton 7	1170	130	77,000
Southampton Floating	960	130	50,000
Durban	1157	110	48,200 (for 900ft)
Esquimalt	1138	135	72,500
Quebec	1158	120	68,700
St John NB	1140	131	71,500
Sydney (1945)	1096	146	
Cape Town	1181	146	

Most Admiralty docks had a slightly tapered entrance, so the maximum beam of the largest ship which could be docked might be less than the waterline beam. Lengths could be increased 30ft or more in some cases by putting the caisson in the outer stop. Floating docks could take longer ships with overhang.[17]

Appendix 10
Shore Bombardment

It was often argued in the second half of the war that shore bombardment was invaluable and a major role, justifying the battleship. This argument has been accepted by most writers without any detailed consideration of the evidence. An example often quoted is the silencing of the Longues battery by *Ajax* on D-Day. She fired 150 6in shells between 0557 and 0620hrs (*Argonaut* later fired 29 rounds of 5.25in). Two German guns were hit by 6in shells entering the embrasure. The Naval Staff history considers this was due to chance since there were few craters around the battery.[18] There is a vivid account of D Day bombardments by a spotter pilot. He maintains that battleship shells often missed by more than a mile.[19] On 4 May 1945 the *King George V* and *Howe* bombarded Hirara airfield on the Sakashima Gunto.[20] The battleships fired at 25,000yds. The carriers were deprived of gunfire support and suffered heavily from air attack. Damage to the airfield was slight.[21]

During the closing phase of the war with Japan there were a number of bombardments with industrial sites as

15 The Mk IV 4.5in RP 50 Mk V in later 'Cs' could fire 18 rounds in the first minute, until the ready-use ammunition ran out.

16 It is arguable that the same applies to heavy AA guns and that battleships should have had nothing between main armament and Bofors.

17 I am grateful to Dr I L Buxton for supplying these figures. It is surprising, in the light of the importance attached to the subject, how much the figures quoted varied from one paper to another.

18 *Landings in Normandy*, HMSO, London, 1994, Section 47.

19 Cdr R M Crosley, *They gave me a Seafire* (Shrewsbury 1986), Chapter 16. In a later book Crosley expands on the inaccuracy of naval gunfire, which he blamed on gyroscopic effects. This led to a lengthy correspondence with entrants from both sides of the Atlantic. In general, gyroscopic effects were not regarded as the cause and worn rifling thought more likely: Cdr R M Crosley, *Up in Harm's Way* (Shrewsbury 1986), Appendix 2.

20 E Gray, *Operation Pacific* (London 1990), p218. Also J Winton, *The Forgotten Fleet* (London 1969), p140. The ships fired 195 rounds of 14in, 598 6in and 378 5.25in.

21 It has been suggested that had the fighters used to escort the bombarding ships been used as fighter-bombers, they would have done more damage.

the prime target. Initial claims of severe damage were not generally supported by detailed photographic analysis or post-war inspection. The damage caused by a large HE shell was generally much less than by a large bomb, *eg* a 16in HE will damage 1400ft^2 of a steel framed building, a 2000lb bomb 8800ft^2. A similar shell will damage machine tools over 4900ft^2 whilst a 1000lb bomb damages 8500ft^2. Firing was generally at about 23,000yds at which range 1 per cent hits were obtained. Lighter shells were even less effective. Post-war questioning suggested that the effect of gunfire on morale was greater than that due to bombing–conversely, it was said that bombardment was good for the morale of the crew of attacking ships!

During the whole of the Falklands War the RN fired 8500 4.5in shells which, it is claimed, made a major contribution to victory. When one realises that during the build up to the battle of the Somme some 10,000 shells were fired each hour one may doubt the Falklands story.

Top left: Warspite at Normandy 1944. Note that X turret is unusable following earlier damage. (Imperial War Museum: A23916)

Middle left: Rodney at Normandy. (Imperial War Museum: A23978)

Lower left:Orion at Normandy. (Imperial War Museum: A24201)

Lower right: Howe at Havraki Gulf, 1945. (Author's collection)

Appendix 11

Admiral Sir Reginald G H Henderson, Controller 1934-9

Both as Rear-Admiral Carriers and as Controller, Admiral Henderson contributed greatly to the Royal Navy's readiness for war.[22] He was born on 1 September 1881 to a family with strong naval connections. After training in *Britannia* he joined his first ship, *Mars*, in 1897. A gunnery specialist, he was the commander of *Erin* at Jutland and was then brought to the Admiralty by Jellicoe in 1916 to head the anti-submarine division. Whilst in this post he spotted the fallacy in the statistics of merchant ship movements which vastly over estimated the number of ships entering and leaving port at 5000 per week. The new figures of 120-140 showed that convoy was indeed feasible.

From 1926 to 1928 he commanded the carrier *Furious* and, after promotion, became the first Rear-Admiral, aircraft carriers. With three carriers under his command he developed the tactics of a carrier task force in the RN. He encouraged his pilots in developing the tactics of dive bombing which led to the procurement of the Skua, the first dive bomber to sink a major warship.

These two appointments showed him that naval warfare was changing.

In April 1934, Henderson, now a vice-admiral, became Controller. It is interesting that he pressed for heavy armament at the expense of armour in the *King George V*, being over-ridden by Chatfield,[23] but the armoured hangar carrier was very much Henderson's creation. He worked directly through W A D Forbes, ADNC Carriers, to develop the *Illustrious* without any formal requirement. Henderson was also insistent that *Unicorn* should have most of the features of an aircraft carrier. He realised the problems of producing all the armour needed in the rearmament programme and much increased UK capacity, and led the visit to Vitcovice which obtained a large amount of armour (c11,000 tons) from Czechoslovakia.

Henderson was full of enthusiasm for new ideas such as motor torpedo boats,[24] while in 1937 he suggested cabins for petty officers.[25] As Controller, he supported and encouraged the development of radar from August 1935 when he directed the Signal School to start work.[26] Henderson was promoted to full admiral in January 1939 and raised to GCB but his health failed, forcing his resignation in March 1939, and he died on 2 May 1939.

22 On the death of Sir Reginald Henderson, Sir Vincent Baddeley, a former Deputy Secretary, wrote an entry for the Dictionary of National Biography and this entry forms the background to this appendix. Several drafts written within DNC Dept have survived giving a fuller story of Henderson's interaction with DNC (referenced as DNB draft).

23 See Goodall 13 Mar 1936, quoted in Chapter 1. Also DNB draft Stanton, Forbes & Pengelly.

24 When Goodall met the new Controller, Fraser, he said that he had only disagreed with Henderson on two points, Scott-Paine and East coast dock. 1 Mar 1939.

25 Goodall 18 Jan 1937.

26 D Howse, *Radar at Sea* (Basingstoke 1993). It is interesting that radar was still secret when Baddeley wrote his note and is not mentioned in the DNB entry.

As Rear-Admiral, Carriers Henderson developed tactics with *Furious*, *Courageous* (nearest centre, note the rear-admiral's flag) and *Glorious*. (Author's collection)

Appendix 12
The Strength of Ships

By the beginning of the nineteenth century there was an understanding of the way in which a ship is supported by the sea and the loads imposed on the structure by that support.[27] This approach was put on a sound theoretical basis by Rankine in 1866 and a practical design method was devised by Edward Reed and his assistant, William White.[28] It was recognised that the worst loading experienced by a ship is when it is end on to waves whose length, crest to crest, is the same as that of the ship. Two cases are considered, one with a wave crest at each end and a trough amidships referred to as sagging and the other case with a crest amidships and the ends drooping into troughs–hogging. This method, refined in detail, was used during the whole of the period covered by this book.[29]

Loading

Even in still water the weight of any section along the length may not be equal to the buoyancy of that section. Hence at any section there will be a vertical force on the structure due to this difference which is known as the shearing force. When in waves, the difference between weight and buoyancy is much increased and the shearing force in the side plating also increases.

The first step is to calculate the longitudinal distribution of weight. The ship is divided into sections (usually twenty for warships) and the weight in each determined. British warship practice was to adjust movable weights –fuel, stores etc–to give a worst case, *ie* weights are removed from the ends in the sagging case and from the middle when hogging. The ship is then 'balanced' on a wave of its own length and of a height equal to $\frac{1}{20}$ of its length so that the total buoyancy is equal to the weight and the centres of weight and buoyancy lie in the same vertical line.[30] This is a tedious task without a computer and has to be done first for hogging and then again for sagging.

The loading (weight minus buoyancy) at each section is then obtained and plotted on a base of length. Summing up the load along the length ('Integrating') gives a curve of shearing force. The shearing force is then integrated to give the bending moment (M) which leads to the stresses in deck and keel. (See diagram on page 32 of *Warrior to Dreadnought*.)

Structure and stress

In resisting these loads, the hull of the ship will act as a hollow box girder with the deck and bottom forming the flanges and the sides forming the web. The effectiveness of such a girder is measured by the second moment of area of the section. The second moment of area (I) is obtained by multiplying the cross-sectional area of every item which contributes to longitudinal strength by the square of its distance from the neutral axis (the axis about which the ship flexes).[31] There are two main problems with this work; the first is that the position of the neutral axis about which the ship bends is not known. This is easily overcome by assuming a reasonable position and calculating the moment of area about it. This leads to a small correction to obtain the true axis.

The second problem is more difficult; that of deciding which items contribute to longitudinal strength. Short girders between hatches are not effective. Rivet holes weakened the plate and, to allow for this, it was usual to deduct $\frac{1}{7}$th of the area of the section in tension from the strength calculation.[32] The design of heavily loaded, riveted joints was complicated in maximising their strength. Wood decking contributed to strength and its contribution was taken as $\frac{1}{16}$th of that of the corresponding cross-sectional area of steel.

Armour was more difficult; thick side armour would be included in compression when the butts would be pushed together but neglected in tension when joints would open up. Thin plating could be made fully effective. Deck armour was usually arranged to be effective. In the design of the *King George V* class the strength was investigated with all structure above the armoured deck destroyed. In this condition she was expected to withstand a wave whose height was L/40.[33]

There is then a relationship used in all branches of structural engineering between the bending moment (M), the second moment of area (I) and the stress (p) at a distance (y) from the neutral axis.

$$p = \frac{M.y}{I}$$

This simple calculation is only an approximation to the actual loading on a ship in a seaway. More recent work has shown that even as first introduced it was a very good approximation shown by the few cases of structural failure in normal service. In particular, it was realised that there were few very long waves with a height equal L/20 length so it was customary to accept higher stresses in long ships. For example, the nominal stresses for *Hood* were–hogging, 9.8 tons/in² in the deck, 9.05 keel (*c*5 sagging).[34] The success of this calculation depended on comparison with similar ships which had given satisfactory service, *eg* if previous destroyers had behaved well with calculated stresses of 8 tons/in², then the next class could be designed for a similar stress. Failure, if any, usually took the form of broken rivets and was unlikely to be catastrophic. Second World War destroyers were over-stressed and their single riveted joints on the forecastle deck would leak making life miserable in the forward mess decks whilst leaks into the feed water tanks were more dan-

27 The early development of the theory of ships structures is described in more detail in *Warrior to Dreadnought*, Chapter 2 and Appendix 6. The first part of this appendix repeats some of the earlier book but the later sections outline new work of the period covered by this book.

28 W J M Rankine, *Shipbuilding, Theoretical and Practical* (London 1866) and E J Reed, 'On the unequal distribution of weight and support in ships and its effects in still water, waves and exceptional positions', *Phil Trans Royal Society* (London 1871)

29 It is not very different from that used today. Dr D W Chalmers, *The Design of Ships' Structures* (MoD London 1993).

30 The height of L/20 was standardised for warships after Biles' work on the TBD *Wolf*; today 8 metres height is used for all ships (*Warrior to Dreadnought*, Chapter 11). The theoretical limit on steepness is L/7.

31 For a more detailed explanation of second moment see D K Brown, *The Grand Fleet*, Appendix 5.

32 Biles' work on the *Wolf* trials showed that this correction was not strictly necessary but it was retained for the sake of consistency.

33 Not unreasonable! In a sea rougher than this hits would be few.

34 It was quite rough when she was sunk and the high bending stresses may have contributed to her breaking in half.

35 Goodall 1 Mar 1940. 'Am concluding destroyers are too flimsy for the rough work on which they are employed in this war'.

36 It was assumed that a strip of plating with a width equal to 25 times its thickness (t) each side of the stiffener would be effective. In a panel of plating with parallel stiffeners there was evidence that all plating would be effective if the stiffeners were 80t apart so the 2x25t assumption was conservative.

gerous,[35] Some other navies accepted much higher stresses. For example, the French *Mogador* had stresses between 9.0 and 10.3 tons/in². It is, perhaps, not surprising that the small French destroyer *Branlebas* broke in half in a moderate gale off Dartmouth in December 1940.

If one flange (deck or bottom) only of the girder is strengthened, the neutral axis will move towards the stiffening, increasing the stress on the other flange. This was the problem with *London*, discussed in Chapter 4. The strength of many parts of the structure was governed by local loading, *eg* waves on the forecastle deck and impacting on the fore side of the superstructure.

Buckling

When in compression, a panel of plating, with its stiffeners, could buckle and collapse completely. Designers were well aware of this as a possible mode of failure but it was not possible to calculate with accuracy until the introduction of the computer. The best that could be done was to consider a single longitudinal girder with an associated strip of plating as a strut.[36] Again, such calculations were only comparative but there were no such failures in British ships in normal service though

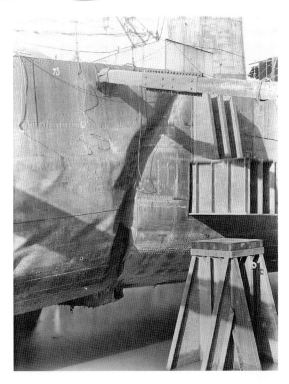

Albuera was loaded till she failed in dry dock. The final collapse began with shear wrinkles in the side of the hull (clearly seen in the close-up). (Author's collection)

buckling was a serious problem under explosive loading. It is likely that this simple design process, used with caution, led to structures heavier than would now be used. Comparison is not easy but it would seem that the weight of hull structure in a Second World War riveted structure is nearly double that of a modern welded ship of the same dimensions.

It was also possible for side plating to buckle at the point of maximum shearing force, roughly ¼ and ¾ length. A check would be made but there was little evidence of any trouble in normal service. Shear buckles were seen on many ships after target trials (see Chapter 10). In particular, the cancelled, uncompleted 'Battle' class destroyer *Albuera*, loaded to failure in dry dock in post-war trials, failed by shear buckling.

Sharp corners, stress concentrations and continuity

In 1913 Inglis read a paper showing mathematically that stresses increased very considerably at a sharp corner while at the same meeting Professor Coker obtained similar results using an optical strain method.[37] The importance of these papers was recognised and they were summarised in the constructors' course notes at the RN College, Greenwich, the same year. However, the draughtsmen responsible for detailed drawings of structure seem to have been unfamiliar with the need to avoid sharp corners and checking all too often failed to detect such errors. Goodall wrote '. . . square corner vent hole in stringer which makes me mad.'[38] These stress concentrations did not extend far and if a crack started it would usually stop as soon as the stress reduced. However, the steels then in use became brittle at low temperatures (sometimes not all that low), something not then known and cracks could extend very rapidly over a whole plate. They would almost always stop at a riveted joint.[39]

There was a similar stress concentration at the break of forecastle and if, as in most destroyers and cruisers, this was close to amidships, local cracking was likely.

The 'Town' class cruisers were particularly bad as the armour deck stepped down very close to the break of forecastle making a major discontinuity of structure (Goodall – 'these *Southampton*s are a groggy lot').[40] Failure at the break of forecastle was all too common after an underwater explosion, *eg Belfast* (see Chapter 10).[41] Pre-war tests against underwater attack had usually involved short test sections such as Job 74. These failed to show how the whole ship would flex violently causing major buckling failure particularly at discontinuities such as the break of forecastle.[42]

A somewhat similar problem could arise at the end of long superstructures. The superstructure formed a fairly strong box which resisted the flexing of the main hull so that the ends tended to tear away from the deck. Such problems could usually be avoided by ensuring that superstructure endings rested on main transverse bulkheads. It was also possible to divide the superstructure into short blocks by expansion joints; divisions with a splash-tight cover. The stress could be high at the bottom of expansion joints. (See Chapter 2 for discussion of open hangar carriers with expansion joints.)

This brief note omits the many strength calculations carried out on pillars, gun supports, rudders, shaft brackets and many other items. Masts, directors etc were supported directly over main bulkheads. (Sometimes, a minor bulkhead would be strengthened to provide support.) Bulkheads were designed to withstand a head of water up to an assumed damaged waterline and some would actually be tested to that condition.

While it is fair to say that more attention should have been paid to structural design it must be recognised that many problems could not be solved without a computer. British failings in normal service were annoying but the RN did not suffer major failures as in some foreign navies. Part of the problem was that peacetime exercises were held at a time and place where reasonable weather would be expected. The author has long advocated the creation of a squadron which would always steam at high speed, even in bad weather, to see what broke.

37 C E Inglis, 'Stresses in a plate due to the presence of cracks and sharp corners' and Prof E G Coker and W A Scoble. 'The distribution of stress due to a rivet in a plate' *Trans INA* (1913).

38 Goodall 12 Mar 1941.

39 For this reason, British riveted escort carriers were preferred for the North Russian route over the welded US-built ships.

40 Goodall, 28 Jan 41 also 15 Mar 1940. 'Lillicrap re *Edinburgh*. He thinks termination of armoured deck is the cause of the trouble. I think nasty corner of the sheer strake is the reason.' 29 Mar 1940. 'Final go at *Edinburgh*. Stresses forward of belt are higher than original calcs as lower deck armour was taken in and should not have been. I expect we will find trouble in OB (Outer Bottom).' 20 Jul 1940. 'bad design in troubles with *Manchester*.'

41 Warship Supplement 87 (World Ship Society 1986).

42 We were not the only ones to get this wrong. The ex-German destroyer *Nonsuch* (*Z38*) failed early at the break.

Appendix 13
Notes on Damage to RN Armoured Hangar Carriers

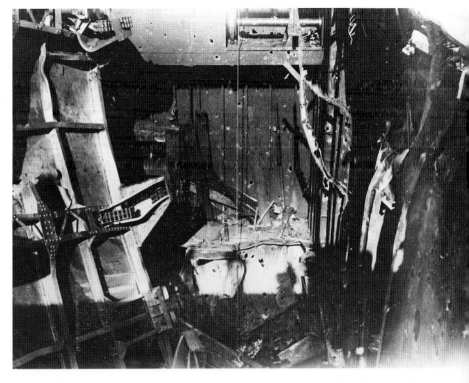

Illustrious's lift well after attack by German dive bombers. (Author's collection)

Ship	Date	Description
Illustrious	10 Jan 41	8 bombs (550kg) hit S2 pom pom, forward flight deck, aft lift, thro' armour, lift, P1 pom pom, near miss stbd, aft, lift.
	16 Jan 41	2 bombs (550kg), flight deck aft, near-miss port.
	6 Apr 45	Kamikaze, grazed island, bomb exploded under water, severe damage.
Formidable	25 Jun 41	2 1000lb bombs (a). Severely damaged under water. Spall from flight deck armour pentrated centre M/C space.
	4 & 9 May 45	2 Kamikaze on flight deck. One 9ft to port of CL Fr 79. Depression 24 x 20ft, hole 2ft square. Deep beam buckled. 3 fragments pierced hangar deck, one went through BR to DB (b). Second port of CL Fr 94. Deck depressed 4½in, beam distorted 3in. Heavy fire in parked aircraft (c).
Victorious	12 Aug 42	Small bomb broke on flight deck.
	9 May 45	3 Kamikaze, remained operational. First hit deck abreast island diving from stbd to port. Bomb exploded in sea, no damage (d). 2nd detonated on deck at Fr 30 between lift and B 4.5in turret at junction of 3in and 1.5in D plates over longitudnal bulkhead, 3in depression and pierced. Hole 25 sq ft, depression 144 sq ft. Bulkhead buckled, accelerator broken. Small fires (e). 3rd hit port side of CL, Fr 135; no damage (f).
Indomitable	12 Aug 42	2 hits, 3 near misses, 550kg SAP. Hits on flight deck just fore and aft of armour. One near miss caused extensive damage.
	11 Jul 43	Torpedoed, fragments of belt went into engine room.
	4 May 45	1 Kamikaze abreast island, no serious damage
Indefatigable	1 Apr 45	Kamikaze. Hit starboard side of island. Deck indented over 15 sq ft by up to 2in. No penetration. Short but impressive fire (g). Flight deck repaired in 30 min, island in 1 month.

Notes
(a) Probably 550kg–I have quoted the official reports.
(b) Fully operational.
(c) Might not have pierced even an unarmoured deck.
(d) As c.
(e) Deck protection invaluable. Temporary repairs while operating. Back in action after 2 days.
(f) As c.
(g) As c.

Based on a Pacific Fleet report, dated May 1945, on the value of armoured decks. 'Without armoured decks, TF 57 would have been out of action (with 4 carriers) for at least 2 months.'

Appendix 14

Wartime Cruiser Building

For completeness, the programmes for all *Dido* and *Fiji* classes and derivatives are listed.

Dido class

1936	*Dido, Naiad, Phoebe, Euryalus, Sirius*
1937	*Bonaventure, Hermione*
1938	*Charybdis, Scylla, Cleopatra*
1939 War	*Argonaut* also five more which became the modified *Dido* or *Bellona* class *Bellona, Black Prince, Diadem, Royalist, Spartan*

Fiji classes

Original design

1937	*Fiji, Nigeria, Kenya, Mauritius, Trinidad*
1938	*Jamaica, Gambia*
1939	*Bermuda,* also two unnamed to be built in Dockyards, cancelled.

Uganda **class,** 62ft beam, nine 6in

1938	*Uganda, Ceylon*
1939	*Newfoundland*

Swiftsure **class** (originally *Minotaur*) 63ft beam, nine 6in

1941	*Swiftsure, Ontario* (ex *Minotaur*), *Bellerophon* (renamed *Tiger**, 64ft beam)

Tiger **class,** 64ft beam, nine 6in. * completed post war to much modified design, four 6in

1941 Supp	*Superb, Defence* (renamed *Lion**), *Tiger* (renamed *Bellerophon,* changed to *Neptune* design and cancelled)
1942	*Blake*, Hawke* (cancelled 1945), four more cancelled in 1942

Appendix 15

D Quality Steel

A new, strong steel was introduced in 1922 known as 'D' quality.[43] It was used to save weight which made it seem of great value following the Washington Treaty which limited the size of warships but it was almost certainly under development before the Treaty was discussed. A variant, D1, was also introduced.

The carbon content of D quality was rather high for welding and a lower carbon steel, DW, was developed with the Institute of Welding during the war which could be welded reliably though it was slightly less strong. A steel for submarine pressure hulls, 'S', was also developed.

The properties of these steels are compared in the table below but some definitions are needed.

Ultimate Tensile Strength (UTS): The load per unit area of the test piece which will break it (tons/sq in).
Elongation: The percentage increase in length just before breaking.
Elastic limit test: When the load on D and D1 was increased from 4 tons/sq in to 17 and back to 4 it was required that the permanent stretch must not exceed 0.0004in on a length of 8in. DW had a similar test but the maximum load was 16 tons/sq in for plates up to 1in and 15 for thicker plates. S quality was required to be loaded to 17 tons/sq in without permanent stretch.
Bend test: A strip of D quality (DW and S the same) 1½in wide had to be bent double over an inner radius of 1½ times the thickness of the plate. D1 had to pass the same test with a 3in strip; a rather more severe condition.

	Mild Steel	D	D1	DW	S
UTS (tons/sq in)	26-32	37-44	37-44	35-41*	30-34
Elongation (%)	20	17	17	17	20**

* 33-39 for plates over 1in
** 18 per cent for plates under ¼in

Comments

The weight saving from the use of D quality was not great; for the 'Hunt' class it was estimated at 13 tons in a total hull weight of 475 tons compared with mild steel. In a formula in use just before the war, hull weight was assumed to vary as $1/(\text{working stress})^{0.175}$. The weight saving from welded construction in mild steel would have been much greater. The use of S quality in submarines was much more beneficial giving an extra 50ft on diving depth.

Aluminium

During the 1930s, aluminium was used extensively in fittings to save weight – vent trunks, valves, side scuttles, lockers and many others. In 1940 it was decided that virtually all aluminium was to go to aircraft. It was estimated that this decision added 100 tons to the displacement of a cruiser and was equivalent to a twin 4.7in mount in a destroyer.

43 This appendix is mainly derived from Sir S V Goodall, 'Some Recent Technical Developments in Naval Construction', *Trans NECI* (1944).

44 This appendix is largely based on research and drafts by P Pugh to whom I am grateful.

45 R D Layman, 'The Day the Admirals Wept', *Warship 1995* (London 1995), R S Egan et al, 'SMS *Ostfriesland'*, *Warship International* 2/75. G T Zimmerman's section is unclear as to the number of hits scored. On the first day there were nine hits of which two exploded out of twenty-three (thirty-three) dropped. Damage was slight. On the second day three out of six 1000lb hit, followed by two near-misses out of six 2000lb bombs dropped.

46 Introduction.

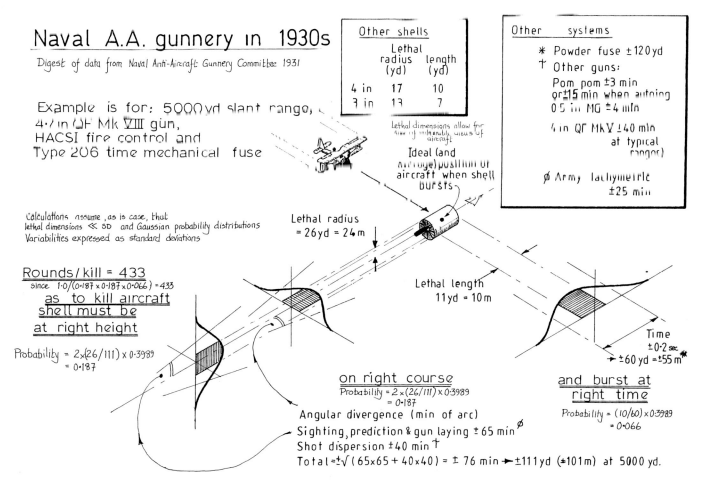

Naval A.A. gunnery in 1930s

Digest of data from Naval Anti-Aircraft Gunnery Committee 1931

Example is for: 5000 yd slant range,
4·7 in QF Mk VIII gun,
HACSI fire control and
Type 206 time mechanical fuse

Calculations assume, as is case, that
lethal dimensions ≪ SD and Gaussian probability distributions
Variabilities expressed as standard deviations

Other shells

	Lethal radius (yd)	length (yd)
4 in	17	10
3 in	13	7

Lethal dimensions allow for size of vulnerable areas of aircraft

Other systems

* Powder fuse ±120 yd
† Other guns:
Pom pom ±3 min
or ±15 min when autoing
0·5 in MG ±4 min
4 in QF Mk V ±40 min
at typical ranges
∅ Army tachymetric ±25 min

Ideal (and average) position of aircraft when shell bursts

Lethal radius = 26 yd = 24 m

Lethal length 11 yd = 10 m

Rounds / kill = 433
since 1·0/(0·187 × 0·187 × 0·066) = 433
as to kill aircraft shell must be at right height

Probability = 2 × (26/111) × 0·3989
= 0·187

on right course
Probability = 2 × (26/111) × 0·3989
= 0·187

Angular divergence (min of arc)
Sighting, prediction & gun laying ± 65 min ∅
Shot dispersion ±40 min †
Total =±√(65×65 + 40×40) = ± 76 min → ±111 yd (±101 m) at 5000 yd.

Time ±0·2 sec
±60 yd =±55 m *

and burst at right time
Probability = (10/60) × 0·3989
= 0·066

Appendix 16

Anti-Aircraft Warfare between the Wars[44]

The evolving threat from the air, first from airships and then from aeroplanes had been recognised by the mounting of anti-aircraft guns even before the First World War and the number and size of such weapons increased considerably during the war. These guns relied on 'eye shooting' and post-war analysis showed that some 3-4000 rounds were fired for each aircraft brought down. No large warship was lost to air attack during the war but the potential of aircraft was evident in the rapid growth in the size of bombers and of their weapons.

After the First World War the subject of air attack on ships became a matter of heated – and often ill-informed – public controversy as proponents of air power claimed that battleships were highly vulnerable to attack by new and larger bombers entering service as the war ended. In particular, much was made of the bungled trial on 21 July 1921 in which the elderly ex-German battleship *Ostfriesland* was sunk by US

bombers.[45] It was claimed that the most modern battle-ships could be sunk by a few cheap aircraft. A more correct lesson of this and of British trials was that it was very difficult to hit a ship, even when stationary and undefended.

The RN carried out a considerable number of investigations and full scale trials to clarify the perceived lessons of the war and to seek solutions to the problems revealed.[46] Anti-aircraft warfare (AAW) can be divided into active defence, shooting down or driving off the attacker, and passive defence, the ability of the ship to withstand the damage inflicted by enemy weapons. In the earlier trials of passive defence, obsolete ships were bombed by individual aircraft or by formations, flying straight and level at high altitude, in conformity with doctrines accepted by all air forces.

In the 1920s it was soon realised that the chance of any one bomb hitting a large ship, even when stationary and undefended, was remote. For example, in the 1924 trials with *Monarch* as the target, formations of aircraft, flying at 8000ft, first used practice bombs to establish wind and other corrections before dropping fifty-seven large bombs which scored eleven hits. In consequence, later trials were carried out in two stages. Firstly, bombs

AA Warfare. (Diagram by Phillip Pugh.)

would be fired from a howitzer against a target representing deck protection and the penetration recorded. Secondly, bombs would be placed at realistic positions within the trial ship and detonated electrically. The lessons read from these trials were that only large bombs, dropped from a considerable height, would cause serious damage to a battleship.[47] Few such bombs could be carried and the chance of hitting a fast manoeuvring ship was slight, particularly when the bomb aimer was distracted by gunfire. It was thought that the chance of hitting a destroyer was negligible. To stand any chance of causing serious damage to larger vessels the attacking aircraft had to fly high, straight and level, with many aircraft in close formation, dropping simultaneously. Forecasts that level, formation bombing would prove ineffective proved valid; for example, RN operations in the Mediterranean were little affected by the well-trained, high level bombers of the Regia Aeronautica.

Active AAW defence concentrated on this high-level threat; note that the 'County' classes had the heaviest AA armament of any early 'Treaty' cruiser. Even their 8in guns were intended to have an AA capability and, had the multiple pompom been put into production in time, they would also have had the best close-range AA as well. It is important to realise that the overall effectiveness of a system depends on its weakest link. The AAW 'system' comprises;

Detection. Visual sighting only until the introduction of radar in two ships just before the war. Exercises showed visual sighting in average conditions would be at about 12-16,000yds for single aircraft and 20,000yds for formations. Reporting by airborne scouts or outlying escorts were useful means to earlier detection. (About 4-5 minutes for the 120kt aircraft of the mid-1930s.)
Control. Estimating angles of elevation and training for the gun so that the shell would meet the aircraft after a time of flight of between 5 and 50 seconds.
Guns which could be trained and elevated quickly and could sustain a high rate of fire at all angles.
Fusing which would explode the shell close enough to the aircraft to cause lethal damage or, at least, put the bomb aimer off.

In 1921 the weakest link was identified (correctly) as the fuse. Next came the control subsystem which became the weak link after the introduction of the proximity fuse during the war. Fire control was difficult since the ship was likely to be pitching, rolling, heaving, swaying, surging and yawing in a seaway whilst the ship's hull would bend several inches in a big wave and about the same due to solar heating of the upper deck, disturbing the alignment of the director with the guns. Then, any practical system had to assume that, during the flight of the shell, the plane would fly straight at a steady speed even though it could in fact vary speed and direction in three dimensions.[48]

Even this simplified case was demanding since a plane detected at 15,000yds and flying at 100kts would be overhead in about 5 minutes. Height, range and bearing were measured using instruments similar to those for surface action but with optics which could be trained in elevation as well as bearing. Aircraft course and speed was initially guessed and then refined using successive measurements with the aid of mechanical calculators. It was highly desirable that the sight or director should be stabilised. Early attempts to stabilise the whole ship using a gyroscope (*Vivien*, 1921) were not successful; later attempts using fin stabilisers (*Bittern*, Chapter 7 and Appendix 19) were more promising but not entirely successful. During the 1920s the Admiralty Research Laboratory (ARL), at Teddington carried out a good deal of work on stabilised sights but control theory, servo mechanisms and gyros were all in their infancy and the problems were not overcome. The Germans pursued this line during the 1930s and produced a director system which was good when it worked but it was unreliable and too heavy for small ships.

If a fully-stabilised line of sight could be established, then the angular rates at which it moved could yield aircraft speed and course more rapidly. This approach, known as tachymetric, was first used by the British Army in the 1920s and was successfully developed for use at sea by the USN in the Mk 37, the best director of the Second World War.

It takes about 10 years to develop a weapon system and the RN fought the war with systems planned about 1930. In fact, there was a major review of AAW by the Naval Anti-Aircraft Gunnery Committee in 1931. The RAF were represented by a Squadron leader, a very junior officer, which seems to show that they did not take the matter seriously or wanted to be able to disavow his views later. Thinking in the RAF and in other air forces was that they were independent services who could win a war through strategic bombing. Though they were aware of the potential of the dive bomber by 1931, they advised that this form of attack was difficult and hazardous with any but purpose-built planes of little value for other purposes and hence their widespread deployment was unlikely.

Dive bombing had been developed in the USN from about 1924 in response to Marine Corps requirements for the support of landing operations, and initially, fighters were used carrying only small bombs. The RN recognised that fighters, which might be escorting bombers, could attack ships in a shallow dive using machine guns and bombs. A high percentage of hits could be expected but with bombs of only 20lb weight, little damage would be expected. The USN thought that such attacks could disable the crews of AA guns making the task of the high level bombers easier. They soon realised that dive bombing was far more accurate than high level bombing and by about 1930 the USN had dive bombers carrying 500lb bombs which could sink

47 With hindsight, these lessons seem valid for the 1920s and even for much of the 1930s.

48 There were too many unknowns with too few data for any other approach.

49 This name appears in almost every technical advance of the age.

50 Major R T Partridge, *Operation Skua* (Yeovilton 1983).

51 Vice-Admiral H G Bowen, *Ships, Machinery and Mossbacks* (Princeton 1934).

unarmoured ships and inflict serious damage even to the best protected. A little later, the Luftwaffe developed the doctrine of operating not as an independent service but of acting as flying artillery for the German army. It procured large numbers of increasingly effective dive bombers and soon realised their potential against ships.

The RN used fighters in the dive bomber role during the war in the Mediterranean. Rear-Admiral Henderson[49] commanding the carriers pressed for a purpose-built dive bomber. This materialised as the Blackburn Skua in 1937 (Requirement 1934) which was also described as a fighter it did shoot down the first German aircraft in the war! The Skua could carry a 500lb bomb and could be controlled accurately in a steep dive.[50] It was also the first dive bomber to sink a major warship; the *Königsberg* in Bergen in 1940. The RN's respect for the dive bomber also showed in the increasing number of multiple pompoms being fitted to their ships.

The 1931 Committee made some specific recommendations which had a considerable influence on destroyer design. In particular, they said that '. . . destroyers can assist in the defence of the fleet in the same way but, since they are not likely to be the object of high level bombing or torpedo attack. Their long range guns need not have great elevation'. The argument was that destroyers would not be firing on planes attacking themselves but against planes passing by on the way to attack capital ships. Then, for example, a typical target would be an aircraft at 5000ft and 5000yds away thus having an elevation of only 18° above the horizon. The committee also recognised the loading problem of dual purpose guns and recommended that 'future destroyers should not be fitted with a dual purpose armament' except that they did recommend a 40° mounting.

They also said that 'Improvements in long range defence should, in general, take precedence over those in close range defence since the former provides an increase in the defensive power of the fleet as a whole whereas close range defence can, as a rule, only increase that of individual units and is impotent against high bombing aircraft'. The committee was keen that long-range gunnery should break up formations since single aircraft at high altitude were unlikely to score hits. They provided table showing the hit probabilities for various guns:

Single hit probability

Range (yds)	4in Mk V %	4.7in Mk VIII %
2500	0.76	
3500	0.36	0.74
4500	0.27	0.44
5500	0.15	0.28
6500	0.14	0.21
7500	0.13	0.30

These figures equate to a chance of between 7 and 12 per cent of killing a single aircraft flying towards the ship at 6500ft and 110kts. While this does not sound very impressive, it means that four guns, which the committee recommended should bear in any direction, had a probability of over 99 per cent of shooting down one out of a formation of eighteen, so disrupting a formation bomb drop. For smaller formations, the probability of killing one aircraft was less but still good in relation to the probability of a successful bomb attack.

The Navy was slow in recognising the growing deficiencies in AAW as aircraft performance improved, possibly because those operated by the Fleet Air Arm were so mediocre in performance. The first major alarm came in 1937 with the introduction of the radio-controlled Queen Bee aircraft, a converted Tiger Moth. One such plane was able to fly straight and level at 85kts for an hour or so over the whole Mediterranean fleet without being hit! Even in the early months of the war *Ark Royal*'s fighters were kept in the hangar to keep the guns free to deal with enemy aircraft. (Since the fighters were Skuas, this may have been wise in the light of their poor performance in that role.)

There is little doubt that the RN's AAW capability was inferior to that of the USN, the Germans and the Japanese during the early years of the war, but the operation significance of this must not be exaggerated. The change from wood and canvas biplanes to the monocoque, all-metal monoplane at the outbreak of the war had so improved aircraft performance that they were very difficult targets for even the best systems until the introduction of the proximity fuse. In February 1941, even shore-based anti-aircraft guns, with a good tachymetric director and on a firm base, needed 3000 rounds per kill. The major cause of the inferiority of the RN's AAW provisions seems to have been the opposite of the 'reactionary' attitude so often blamed. The RN was the first to try a good close-range weapon, the multiple pompom, but production was delayed by a very rare Treasury block and by 1939 it was obsolescent. Similarly, the 1931 committee was a little early and only two years later would have recognised the threat posed by the dive bomber and the weakness of the fleet's AA defences against it (particularly apparent in the *Dido*s and 'Hunts'). It is one of those not-uncommon cases in which a number of decisions, individually correct or, at least justifiable, add up to an incorrect solution overall. Or rather, where the solution decided upon proves to be the answer to the wrong question. Air attacks of the kind postulated by the RAF in 1931 were, in the event, countered quite well by the AA systems of the RN. These systems were, however, of little utility against the Luftwaffe's dive bombers.

Appendix 17

USN Destroyer Machinery

Until the early 1930s US destroyer machinery was very similar to that of the RN which is hardly surprising since the principal US shipbuilders all built Parsons turbine designs under licence. The *Farragut*s were the first post-war design and they used steam at 400lbs/in² and 650°F (200° superheat). They also introduced alternating current main supply. The shipbuilders only built small numbers of machinery units and hence could not invest in research or development, relying entirely on Parsons who were described as extremely conservative. The USN were concerned that Parsons were passing information on new American designs to the Admiralty and in 1935 the Head of the Bureau of Engineering, Rear-Admiral S M Robinson, invoked the Espionage Act to prevent further dealings with the firm.[51]

By 1935, the US builders of power stations such as General Electric, Westinghouse and Allison-Chalmers had made enormous advances in the design of steam plant. Such developments were an integrated whole with improved boilers, controlled superheaters, piping, turbines and gearing, Bowen pointing out that Parsons turbines were large, operated at low speed and had a large number of blades making them unsuitable for high steam conditions. In contrast, the power station plants were compact, fast running and had a small number of blades, suiting them for high steam pressure and temperature.

The first six *Mahan*s were ordered in pairs from Bath Iron Works, United Shipyards and US Steel and it was a requirement that the ships and their machinery should be identical. None of the builders had the design capability needed so it was agreed that Gibbs and Cox should prepare the design. At that time they had very little warship experience but they had designed a number of merchant ships with advanced steam machinery plants taking advantage of the developments in power stations. As a result the *Mahan*s showed a considerable step forward in machinery with steam at 400lbs/in² and 700°F and double reduction gearing but the machinery spaces were very congested. This was unfortunate since President Roosevelt had used (quite properly) some $281 million from the National Industrial Recovery Act to strengthen the Navy as a result of which twenty-six *Mahan*s were built and their cramped machinery helped to give advanced plants a bad reputation. The *Mahan* turbines turned at about double the speed of earlier engines using double reduction gearing.

There were further important advances in the *Somers* class with controlled superheat and air-encased boilers which meant that open stokeholds (fire rooms) could be used which were much more convenient and safer under gas attack. The boilers were designed to deliver steam at 600lbs/in² and 850°F, one boiler being tested on shore to 40 per cent overload. One complete set of *Benham*'s machinery was set up on shore and tested exhaustively. The turbines had many fewer blades than the older Parsons design and the rotor was 25 per cent shorter, machined from a solid forging instead of built up. Westinghouse had spent very large sums on R & D and members of their staff had made major advances in the study of vibration of the blades and rotor which had led to many failures in earlier units (probably HMS *Acheron*'s problem). It is interesting that, though this work was published in the American Society of Mechanical Engineers, it does not seem to have been applied elsewhere. Westinghouse also made much more use of X-ray examination of castings and forgings, used advanced steel alloys and developed much improved pipe joints which did not lead to the infuriating steam leaks so common in British ships.[52]

The trials of *Somers* in November 1937 were a revelation even though she was operating at a cautious 730°F to begin with. Fuel consumption was about 20 per cent less than *Porter* with a similar increase in endurance while the machinery, though more powerful, was 10 per cent lighter. For the same power the machinery would have weighed 130 tons less, equivalent to three twin 5in mounts. Another comparison between *Benham* and *Gridley* showed the former to use 23 per cent less fuel and weighed 12 per cent less. When the temperature was raised to 850°F there was a further gain of 6 per cent in economy and 10 per cent in power, equivalent to a knot on top speed. The *Somers* had 14,730 turbine blades compared with 98,750[53] in *Porter* whist the rotors in the former were 25-33 per cent shorter, making them better able to withstand rapid changes in temperature. Despite all these changes the advanced plant had higher factors of safety in all components than the older plant. Once again, it must be emphasised that the improvement did not lie solely with high temperatures and pressures but a fully integrated design with double reduction gearing, air encased boilers, controlled superheat, economisers, de-aerators etc.

The full range of improvements was introduced from the spring of 1938 in what were known as the 'Bath Changes', in a series of phases, the full temperature being introduced in Phase 4 with DD429 (and four earlier ships which could be caught). Similar changes were made to the machinery of other categories with equal benefit. In one comparison it was found that, at low speeds, *King George V* burnt 39 per cent more fuel than *Washington* which still retained a big advantage at higher speeds. Since the US ship carried more fuel, her endurance at cruising speed was double that of the British and 20 per cent more at top speed and required far less maintenance.

Rear-Admiral H G Bowen's fascinating account of the introduction of these changes shows how they were opposed by vested interests and conservatives and how internal politics confused the issue – at one time he was under investigation for ignoring the Staff Requirement for endurance by exceeding it! The success of the US machinery was due to the determination of the man at the top to take advantage of new developments outside the conventional marine engineering industry. It was also due to the designer's success in producing a fully integrated plant with each component taking advantage of improvements elsewhere and fully matched to the operating conditions making the overall improvement greater than the sum of the parts. The USN also made the wise—but brave—decision to go ahead with a whole class and not mess about with a single prototype like *Acheron*.

Appendix 18
Submarine Stability etc

When fully surfaced, the stability of a submarine has the same features as those of any other surface ship and is measured by the same parameters, metacentric height (GM) and the curve of righting levers (GZ) (see, for example, the introduction to *Design and Construction of British Warships, 1939-45*). A little care is needed to ensure that the unusual shape is properly represented and that the possibility of liquids moving in the numerous tanks is considered (see discussion of 'A' class in Chapter 6).

When the submarine is submerged things are very different. The concept of the metacentre was introduced as an approximation of the effects of the change in shape of the underwater form of a surface ship as it heels. Since a submerged submarine is all underwater, there is no change in shape, no metacentric height and the force of buoyancy acts though the centre of buoyancy (B), now a fixed point. Though this makes life simple in many respects, there are consequences which are not always obvious. Archimedes principle, weight = buoyancy takes on a new significance. The force of buoyancy is given by volume x density and if the density of water changes, weight must be adjusted to equal the new buoyancy.

From the *Odin* onwards, it was decided that submarines should be able to dive in water of specific gravity (sg) 1.00 to 1.030. The difference in buoyancy in *Odin* amounted to 53 tons which had to be compensated for with internal water ballast. Added weights during the war reduced the scope for varying ballast so that range of sg changed first to 1.005–1.03, then 1.01–1.03 and finally 1.015–1.03. Ballast must also be adjusted as fuel, stores, torpedoes and other consumable items are used during a patrol. For water of a given density, there is only one displacement at which the submarine will float in equilibrium.

Submarines are designed with a combination of water and solid ballast which may be adjusted to compensate for changes in weight. Solid ballast can only be moved at refit and is there for used to allow for major changes in equipment fit. Since the solid ballast is usually low down and added weights are higher, any weight addition will raise the centre of gravity (G), lowering BG.

Buoyancy and stability are checked on completion and at intervals during the service life by a 'trim and incline experiment'. With the boat on the surface, water ballast is adjusted so that she is floating at draughts so that when the external ballast tanks are flooded she will float, submerged, in equilibrium. Before diving, a conventional inclining experiment is carried out. Known weights are moved, the angle of heel is measured and the metacentric height deduced. The boat is then cautiously submerged and the water ballast adjusted until she is floating happily. Weights are then moved to deduce the stability, BG. In most cases, the experiment will lead to an adjustment of solid ballast before a stability statement is issued.

Some values of GM and BG[54]

Class	Design		Measured	
	GM	BG	GM	BG (ins)
Oberon			14.75	8.1
Rainbow	11.42	10.2	7.05	8.1
Thames	18.72	10.5	9.83	5.0
Swordfish	16.45	17.1	6.31	6.9
Shark	21.2	19.3	9.0	9.1
Porpoise	14.17	10.4	10.56	9.5

The real problems came in the act of surfacing. There would be a large quantity of water trapped in the casing, high up, and draining only slowly. The amount of water in the ballast tanks was uncertain and changing rapidly. Without a computer there was no way of examining this transient condition and the designer had to do the best he could, based solely on experience. Most submarines were very tender in these conditions, some worse than others—the 'S' class had a bad reputation.

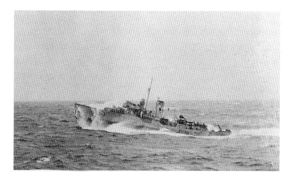

Eyebright taking it green. Probably Sea State 5-6, wave height about 13ft. The 'Flower' class were too short for sustained operations in the Atlantic. (Author's collection)

Appendix 19
Seakeeping

The operational capability of a warship depends to a great extent on seakeeping and this was never more true than in the escort vessels of the Second World War though this was not fully recognised at the time. The North Atlantic is big, cold, rough (sometimes very rough), corrosive and hard when it hits you. In bad weather the fighting effectiveness of a ship falls off quite quickly mainly due to the degradation of the mental and physical abilities of the crew. Damage to the ship can also occur. Asdic domes were vulnerable as were boats and some destroyers lost funnels or had their bridge fronts pushed in.[55] The effectiveness of radar was much reduced in big waves. Surface attacks by submarines would normally be made with wind and sea astern, making life unpleasant for lookout on the escorts. In very big waves, submarines would have difficulty in depth keeping at periscope depth.

The table below gives accepted figures for sea state. This is not directly associated with wind speed. (Sea State (SS) is NOT the same as Beaufort Number which measures wind speed.) The relationship between wind speed and wave height in the table below is very approximate and only valid for a fully developed sea and a long fetch. The probability of occurrence, shown as a percentage of the year, is averaged over the whole year for the whole of the North Atlantic: figures for the winter months or for northerly latitudes will be more severe.[56]

The cause of seasickness was not fully understood during the war but it is now recognised as primarily associated with vertical acceleration from the combined effects of pitch and heave. It is less certain, but probable, that vertical acceleration is also the prime cause of impaired judgement in those not actually vomiting.[57] The amplitude of both pitch and heave in head seas is governed mainly by length, long ships having smaller motions. Vertical acceleration will also depend on the position along the length as that due to pitch will be much more severe at the bow and stern. Conversely, the effects of motion can be reduced by placing vital spaces such as the bridge, operations room etc close to amidships. Sickness also depends on the frequency of the motion occurring most often between 0.15 and 0.30Hz (cycles/second).

British destroyers – position of bridge and A gun

Class	Length (ft)	% of length from bow	
		Bridge	A gun
'M'	267	23	18
'V'	320	29	15
'Tribal'	364.7	34	17
'J'	348	29	14
'L'	354	32	16

These figures explain many of the popular impressions of the behaviour of the various classes. The 'V' and 'Ws' had a bridge much further aft than the earlier ships with less perceived motion as well as dryer. The bridge of the 'Tribals' was far aft which encouraged the COs to drive them hard partially accounting for the slamming damage. It is interesting that the Canadian 'Tribals' were strengthened but they had similar damage as they were driven harder (Goodall, 8 Apr 1943). The bridge of the USN *Sumner* class was only 13 per cent from the bow accounting for their reputation as poor sea boats. Note that most crew accommodation in Second World War escorts was right forward, the worst possible place.

The performance of even a modern power-worked gun mounting falls off rapidly in big waves.

The effect of motions on the crew's ability to fight depends on the degree of acclimatisation as well as on ship size. The figures below are based on experience with the *Leander* class frigates, at 360ft much longer than wartime escorts.

Sea State	Wave ht, mean (ft)	Wind speed, mean (kts)	Probability N Atlantic (%)	Period (secs)	Likely wave length (ft)
0-1	0.2	3.0	0.7	-	-
2	1.0	8.5	6.8	7.5	90
3	3.0	13.5	23.7	7.5	90
4	6.3	19.0	27.8	8.8	123
5	10.8	24.5	20.6	9.7	148
6	16.7	37.5	13.2	12.4	238
7	25.0	51.5	6.1	15.0	350
8	38.3	59.5	1.1	16.4	424
9	46.7	63.0	0.05	20.0	615

Sea State	% Loss of Capability (Leander)	Wave height (from) (ft)
0-4	0	
5	10	8
6	30	12.5
7 & over	95	20

Making a number of approximations these figures may be applied to escort vessels of the Second World War. Firstly it is assumed that loss of capability is directly proportional to vertical acceleration. Using the earlier table the percentage of a year when waves of different height occur is known. Multiplying probability of occurrence and loss of capability gives a figure for equivalent loss of days.[59] For the main classes this gives:

Class	Days lost/year
'Flowers'	28
'Castles'	21
'Rivers', old destroyers	15
Leanders	9

The 'Castle' class OPVs were designed for a level of motion, averaged over the year, similar to that which had been found acceptable in previous ships.[59] To allow for rising expectations a margin was added and this led to a length of 75 metres being selected.[60] It was no surprise that this simulation showed the 'Flowers' to be too short, an assessment fully supported by many subjective accounts.[61]

Severe pitching will cause the bow to come out of the water and, when it re-enters fast, there is a severe impact known as slamming which can damage Asdic domes and even the hull.[62] It is a very complicated phenomena but the table below, based on more recent ships, shows the speed which might be reached without unacceptable slamming as a function of draught. In general, slamming would be rare in corvettes, frigates and sloops at the speed which they could maintain in Sea State 6. Surprisingly, many accounts refer to the 'Flowers' as superb sea boats and it can only be assumed that this refers to their lack of slamming.

Speed at which slamming is severe in SS 6 (with considerable variation)

Draught (ft)	Speed (kts)
8	10
9	12
10	14
12	18

Destroyers were longer, shallower and much faster and likely to slam quite often from Sea State 5 upwards. Their highly stressed hulls would shudder and shake, worrying to both captain and crew. Rivets would be loosened, particularly in single riveted seams, causing troublesome leaks.[63] Pitching also caused interference with the Asdic due to the rapid flow of water, full of air bubbles, past the dome.

Sailors have always said 'One hand for yourself, one hand for the ship'. More recently, it has been shown that the ability to carry out manual work, such as loading depth charges, is mainly governed by lateral acceleration associated with rolling. Rolling is a complicated motion influenced by the size and frequency at which waves meet the ship (which depends on course and speed), on the metacentric height and on the resistance to roll provided by bilge keels etc. Though sufficient metacentric height is needed to ensure that the ship will not capsize in extreme seas, excessive values are to be avoided as they lead to rapid rolling with high accelerations. The basic theory had been set out by William Froude in 1860 but it could not be used directly until computers were available. A considerable amount of experimental work had been carried out on rolling before the war but there was still much that was not understood or at least quantified.

52 Vice-Admiral Sir L L Halley, *The Man around the Engine* (Emsworth 1990).

53 These are the figures given by Bowen. They seem very high and probably refer to both shafts, ... g turbines.

54 A N Harrison, *The Development of HM Submarines* (BR 3043: Bath 1979).

55 Motor cutters were replaced by whalers in the 'S' class as so many were washed away!

56 A more comprehensive table is given in D K Brown, 'Atlantic Escorts 1939-1945', S Howarth and D Law *The Battle of the Atlantic* (London 1994), p452.

57 It is no coincidence that the word *nausea* derives from the Greek word for ship!

58 Fully described in D K Brown, 'Atlantic Escorts 1939-1945' (thanks to Dr Adrian Lloyd).

59 The parameter averaged was 'Subjective Motion Magnitude'. See D K Brown and P D Marshall, 'Small Warships in the RN and the Fishery Protection Task', *RINA Warship Symposium* (London 1978), p47.

60 Based purely on historical evidence I would have chosen 80m. The new 'Castles' have won high praise in service. D K Brown, 'Service experience with the Castle Class', *The Naval Architect* (September 1983), ppE255-E257

61 N Monserrat, *The Cruel Sea* (London 1954). Probably the best account of life in a 'Flower'.

62 Slamming may cause local damage such as split plates or seams but it will also increase the overall bending load on the hull which will become manifest in earlier fatigue failures.

63 N G Holt and F E Clemitson, 'Notes on the Behaviour of HM Ships during the War', *Trans INA* (London 1949).

Nubian during rolling trials in 1939. Men ran backwards and forwards across the platforms either side of the after funnel. The trial gave valuable information on the efficacy of bilge keels and on the accuracy of model tests. Half a century later I had them re-analysed and used to check the accuracy of modern computer estimates – man power won! (Author's collection)

A ship which is too stiff will roll to only slightly larger angles than one with a smaller metacentric height but the roll will be much more rapid, increasing the lateral acceleration and making work more difficult. The stability of some older destroyers was marginal and they needed strict control of topweight and some ballasting.[64] On the other hand, the 'Captain' class were much too stiff, making work dangerous, and had to be taken out of service for bigger bilge keels and more topweight. The commander of HMS *Duckworth* wrote in the Ship's Cover:

> . . . since this report is written at sea it is difficult to describe with reticence the nauseating movement of the vessels in the open sea . . . it is influenced by excessive and uncontrollable rolling which is a factor which obscures every virtue these ships may possess.

The bilge keels were increased in depth from 18 to 24 inches and extended aft and the number of depth charges increased from 100 to 160. Weights were arranged as far from the roll axis as possible to increase the polar moment of inertia. Two of the diesel engined ships went to sea together, one modified, the other not with the results shown below.

Ship	Version	Double angle of roll (deg)	Period (secs)
Cooke	Original	56	8
Kempthorne	Modified	40	7½

The 'Flower' class also suffered from heavy rolling; 'They would roll on wet grass' (Monserrat). More prosaically, A W Watson gives the following figures;

'Flower' class

Ship	Wind force	Sea	Swell	Amplitude out-out (deg)	Full period (secs)	GM (ft)
Heather	7-8	5	3	17	4.8-8.4	2.6
Salvia	4	3	2	16	6.6-8.4	2.4

Sea condition

Sea Condition	Stabilised		Unstabilised	
	Angle°	Roll vel (Deg/sec)	Angle°	Roll vel (Deg/sec)
Slight sea, 200ft swell 10ft high, beam	2.3	0.35	10	1.53
Short, steep confused, 150ft, 10ft high, beam	2.6	0.74	9.3	2.02
Small, confused, following	2.3	0.09	6.5	0.7
Heavy, confused. Wind force 9	8.2	0.95	19	2.75

The natural roll period was about 10-10¼ seconds so Watson's figures refer to forced rolling in the period of wave encounter. The 'Flowers' were later fitted with bigger bilge keels. Most RN destroyers had 18in bilge keels (about the biggest possible with a single plate) though the 'Ls' and the Canadian 'Tribals' had 24in. Other nations were generally similar though the Dutch *Isaac Sweers* had 36in keels.

By modern standards, most Second World War ships had bilge keels which were too small. There seems to have been a feeling that ships always roll, that sailors are tough – and naval architects were aware that big bilge keels needed to be very strong and might reduce speed.

The *Bittern* was fitted with a Denny-Brown active fin stabiliser to reduce roll and similar stabilisers were fitted in the *Black Swan* class. A trial, with and without fins operating showed they could be very effective. Goodall was a very great enthusiast for the fin stabiliser.[65]

These trials would have been carried out in the presence of experts who would tune the control settings for optimum performance. Results in normal service were not as good. Some 'Hunt' and 'Battle' class destroyers were fitted with fins but, in most, the space was used for extra fuel.

Wetness due to green seas over the fore end of the ship could make open gunmountings and Hedgehog positions unpleasant and even dangerous to operate and could lead to exhaustion on open bridges. Adequate freeboard is the main factor in keeping ships dry. A rule of thumb introduced at the end of the Second World War, based on the number of complaints received, was that freeboard should equal 1.1 times the square root of the length (ft). Ships whose freeboard exceeded this value rarely complained. Flare, knuckles and breakwaters can help. All cruisers built between the wars had a knuckle with the exception of the *Birmingham*.[66]

Freeboard, RN Destroyers

Class	Length (ft)	Freeboard (ft)	1.1 Sq rt L ft
'M'	270	17	16.4
'V & W'	300	18.8	17.3
'I'	320	16.8	17.9
'Tribal'	364.7	18.2	19.1
'J'	348	19.7	18.6

The 'Tribals' were the only class in which the freeboard was less than the guideline and, sure enough, they were said to be wet.

Part of the problem was that as already noted between the wars exercises were held at a time and place where bad weather was unlikely. If bad weather did occur, the exercise would be stopped.[67]

64 D K Brown, 'Stability of RN Destroyers during World War II', *Warship Technology* 4/89.

65 Goodall, 4 Feb 1937. 'Told Controller of Denny Brown stabiliser, DNO present, both keen.' 6 Mar 1937. 'Woollard back. Gave me the impression that anti rolling gear in *Bittern* won't be all violets.' 1 June 1938. 'Told [Australian liaison officer] of success of stabiliser. I was of the opinion that they were wasting their money building an unstabilised sloop.'

66 The value of knuckles is a matter of debate, often heated. The author's view is manifest in the 'Castle' class – though I may have overdone it a little in these ships. The near universal fitting of knuckles in cruisers but not elsewhere illustrates the independence enjoyed by ship sections.

67 Roskill I p534.

Appendix 20
The Fleet Train

The numbers actually built or converted were:

Fleet Repair Ships	3
Heavy Duty Repair Ships	2
SRR(D) Accommodation Ships	2
Hull Repair Ships	2
A/C Maintenance Ships	2
A/C Engine Repair Ships	1
A/C Component Repair Ships	2
Escort Maintenance Ships	5 (1 cancelled)
LST Maintenance Ships	3
LC Maintenance Ships	4
Motor Craft Maintenance Ships	2 (1 cancelled)
Coastal Force Maintenance Ships	1
Armament Maintenance Ships	1 (1 cancelled)
Minesweeper Maintenance Ships	2
Seaward Defence Ship	1
Amenity Ship	1 (1 Cancelled)
Spare S/M Crew Accom Ship	1
	35

In addition, there were tankers, store carriers, tugs, harbour craft, hospital ships and floating docks. Comparatively few completed in time for service during the war.

In the Pacific

In July-August 1945 the Fleet Train consisted of; 1 destroyer repair ship, 2 repair ships, 3 maintenance ships, 1 boom defence vessel, 14 tankers, 4 water tankers, 4 small tankers, 3 armament store carriers, 10 armament stores issuing ships, 1 naval stores issuing ship, 4 victualling stores issuing ships, 5 naval store carriers, 5 accommodation ships, 1 deperming ship, 2 salvage ships, 1 distilling ship, 4 hospital ships, 5 tugs, 1 collier, 2 floating docks, 1 aircraft maintenance ship, 1 aircraft component repair ship, 1 aircraft repair ship, 1 aircraft stores issuing ship, 6 escort carriers, 1 destroyer depot together with 37 escort vessels.

Review of Principal Sources

While the principal sources are listed below, many others which deal with specific points will be found in the footnotes.

Public Record Office papers

I am particularly grateful to George Moore for his research into both the Admiralty papers (ADM Series), which have been used by earlier writers and the Cabinet Office series (CAB) which have not been trawled to the same extent.

Ships' Covers

Held in the National Maritime Museum (Woolwich annex). They are an invaluable source of information on the development of the design but, as described in Appendix 3, they may be the 'Truth and nothing but the Truth' but they are not the 'Whole Truth'. Also manuscript work books, particularly C S Lillicrap on cruiser design.

Goodall Diaries

British Library (see Appendix 1). An unusual view from the top.

Published Works

Transactions of the Institution of Naval Architects (Trans INA) (London). Particularly C E Inglis, 'Stresses in a Plate due to the Presence of Cracks and Sharp Corners' (1913); C E Sherwin, 'Electric Welding in Cruiser Construction' (1936); S V Goodall, 'Uncontrolled Weapons and Warships of Limited Displacement' (1937); S V Goodall, 'HMS *Ark Royal*' (1939); A P Cole, 'Destroyer Turning Circles' (1938); A Nicholls, 'The All-welded Hull Construction of HMS *Seagull*' (1939); A J Sims, 'The Habitability of Naval Ships under Wartime Conditions' (1945); J Lenaghan, 'Merchant Aircraft Carriers' (1947); N G Holt and F F Clemitson, 'Notes on the Behaviour of H M Ships during the War' (1949); R Baker, 'Ships of the Invasion Fleet' (1947); D B Fisher, 'The Fleet Train in the Pacific War' (1953); J H B Chapman, 'The Development of the Aircraft Carrier' (1960).

Note: there are many other important papers in the 1947 Transactions which were based on chapters of *Design and Construction of British Warships*.

A D Baker III (ed), *Allied Landing Craft of World War II* (London 1985)

le Bailley, Vice-Admiral Sir Louis, *The Man around the Engine* (Emsworth 1990). An autobiographical and very critical account of life as an engineer officer. Also *From Fisher to the Falklands* (London 1991). A more general review of the position of the naval engineer.

H G Bowen, *Ships Machinery and Mossbacks* (Princeton 1934)

D K Brown, *A Century of Naval Construction* (London 1983). The history of the Royal Corps of Naval Constructors.
Also *Design and Construction of British Warships* (London 1995)
Drafted as the official history of DNC department in the Second World War Each chapter was written by the appropriate section so that the quality is variable. Though checked on numerous occasions there are still errors.
The Grand Fleet: Warship Design and Development 1906-1922 (London 1999)
The predecessor to this volume.
'Naval Rearmament, 1930–41: the Royal Navy' in J Rohwer (ed), *The Naval Arms Race* (Stuttgart 1991)
'Stability of RN Destroyers during World War II', *Warship Technology* 10 (1989)
A more technical review of the subject.
'Ship Assisted Landing and Take Off', *Flight Deck* (Yeovilton 1986)
A very detailed account of catapults, arrester gear etc. (Partially reproduced in *Warship 49*)
'The Cruiser' in R Gardiner (ed), *Eclipse of the Big Gun* (London 1992)
'Armed Merchant Ships–A historical review', *RINA Conference Merchant Ships to War* (London 1987)
'Attack And Defence', *Warship 42-44*
– – – & P D Marshall, 'Small Warships in the RN and the Fishery Protection Task' *RINA Warship Symposium* (London 1978)

J D Brown, *Aircraft Carriers* (A WWII Fact File)
A most useful reference for the equipment of carriers; lift sizes, petrol stowage etc, figures not often quoted.

R A Burt, *British Battleships of World War I* (London 1986)
Very good on trials of protection.

I L Buxton, *Warship Building and Repair during the Second World War* (Glasgow 1997)
A very detailed survey of the performance of industry during the war.
Also 'Landing Craft Tank Mks 1 & 2', *Warships* 119 (London 1994)

H C Bywater, *The Great Pacific War* (London 1925)
A fictional account of war out in the Pacific in 1931. Much of the background is RN pub gossip and is of interest concerning gas warfare, diesel engines etc.

C R Calhoun, *Typhoon, the other Enemy* (Annapolis 1981)
Written by one who survived.

J Campbell, *Naval Weapons of World War II* (London 1985)
Used throughout as the reference for weapon data.

D W Chalmers, *The Design of Ships' Structures* (MoD London 1993)

E Chatfield, Admiral of the Fleet, Lord, *It Might Happen Again* (London 1947)
The second volume of his autobiography covering his term as Controller and as First Sea Lord.

G C Connell, *Valiant Quartet* (London 1979)

R M Crosley, *They gave me a Seafire* (Shrewsbury 1994) and *Up in Harm's Way.* (Shrewsbury 1986)
Very interesting account and strong views.

A B Cunningham, Viscount, *A Sailor's Odyssey* (London 1951)
A personal view.

P Dickens, *Night Action* (London 1974)
Exciting account by one of the most successful MTB captains.

P Elliott, *Allied Minesweeping in World War 2* (Cambridge 1979)
A most valuable reference with detail and illustrations not available elsewhere.

J English, *Amazon to Ivanhoe* (Kendal 1993)

B H Franklin, *The Buckley-Class Destroyer Escorts* (London 1999)
A very good account of the history both of the class and of individual ships – he has even found a photo of every one.

N Friedman, *British Carrier Aviation* (London 1988); *US Destroyers* (Annapolis 1982); and *Carrier Air Power* (London 1981)

W H Garzke & R O Dulin, Battleships – *Allied Battleships in World War II* (Annapolis 1980)
Detailed and accurate account of the technology.
Also 'The Sinking of the *Bismarck*', *Warship* 1994

G A H Gordon, *British Sea Power and Procurement Between the Wars* (Basingstoke 1988)
Covers much the same ground as Peden but from the Admiralty point of view. Happily, they agree on most points.

P Gretton, *Convoy Escort Commander* (London 1964)
An interesting account of the U-Boat war. My paper on stability of RN destroyers was partly inspired by this book.

W Hackmann, *Seek and Strike* (London 1984)
A complete and interesting study of A/S weapons and sensors.

S Howarth and D Law (eds), *The Battle of the Atlantic 1939 1945* (London 1994) Papers read at the 50th Anniversary conference, Merseyside, 1993. An invaluable source.

A Hague, *Sloops 1926–1946* (Kendal 1993)
General background and individual ship histories.

A N Harrison, *The Development of HM Submarines from Holland No 1 to Porpoise* (London 1986)
Full of technical detail.

D Henry, 'British Submarine Policy 1918-1939' in B Ranft (ed), *Technical Change and British Naval Policy 1860–1939* (Sevenoaks 1977)
An excellent and thought-provoking essay.

W J Jurens, 'The Loss of HMS *Hood* – a re-examination', *Warship International* 2/87.

E Lacroix and L Wells, *Japanese Cruisers of the Pacific War* (London 1997)

J D Ladd, *Assault from the Sea* (Newton Abbott 1966)

J H Lamb, *The Corvette Navy* (London 1979)

J Lambert and A Ross, *Allied Coastal Forces of World War II* Vols I & II (London 1990-3).

J R P Lansdown, *With the Carriers in Korea* (Worcester 1992)
A very detailed record of Fleet Air Arm Operations.

R D Layman, *The Hybrid Warship* (London 1991)
An account of the many (unsuccessful) attempts to merge the carrier with gunpower.

D J Lyon, 'The British Tribals' in A Preston (ed), *Super Destroyers* (London 1978)
A novel and interesting approach to these ships.

K McBride, 'Eight Six inch guns in Pairs. The *Leander* and *Sydney* class Cruisers', *Warship* 1997-98.

B Macdermott, *Ships without Names* (London 1992)
A detailed record of LST history.

L E H Maund, *Assault from the Sea* (London 1949)
Particularly good on the early days of combined operations.

MoD (N), *War with Japan* (London 1995)

N Monserrat, *HM Frigate* (London 1946)
Interesting comparison of the US-built 'Colony' class frigates with the British 'Rivers' from which they were derived. Also *The Cruel Sea* (London 1954). Fiction but the best account of conditions at sea in a small ship.

G C Peden, *British Rearmament and the Treasury 1932–41* (Edinburgh 1979)
An invaluable view of tri-service rearmament from the Treasury viewpoint.

H B Peebles, *Warship Building on the Clyde* (Edinburgh 1987)
A detailed analysis of the financial background to warship-building.

A Preston, *V & W Class Destroyers 1917-1945* (London 1971)

P Pugh, *The Cost of Seapower* (London 1986)
An excellent analysis of the cost of maintaining a navy. An unusual but very interesting approach.

A Raven & J Roberts, *British Battleships of World War II* (London 1976) and *British Cruisers of World War II* (London 1980)
The definitive books on British battleships and cruisers. Also *V & W Class Destroyers*. Man o'War 2 (London 1979)

D A Rayner, *Convoy Escort Commander* (London 1964)
A personal account by a successful commander.

S Roskill, *Naval Policy between the Wars*, Vols I & II (London 1976)
The strategic and administrative background to Admiralty policy.

J D Scott, *Vickers – A History* (London 1962)
Some useful material on armour.

J P M Showell, *U-Boat Command and the Battle of the Atlantic* (London 1989)
The strategy of the Battle of the Atlantic from a German point of view.

I A Sturton, 'HMS *Surrey* and *Northumberland*', *Warship International* 3/1977

J Winton, *Air Power at Sea* (London 1987)
General history of operations.

Periodicals of particular value are: *Warships* (Formerly Warship Supplement, World Ship Society), *Warship* (Conway quarterly and annual), *Warship International*, *Warship World*. Key articles are listed in this section, others dealing with specific aspects will be found as footnotes.

Glossary and Abbreviations

AA: Anti-aircraft

AAW: Anti-aircraft warfare

Accelerator:
    Fitted in some carriers to accelerate aircraft to flying speed while resting on their wheels. Often mistakenly called a catapult (*qv*).

ACNS: Assistant Chief of Naval Staff

AEL: Admiralty Engineering Laboratory

AEW: Admiralty Experiment Works. Ship model tanks at Haslar

AIO: Action Information Organisation. Ship's operations room and annexes.

Amatol: High explosive used in underwater weapons – 50/50 ammonium nitrate/TNT

APC: Armour Piercing Capped (shell)

AP: Armour Piercing

ARL: Admiralty Research Laboratory, Teddington

A/S: Anti-submarine

ASI: Admiralty Supply Item. Equipments bought in bulk and supplied to shipbuilders

ASNE: American Society of Naval Engineers

ASW: Anti-submarine Warfare

B: Bomb intended to be dropped ahead of the target ship and come up under the bottom

BD: Between Deck (gun mounting)

BG: Separation of the centres of Buoyancy and Gravity, a measure of submerged stability in submarines.

bhp: brake horsepower

BL: Breech-loading or, later, bag loading.

Board: (of Admiralty)

Boiler formula:
    A simple measure of pressure hull strength.

BR: Boiler Room

Bulbous bow:
    A projecting 'knob' on the forefoot which can, at certain speeds, reduce the size of the bow wave and hence resistance.

BYMS: USN equivalent to MMS (*qv*).

C: Cemented armour (face hardened)

°C: Degrees Celsius (though in the period covered it would have been called Centigrade).

Cal: Calibre of gun *eg* 6in. The length of the barrel is then given in calibres *eg* 50cal.

Catapult: Fitted in large ships (including aircraft carriers) to launch aircraft which were held in a cradle.

Chatham Float:
    A big pontoon carrying large models for tests of underwater protection.

C-in-C: Commander-in-Chief.

CMB: Coastal Motor Boat. A First World War torpedo boat

Cordite: British propellant. SC was the normal material: nitrocellulose 49.5 per cent, nitro-glycerine 41.5 per cent, centralise 9 per cent.

CPC: Common Pointed Capped (shell). Replaced with SAP (*qv*).

CPO: Chief Petty Officer.

crh: Calibre radius head. The longitudinal radius of the head of a shell expressed in units of its calibre.

cyl: Cylinder.

D: Depth from keel to uppermost continuous deck.

D of D: Director of Dockyards, a naval post.

D, D1, DW:
    High strength steels. See Appendix 15.

DAM: Director of Air Material.

DC: Depth charge, also Direct Current.

DE: USN Destroyer Escort (RN 'Captain' class frigates).

DE: Diesel-Electric propulsion.

DGD: Director Gunnery Division.*

Displacement, deep:
    All up weight with all fuel stores etc.

Displacement, standard:
    Roughly, deep displacement with all liquids removed. Defined under Washington Treaty.

dspt: Displacement.

diving depth:
    Original meaning seems to have been the depth at which collapse was likely. From the early 1920s it was a safe operational depth, often half the collapse depth. See Chapter 6.

DNC: Director of Naval Construction. See Appendix 2.

DNO: Director of Naval Ordnance.

Downflooding angle:
    The angle of heel at which water would flood into permanent openings. Values of GZ beyond this angle are meaningless.

DTM: Director of Torpedoes and Mining.

DTSD: Director of Tactical and Staff Duties.

Duplex pistol:
    A torpedo pistol which would explode the warhead as the torpedo passed under a target sensing the ship's magnetic field. Used only in air-dropped torpedoes and not very successful.

EA: Electrical Artificer

ehp: Effective horsepower. The power required to pull a bare hull through the water at a given speed.

E-in-C: Engineer-in-Chief.

ER: Engine Room.

ERA: Engine Room Artificer.

°F: Degrees, Fahrenheit.

FIDO: See Mine, Mk 24.

FOSM: Flag Officer, Submarines.

ft: feet.

GM: Metacentric height. A measure of stability for small angles of heel.

GP: General Purpose (bomb)

GZ: Righting lever. A measure of stability for large angles of heel.

HA: High Angle (gun)
HACS: High Angle Control System.
HE: High Explosive.
Hedgehog: A/S mortar.
Hogging: Ship bending in a seaway with most of the support amidships.
HT: High Tensile (steel).
HTP: High Test Peroxide (H$_2$O$_2$).

Immunity zone: The zone between the maximum range at which the side armour can be penetrated and the minimum range at which the deck armour is vulnerable. It may be negative!
in(s): inch(es).
INA Institution of Naval Architects.

Job 74 A very large pontoon on which full scale systems of protection could be tested.
Job 81 } Replica submarine test sections to examine
Job 9 } resistance to shock.

kt(s): knot(s)

lbs/in²: pounds per square inch (pressure).
LA: Low Angle (gun).
LC: Landing Craft.[1]
LS: Landing Ships.[2]
Lyddite: High explosive–picric acid.

M/C: Machinery.
MASB: Motor Anti Submarine Boat.
MC: Medium Case (bomb).
MGB: Motor Gun Boat.
Mine Mk 24: US A/S homing torpedo, the first (also FIDO).
Minol: High explosive–amatol enhanced with 20 per cent aluminium.
ML: Motor Launch.
MMS: Motor Mine Sweeper.
MS: Mild Steel.
MTB: Motor Torpedo Boat.

NC: Non-Cemented armour.
NECI North East Coast Institute.
Nitro-cellulose: USN propellant.
Normal (impact): Perpendicular to the surface struck.

OA: Ordnance Artificer
OPV: Offshore Patrol Vessel.

pdr: pounder, *eg* 6pdr gun.

Period: The time for a complete oscillation, *eg* roll from out to out *and back*.
Permanent Secretary: The senior administrative civil servant in a Ministry, *eg* Secretary of the Admiralty.
PO: Petty Officer.
pp: Length between perpendiculars. (Note that in this era the after perpendicular was the rudder stock.)
PRO: Public Record Office (Kew).
PSO: Principal Ship Overseer. RCNC officer responsible for overseeing in a shipyard.

QF: quick-firing gun, *ie* firing ammunition where shell and propellant are combined.

RA(S): Rear-Admiral (Submarines)
RCNC: Royal Corps of Naval Constructors.
RDF: Radio Direction Finding. British term for Radar.
rpm: rounds per minute

S Quality: High-tensile steel for submarines. See Appendix 15.
Sagging Bending of a ship in a seaway supported mainly at the ends.
SAP: Semi Armour-Piercing (shell).
Shark: 96lb A/S projectile fired from 4in gun, 24lb torpex charge.
shp: Shaft horsepower
S/M: Submarine.
SNAME: (US) Society of Naval Architects and Marine Engineers
STAAG: Stabilised Tachimetric AA Gun – twin Bofors.
Squid: Three-barrel A/S mortar.
SRR(D): Special Repair Rating (Dockyard).
SS: Submarine.

T: Draught.
TE: Turbo-Electric propulsion.
TNT High explosive – Tri nitro toluene.
Torpex: High explosive for underwater weapons: 37-41 per cent TNT, 41-45 per cent RDX, 18 per cent aluminium.

UD: Upper deck mounting.
USN: United States Navy.

VCNS: Vice Chief of Naval Staff.

wl: Waterline length.
WPS: Warship Production Superintendent. A senior RCNC officer responsible for production of ships and their equipment over a wide area.
W/T: Wireless Telegraphy (Morse code).

yds: yards.

* The Naval Staff was split into Divisions; Controller's organisation into Departments.

1 A Assault, F Flak, G Gun, I Infantry, M Mechanised, P Personnel, P(R) personnel (ramped), VP Vehicle and Personnel, T Tank, T(E) Engineering.

2 As for landing craft plus SS Stern Chute, G Gantry, H headquarters.

Index